The Tendering Presence

Essays on John Woolman

In Honor of

Sterling Olmsted and Phillips P. Moulton

The Tendering Presence

Essays on John Woolman

In Honor of
Sterling Olmsted &
Phillips P. Moulton

Edited by Mike Heller
Roanoke College

Paul Anderson
Michael L. Birkel
Philip L. Boroughs, S.J.
Anne Dalke
Vernie Davis
Susan Dean
J. William Frost
Lisa M. Gordis
Michael P. Graves
Mike Heller
Paul A. Lacey
Mary Moulton
Phillips P. Moulton
Anne G. Myles
Sterling Olmsted
Mary Rose O'Reilley
Gerald W. Sazama
Neil Snarr
Jean R. Soderlund
Margaret E. Stewart
Christopher Varga

Pendle Hill Publications
338 Plush Mill Road
Wallingford, PA 19086
800-742-3150 x 2
bookstore@pendle Hill.org

Cover art by Rachel Phillips*

Library of Congress Cataloging-in-Puiblication Data

The tendering presence : essays on John Woolman : in honor of Sterling Olmsted & Phillips P. Moulton / edited by Mike Heller
p. cm.
Includes bibliographical references.
ISBN 0-87574-940-2
1. Woolman, John, 1720-1772. I. Olmsted, Sterling. II. Moulton, Phillips., 1909-. III. Heller, Michael Alan.

BX7795.W7T46 2003
289.6'092-dc22

20033062372

**Rachel Phillips is a former resident student at Pendle Hill. She practices art using a wide variety of media and understands the creative process to be a channel for spiritual healing and revelation. She currently grows organic vegetables in North Yorkshire, England.*

PERMISSIONS

Much appreciation to the following for their permissions to use material in this collection:

Women's Studies: An Interdisciplinary Journal for permission to use portions of Anne Dalke's "Outside the Mainstream/In the Well of Living Water: Toward a Feminist Quaker Pedagogy" Vol. 28 (1999): 473-501.

Peter Lang Publishing, Inc. for permission to use portions of Anne Dalke's *Teaching to Learn/Learning to Teach: Meditations on the Classroom* (studies in Education and Spirituality, Vol. 4, 2002).

For the map used in Jean Soderlund's "African Americans and Native Americans in John Woolman's World," appreciation for permission from the Smithsonian Institution. The map is an enlargement from Ives Goddard's "Delaware," *Handbook of North American Indians,* Vol. 15., Northeast. Ed. Bruce G. Trigger (Washington: Smithsonian Institution, 1978), p. 214.

Philadelphia Yearly Meeting Religious Education and Pendle Hill for permission to build this collection around the autumn 1994 Monday Evening Lecture Series and the resulting study guide: *John Woolman's Spirituality and Our Contemporary Witness*, Ed. Shirley Dodson (Philadelphia: Philadelphia Yearly Meeting Religious Education Committee and Pendle Hill, 1995), which included earlier versions of essays by Philip Boroughs, Mary Rose O'Reilley, Anne Dalke, and Susan Dean.

Friends Association for Higher Education to publish Phillips P. Moulton's and Sterling Olmsted's essays, originally published in the *Conference on Quaker Studies on Human Betterment Proceedings, Swarthmore College, June 16-18, 1988,* Ed. Jim Nichols (Philadelphia, PA: Friends Association for Higher Education, 1988). Also thanks and regards to Mary Moulton for permission to publish Phil Moulton's essay.

The regular Quaker practice of corporate worship and of private prayer furnished a means "to keep to the root," as he expressed it. But more important still was this constant attempt on his part to live close to the root, close to the inward teacher, close to the tendering presence that he had known and felt.

—Douglas V. Steere
"The *Journal* of John Woolman,"
Doors into Life 96

Contents

I. John Woolman's Spirituality

II. Literary, Historical, and Economic Contexts

III. Issues of Oppression, Social Change, and Education

IV. Scholars Who Became Disciples

Preface

John Woolman (1720-1772), Quaker social reformer, challenged slavery and its economic injustice and called the Religious Society of Friends to stand in a corporate testimony against the practice. He felt called to do so out of a real and ongoing experience of the tendering presence of God at work in his life. His life, his faith, and his social witness exemplify a model to replicate today to help make a positive difference in the ongoing social ills of war, poverty, and environmental destruction. The purpose of this essay collection is to deepen our understanding of John Woolman's writings and their implications, particularly as they affect our common humanity and universal, spiritual love. Woolman holds a distinctive place in American history, religion, and literature. Woolman's *Journal* is often placed among the world's classic spiritual autobiographies. His essays on slavery, war-tax resistance, labor and economics, the poor, and environmentalism— long before environmentalism was fashionable—have had a major influence on Quakers, people of other faiths, those working for social and economic reform, and advocates of nonviolence and conscientious objection.

Woolman's interests knew no boundaries between the spiritual, the social, and the political. The breadth of his concerns is reflected today in the interest of readers across academic disciplines of history, literature, religion, economics, peace studies, and sociology, which are represented in this collection. Perhaps most importantly, these essays model that scholarship which seeks to practice dispassionate research at the same time that it recognizes that, as scholars, our lives also are touched personally and spiritually by Woolman's writings. The belief underlying these essays is that there is no reason why reading Woolman sensitively should prevent us from asking hard questions, as indeed Woolman did. The kinds of questions we ask, however, are at the heart of our scholarship. This book grows out of our recognition of Woolman's importance in his own right for what he has yet to teach us and it demonstrates our efforts to apply our best scholarship to a writer and thinker who forces us to question the limits of our disciplinary approaches.

1

Like Teresa of Avila, William Wilberforce, Dorothy Day, and Mohandas K. Gandhi, to whom Woolman has been compared, Woolman would credit his accomplishments to the inner leadings of the spirit of God. Describing "Holy Obedience" in *A Testament of Devotion*, Thomas Kelly writes that

> Only now and then comes a man or a woman who, like John Woolman or Francis of Assisi, is willing to be utterly obedient, to go the other half, to follow God's faintest whisper. But when such a commitment comes in a human life, God breaks through, miracles are wrought, world-renewing divine forces are released, history changes. (52)

Woolman's account of the personal, lived experience of this spiritual commitment has served as a model for people of all faiths who are interested in the contemplative and mystical traditions and who seek that ethical life guided by their own experiential knowledge of that of God within. As Douglas V. Steere notes: "The regular Quaker practice of corporate worship and of private prayer furnished a means 'to keep to the root,' as he expressed it (PM 117). But more important still was this constant attempt on his part to live close to the root, close to the inward teacher, close to the tendering presence that he had known and felt" (96). Woolman's achievements are all the more striking because of the dignity he granted to those with whom he disagreed. He has inspired generations working to alleviate violence, oppression, inequality, economic injustice, and poverty. Woolman continues to teach readers today through his remarkable empathy, his commitment to plainness and simplicity, and, as Phillips P. Moulton says, through "his capacity to see the long-range effects and implications of an act" ("Exemplar of Ethics" 85).

Woolman's *Journal* is one of the most cherished documents of Quaker devotional literature. By the time Woolman began writing his *Journal* in the 1750s, Friends' journals had evolved over the preceding one hundred years into a distinctive form of spiritual autobiography. The spiritual journey was usually seen as a gradual evolution of one's life's work, expressed as a faithful response to the leadings of the inward spirit. These writers often chose self-effacing, passive diction and syntax to express their sense of humility and the experience of surrendering to "the motion" of "that of God within." This language in turn evoked that experience for readers.

Quakers, formally referred to as the Religious Society of Friends, had no liturgy in their "silent" worship, no hymns, and no truly sacred literature except the Bible. Quakers were often attacked and persecuted, especially in the seventeenth century, because they discovered authority in the personal experience of the divine as well as in scripture. Out of that personal experience came the God-given messages spoken in worship as well as one's direction for action in the world. The Quaker ideal, expressed as "let your lives speak," placed writing on the same plain as social action.

The journal, telling the story of one's spiritual growth and personal transformation, was the perfect form for the Society of Friends. Quakers valued and read these journals as their most prized form of literary expression. As evidenced by recent publications such as Catherine Blecki and Karin Wulf's edition of *Milcah Martha Moore's Book,* colonial Quakers showed more enthusiasm for poetry than we previously thought, but that interest was still relatively limited, and there is even less evidence that they were interested in fiction or drama. Friends read pamphlets and essays, and they had a keen interest in written descriptions of death-bed experiences as published in the series *Piety Promoted.* The narrative of the life told in the journal seems to have held a power for readers beyond that of these other genres. Howard H. Brinton has shown, in *Quaker Journals: Varieties of Religious Experience among Friends,* that in the published journals, which eventually numbered in the hundreds, as well as the numerous journals circulated in manuscript, Friends' journals were a highly successful and widely-read literary genre.

As becomes obvious in the essays in this collection, Woolman's *Journal* and essays stand out among Quaker writings. Through his *Journal*, his other writings, as well as his itinerant ministry, he was a major figure in a movement to bring about change within the Society of Friends. He became an eloquent writer on the evils of slavery as well as on the interconnectedness of war, affluence, poverty, and destruction of the environment. Because he was not of the wealthy, merchant class of Philadelphia, but a humble tailor, part-time orchard keeper, and itinerant minister, the eloquence of his *Journal* was unexpected and from the outset all the more admired. Frederick Tolles and other historians have claimed that Woolman was responsible, more than any other single individual, for moving the Quakers to emancipate their slaves (Tolles, "Introduction" viii), not only at a time when some signers of the Declaration of Independence were themselves slave owners, and but also some ninety years before the Emancipation Proclamation. In Woolman's and other Friends' early efforts against "slave keeping," out of which emerged the earliest American anti-slavery societies, we can also see roots of the nineteenth-century women's movement and the twentieth-century civil rights movement.

Although most literary criticism has focused on John Woolman's *Journal,* his essays apparently had a profound effect on his contemporaries and later generations. He seems to have taken the genre of the essay as seriously as he did the genre of spiritual autobiography. In addition to two major essays on slave keeping and a major essay, entitled "A Plea for the Poor," he wrote other essays on topics such as trade, "Pure Wisdom and Human Policy," "the True Harmony of Mankind," and the ministry. Woolman's essays seem to have been extraordinarily effective partly because he sought not to condemn the slave owner, the wealthy, or the landowner, but rather to appeal to the readers' higher interests. Woolman's first essay, "Some Considerations on the Keeping of Negroes," published in 1754, particularly influenced the antislavery decisions of the Philadelphia Yearly Meeting of 1758 (James 130-38).

2

Woolman's writings challenge us to respond in new ways. How, for example, do we square a critical response to Woolman's deeply spiritual writings with his expressed intention of deepening the reader's passionate, personal response? Must we separate our experiential response from an academic response, grounded in our disciplinary methods while maintaining "objective" distance? Is it true, as some would argue, that reading Woolman from a position of faith prevents a person from asking the hard questions? Or can the experiential response enhance the disciplinary response? It would seem that Woolman's writings especially call for us to look for new ways to live in our spirituality, to act upon our concerns for human betterment, and to contribute to our disciplines. In our disciplines, we need to discover how to read and respond to texts like Woolman's, recognizing that which in our traditional methodologies is useful and that which will lead us to expand our "ways of knowing." All of the essays included in this collection are grounded in the writers' academic disciplines; all are sensitive to the dynamics of early Quaker writings.

Because of the high regard for Woolman's *Journal* and because of the way Quaker journals functioned for readers in the Society of Friends, scholarship on Woolman in the past has often been sentimental, homiletic, or hagiographic. It is interesting that we no longer just dismiss such responses. We want to understand, within the historical and cultural context of eighteenth-century American Quakerism, how Woolman approached writing in order to affect readers, and we want to understand why and how his writings continue to speak to readers across the centuries. Somewhere or somehow he learned to write remarkably effective prose that continues to invite readers to reflect upon their own spiritual lives. Reading "experientially" seems to go counter to much of the last hundred years' scholarship, in which our academic disciplines in the humanities and social sciences have compared themselves to the sciences and have strived to establish objective methods of inquiry. Yet, the issue of "experiential reading" is inseparable from the genre of the Quaker journal. George Fox, the seventeenth-century writer of the other most famous Quaker journal, saw how Friends' journals had a "mirroring" effect upon readers, who "experienced" in the text something of the spiritual life of the journal writer as well as some connection with the truth of their own spiritual lives. Modern scholarship routinely resisted these directions. Yet Woolman's writings invite us to rethink how we approach such texts holistically with our intellect, intuition, and spiritual being. Only in recent years have scholars acknowledged that there is a place in our scholarly approaches for situating ourselves in our own spiritual lives. The writers in this collection approach this issue from various perspectives; all of them are sensitive to how their scholarship is affected by their encounter with texts, which openly engage the reader's spiritual experience.

Quaker journals were never free from issues of censorship. The Overseers of the Press, in Woolman's time, edited out dreams and other personal expressions, which the Overseers (who were actually Woolman's peers and friends) believed were a detraction from the journal's didactic purposes. These editorial revisions were carried out in the name of making the journals uplifting for the community for which they were to be published. Woolman also willingly submitted his essays to the Philadelphia Yearly Meeting's Overseers of the Press, because he wanted their approval and support, although he sometimes struggled with the conflict of interest created by that support (PM 117-18, 195-96). The community's expectations for publication may seem to us to have devalued that which was idiosyncratic and individualistic, as well as that which was not easily understood, such as dreams. In the case of women's journals, the editing seems at times to have been oppressive. The community pressures under which Quaker writings were published are not entirely different from our own struggles today to find valid forms of expression and publication.

3

This collection of essays exemplifies studies on Woolman today. The essays touch on a wide range of issues. The writers of the essays address their understanding of Woolman's contributions to a body of literature, which emerged within this religious community—a literature that originally was written to enhance and reclaim the experience of the spirit, which guides one's actions in the world. For Quakers these spiritual leadings often directed one to work for social reform. The essays exemplify that scholarship, nurtured by the Friends Association for Higher Education and stated in the organization's goals, which include "the ideal of integrating spiritual commitment, academic excellence and social responsibility," and the forwarding of "research directed toward perceiving and achieving a more perfect human society."

The book's first three sections are organized around major facets of Woolman scholarship: "John Woolman's Spirituality";"Literary, Historical, and Economic Contexts"; and "Issues of Oppression, Social Change, and Education."

The book's final section honors two men who have made the most important contributions to Woolman scholarship: Phillips P. Moulton and Sterling Olmsted.

Phil Moulton's edition of *John Woolman's Journal and Major Essays* (Oxford University Press, 1971; reprinted, Friends United Press, 1989) became the authoritative text, which corrected many errors introduced by the original editorial committee that had been carried forward in subsequent editions. The Moulton text restored the dreams that had been omitted and made extensive corrections based upon his study of the manuscripts. Mary Moulton, his wife, explains in her essay that in dedicating his career to the study of ethics, Phil found that Woolman opened "vistas of creative thought and action" as he sought to apply his faith to everyday experience.

In his essay honoring Sterling Olmsted, Neil Snarr describes how Sterling has devoted much of his scholarly life to understanding what

Woolman has to teach us about the connections between the spiritual life and nonviolent social change. In his essay, Sterling has shown how John Woolman and Mohandas K. Gandhi were transformed by their spiritual experiences and believed their work for social justice was above all a spiritual endeavor. Sterling writes in his introduction to Woolman's "Conversations" that Woolman's deeply felt concerns were for the rich as well as the poor: "He was able, therefore, to deal with rich oppressors as a friend rather than an enemy. It is important to note, however, that the reforms Woolman called for were not minor. He was interested in total and radical change—in people and in the economic arrangements of his time" (4).

Acknowledgements

Four of the essays in the collection were first delivered in the autumn 1994 Pendle Hill Monday evening lecture series on John Woolman, which was organized by Peter Crysdale, and which appeared in earlier form in a study guide entitled John Woolman's Spirituality and Our Contemporary Witness, edited by Shirley Dodson. I thank the Philadelphia Yearly Meeting Religious Education Committee and Pendle Hill for permission to create this collection around that initial lecture series and study guide. Working on this book with all of the contributors has been for me a gift and a spiritual journey. I wish to express my appreciation to Roanoke College for grants in time and funds, which supported work on this volume. I thank Joe Mathews of Leesburg, NJ, Patricia Scott in the Fintel Library at Roanoke College, and my colleague in the Roanoke College English department, Katherine Hoffman, for their invaluable assistance. Heart-felt appreciation goes to Neil Snarr, Mary Moulton, and Barbara Olmsted for their gentle and wise words of encouragement and faith. I thank Rebecca Kratz Mays, Eva Fernandez Beehler, Holley R. Webster, Bob McCoy, and the staff at Pendle Hill for all of their labors to publish this book. I also owe more than I can say to the support of my wife Rebecca A. Heller.

—Mike Heller
Roanoke College

WORKS CITED

Blecki, Catherine La Courreye, and Karin A. Wulf, eds. *Milcah Martha Moore's Book: A Commonplace Book from Revolutionary America.* University Park, PA: The Pennsylvania State University P, 1997.

Brinton, Howard H. *Quaker Journals: Varieties of Religious Experience among Friends.* 1972. Wallingford, PA: Pendle Hill Publications, 1983.

Dodson, Shirley, ed. *John Woolman's Spirituality and Our Contemporary Witness.* Philadelphia: Philadelphia Yearly Meeting Religious Education Committee and Pendle Hill, 1995.

Fox, George. *The Journal of George Fox.* Ed. John L. Nickalls. 1952. Philadelphia: Religious Society of Friends, 1985.

James, Sydney V. *A People Among Peoples: Quaker Benevolence in Eighteenth-Century America.* Cambridge: Harvard UP, 1963.

Kelly, Thomas R. *A Testament of Devotion.* NY: Harper & Row, 1941.

Moulton, Phillips P. "John Woolman: Exemplar of Ethics." *Quaker History* 54 (1965): 81-93.

Steere, Douglas V. *Doors into Life: Through Five Devotional Classics.* NY: Harper & Brothers, 1948.

Tolles, Frederick B. "Introduction." *The Journal of John Woolman and A Plea for the Poor.* Secaucus, NJ: Citadel P, 1961.

Woolman, John. *A First Book for Children.* Philadelphia: Crukshank, n.d. [1774?]

—-. "Conversations on the True Harmony of Mankind And How It May Be Promoted." Ed. Sterling Olmsted. Philadelphia: Wider Quaker Fellowship, 1987.

—-. *The Journal and Major Essays of John Woolman.* Ed. Phillips P. Moulton. 1971. Richmond, IN: Friends United P, 1989.

ABBREVIATIONS

The following abbreviations are used to refer to John Woolman's works frequently cited:

AMG *The Journal and Essays of John Woolman.* Ed. Amelia Mott Gummere. New York: Macmillan, 1922.

PM *The Journal and Major Essays of John Woolman.* Ed. Phillips P. Moulton. 1971. Richmond, IN: Friends United P, 1989.

I.

John Woolman's Spirituality

1

John Woolman's Spirituality

Philip L. Boroughs, S.J.

JOHN WOOLMAN INSPIRES ME. When I read his *Journal* or essays I find that his witness to that of God within him stirs that of God within me. Consequently, my faith grows stronger and I experience hope. Furthermore, I am moved by his availability for God: his openness to let God direct him, transform him, and empower him. I am impressed by his rich prayer life, his deep devotion to his religious tradition, and his active commitment to living publicly the principles he professed.

While inspired by Woolman, I also recognize that I am challenged by him. His intense faith, his radical integrity, and his courageous ministry make me uncomfortable, as they did many of his contemporaries. Woolman prompts me to look more critically at my own life and that of my faith community as we attempt to live out Gospel values in our time.

John Woolman invites me to examine more carefully the implications of Christian spirituality. He begins his *Journal* by saying: "I have often felt a motion of love to leave some hints in writing of my experience of the goodness of God. . ." (PM 23). Woolman experienced God as loving and good and, in response, searched for life-giving ways to enter into a deeper relationship with God by following the example of Jesus. Woolman believed that God created the human person with the potential to live in union with God and, concomitantly, in union with all other human beings. In his second essay "On Keeping Negroes," he writes:

> There is a principle which is pure, placed in the human mind, which in different places and ages hath had different names. It is, however, pure and proceeds from God. It is deep and inward, confined to no forms of religion nor excluded from any, where the heart stands in perfect sincerity. In whomsoever this takes root and grows, of what nation soever, they become brethren in the best sense of the expression. (PM 236)

As a contemplative in action, Woolman emphasizes that spirituality deals not only with how God comes to us, but how we respond to God in prayer and in loving relationship with others. Spirituality, then, seems to be a matter of gift *and* response: the gift of God's faithful love for us and our creative response to God's love in our lives. For Woolman this is communal, as a participant in the Society of Friends; social, as a member of the human family within creation; and personal or individual, as a man of deep faith. Consequently, I will describe John Woolman's spirituality, or his response to God's goodness in his life, from these three distinct but interrelated dimensions:

> The Communal: Woolman's spirituality as a member of the Society of Friends, his Quaker identity, and how his religious tradition shaped and was shaped by Woolman.
>
> The Social: Woolman's spirituality as a member of the human family within creation and the implications of his faith for the transformation of his world.
>
> The Individual: The uniquely personal aspects of Woolman's spirituality, how he experienced God in his life, and how his spirituality grew and developed.

These three dimensions of Woolman's spirituality developed simultaneously, and no one dimension of his spirituality adequately can be understood if separated from the others. I distinguish them here only to clarify the richness of his holistic spirituality. Furthermore, Woolman continues to inspire many of us today because of the creative synthesis he achieved blending these three dimensions of his religious life. Each perspective functioned as a critique of the other two and continually kept him growing and developing spiritually.

The Communal Dimension of Woolman's Spirituality

Born in 1720, John Woolman grew up during a period Howard Brinton has called "the Golden Age of Quakerism in America" in a rural New Jersey village which Amelia Mott Gummere has described as one of the most conservative Quaker communities of the time (*Friends for 300 Years* 183, AMG 14). While Burlington County, New Jersey, had moved beyond the rigors of early colonial settlement, it was just far enough away from the temptations of more sophisticated Philadelphia to maintain its religious character.

Woolman never questioned his Quaker identity and, following a period of adolescent turmoil, he reappropriated it with quiet intensity. Quakerism defined Woolman's world view, provided his community life and social world, and was the primary influence on his sense of self and personal spirituality. His love of silence and prayer, his ongoing commitment to discerning God's plan, and the importance he placed on living, in very practical terms, the principles he professed were all grounded in his religious tradition.

Consequently, as a Quaker by profession and an idealist by personality, Woolman was concerned about the religious integrity of his faith community. In the second paragraph of the *Journal* he expressed his early concern for the spiritual condition of the Society of Friends:

> From what I had read and heard, I believed that there had been in past ages people who walked in uprightness before God in a degree exceeding any that I knew, or heard of, now living; and the apprehension of there being less steadiness and firmness amongst people in this age than in past ages often troubled me while I was a child. (PM 24)

This theme of reform would permanently mark his life and repeatedly surface in his writings. Woolman so loved his religious community that he wanted it to be authentic.

Walter Brueggemann, in *The Prophetic Imagination,* offers a poignant insight which might describe Woolman's relationship with the Society of Friends:

> . . . the prophet is called to be a child of the tradition, one who has taken it seriously in the shaping of his or her own field of perception and system of language, who is so at home in that memory that the points of contact and incongruity with the situation of the church in culture can be discerned and articulated with proper urgency.

Deeply committed to his Quaker heritage, Woolman observed many points of incongruity in the practice of eighteenth-century Friends, and he worked diligently to develop a renewed commitment to Quaker principles in the life of his religious community.

On occasion, Woolman has been characterized as a lone prophet single-handedly preaching religious conversion and social transformation. In fact, although Woolman was a significant voice in calling for the reformation of American and, later, English Quakerism in the 18th century, he was not alone in this work nor were his sensitivities unique. Woolman was part of a larger movement which included Anthony Benezet, John Churchman, Daniel Stanton, Israel and John Pemberton, and many others. Considered controversial at times, their ministry was sanctioned by the Society of Friends, and all of these men were highly involved in the internal workings of their monthly, quarterly, and yearly meetings. While they clearly critiqued the practice and values of their co-religionists, they did so within the appropriate structures and procedures of their faith community.

From Woolman's *Journal* it is clear that he followed his leadings with intense sincerity. His path was far more stringent than most, and his witness was challenging. The simplicity of his life, his undyed clothing, and his persistent social critique were noteworthy and, at times, off-putting. However, he had great credibility within the Quaker community. In addition to his personal integrity, Woolman was so heavily involved with the internal structures and procedures of the Society of Friends that his voice was respected. His positions of leadership reflect not only his deep commitment to the Society of Friends, but also its trust in him. Since Woolman doesn't reveal much about these positions in the *Journal*, it is necessary to examine meeting minutes to discover just how involved he was. Here is a listing of Woolman's meeting involvement:[1]

1740s:	Representative to Burlington Quarterly Meeting and Philadelphia Yearly Meeting
1743:	Recommended minister and member of the Burlington Quarterly Meeting of Ministers and Elders
1750-63:	An editor of letters from Philadelphia Yearly Meeting to other Yearly Meetings in America
1752-69:	Clerk of Burlington Quarterly Meeting of Minsters and Elders
1756-72:	Member of the Overseers of the Press for Philadelphia Yearly Meeting
1764-72:	An editor of the important yearly epistle to London Yearly Meeting

Furthermore, Woolman was heavily involved with special tasks and committees on matters of discipline for the Burlington Monthly Meeting and the Philadelphia Yearly Meeting. This work included care of couples preparing for marriage, the evaluation of marriage ceremonies, support for families with financial problems, assistance for those seeking to join the Society of Friends as well as drafting letters of removal for others, the ministry of family visiting, and work on educational issues.

In addition to internal concerns, the increasingly complex political situation moved Woolman to join committees which treated the critical issues facing the Quaker community. In 1755 he was a member of the Committee to Revise Queries for Discipline for the Philadelphia Yearly Meeting and Committee to visit Monthly and Quarterly Meetings to apprise adherence to discipline and suggest improvements. In 1756 he participated on the committee which proposed establishing the Meeting for Sufferings and the committee which reviewed issues regarding taxation and war effort. From 1758 to 1762 he was a member of the committee of the Philadelphia Yearly Meeting which visited slave-owning families; and in 1758 he was part of the committee established to investigate those who leased wagons for the French and Indian War effort. In 1760 he was asked to join the Committee to revise the Minutes for Discipline for the New England Yearly Meeting.

As this list makes clear, Woolman was not a lone prophetic figure out of step with the mainstream of the Quaker community. Rather, Woolman was heavily committed to a spirituality of daily life, especially as connected with disciplinary matters. In many ways I think that his radical social positions and his symbolic ascetical practices were tolerated or even accepted by other Friends because of his personal integrity and his obvious commitment to the whole of Quaker life. He spent so much time talking to individuals and families about matters of importance that people came to know him as a man of intense faith, remarkable charity, and deep humility. This more mundane side to his ministry gave him depth and authenticity. People knew they could trust him, so they took seriously the more challenging dimensions of his prophetic witness.

Finally, while Woolman was heavily involved in the disciplinary concerns of Quakerism, he was also remarkably open to other denominations. He writes: "I found no narrowness respecting sects and opinions, but believed that sincere upright-hearted people in every Society who truly loved God were accepted of him" (PM 28). For Woolman, sincere authentic living was more important than religious affiliation. Therefore, in a variety of circumstances he displays great openness to people of various faiths: Presbyterians, who often opposed Quakers politically (PM 41-2); New Light Presbyterians who, with some Quakers were involved in educating slaves even when against the law (PM 65); Moravians, as evidenced in the Wyalusing experience (PM 122-37); Dutch Mennonites, some of whom also opposed slavery (PM 73-4); Catholics, note his reference to Thomas à Kempis and religious reform and how he used some Jesuit writings to understand and describe the brutality of slave trade (PM 75, 210-11); and even Deists who lived sincerely (PM 210). For Woolman, ecumenical openness was a logical consequence of a religious perspective which preached God's universal love and cherished "that of God in everyone."

The Social Dimension of Woolman's Spirituality

John Woolman was not only interested in the internal reformation of his religious community, but he worked to ensure that the theological values of his tradition were consistently applied by Quakers in business, politics, and social customs. Because of his religious beliefs, Woolman felt compelled to identify the systems of accepted oppression which characterized colonial life.

Once again, Walter Brueggemann unwittingly describes John Woolman when he writes:

> The prophet does not scold or reprimand. The prophet brings to public expression the dread of endings, the collapse of our self-madeness, the barriers and pecking orders that secure us at each other's expense, and the fearful practice of eating off the table of a hungry brother or sister. (50)

Woolman was committed to raising to public consciousness the pain and sinfulness of slavery, the tragedy of war, and the abuse of Native Americans. In less systematic ways, he was also concerned with the treatment of animals and, on occasion, air pollution and disregard for the earth. As he explored each of these issues, he always returned to the same root cause: social injustice primarily was a consequence of greed and economic injustice. Significantly, his economic and social theories were grounded in his theology and spirituality.

About 1763-64 Woolman composed an essay originally entitled "A Word of Remembrance and Caution to the Rich" which today is better known as "A Plea for the Poor." This essay addresses the issue of economic justice and the distribution of the resources of the earth. It also provides a number of theological principles on which Woolman based not only his economic perspective, but his social concerns, as well. These theological principles appear throughout his *Journal* and his other essays. For Woolman these principles were not simply intellectual ideas or abstractions; rather they were deeply felt values which offered him a lens through which he saw reality and constructed his world view. As he applied them in concrete circumstances, they illuminated his eventual course of action.

I will highlight five principles—each of which ultimately overlaps:

1. God is the true proprietor of the earth

> The first people who inhabited the earth were the first who had possession of the soil. . . . But our gracious Creator is as absolutely the owner of it as he was when he first formed it out of nothing, before man had possession of it. (PM 260)

In Woolman's time the term "proprietor" usually designated the descendants of William Penn who originally owned the colony of Pennsylvania and to whom special quitrents or taxes were owed. Woolman is suggesting a much different concept of ownership; he is emphasizing the conditional not absolute character of the ownership of property. Woolman believed in stewardship more than ownership, and the more one stewarded, the more responsibility one had towards the needs of others.

2. God has a gracious design for creation

While Woolman never delineates just how one comes to know the specifics of God's design for creation, he believed that God had ordered creation with harmony, peace, and equality in mind. Therefore it is vital for people to live reflectively, not compulsively, discerning God's will in each circumstance. He maintained that God has adequately provided for the needs of all if the resources of creation are appropriately distributed and people live simply. (PM 226, 256, 263)

3. God is "no respecter of persons," rather God loves all people universally (PM 66)

Woolman believed that society should be structured to reflect God's universal love, that God does not favor one race over another, nor the affluent over the poor, and that liberty is the right of all people equally. Therefore, personal interest can never be separated from the common good. Individual needs and desires must be situated within the context of the legitimate needs of others.

4. Trust in the providence of God

Woolman maintained that God has adequately provided for the needs of all and one must trust in a God whose ways are not always clear. As he says in his essay, "On the Right Use of the Lord's Outward Gifts:"

> These Things which he beholds necessary for his People, he fails not to give them in his own Way, and Time: but as his Ways are above our Ways, and his Thoughts above our Thoughts, so imaginary Wants are different "from these Things which he knoweth that we have need of." (AMG 395)

Woolman also believed that moderate work complemented this trust. Moderate work allowed time for leisure, prayer, reflection, and social contribution. Neither the poor nor the rich should work too hard nor too little. Consequently, Woolman was deeply troubled by the growing affluence of some members of the Society of Friends and the oppression of others which helped produce that affluence. He believed that greed was the primary source of social evil, and he described the consumerism of his age as a form of idolatry which placed possessions before God and God's design for the good of all. He recognized that "with an increase of wealth the desire for wealth increased" (PM 35).

Of major concern to Woolman was the issue of inheritances. So often, he noted, good people lived inappropriately or condoned social injustice directly or indirectly because they wanted to provide for their children's security. Woolman believed that inheritances often spoil and ruin children (PM 247-50). What better inheritance could parents offer their children than a commitment to justice, a good education, and training for decent work?

5. Follow the pattern of Jesus

Woolman describes Christian discipleship in this way:

> Leave everything which our Lord Jesus Christ does not own. Think not his pattern too plain or too coarse for you. Think not a small portion in this life too little, but let us live in his spirit and walk as he walked, and he will preserve us in the greatest troubles. (PM 255)

Woolman believed that just as Jesus was concerned with the weak, poor, and the helpless, so too his disciples should live with the same compassion, abiding in the pure principle of universal love. In addition, Woolman was concerned that the bad example of affluent Quakers weakened the integrity of the Society of Friends and encouraged others to do the same.

Woolman appropriated these theological principles as living truths which guided his choices, positions, and actions. However, his real genius was neither the content of his positions nor his methodology for religiously motivated social change. Friends before him and many of his contemporaries were equally involved in the issues of slavery, peace, Native American rights, and simplicity of life. Woolman's genius, it seems to me, was his ability to grasp the interconnection between various forms of social oppression and injustice:

> Wealth is attended with power, by which bargains and proceedings contrary to universal righteousness are supported; and here oppression, carried on with worldly policy and order, clothes itself with the name of justice and becomes like a seed of discord in the soil; and as this spirit which wanders from the pure habitation prevails, so the seed of war swells and sprouts and grows and becomes strong, till much fruits are ripened. Thus cometh the harvest spoken of by the prophet, which is "a heap in the day of grief, and of desperate sorrow" [Isaiah 17:11]. (PM 255)

Woolman's commitment to the reformation of Quakerism was intimately connected with his deep concern for suffering humanity: for slaves, Native Americans, settlers pushed to the frontier because of high rents in settled areas, sailors, post boys, and women in factories. He believed that if his religious community truly lived what they professed, they would engage these concerns in socially transformative ways. Thus, others beyond the Society of Friends would benefit from their integrity.

The Individual Dimension of Woolman's Spirituality

The individual or uniquely personal dimension of Woolman's spirituality can best be described by examining five different themes or perspectives: ethical mysticism, stages in spiritual development, prayer, identification with the poor and oppressed, and the cross of Christ.

1. Ethical Mysticism

Howard Brinton has described Quakerism as an ethical mysticism by which he means:

> ... that type of mysticism which first withdraws from the world revealed by the senses to the inward Divine Source of Light, Truth, and Power, and then returns to the world with strength renewed, insight cleared, and desire quickened to bind all life together in the bonds of love. These bonds are discovered by this process of withdrawal and return because the one inward Divine Source is itself the creative unity which seeks to bind all life together. (5)

This dynamic of withdrawal and return truly characterized Woolman's spirituality. His prayer consistently sent him out into the world to live by the spiritual insights he had received. Similarly, his return to the world consistently raised issues for him which he found challenging and overwhelming. Consequently, he withdrew to prayer, again seeking God's support and help to respond to the conflicts he encountered.

Woolman's *Journal* reveals that he enjoyed deep union with God. While this union didn't protect him from times of fear, difficult questions, or even mistakes, it did carry him through these difficulties into a deeper and more radical peace. As a consequence of his union with God, Woolman began to see the world as God sees it, and he learned to love the world as God loves it, without respect to persons, race, or economic status. This is one sign of the true mystic: someone who enters into the heart of God and loves what God loves. Woolman appropriates Jesus' love command in the following way:

> . . . when we love God with all our heart and with all our strength, then in this love we love our neighbors as ourselves, and a tenderness of heart is felt toward all people, even such who as to outward circumstances may be to us as the Jews were to the Samaritans. (PM 177)

Woolman was a mystic and a prophet: a mystic because of his intense union with God, and a prophet because he was able to discern where God was moving in 18th century colonial America. As William Johnston writes:

> . . . Mysticism, the core of all religious experience, has led to the most dynamic and revolutionary action the world has known . . . the great prophets were mystics in action—their inner eye was awakened so that they saw not only the glory of God but also the suffering, the injustice, the inequality, the sin of the world. . . . and just as the great prophets were mystics, so the great mystics had a prophetic role. . . .

It is comforting to know that Woolman did not always know what God wanted in every situation. In one of my favorite quotations he says:

> . . . I have gone forward, not as one travelling in a road cast up, and well prepared, but as a man walking through a miry place, in which are stones here and there, safe to step on; but so situated that one step being taken, time is necessary to see where to step next. (AMG 315)

Often, Woolman relates that his way only became clear as he walked it. By taking each step as it surfaced and continually looking for the next, he entered more deeply into the love of God, while at the same time he became more involved in the religious and social needs of his era. As a hallmark of his spirituality, then, Woolman is a man who is constantly seeking and making connections. He consistently reflects on the necessary relationship between love of God and love of neighbor, the importance of linking authentic principles and practice, and the interconnectedness of social issues themselves.

2. Stages in Woolman's Spiritual Development

As I read the *Journal* I notice that when Woolman describes the first half of his life much of the focus centers on his interior struggles: his adult reaffirmation of his faith, his call to ministry, overcoming fears about speaking out, and learning to follow his conscience without becoming overly preoccupied with the opinion of others. However, in the second half of his *Journal* Woolman says increasingly less about his interior struggles and spends more time focusing on the needs and concerns of others. His attention becomes increasingly other-oriented. After the crisis of the French and Indian War, he seems more settled in his role as a Quaker reformer, and he is more peaceful even in the face of significant difficulties.

Ironically, at the same time he progressively becomes less concerned with success in his ministry and more concerned with simply following God's will:

> Travelling up and down of late, I have had renewed evidences that to be faithful to the Lord and content with his will concerning me is a most necessary and useful lesson for me to be learning, looking less at the effects of my labour than at the pure motion and reality of the concern as it arises from heavenly love. In the Lord Jehovah is everlasting strength, and as the mind by humble resignation is united to him and we utter words from an inward knowledge that they arise from the heavenly spring, though our way may be difficult and require close attention to keep in it, and though the manner in which we may be led may tend to our own abasement, yet if we continue in patience and meekness, heavenly peace is the reward of our labours. (PM 72)

As he grew spiritually, Woolman's ability to wait patiently in silence for God to speak and for clearness to surface moved him toward complete resignation to God and to a mature happiness. He also realized that his inner conflicts were often the result of his lack of full resignation to God's will. Finally, Woolman's inner freedom seems to correspond to the gradual simplification of his life, especially as he tried to rid himself of anything which was connected with the oppression of others.

3. Prayer

Just as there is a definite movement from self-concern to concern for others in the *Journal*, so too I detect distinct development in Woolman's prayer life throughout the *Journal*. Woolman uses at least four different forms of prayer: prayer of petition which expresses his need for God's help, mercy, strength; prayer of resignation where he surrenders to God's will; prayer of thanksgiving in appreciation for what God is doing in his life and in his world; and prayer of adoration where he praises God for God's goodness and love. While each form of prayer is present in every stage of his life, there seems to be a progression from his early years which predominately center on a prayer of petition, to his later years which increasingly reveal a prayer of adoration and praise.

Also, Woolman's prayer was often quite emotional. At times he shed tears of sorrow both in private and in meeting. At other times he was filled with elation and joy. He seems to have experienced growing humility before God and increasing freedom as he let God take control of his life. For a man whose lifestyle was rather austere, his spiritual life was rich with feeling.

However, there are some things Woolman does not tell us about his prayer. Missing are descriptions of how God works within him and how Woolman discerns what action to take. We know that God does work and that Woolman himself discerned carefully his decisions, but he says little about how God works in him and how he discerns what God is asking of him. The *Journal* really does not center on Woolman's unique religious experience, but rather emphasizes the reality of God's action in itself. Woolman writes his *Journal* not to provide a normative experience, but as an encouragement to others to let God work in them.

4. Identification with the Poor and Oppressed

In the *Journal* one can see in Woolman a gradual movement from sympathy to empathy. As his social consciousness begins to awaken, he describes his emerging concern for the poor from the perspective of one who cares about the needs of others while remaining personally secure and comfortable. However, as Woolman increasingly becomes involved in social issues, he begins to alter his lifestyle in accord with the principles he preaches. Consequently, he begins to share at least some of the reality of the oppressed, and he speaks with greater sensitivity.

For example, Woolman's developing concern over slavery gradually leads him to simplify his life radically. His decisions, both practical and symbolic, not only commit him to some discomfort, but also occasion some misunderstanding, ridicule, and rejection, experiences well known to slaves or the poor. Or, when he makes the dangerous journey to the Native American community at Wyalusing during Pontiac's Rebellion, he explains that he discerned that he was called to learn more about Indian spirituality and to share his own faith with them. The dangers and difficulties of the journey helped him to understand the hardships facing Native Americans, particularly as a result of colonialization.

During the latter years of his life, when his health was fragile, he undertook most of his religious journeys on foot in order to identify more closely with the poor and oppressed. On his final journey, he traveled to England in steerage out of a deep desire to live simply and to share the lot of the sailors. When he arrived in England, he refused to use the stage system or even receive mail conveyed on it because of the oppressive treatment of the post boys, drivers, and horses. Furthermore, some English Quakers, uncomfortable with his undyed clothing and simple faith, found it difficult to accept him until they gained some sense of his depth and holiness.

I think Woolman would agree with the adage that "where you stand determines what you see." He stood with the poor, and tried to respond to the Gospel and God's call as he heard it standing in their reality.

5. *The Cross*

Finally, the cross functioned as a vital image or symbol for Woolman and he used it frequently. The cross carried three levels of meaning for him. First of all, it was an image which represented God's unconditional love for humankind. Secondly, it was a symbol which helped Woolman to unite his suffering with the suffering of Christ. Finally, it offered a standard against which he measured the values of the world and the quality of his discipleship in the world.

Like St. Paul, Woolman believed that Christ's sufferings continue in the sufferings of his disciples:

> Now I find that in pure obedience the mind learns contentment in appearing weak and foolish to that wisdom which is of the world: and in these lowly labours, they who stand in a low place, right exercised under the cross, will find nourishment.
>
> The gift is pure; and while the eye is single in attending thereto, the understanding is preserved clear; self is kept out; and we rejoice in filling up that which remains of the afflictions of Christ for his body's sake, which is the church. (AMG 315)

Woolman maintained that submitting to the power of the cross would lead Christ's disciple to let go of attachments which blind one to God's will and would prepare one to enter into deeper union with God. Woolman also believed that suffering was part of the life of the disciple, just as it had been part of Christ's life. However, total resignation to God's will would issue in new life. This is most clearly stated in that powerful incident, really a mystical experience, which he relates near the end of the *Journal* when he was ill with pleurisy. While trying to figure out the meaning of the voice which said, "John Woolman is dead," he finally concludes, "I am crucified with Christ, nevertheless I live; yet not I, but Christ that liveth in me, and the life I now live in the flesh is by faith in the Son of God, who loved me and gave himself for me" [Gal 2:20]. And he goes on to conclude, "that language that John Woolman is dead meant no more than the death of my own will" (PM 186). Once again, William Johnston offers a helpful interpretation of this paradigmatic Christian experience:

> In a Christian context, mystical action reaches its climax when I surrender to the Spirit so totally that I can make my own the words of Paul, "It is no longer I who live, but Christ who lives in me" (Gal 2:20). When these words live in me the Spirit of Jesus governs my life, my action is no longer my own, and what appears to be conscious effort is the activity of a deeper power which dwells within. (155)

Conclusion

John Woolman's spirituality is so worthy of our study because it reflects a creative synthesis of the values of his religious tradition, the social expression of those values, and a rich prayer life. Each dimension of his spirituality critiques and authenticates the others. Thus, Woolman's identity as a Quaker was challenged by the social needs of his time and the ongoing and increasingly radical call he received from God in prayer. His social concern was grounded in the spiritual values of his tradition and sustained by his own discipline of prayer. And his interior life both shaped and was shaped by his tradition and his response to the social needs of his time.

John Woolman provides us with a wonderful example of a truly holistic spirituality, and his spirituality both inspires and challenges us to live our lives with greater integrity as individuals, as participants in faith communities, and as members of the human family within creation.

NOTE

[1]The meeting minutes consulted include: Burlington Monthly Meeting Minutes, 1737-56, 1757-70, 1770-81; Burlington Quarterly Meeting Minutes, 1686-1767 (minutes from 1767-95 are missing); Burlington Quarterly Meeting—Ministers and Elders Minutes, 1717-96 (Vol. A); Philadelphia Yearly Meeting Minutes, 1681-1746, 1747-79; Philadelphia Yearly Meeting—Ministers and Elders Minutes, 1734/5-1774; Philadelphia Yearly Meeting—Meeting for Sufferings, 1756-75; Friends Historical Library, Swarthmore College, Swarthmore, PA.

WORKS CITED

Brinton, Howard H. *Ethical Mysticism in the Society of Friends.* Pendle Hill Pamphlet, no. 156. Wallingford, PA: Pendle Hill, 1967.

—. *Friends for 300 Years.* 1952. Wallingford, PA: Pendle Hill, 1983.

Brueggemann, Walter. *The Prophetic Imagination.* Philadelphia, PA: Fortress Press, 1978.

Johnston, William. *The Inner Eye of Love.* San Francisco,CA: Harper, 1978.

Meeting Minutes. Friends Historical Library, Swarthmore College, Swarthmore, PA.

Woolman, John. *The Journal and Major Essays of John Woolman.* Ed. Phillips P. Moulton. 1971. Richmond, IN: Friends United Press, 1989.

2

The Spiritual Formation of Young John Woolman

Paul Anderson

When we think of John Woolman's contribution, we might think first about his advocacy for the poor and his opposition of slavery. But whence did his concerns emerge, and how did his spiritual sensitivities develop? A remarkable thing about many Quaker autobiographies is the fact that one can trace early on in the experience of an eventual leader the clear promptings of the Deity, coupled with the individual's responses of faith. Certainly it was true for George Fox and others, but the narrated memory of childhood openings and reflections upon youthful spiritual development is even clearer in the *Journal of John Woolman*. The thesis could even be argued that young Woolman's spiritual openings formed the pattern for his later social concerns—either in content or in process—but the interest of this essay is other. It seeks to examine the spiritual formation of young John Woolman with the particular interest of finding out what can be learned about the spiritual development and experience of children and young adults—then and now.

Of course, distinguishing the historical Woolman from the narrated Woolman may be a finally impossible venture, but for the purpose of this essay, one will take the *Journal* reportings pretty much at face value. In doing so, however, one is neither assuming nor doubting their historicity but is simply responding to the narrated memory of earlier events, keeping the authorial interest of the written form at least somewhat in mind. This purpose is most clearly articulated in Woolman's introductory sentence: "I have often felt a motion of love to leave some hints in writing of my experience of the goodness of God, and now, in the thirty-sixth year of my age, I begin this work" (PM 23). From this declaration of intent one may infer Woolman's primary purpose was to record his experience of "the goodness of God" in order that future readers may be inspired and moved toward like encounters. In that sense, his narration serves the function of forming—every bit as much as informing—the reader in ways spiritual. An analysis of Woolman's treatment of both of these interests in the narration of his first twenty-three years, thus comprises the interest and scope of this essay.

So how does one approach such an endeavor, letting Woolman's text speak for itself? In order to best get at the content, three tasks may help. First, breaking his learnings into appropriate units, largely following his own paragraph structuring, helps one consider them individually. This also facilitates considering the source(s) of each of Woolman's impressions, suggesting something of the formation process itself. Second, identifying phases and developments in terms of content enhances one's appreciation of Woolman's spiritual learnings and insights. Third, from considering these two analyses together, then, observations and insights emerge regarding the spiritual formation of young John Woolman in ways instructive for our times as well.

An impressive thing about Woolman's writing is the way he characteristically develops fully a single idea within a single paragraph. His learning shows. This makes it possible largely to follow his own paragraph structure (and Moulton's editing of it) as it relates to isolating the spiritual learnings and impressions themselves. Each paragraph is often hemmed by markers of time or space, or both, or at least the introduction of a new theme or a further development of an earlier theme. This contributes to the identifying of 30 narrations of spiritual insight within the 32 paragraphs of Woolman's first chapter. With such exceptions as finding two learnings in the second, twelfth, and thirteenth paragraphs, and event/reflection combinations of paragraphs 3/4, 5/6, 9/10, 16/17, and 31/32, the rest of the paragraphs in Woolman's first chapter correspond one to one with narrations of particular spiritual learnings.

While more than one source is often mentioned within each paragraph, attention has been focused on the primary one serving as the prevalent source of formation in that particular instance. Of course, as such a procedure is always based on subjective impressions and is thus somewhat inexact, the findings ought to be taken as suggestive indications rather than conclusive ones. On the other hand, categorization and analysis does lend valuable insight as to the character and origin of each of Woolman's early spiritual impressions. So let's proceed.

Sources of Spiritual Impressions

In Woolman's first chapter spiritual impressions emerge from basically eight distinctive sources. At times these are combined, such as Scripture, meeting, and reflection producing a singular opening, but mostly each insight tends to have emerged from a primary source, and taking note of such is telling. These also range in frequency from once (a dream and the helpful fellowship of supportive friends) to nine times (divine address and help received). Of course, these sources of openings worked in complementary ways, such as an event or experience leading to reflection or the sense of divine help, for instance, so some of those confluences will be at least touched upon. While one could approach these sources numerically, from most frequent to least frequent or vice versa, a simpler way to approach these is to follow the sequence of the category's first appearance in the *Journal* itself and then to discuss other references along that same motif. Nonetheless, the number of each appearance is as follows:

Table 1: *"Sources of Woolman's Early Spiritual Impressions and Learnings"*

Source	Number of Times Mentioned
Readings of Scripture or Other Good Books	7
Parents' Counsel and Instruction	3
A Dream	1
Events and Life Experiences	7
Divine Address and Help	9
Corporate Meetings for Worship and Private Worship and Prayer	3
Observation and Reflection	3
The Helpful Fellowship of Supportive Friends	1

a) The Reading of Scripture or Religious Books.

Woolman's first reported spiritual impression came from the reading of Scripture, and six other ones emerged from either reading the Bible, "pious authors" or "good books." In fact, this medium of inspiration (along with learnings derived from experiences or events, which also numbers seven) is second only to the noting of receiving divine address or help which Woolman cites nine times in his first chapter. It also occupies an important place early in his personal experience. The prevalence and chronological primacy of Scripture in Woolman's spiritual formation is thus extremely significant.

As a six- or seven-year-old reading the 22nd chapter of Revelation, Woolman reflects: "And in reading it my mind was drawn to seek after that pure habitation which I then believed God had prepared for his servants. The place where I sat and the sweetness that attended my mind remains fresh in my memory" (PM 23). Clearly, he was warmed to a vision of the people of God and "a pure habitation" which began to form his own identity and aspirations. This opening was followed by a habitual pattern of reading, both of Scripture and "good books," which Woolman conducted after meeting and otherwise. It is even possible that one of these may have been the *Journal of George Fox,* as Woolman makes good use of such reminiscent terms as "openings" and the seeking out of deserts and "lonely places." His later reflections on friendship likewise suggest familiarity with St. Augustine's *Confessions.*

At several times, Scripture provided a source of guidance in ways which spoke existentially to the condition of young John Woolman. For instance, as a convicting parallel to his killing of the baby birds, the words of Proverbs 12:10 rang true: "The tender mercies of the wicked are cruel" (PM 24f.). Likewise, after having spent part of a day "in wantonness," Woolman picked up a Bible by his bed, and his eye landed on a passage which bespoke his situation: "We lie down in our shame, and our confusion covers us" [Jer. 3:25], (PM 27). The telling connection here is that Woolman experienced his own situation being "read" by the inspired text. It was as though the divine author of the Scriptures were speaking to his situation directly as he read, and such contributed considerably to Woolman's early formation.

As well as these explicit references, many indirect biblical images present themselves throughout Woolman's presentation of his early life. The white stone and new name of Revelation 2:17, for instance, mark his understanding of the blessing awarded the faithful, and "to bear the cross" becomes for Woolman a meaningful daily motif denoting the cost of discipleship (PM 29). Likewise, "the spirit of supplication" [Romans 8], (PM 30) becomes a description of divine enablement, and being addressed by "that Word which is as a fire and hammer" (PM 26) describes the convicting power of God's spirit. It would be a mistake to identify Woolman as a biblicist, and yet, the Scriptures undeniably played a major role in his early spiritual formation. While known primarily for his social impact and sensitivities, one must ponder whether these would have developed the way they did had young John Woolman not early on engaged—and been engaged by—the Scriptures.

b.) Parents' Counsel and Instruction

The second source of influence mentioned by Woolman is the counsel received from his parents. It was his parents whom he describes as:

> . . . having a large family of children, used frequently on First Days after meeting to put us to read in the Holy Scriptures or some religious books, one after another, the rest sitting by without much conversation, which I have since often thought was a good practice. (PM 23f.)

From this, Woolman "believed there had been in past ages people who walked in uprightness before God in a degree exceeding any that I knew, or hear of, now living" (PM 24). Early on, his parents advised him to take seriously the life of the Spirit and the way of piety. Apparently, young Woolman took this counsel to heart and aspired to live his life in accord with such standards.

Suggestive of Woolman's sensitivity, when his father later corrected him for making "an undutiful reply" to his mother, Woolman reports:

> . . . the next First Day as I was with my father returning from meeting, he told me he understood I had behaved amiss to my mother and advised me to be more careful in future. . . . Being thus awakened to a sense of my wickedness, I felt remorse of mind, and getting home I retired and prayed to the Lord to forgive me, and do not remember that I ever after that spoke unhandsomely to either of my parents, however foolish in other things. (PM 25)

Clearly, his personal sensitivity was formed significantly by his parents' direction, as young Woolman quite early on developed a keen sense of high moral standard encompassing both outward and inward measures.

c.) Dreams

The third source of spiritual formation for Woolman was a dream he had during his ninth year. While he records other dreams during later times of his life, this was the only one he mentioned during his early years. The actual implications of the dream are left unmentioned, and one can appreciate why the dream has been omitted from MS. A (PM 24). And yet, Moulton rightly includes it, as an author's somewhat opaque contributions deserve also to be considered by later readers as well as the more memorable ones.

The importance of this dream lies not so much in the direct content it conveys, but the impression of one who sees God at work radically in the world. One could even use the words "eschatological" and "apocalyptic" to describe Woolman's emerging world view. It is apocalyptic (*apocalypsis* = revelation) in that it assumes the unveiling of God's purposes and workings transcending and invading the physical world. It is also eschatological (*eschaton* = last) in that it expects God to act with finality in the lives and affairs of humans. The believer is called to partner with God in the unfolding of God's saving/redeeming purposes in the world. Such understandings are not incidental to Woolman's ethical and social stands; they are central and foundational to them.

d.) Events and Life Experiences

Tied with the reading of Scripture and good books, the second most frequent source of spiritual formation mentioned by Woolman in the first chapter of his *Journal* is events and life experiences. He mentions seven such episodes, which involve reflection upon the common happenings of life. The first and last of these in Woolman's first chapter are the most dramatic, while the middle ones tend to address his struggles with social temptations and other trials.

The first of these involves an event in the life of young Woolman as a child, when he killed a robin with a stone. Feeling terrible about the incident and taking pity on the chicks, he killed them all rather than leaving them to a drawn-out demise. And yet, he records his anguish over the incident: "but for some hours [I] could think of little else but the cruelties I had committed, and was much troubled" (PM 25). From reflecting on this event and his own feelings about it, Woolman concluded God had "placed a principle in the human mind which incites to exercise goodness toward every living creature; and this being singly attended to, people become tender-hearted and sympathizing" (PM 25).

The middle events and experiences from which Woolman derives spiritual insight tend to involve his struggles with social pressures and worldly temptations. At this point, one must guard against the inclination to contextualize such trials. All too easily, later audiences read of earlier struggles and minimize their sway because they seem archaic or irrelevant. Too facilely, the modern or post-modern interpreter declares with patronizing smugness, "Yes, well, those people back then struggled with X or Y (obviously they didn't know any better, as we do today, of course) but despite their moral unsophistication we can distill certain values. . . ." Nonsense. We don't need to know the specifics of Woolman's social temptations to appreciate their sway. The fact is that he reports struggling greatly—more so with this set of issues than any other—and if we want to glimpse the core of young Woolman's spiritual formation, we must take seriously his narration of backsliding struggles as indeed being such. Consider his sensitive introduction to the issue:

> Having attained the age of sixteen years, I began to love wanton company, and though I was preserved from profane language or scandalous conduct, still I perceived a plant in me which produced much wild grapes. Yet my merciful Father forsook me not utterly, but at times through his grace I was brought seriously to consider my ways, and the sight of my backsliding affected me with sorrow. But for want of rightly attending to the reproofs of instruction, vanity was added to vanity, and repentance to repentance; upon the whole my mind was more and more alienated from the Truth, and I hastened toward destruction. While I meditate on the gulf toward which I travelled and reflect on my youthful disobedience, for these things I weep; mine eye runneth down with water. (PM 25)

Several things emerge as Woolman's adolescent struggles with temptations arise. The first is that he found himself "estranged" from the Holy Scriptures rather than finding comfort in them. Second, he felt himself "going from the flock of Christ" and associating with those running down the same road "in that which is reverse to true friendship" (PM 25f.). Along "this swift race," however, he reflects "it pleased God to visit me with sickness, so that I doubted of recovering" (PM 26). Upon the affliction and estrangement that ensued, Woolman reflects: "in a deep sense of my great folly I was humbled before him, and at length that Word which is as a fire and a hammer broke and dissolved my rebellious heart" (PM 26).

Over the next few years, Woolman gained and lost ground in his struggles with "giving way to youthful vanities" and "getting with wanton young people." The tension is described well:

> I was not so hardy as to commit things scandalous, but to exceed in vanity and promote mirth was my chief study. Still I retained a love and esteem for pious people, and their company brought an awe upon me. (PM 26)

Another example of the tension is described in the following passage:

> Now though I had been thus strengthened to bear the cross, I still found myself in great danger, having many weaknesses attending me and strong temptations to wrestle with, in the feeling whereof I frequently withdrew into private places and often with tears besought the Lord to help me, whose gracious ear was open to my cry. (PM 29)

This development of an autonomous spiritual identity became tested and strengthened by the experience of being hired to tend shop and keep books by a local shopkeeper and baker when Woolman was in his twenty-first year. He moved out of his family home and into the shop he was tending, and this event proved a testing ground for his moral commitments and resolve. When several young people he had known before "who knew not but vanities" came to visit him, Woolman says, "I cried to the Lord in secret for wisdom and strength. . . . And as I had now left my father's house outwardly, I found my Heavenly Father to be merciful to me beyond what I can express" (PM 30).

Two final events in this early chapter of Woolman's life involved actions of others, personalizing the slave trade, which troubled him and called for action and reflection. The first was a Scotch manservant, purchased from a vessel and brought to Mount Holly by Woolman's master. This man was terribly ill, and Woolman tended to his needs as he became delirious and eventually died. His second recorded encounter with the anomalies of slavery involved his employer's selling a Negro woman and directing Woolman to write a bill of sale for the man who bought her. Woolman recalls his unease with writing "an instrument of slavery" and reflects: "so through weakness I gave way and wrote it, but at the executing it, I was so afflicted in my mind that I said before my master and the Friend [buying the slave] that I believed slavekeeping to be a practice inconsistent with the Christian religion" (PM 33). Later, in a conversation with a purchaser, Woolman heard him also express his doubts about slavery, and one must surmise such experiences with the personal reality of the issue cannot but have affected Woolman's later position on the matter over the rest of his life.

From this sequence of event or experience and reflection, one can detect a clear pattern of learning and discernment which becomes a friend to Woolman all of his life. As a reflective practitioner in terms of ethics and matters of morality, young John Woolman acquired the twin abilities of allowing the roots of conviction to go deep into his being and becoming willing to stand against the tide of popular opinion when Truth demanded it. These became trademarks of his life.

e.) Divine Address and Help

The most common source of spiritual formation recorded by Woolman regarding his early years may be described as the receiving of divine address and divine help. This is not to say he did not experience intimations of the Divine through the other media mentioned above and below, but at times Woolman simply notes unmediated experiences of divine enablement, which either point out the way he should go or provide the empowerment to walk in what he knows to be the way of Truth. These number at least nine in the first chapter of his *Journal,* and they are often mentioned in tandem with other means of formation.

Consider these accounts:

> Yet my merciful Father forsook me not utterly, but at times through his grace I was brought seriously to consider my ways, and the sight of my backsliding affected me with sorrow. (PM 25)

> . . . I felt the judgments of God in my soul like a consuming fire, and looking over my past life the prospect was moving. (PM 27)

> Thus for some months I had great trouble, there remaining in me an unsubjected will which rendered my labours fruitless, till at length through the merciful continuance of heavenly visitations I was made to bow down in spirit before the Lord. (PM 27)

In the following account, both divine guidance and empowerment are recalled:

> I was now led to look seriously at the means by which I was drawn from the pure Truth, and learned this: that if I would live in the life which the faithful servants of God lived in, I must not go into company as heretofore in my own will, but all the cravings of sense must be governed by a divine principle. In times of sorrow and abasement these instructions were sealed upon me, and I felt the power of Christ prevail over selfish desires, so that I was preserved in a good degree of steadiness. (PM 28)

The following accounts also speak for themselves: "As I lived under the cross and simply followed the openings of Truth, my mind from day to day was more enlightened" (PM 28) ". . . in those times the spirit of supplication was often poured upon me, under which I was frequently exercised and felt my strength renewed" (PM 30). "This truth was early fixed in my mind, and I was taught to watch the pure opening and to take heed lest while I was standing to speak, my own will should get uppermost and cause me to utter words from worldly wisdom and depart from the channel of the true gospel ministry" (PM 31). "In the management of my outward affairs I may say with thankfulness I found Truth to be my support. . ." (PM 31). And finally,

> About the twenty-third year of my age, I had many fresh and heavenly openings in respect to the care and providence of the Almighty over his creatures in general, and over man as the most noble amongst those which are visible. (PM 32)

The above references illustrate graphically Woolman's growing conviction that God seeks to be engaged with humans in an inward dialogue of divine initiative and human response. And, not only is such a dialogue declared a worthy venture by Woolman, but the content of this conviction is also rooted in such a dialectical experience:

> And being clearly convinced in my judgment that to place my whole trust in God was best for me, I felt renewed engagements that in all things I might act on an inward principle of virtue and pursue worldly business no further than as Truth opened my way therein. (PM 32)

And by this standard Woolman sought to live the rest of his life.

f.) Corporate Meetings for Worship and Private Worship and Prayer

Several times Woolman mentions receiving help from corporate meetings and private times of worship. Not that these are the only times worship was mentioned (see, for instance, PM 23f.), but three times especially Woolman describes the formative power of worship:

> I kept steady to meetings, spent First Days after noon chiefly in reading the Scriptures and other good books, and was early convinced in my mind that true religion consisted in an inward life, wherein the heart doth love and reverence God the Creator and learn to exercise true justice and goodness, not only toward all men but also toward the brute creatures. (PM 28)

The mention of quiet evenings alone as a source of sustenance is general (PM 30), and of course the learnings from having spoken "more than was required of me" (PM 31)—and the ensuing reflection—is a classic.

Learnings from meetings for worship are frequently combined with other means of formation such as reading, parental influence, event/experiencc and observation/reflection. In fact, the most extended description of meeting-related formation (PM 30) itself is based on event/experience, reflection, and divine address. At times private worship becomes a source of strength and formation (PM 30), and one gets the sense that the inward strength formed in solitude becomes the core source of later public ministry.

g.) Observation and Reflection

Several times Woolman's spirituality was formed by the process of reflection. In conjunction with reading the Scriptures and other good books and attending meetings for worship, his reflection upon the life of the Spirit contributes significantly to his being "early convinced in my mind that true religion consisted in an inward life" (PM 28). The next time reflection is mentioned, however, it is described as a singular factor:

> While I silently ponder on that change wrought in me, I find no language equal to it nor any means to convey to another a clear idea of it. I looked upon the works of God in this visible creation and an awfulness covered me; my heart was tender and often contrite, and a universal love to my fellow creatures increased in me. (PM 29)

Woolman also observed people "resorting to the public houses" and other sorts of "disorder" and formed a personal conviction against such activities (PM 32). What we see emerging in Woolman is the capacity for being a thoughtful, reflective practitioner in the everyday venues of life. From such reflection emerge insights and convictions central to his emerging ethical stands.

At this point, something must be said about Woolman's understanding of what he calls a "divine principle" or an "inward principle." As this motif is mentioned six times in his first chapter, one could argue this should be considered a separate source of formation, but two facts call for an alternative approach. First, the mention of principle is the result of reflection upon events and experiences, and it simply refers to what is known to be the path pleasing to God—which if taken leads to harmonious and constructive ends; but if rejected leads to "confusion" or infelicitous results. The classic example is the killing of the robin and her young (PM 24f.). Second, the mention of inward or divine principle is used in conjunction with other means of divine address, so that it really cannot be considered a separate means. Rather, "divine principle" functions for Woolman as the abiding truth of God, which is encountered inwardly while brought to awareness by life experiences (PM 25), divine enablement and address (PM 28, 30, 32), and the attending of meeting and the reading of Scriptures (PM 28). Accordingly, Woolman believed heeding such a principle would lead or help one to "exercise goodness toward every living creature" (PM 25), govern the "cravings of sense" (PM 28), have one's heart "enlarged in this heavenly principle" (PM 30), "pursue worldly business no further than as Truth opened my way therein" (PM 32), and to "love God as an invisible, incomprehensible being . . . [and] to love him in all his manifestations in the visible world" (PM 28). So divine principle, for Woolman, functions as the inward locus of God's Truth, which if minded leads to goodness, but if disobeyed leads to destruction.

h.) The Helpful Fellowship of Supportive Friends

One time in particular Woolman mentions the value of supportive friends and fellowship, who apparently supplanted less helpful associations:

> After a while my former acquaintance gave over expecting me as one of their company, and I began to be known to some whose conversation was helpful to me. And now, as I had experienced the love of God through Jesus Christ to redeem me from many pollutions and to be a succour to me through a sea of conflicts, with which no person was fully acquainted, and as my heart was often enlarged in this heavenly principle, I felt a tender compassion for the youth who remained entangled in snares like those which had entangled me. From one month to another this love and tenderness increased, and my mind was more strongly engaged for the good of my fellow creatures. (PM 30)

Again, the reference to the specific sort of help received is left general, but for our purposes, the significant interest is in the source of influence and formation. Here we see Woolman's peer group shifting to one more conducive to his values, and he clearly feels helped by these acquaintances over alternative ones. From such support and reflecting upon his own struggles, Woolman's sensitivity toward others struggling with like issues is accentuated, and one gets the sense help received will later on be translated into help offered in similar settings.

In considering the sources of formation regarding the spiritual development of young John Woolman, one can clearly infer a progression from the influences of Scripture, family, and meeting, to reflection upon events and experiences, to broader issues and engagement in social concerns. Such a progression is entirely understandable, and yet noting the particular development in Woolman's life is instructive. All too easily, his considerable social contributions become the primary focus of study, while the formative factors underlying such sensitivities is all but overlooked. The present analysis continues in examining the particular phases in his formation, with a special interest in the themes emerging at various stages of development.

Phases in Young Woolman's Spiritual Formation

Three particular phases emerge when considering Woolman's narration of his early life, and each of these appears to have two parts to it. In the first and third phases the two parts appear to be somewhat distinct, but in all of them, and especially in the second, a considerable degree of overlapping between the two parts within the phase presents itself. Not that the phases are discontinuous between themselves at all. Indeed, progress established during one phase prepares the way for later developments as well. Here one may feel inclined to analyze Woolman's experience and development within the categories of any number of developmentalist or stages-of-faith theoretical constructs, but such will be resisted in this essay. The interest here is to let Woolman's own formation determine its own classification and markers of boundary first, so as to consider fully its own character, before imposing onto it rubrics of analysis from without. Such ventures can often be helpful, but they can also function to diminish appreciation for the very special quality of individual experience. The three phases are as follows:

Table 2: *"Phases in the Spiritual Formation of Young John Woolman"*

Phase	Parts within each phase	(Approximate ages)
a. Emergence of a Personal Vision of "Uprightness" (ages 6-16)		
	i.) Seeking after "That Pure Habitation"	
	ii.) Awakened to "A Sense of Wickedness"	
b. Finding a Place between Family and Society (ages 16-21)		
	i.) Struggles with "Wantonness"	
	ii.) Learning to "Live under the Cross"	
c. Learning to Speak to the Conditions of the World (ages 21-23)		
	i.) Learning to "Watch the Pure Opening"	
	ii.) Developing a "Feeling Sense of the Condition of Others"	

a.) Emergence of a Personal Vision of "Uprightness"

Explicit within the first three pages of his *Journal* is the emergence of a personal vision of "uprightness" within the consciousness of young John Woolman. He interprets these developments as effects of the operations of divine love, and the resulting vision of what is required of him becomes a calling to live into such an ideal personally. On one hand, the emergence of an ideal becomes the stuff of personal aspiration, challenging Woolman to a life believed to be pleasing to God. On the other hand, the ideal is experienced to be a far cry from his actual inclination and deeds, and such a disparity produces a great deal of consternation for him. These two impulses, and the tension between them, can be seen clearly in the two parts within the first phase.

i.) *Seeking after "That Pure Habitation."* Before the age of seven, young Woolman records, his sights were lifted to a pure and righteous standard to which he should aspire. Through the reading of Scripture and good books, the instruction of his parents, and the example of Friends at meeting his understanding of a life pleasing to God becomes formed, and such a vision becomes a calling to "seek after that pure habitation which I then believed God had prepared for his servants" (PM 23). Woolman was also keenly aware of discrepancies between such a pure standard and the lives of those around him. Instead of playing with peers, he would at times seek out contemplative settings; the "ill language" of boys bothered him; and he was troubled by the lack of "steadiness and firmness" among the people of the present age as contrasted to former times when people "walked in uprightness before God" (PM 23f.).

While the exact role of the dream is unclear, the sense of the transcendent workings of God comes through very clearly in it, and such has direct implications for an emerging sense of moral direction. Inclinations to relativize invariably wither before a lively sense of the ultimate. In all, one can detect clearly the emergence of a personal vision of what sort of life would be pleasing to God during the early years of Woolman's life, and such a vision becomes a sort of compass, pointing to true north amidst confusing times. While Woolman is stricken with a sense of incongruity between his emerging ideals and the lives of those around him, a special set of crises emerge as he is confronted by the disparity between his own actions and his emerging standards. Ironically, a personal sense of righteousness also causes him to be awakened to a personal sense of wickedness.

ii.) *Awakened to "A Sense of Wickedness."* Two primary events are recorded as awakening young Woolman to his own sense of falling short of a standard of life pleasing to God. The first is the killing of the robin and her young. Upon reflection, Woolman felt terrible about having harmed such innocent creatures and interpreted such as the rejection of the divine "principle in the human mind," resulting in the mind shutting itself up "in a contrary disposition" (PM 25). The other experience awakening Woolman to his personal "sense of wickedness" was his "undutiful reply" to his mother's reproof for his misconduct during his twelfth year of age (PM 25). When his father confronted him on the way home from meeting the next First Day about his behaving "amiss," young Woolman felt remorseful, prayed for forgiveness, and reports repentantly he did "not remember that I ever after that spoke unhandsomely to either of my parents, however foolish in other things" (PM 25).

Throughout these reports, Woolman's keen sensitivity shows through, and later interpreters may either question the authenticity of the presentation or consider him too exceptional to be relevant. Presenting the "historical Woolman" versus the narrated Woolman, however, is beyond the purview of this essay, and some embellishment or recasting of former events is always expected within any narration, even historical ones. The fact is Woolman was indeed an exceptional person, which is why his contribution is so impressive and why his life still commands sustained interest. What does indeed come through here is the tension between the emergence of a lofty ideal personally, and the personal sense of inadequacy to live up to that ideal experientially. Rather than proving a final discouragement, however, Woolman seems to have become more keenly aware of his dependence on divine enablement, and this becomes a source of further spiritual connectedness and vitality.

The first phase in Woolman's narrated spiritual development appears thus to be a personal one. The work of establishing a sense of the ideal, of a life believed pleasing to God, catches his imagination and becomes a personal aspiration. Indeed, such aspiration then becomes the stuff of personal awareness of shortcomings, leading to further spiritual struggle and maturation. While Woolman must have had other spiritual experiences before those narrated in his *Journal*, the emergence of a personal vision of wholeness becomes the beginning juncture for narrating his story of the operations and motions of divine love upon his life.

b.) Finding a Place between Family and Society

From the age of sixteen into his early twenties, Woolman records many and repeated struggles to find a place between family and society. He recalls the beginning of this phase like this: "Having attained the age of sixteen years, I began to love wanton company, and though I was preserved from profane language or scandalous conduct, still I perceived a plant in me which produced much wild grapes" (PM 25). This phase continues even after Woolman's moving out of his parents' home and into the shop at which he worked. While this phase also has two main parts to it, it is unlike the first in that the two parts are described as greatly interwoven. Woolman describes struggles with wantonness throughout these five years or so, and he also narrates his learning to live under the cross into his twenty-first or twenty-second year with varying degrees of success.

i.) *Struggles with "Wantonness."* On one hand, one may consider this time in Woolman's life as the healthy development of peer relations and the needed work of individuation, moving from parental values to the establishing of one's own. Some of that does indeed happen here. In a couple of ways, however, such a task is inadequate to describe Woolman's situation. First, he has already come to own personally many values, some of which are rooted in parental instruction and some of which are not. So a fair degree of individuation and autonomy is already in place by this time in Woolman's life. A second disparity is that Woolman for some time appears to have had no genuinely supportive peer group or extra-familial locus of authority from which to receive support. He describes emerging social contacts as "wanton young people" (PM 26), "several young people, my former acquaintance, who knew not but vanities" (PM 30), and "youth who remained entangled in snares" (PM 30). And yet, it is also clear that Woolman numbers himself among them in the promoting of mirth and vanities and in the pursuit of wantonness. In that sense, the second part of the first phase continues into the first part of the second. Struggles with personal matters of morality now become wrestled with in social contexts, and such struggles continue over several years.

Again, basic ignorance of the specific issues of morality here is not problematic, as contextualizing too easily relativizes the values at stake and diminishes later readers' esteem for the gravity of the narrated struggles. The fact is Woolman reports struggling, intensely and repeatedly, and such deserves to be accorded its full weight by later readers, whatever the issues might have been.

ii.) *Learning to "Live under the Cross."* Learning to bear and live under the cross becomes Woolman's way of describing the yielding of his will to God, wherein he humbly draws on God's grace and chooses to mind the leading he knows to be true. As an inward effect of young Woolman's hastening "toward destruction," he reports his way growing more difficult: "Though I had heretofore found comfort in reading the Holy Scriptures and thinking on heavenly thing, I was now estranged therefrom" (PM 25). In the midst of this sense of estrangement, Woolman interprets the visitation of illness as a divine means of humbling and drawing him back to God. He reports:

> . . . in a deep sense of my great folly I was humbled before him, . . . then my cries were put up in contrition, and in the multitude of his mercies I found inward relief, and felt a close engagement that if he was pleased to restore my health, I might walk humbly before him. (PM 26)

It is unclear to what degree the above experience defines his later conviction that the way forward spiritually and morally is to live humbly under the cross, but Woolman discusses his reflection over these events in the next paragraph: "After my recovery this exercise remained with me a considerable time" (PM 26). The dialogue between experience and reflection here continues, and Woolman's understanding of what it means to live under the cross is connected centrally to this dialectic. Later, having "lost ground" and having felt "the judgments of God in my soul like a consuming fire" (PM 26f.) he reports:

> In a while I resolved totally to leave off some of my vanities, but there was a secret reserve in my heart of the more refined part of them, and I was not low enough to find true peace. Thus for some months I had great trouble, there remaining in me anunsubjected will which rendered my labours fruitless, till

> at length through the merciful continuance of heavenly visitations I was made to bow down in spirit before the Lord.
>
> I remember one evening I had spent some time in reading a pious author, and walking out alone I humbly prayed to the Lord for his help, that I might be delivered from all those vanities which so ensnared me. Thus being brought low, he helped me; and as I learned to bear the cross I felt refreshment to come from his presence. (PM 27)

This appears, in the first chapter of Woolman's *Journal,* to be the closest thing we find to a conversion experience. Notice the sense of need, the coming to God humbly in faith and the sense of transformation emerging from the experience of divine grace and presence. Note also, however, that this was by no means a first religious experience. It follows at least a decade of human/divine dialogue, but the change here appears to be connected to Woolman's offering his "unsubjected will" to God and learning to "bow down in spirit before the Lord." This results in a sense of restored fellowship with God, and it represents the learning of an important spiritual lesson. One can choose to approach God humbly and authentically, with lowliness of heart, thereby finding help, and this is what it means to "bear the cross" (PM 27). On the other hand, such an encounter, real though it may be, is never the last leg of the journey. Woolman records losing ground again but also reports humbly craving help from God, to the effect that: "And I may say with reverence he was near to me in my troubles, and in those times of humiliation opened my ear to discipline" (PM 28). Learning to bear the cross, therefore, first implies humbly turning to God and conforming one's will to the divine principle, whence one encounters the inward "power of Christ to prevail over selfish desires" (PM 28).

A second association with "living under" and "being humbled and disciplined under the cross" (PM 28, 31) has to do with following "the openings of Truth" (PM 28). The first reference appears to relate to living in ways upright, which seems to have produced an inward change in Woolman beyond what he can describe. His heart was filled with a sense of awe toward God and a sense of universal love for fellow creatures (PM 29). The next mention of the cross is set in the context of discerning the leadings of the Spirit within the meeting for worship. Having felt led to speak, though, Woolman reports, ". . . but not keeping close to the divine opening, I said more than was required of me; . . . I was afflicted in mind some weeks without any light or comfort, even to that degree that I could take satisfaction in nothing" (PM 31).

Nonetheless, he eventually felt God's comfort and forgiveness and then recalled:

> And after this, feeling the spring of divine love opened and a concern to speak, I said a few words in a meeting, in which I found peace. This I believe was about six weeks from the first time, and as I was thus humbled and disciplined under the cross, my understanding became more strengthened to distinguish the language of the pure Spirit which inwardly moves upon the heart and taught [me] to wait in silence sometimes many weeks together, until I felt that rise which prepares the creature to stand like a trumpet through which the Lord speaks to his flock. (PM 31)

Distinctive to the second narrated phase of Woolman's spiritual formation is the interplay between the two parts. His pursuit of "wantonness" leads to a desire to learn what it means to "live under the cross," and eventually young Woolman makes progress. Just as the first phase leads into the second, so the latter part of the second phase leads directly into the third. Rather than reflecting the personal inculcation of values or the finding of one's place beyond the family circle, the third phase brings Woolman's keen sensitivities directly to bear on the acute needs of the world. More specifically, learning to live under the cross brings with it the vocation to discern the leadings of the Spirit as they bear upon the personal and social conditions of the world, and this takes us into the next phase of young Woolman's spiritual formation.

c.) Learning to Speak to the Conditions of the World

While maturation is clear as Woolman moves from personal to peer to societal issues, it must be kept in mind that the ability to function within later phases leans heavily upon the skills and learnings of prior phases. This set of connections obviates at least one reason the spiritual maturation process is approached within stage-development frameworks by many analysts, as later developments are often made possible only as earlier ones are established. Indeed, the value of considering Woolman's convictions from the narrated perspective of devotional autobiography is that one can identify the struggles behind and evolutions of eventual stands. This provides the history behind the story, which allows the narration to have a far richer impact than a one- or a two-dimensional presentation of convictions or concerns. Again, such an analysis makes it clear that Woolman's later radical ministries emerged out of earlier radical discoveries, and the connections between these must not be overlooked. A clear case in point is the bridge between phases two and three. For Woolman, sensitivities to the Spirit's leading with regard to personal morality was undoubtedly foundational to sensitivities regarding social concerns and later being able to address the conditions of the world.

i.) *Learning to "Watch the Pure Opening."* Woolman himself marks the transition from his concerns to mind the truth for his own sake and the desire to do so for the well-being of others. He describes the growth of his compassion for youth who had "remained entangled in snares like those which had entangled me" (PM 30). One gets the sense Woolman will invest a good deal of his life in the formation of other young lives, and indeed his school teaching and other work with young people attest to that calling. Another clear image is the description of inspired vocal ministry as feeling "that rise which prepares the creature to stand like a trumpet through which the Lord speaks to his flock" (PM 31). Notice the locus of import has shifted here to addressing meaningfully the conditions of the world. Thus, minding the Spirit's leading becomes valued primarily for the sake of ministry, which Woolman describes lucidly:

> From an inward purifying, and steadfast abiding under it [the cross], springs a lively operative desire for the good of others. . . . The outward modes of worship are various, but wherever men [and women] are true ministers of Jesus Christ it is from the operation of his spirit upon their hearts, first purifying them and thus giving them a feeling sense of the conditions of others. This truth was early fixed in my mind, and I was taught to watch the pure opening and to take heed lest while I was standing to speak, my own will should get uppermost and cause me to utter words from worldly wisdom and depart from the channel of the true gospel ministry. (PM 31)

The description of ministry here is classic. Ministry is not a set of programs or a platform of human initiatives to effect a task; rather, like authentic worship, it is from the operation of the Spirit upon people's hearts. This operation purifies the individual, and such heightened sensitivity becomes the fountain of one's "feeling sense of the condition of others." True ministry thus becomes the addressing of human needs in ways spiritually sensitized and empowered. Central to this work is the ability to attend, discern, and mind the promptings of the Spirit, lest worldly wisdom detract from the "channel of the true gospel ministry."

This endeavor of watching for the "pure opening" carries beyond the meeting for worship and extends to the workplace. Thus, Woolman reflects on this venture and its effect: "In the management of my outward affairs I may say with thankfulness I found Truth to be my support, and I was respected in my master's family, who came to live in Mount Holly within two year[s] after my going there" (PM 31). Woolman reportedly received in his twenty-third year "many fresh and heavenly openings in respect to the care and providence of the Almighty over his creatures in general, and over man as the most noble amongst those which are visible" (PM 32). This sentence clearly suggests he was becoming more and more sensitized to the conditions of animals and humans around him, and one infers the development of social consciousness which becomes the foundation of later concerns and actions. Being confirmed in his decision to place his whole trust in God, Woolman applies the same rigorous standard guiding vocal ministry to the workplace: ". . . I felt renewed engagements that in all things I might act on an inward principle of virtue and pursue worldly business no further than as Truth opened my way therein" (PM 32). So in the religious life and beyond it, young Woolman set his attention to watching for, and heeding, the pure opening.

ii.) *Developing a "Feeling Sense of the Condition of Others."* Not only does this phrase render a fitting description of gospel ministry, but it describes Woolman's own actions during the last part of this chapter. In particular, Woolman becomes concerned about two situations wherein the well-being of others is threatened, and he addresses each with intentionality. It is fair to say that in neither of these actions can Woolman's actions be deemed highly successful, or even significant. But two considerations remain: his first concern was to be faithful to a sense of principle and divine leading. In that sense, "success" deserves to be interpreted in terms of sensitivity to ills needed to be addressed and one's willingness to act meaningfully toward such ends. A second consideration is that from the early development of social concerns, later plans of action flow. Over the long-term perspective, world-changing movements were beginning to coalesce.

The first concern had to do with corruptions and vanities associated with drinking at public houses. Feeling led to go and speak to the master of a particular pub, Woolman paused because he was not aware of other more mature Friends raising this concern first, and yet the "duty" was laid upon him to do so. Likening himself to Ezekiel, the watchman on the tower, he carried forth his prophetic charge. He spoke to the man, who actually received his concern warmly, and Woolman was very pleased to have done so because, shortly thereafter, the man died. This confirmed the timeliness of faithful responsiveness to the pure opening, and Woolman felt grateful for God's guidance and support in the matter (PM 32).

The second concern relates to being asked to write a bill of sale for a Negro woman who was being sold by his master to a Friend, an elderly man in the community. While Woolman considered it weakness to have written it, he reports: "I was so afflicted in my mind that I said before my master and the Friend that I believed slavekeeping to be a practice inconsistent with the Christian religion" (PM 33). Woolman felt good about having at least said something, but he still felt bad about having written "an instrument of slavery." At the next opportunity to write a bill of purchase for a slave owner Woolman objected. "I told him I was not easy to write it, for though many kept slaves in our Society, as in others, I still believed the practice was not right, and desired to be excused from writing [it]" (PM 33). Apparently he was excused, and he even found some resonance within the heart of the man making a "gift" to his wife. Addressing the conditions of others leads to specific, direct action for Woolman, and this begins the public chapter of his long life of spiritual and social service and reform.

Throughout the three phases of Woolman's early spiritual formation one sees the progression between the emergence of a personal sense of uprightness—the stuff of aspiration, to struggles with living up to those standards—personally and in the world, to a place where he could say "I found Truth to be my support." The habitual vision of greatness central to the life of every great person here becomes a paradoxical reality. The only way forward is the way of the cross, and sensitivities gained in personal struggles become the sharpened implements of social reform. While the phases overlap to some degree and appear to have a couple of parts within each, they also build upon each other in ways significant. To tease out the implications, a bit of final analysis is in order.

Analysis and Observations

Upon considering the sources and phases of young Woolman's spiritual formation, several observations deserve to be drawn out. Many of these may appear to be obvious, and indeed rational analysis may at times detract from the emotion and aesthetic experience of simply letting the text speak for itself, but my belief is that such a venture serves the reader well. The following analysis and observations attempt to draw together some of the findings of the above work in ways which not only distill learnings from Woolman's spiritual formation, but they also do so in ways which have meaningful implications for spiritual formation work today.

The first thing one notes is the importance of outward sources of formation upon the early spiritual life of John Woolman. The reading of Scripture and good books, the loving instruction of parents, guidance received from Friends at meeting, and the social support received from helpful friends all played extremely significant roles in his spiritual formation. This input forms the stuff of spiritual aspiration, and it becomes a central source of later encouragement along the way. Hence, "take up and read" was not only the invitation received by St. Augustine over thirteen centuries earlier, but its echoes also ring clearly in the experience and formation of the young John Woolman.

What if Woolman had not read the Bible and been warmed to the lofty idealism of Revelation? What if his parents had not insisted on the attending of meeting or had not expected high standards regarding respect for others, honesty, and integrity? What would have come of Woolman's first formative phase? Would he have ever become as sensitive to his own need or the condition of the world around him? These may be impossible questions to answer, but they are highly significant as educators and formers of young lives today consider their callings. Steady, consistent, loving input appears to be foundational to spiritual formation if the life of Woolman serves as any sort of an example.

A second observation takes seriously the growing internalization of values and the ability to trust God inwardly within the maturing spiritual experience of young John Woolman. His dream, events, and experiences, receiving divine impressions and help, and reflection upon these experiences all produced a growing ability to trust one's inward estimation of the Truth. At times, Woolman called this a divine or inward principle, and at times he described it as "the pure opening," or the leading of the Spirit. Eventually, this battle becomes defined as the willingness to trust God versus clinging to one's "unsubjected will," and growth in small increments leads to larger ones. Implications for spiritual formation today include the importance of facilitating autonomy in the spiritual experiences of young people. As valuable as external sources of formation are, the central goal is to prepare emerging leaders to be able to attend, discern, and heed the promptings of the divine presence. Trust becomes the way forward, and moving one's life from an unsubjected will to a creative "yes" to God becomes the goal.

Note the tremendous importance of the peer group in the process of young Woolman's spiritual formation. From his middle teens to his early twenties, the greatest source of diversion and "confusion" (a term for spiritual lostness) is the influence of "wanton" young people. The conflict involved the healthy individuation by means of socialization outside the family, combined with the fact that peer values went against many of those of Woolman's family, as well as his own, and this produced major and repeated crises. While young Woolman was undoubtedly strengthened by his repeated seeking of God rather than the world and its wantonness, one is reminded that he finally found his way as he developed friendships supportive of his values and moral commitments. Implications for today are twofold. First, young people must be given support to stand up for values and convictions, especially other than those embraced by prevalent peer groups. Second, the organizing of social contexts where peers can be of mutual support, spiritually and morally, is extremely valuable in the successful formation of personal positive identity. Apparently, young Woolman found his own set of supportive relationships, independent of assistance, but one wonders what might be done by others to facilitate such developments for emerging leaders today.

One is impressed at the processive way Woolman's spiritual commitments developed. The fact that all people develop in their own distinctive ways should be an instructive point to remember. Notice that Woolman's becoming established in his faith really took over half a decade, from the first commitments of his will to God to the sense of finding victory in the Spirit. This does not fit some instantaneous doctrines of transformation wherein one "gets it right" the first time and has no more struggles thereafter. Apparently, Woolman's experience went up and down many times, and it finally leveled off into a more matured set of commitments and experiences. This is to say that his "conversion experience" appears to have been more like a "conversion process," and this ought to allow us some liberty when people don't appear to fit one's understanding of how it "ought to" take place. At this point, however, a caution in the other direction is also fitting. Neither should one expect a five-year process to be normative just because things happened something like that for John Woolman. Transformational work may indeed take shorter or longer, depending on the individual and her or his situation. From Woolman's example, present readers find liberty to value fully the particular ways spiritual experience and formation emerge—or don't emerge—within the life of each person. This sets us free to face authentically into the places we seem to be, and to respond appropriately to the Truth as understood and needed.

One is greatly impressed at the spiritual sensitivity of young John Woolman, both in relation to his personal state of being and to the condition of others in a hurting world. One cannot escape his acute moral sensitivity, and the tendency to consider such exaggerated or to disregard it as extreme should be resisted at all costs. One is mindful that his social sensitivities were also experienced thusly, especially by those who would rather not have had the boat rocked too much. But the prophet always sings a solo, at least for a while, and in retrospect we wonder why more people had not made the stands Woolman did before or even during his time. Put otherwise, why were not more people sensitive to the terrible abuses of humanity endemic to the slave trade and other social ills? Were their hearts hardened? Were they desensitized by those who thought rocking the boat socially to be extremist? Or, were they never given the opportunity to develop personal moral sensitivities because no one gave them the chance? Whatever the case, one is struck that personal moral sensitivity provides the early framework for later social concern, and it is never too early to develop such sensitivities and foundations for later contributions.

One is also taken by Woolman's acute desire to mind, above all else, the pure openings of Truth, both in the meeting for worship and in the workplace. This commitment to be a seeker and minder of the Truth becomes the trademark of Woolman's maturing spiritual life. He felt terribly distraught over having spoken "more than was required" of him, and out of the repentant weeks following that episode, he came to exercise faithfulness once more, leading to the experience of being used as a trumpet of the Lord, sounding the clarion call of the Word of the Lord within the world. Likewise, in the business world, rather than seeing such as off limits to the workings of the Spirit, Woolman aspired to live in ways truthful and to behave in all ways beyond reproach. Implications for spiritual formation today involve the paramount importance of living with integrity and seeking to be truthful in small things as well as large ones. The seeking of Truth, then, becomes not only the end goal of spiritual formation, but also its beginning.

A final observation involves the priority of faithfulness to divine principle over outward measures of success. Impressive about many of young Woolman's socially moral stands is that many of them appear to have had very little impact on the outcome of events, if any. From this one may be inclined to consider them failures, but as in war, the only really important battle is the last one. All too easily, prophetic work is measured by early receptions rather than lasting contributions, and the example of young Woolman's faithfulness helps later audiences take heart. He indeed felt pleased at least to have spoken to people about his concerns, even though no appreciable changes appeared to have resulted from such conversations. On the other hand, world history was changed by the long-term example of Woolman and by his compelling narration of his experiences. Implications for later generations are rife. The central issue is faithfulness to the Truth and the embracing of what is known to be divine principle. Having done so, apparent successes and failures become glimpsed through a different prism—refracting our fractured sight, until the whole is fully seen.

Considering the spiritual formation of young John Woolman grants insight into the foundational set of experiences which produced one of the most effective agents of change in American history. It also reminds us of an often-overlooked fact in this age of pluralism and the conscious or unconscious diminishment of the religious self: that Woolman's great social impacts had their roots deeply embedded in spiritual soil, without which such contributions might not have been made, certainly not in the same way. The central implication may be put better in the form of a query: "In desiring to change the world for the good, today and tomorrow, how well are we doing at forming the spiritual lives and sensitivities of emerging generations of young people?" From reading anew the first chapter of John Woolman's *Journal*, many fresh insights emerge. As we consider this record of "the operations of divine love," we too may feel "a motion of love" to leave some hints of the goodness of God in the world, ourselves. When this happens, we become mindful that these "hints" extend beyond the written page to the life of the reader, and information extends to formation—our own.

WORK CITED

Woolman, John. *The Journal and Major Essays of John Woolman.* Ed. Phillips P. Moulton. 1971. Richmond, IN: Friends United Press, 1989.

3

"Stranger Friend": John Woolman and Quaker Dissent

Anne G. Myles

WHAT DOES IT MEAN TO DISSENT? The word "dissent" is derived from the Latin *dissentire,* meaning "to think or feel differently." To be a dissenter is to be in opposition to something, intellectually and/or emotionally, but the meaning and experience of being a dissenter cannot be adequately defined by the principles or institutions that are opposed. To be a dissenter is a complex, encompassing form of selfhood and experience, an identity shaped by the profound, transformative act of stepping aside from the orthodoxies or mainstream views of one's society, and bearing the difficult consequences of so doing. To live out dissent becomes a transformative initiation into marginality.[1]

In the early years of Quakerism to be convinced as a Friend was not only to take on a new religious identity but also a dissenting one. To declare oneself a Quaker was a spiritual rite of passage, adopting the distinctive Quaker testimonies of speech, behavior, and dress meant accepting the sufferings of mockery, state persecution, and occasionally physical violence that marked the heroic Quaker life. The spiritual intensity of individuals who had come through this passage, I would suggest, came from the transformative impress of this experience as well as from the sense of certainty and liberation Friends found in their worship and belief. Such intensity and bonding marked the early years of the Religious Society of Friends as a dissenting community. This kind of collective dissenting identity was not, of course, unique to Friends; most Puritan groups claimed it too, as part of their heritage if not their daily reality. But the experience was especially dramatic for early Friends, given their radical revision of Christian theology, their often confrontational forms of public witness, their openness of worship and bold response to opposition, and nowhere was it more pronounced than among Friends who entered the American colonies prior to the settlement of Pennsylvania in 1682.[2]

But by the eighteenth century, especially in the Philadelphia area, things had changed in conspicuous ways. Friends had become a politically powerful and economically dominant group. Even in most other areas of the colonies, they now constituted but one more sect in an increasingly tolerant, diverse, and secularized public sphere. To define oneself as a Friend—especially if one was born within the Society—no longer implied that one would encounter oneself as marginal to any meaningful degree. Grateful as they were that the days of religious persecution were past, Friends realized that something crucial had been lost, and that Quakerism's distinctive oppositionality was in danger of being swallowed by secularization and participation in the emerging capitalist ethos. How could spiritual renewal be obtained? Laments over the decline of piety and the dangerous growth of "selfishness" were ubiquitous among Protestant groups in this period, but for no group was the dissenting heritage and the connection of dissenting suffering to spirituality more central than they were for Friends. Thus the dilemma facing Friends—even if they would not have defined it in precisely these terms—was, how could they possibly regain the religious and community-building power of dissent within the comfortable setting of the eighteenth-century Mid-Atlantic?

John Woolman's work is shaped by this conflict over the loss of Quakerism's dissenting witness, a conflict he felt in an urgent and personal way and strove throughout his life to resolve. On the surface, Woolman does not fit the obvious model of a dissenter: neither a rebel nor in most senses an outsider, he broke no laws, suffered no rebuke, and never acted without the approval of his religious community. Yet he can be seen as a dissenter in a double sense, for he was at once the prime exponent of his tradition's historic dissent to the norms of American society and the most critical and prophetic voice to speak to that tradition. What I will suggest in this essay is that to understand Woolman as a dissenter we need partly to invert our standard perception that, for him as for other Friends, spiritual experience gave rise to the ability to witness in words. While this view remains accurate, I want to emphasize the paradox that, for Woolman, the act of witnessing was itself an indispensable source of spiritual transformation. To put it more particularly, it was through the difficult process of speaking out as a dissenter within and against his own community that Woolman came to understand the plight of society's "strangers," an understanding that would constitute the heart of his religious and social message to eighteenth-century Friends.

The first chapter of *The Journal of John Woolman* shows Woolman beginning to form his response to his historical situation.[3] As a starting point, it is useful to observe what is absent from the chapter: in recounting his youth and convincement, Woolman says nothing about what it means to him to identify as a member of the Religious Society of Friends, to observe Friends' everyday testimonies of speech, dress, and behavior. About this, apparently, he has nothing to record: as a birthright Friend immersed in a Quaker-dominated setting, it would seem that nothing happened to make this once controversial religious identity a subject of reflection. Near the close of the chapter, however, Woolman recounts an alternative kind of passage, his initiation into thinking and feeling—and acting—differently. First he describes his inner struggle when he finds himself moved to speak to the keeper of a "public house" where he observed drinking and disorder. Then the narrative jumps to a new topic, implying that Woolman was rapidly moved from matters of conventional morality to more demanding social issues, as he describes himself wrestling for the first time with the moral dilemma of writing a bill of sale for a Friend's slave. He recounts the painful progress from what he considers a less to a more adequate response, as he negotiated the complex process of opposing his fellow Friends without breaching harmony, a process that involved determining his responsibility as a social agent, finding a form to express his awareness, and communicating the reason for his actions to those it affects (PM 32-33).

Although Woolman first experienced what it was like to stand out in resistance to the norms of his community in these and many subsequent incidents at home, this experience was deepened when he travelled in the ministry to take his message to Friends elsewhere in the colonies. Confronting the dangers and uncertainties of travel, circulating across the boundaries between colonies and between settlement and wilderness: such experiences gave Woolman some taste of the hardship that would have marked the life of Quaker ministers in the seventeenth century. In travelling with a special concern about slave-holding and economic injustice, however, Woolman was forced into a radical encounter with the threshold between unity and individual resistance. One of the goals of the travelling ministry among Friends was to strengthen the bonds between distant meetings and to build unity and fellowship within the Society. Yet if Woolman was to be faithful to his concern, it meant that he had to declare an unpopular message, and the power of his spoken ministry could not be separated from his personal authority as a messenger. In order to speak convincingly of the need for Friends to renounce what he elsewhere called "the selfish spirit" (PM 252), Woolman had to embody the values he called for. In turn, through the experience of living out his message, the truth and urgency of his message became ever more clear to him.

The relation between travelling and dissent is particularly evident in Woolman's account of a trip he made with his brother to the southern colonies in 1757. The journey began with an intimation of the difficulty he would face. Crossing from Pennsylvania into Maryland, Woolman wrote that "a deep and painful exercise came upon [him]." He explained,

> As the people in this and the southern provinces live much on the labour of slaves, many of whom are used hardly, my concern was that I might attend with singleness of heart to the voice of the True Shepherd and be so supported as to remain unmoved at the faces of men. (PM 59)

The traditional language Woolman uses both reflects and deflects the pain of the choice he believes he must make, between Christ's wordless inward voice, and the faces (and voices) of those he must confront—those who, though he may distance them by the collective abstraction "men," are still Woolman's brethren, by whom he is disposed to be moved. Woolman observed that accepting hospitality from slaveholders would have been a kind of lie, since it would convey an impression of unity with the slave system, and could tend to sway him towards those he morally opposed. His insistence on paying for the accommodations he received was a move that was confrontational and rhetorical without direct speech: by translating the proffered hospitality back into the unlovely terms of monetary value, he was denouncing whatever illusions Friends might have that they were living in a purely spiritual network of relations.

While his behavior resulted in no punishment or physical suffering, Woolman found the prospect of giving offense to well-intentioned hosts an agonizing burden. He is eloquent about the pain it caused him, describing his resolution to persist in his decision in the language of spiritual crisis. This is one of the comparatively few points where he resorts to identification with Biblical figures to communicate the intensity of his experience:

> The prospect of so weighty a work, and being so distinguished from many who I esteemed before myself, brought me very low, and such were the conflicts of my soul that I had a near sympathy with the prophet [Moses] in the time of his weakness, when he said, "If thou deal thus with me, kill me I pray thee out of hand, if I have found favour in thy sight" [Num. 11:15]. (PM 60)

Finally, Woolman writes, "after a time of deep trial, I was favoured to understand the state mentioned by the Psalmist more clearly than ever I had before, to wit: 'My soul is even as a weaned child' [Ps. 131:2]" (PM 60). He proceeds to detail how, "thus helped to sink down into resignation," he negotiated payment for the housing he received.

The language and allusions here are familiar ones within Quaker and Puritan spiritual autobiography, but they nonetheless convey a sense of extreme strain, of going past one's limits, of involuntarily becoming other than one was. What early Friends might have experienced in imprisonment, banishment, or other "sufferings," Woolman encountered in some measure simply in having to choose distance from some of his brethren. The trials Woolman experienced while travelling in the southern states can be read as an internal analogy to what being thrust out into the wilderness was for earlier American dissenters, who were typically banished from the settled colonies in which they resided. I would further suggest that the experience of banishment in the wilderness is less dependent on the literal space into which the dissenter is thrust than the isolation, impoverishment, and transformative spiritual initiation that they experience. This motif of the "wilderness experience"—mingling wilderness as a place and as a spiritual state—is a resonant one throughout Western culture, drawing from Biblical roots and echoed powerfully in many early American texts.

In this experience, Woolman learned what it is like to be destitute, to feel oneself reliant on God for all one's needs. It is at precisely this point in the *Journal* that Woolman describes how, camping outdoors one night and kept awake by damp ground and mosquitoes, he

> was led to contemplate the condition of our first parents when they were sent forth from the garden, and considered that they had no house, no tools for business, no garments but what their Creator gave them, no vessels for use, nor any fire to cook roots or herbs. But the Almighty, though they had been disobedient, was a father to them. . . . (PM 72)

In this passage literal and spiritual need, banishment from the garden and the experiential hardship, are merged. But while Woolman testifies in this passage to the sufficiency of God's providence, he found that even God cannot erase the pain of marginality. He expresses the feeling of isolation that his situation has produced in the words of a Psalm he experiences as deeply authentic: "[I]n my travelling on the road [in Virginia] I often felt language rise from the center of my mind thus: 'Oh Lord, I am a stranger in the earth; hide not thy face from me'" (PM 61). The choice of this verse from Psalm 119, which rises up within him like the readiness to speak in meeting, is significant: when Woolman calls himself "a stranger in the earth" he is establishing several identifications at once, identifications that coalesce into the core of his prophetic message.

What does it mean to be a "stranger"? The word has two different senses within the Biblical sources from which Woolman draws. In the quotation above, the "stranger in the earth" signifies God's servant who is "not of this world," evoking the traditional figure of the Christian as a pilgrim and sojourner. As William Penn explained in his widely-read *No Cross, No Crown* (1668),

> And therefore does the apostle call [God's peculiar people] "strangers" (a figurative speech), people estranged from the customs of the world, of new faith and manners; and so unknown to the world . . . the strangeness lay in leaving that which was customary and familiar to them before. (Penn 131)[5]

The entreaty Woolman cites, "turn not thy face from me," is one of a series of pleas the Psalmist makes for God to help him understand, obey, and witness to the "way of truth."[6] In this first sense, then, being a stranger is simultaneously a metaphor for the individual discipleship that Woolman practices in the course of oppositional witness, the isolation that discipleship produces, and the collective "peculiarity" to which he is recalling the Quaker community—the holy paradox of being at once "strangers" and "Friends."

In other Biblical contexts, however, references to the stranger signify something more literal and more problematic. In the Old Testament, the stranger is one who is a foreigner, not a Jew. This political definition traditionally takes on a host of negative connotations, in which the "strange" is linked with being foreign, improper, without property, without legitimate selfhood.[7] The Biblical attitude towards this kind of stranger is notably inconsistent: at one moment, strangers are figured as the idolatrous foreigners who are fit subjects for slavery; at another, they are needy outsiders to whom Israel has a duty to be compassionate. Woolman was well aware of this Biblical meaning and its moral charge. In his pair of anti-slavery essays, he argues that Friends must regard African-American slaves in light of the latter understanding. In "Some Considerations on the Keeping of Negroes," following a quotation from a Quaker author about the Golden Rule, he elaborates:

> This doctrine . . . hath been likewise inculcated in the former dispensation: "If a stranger sojourn with thee in your land, ye shall not vex him; but the stranger that dwelleth with you shall be as one born amongst you, and thou shalt love him as thyself." Lev. 19:33, 34. . . . If the treatment which many of [those who come by force as strangers among us] meet with be rightly examined and compared with those precepts, . . . there will appear an important difference betwixt them.[8] (PM 203-204)

In other words, Woolman is saying that African slaves are the most obvious Anglo-American analogy to Israel's "strangers," and that Friends' treatment of them falls disturbingly short when held to the standard of the Biblical precept.

"Thou shalt love [the stranger] as thyself": this Levitical command can actually be taken as more demanding socially than the more familiar New Testament version, "love thy neighbour as thyself," since those one commonly registers as "neighbors" tend to be people similar to oneself with whom it is relatively easy to empathize; loving the marked otherness of genuine strangers is a stretch. That Friends are called by God to make this stretch is the message at the heart of Woolman's writing. Yet in the context of Woolman's writing, the phrase becomes even more radical in its implication: if Friends are "strangers" too, then to love the stranger as oneself is natural, indeed tautological. Seen truly, the stranger *is* oneself; the oppositional Christian and the needy foreigner are one. However different they may be outwardly, both kinds of stranger share the category of marginality, and share a knowledge of neediness and pain.

When we recognize and understand Woolman's faith in the natural bond between spiritual and political strangers, we can see why he believed the social reforms he called for and the renewal of Quaker identity to be inseparable. As Woolman points out, the Mosaic law of compassion was based in an appeal to Israel's own experience of oppression. In "Some Considerations on the Keeping of Negroes," he reviews the history of the Old Testament Patriarchs as sojourners among strangers (and hence as strangers themselves) and in other ways subject to "low estate" (PM 206). In "A Plea for the Poor," he makes the appeal to experience more explicit:

> To pass through a series of hardships and to languish under oppression brings people to a certain knowledge of [the workings of justice and injustice]. To enforce the duty of tenderness to the poor, the inspired Lawgiver referred the children of Israel to their own past experience: "Ye know the heart of a stranger, seeing ye were strangers in the land of Egypt" [Ex. 23:9]. He who hath been a stranger amongst unkind people or under their government who were hard-hearted, knows how it feels; but a person who hath never felt the weight of misapplied power comes not to this knowledge but by an inward tenderness, in which the heart is prepared to sympathy with others. (PM 242-243)

Woolman writes that Moses "referred" the Israelites to their experience, as if to a passage in a text: for Woolman experience is, finally, the only text that can truly teach people about power's crushing weight. Reiterating this crucial scripture less than a page later, he again draws the reader's attention to what we might call the epistemology of oppression:

> [H]e who toils one year after another to furnish others with wealth and superfluities, who labours and thinks, and thinks and labours, till by overmuch labour he is wearied and oppressed, such an one understands the meaning of that language: "Ye know the heart of a stranger, seeing ye were strangers in the land of Egypt." (PM 243)

Woolman's syntactic insistence that it is "such [a] one" who understands the need for compassion implies that without experience to translate it the divine law becomes opaque, a mere piece of Biblical verbiage rather than a living meaning. He goes on to rebuke the "many at this day" who, while they may be compassionate when they notice an immediate need, lack a "feeling knowledge" of the hardships experienced by those who labor to provide the substance they expend so lightly, and thus never think of lightening their burden by living less expensively (PM 243-244).

As Woolman counted on his readers to recognize, the Quakers too had once been the children of Israel under a "hard-hearted" government, but were no longer in that situation.[9] The dilemma is, if the moral law is authorized by the empathy born of experience, how can the law be understood when the original conditions for this experience have been lost? Significantly, the paired command and explanation in Exodus—"Also thou shalt not oppress a stranger: for ye know the heart of a stranger, seeing ye were strangers in the land of Egypt"—is given precisely at the point of transition from wilderness to citizenship, when Moses is on Mount Sinai and the Israelites are about to leave their wandering in the desert and enter the Promised Land. Not accidentally, this scripture is a central text in the Jewish Passover ceremony. The Passover is a ritual reenactment of history, binding a people's past and present identity and seeking to infuse present knowledge with the living memory of oppression. Although Woolman may not have known the details of the Passover ceremony, he grasps the way the scriptural text is meant to function, explaining that "to excite [Israel's] compassion" God "reminds them of times past" (PM 207).

The burning question for eighteenth-century Friends was how to accomplish something similar. With no one alive to remember what the experience of persecution and hardship had been, the true meaning of the past stood in danger of being lost. Woolman strives to revivify Friends' historical memory of their Anglo-American experience. Following the scriptural citation above, he entreats his readers to "trace back the steps we have trodden and see how the Lord hath opened a way in the wilderness for us," describing a kind of Quaker Exodus from the "afflictions, reproaches, and manifold sufferings" of the forebears to the "civil and religious liberties" of the present (PM 207). He urges them to use this memory as an incentive for "fruitful returns" and benevolence, since "all this was not done to be buried in oblivion" (PM 207). Such a review of past mercies is a standard part of the Protestant answer to the Passover's renewal of communal identity, the ritualized rhetoric of the "jeremiad," in which the sins of the present are lamented in contrast to the obedience of ages past, and the specter of divine judgment is invoked to spur reformation.[10] Yet Woolman knew that, without personal initiation, memory and exhortation were not alone sufficient to give the Quaker community the transformed perspective that was required for renewal. The clearest solutions to this dilemma were individual ones: if history has not placed one in a position of political oppression or of legal or economic servitude, the *Journal* argues, one must use whatever first-hand experience is available to gain the revitalizing, compassion-engendering knowledge of marginality. The experience of being a prophetic Christian stranger was accessible to all people in all eras—if not as in the early Quaker movement through simply standing by one's faith, then through the always-accessible struggle of being an outspoken witness within one's community.

But if individual solutions were an entry point, they were not the entirety of Friends' attempts to regain the authority of an earlier model of religious identity. In the mid-1750s, Woolman played an active part in the historic political conflict in which Pennsylvania Friends as a body turned back from the course of cultural assimilation. The crisis over Friends' decision to withdraw from participation in government rather than pay war taxes during the French and Indian War became a profound passage of re-initiation, in which Friends learned first-hand just how quickly they could become strangers again on the American scene.[11]

The events of the 1750s express in an outward, collective form deep personal themes in Woolman's discourse. Friends' withdrawal from politics led to profound and lasting changes within the Society. There was a shift from substantial mainstream assimilation of the preceding decades to a renewed sense of what Frederick Tolles calls "Quaker tribalism," but we could as well call "collective dissenting identity." This new identity was shaped by an emphasis on spirituality, simplicity, humility, and various forms of benevolence (see Tolles 230 and 235ff.). Mainstream historians have tended to regard Friends' withdrawal from Pennsylvania politics as a moment of historical failure—failure to engage with worldly realities, to recognize the direction of history, failure to be, above all, American.[12]

Also perhaps more seriously it can be seen as signifying the failure of Penn's "Holy Experiment." But neither of these views is how those who chose this path understood it. They had decided the only way they could retain their identity as a people was to be a people called out. In effect, this "tribalism" signified Israel's attempt to return to the desert within the geographic and institutional bounds of Pennsylvania's Promised Land.

Friends who chose not to pay the war tax faced trials of both an economic and emotional nature. As Woolman reports, "When the tax was gathered, many paid it actively and others scrupled the payment, and in many places (the collectors and constables being Friends) distress was made on their goods by their fellow members" (PM 87). Through a process they had willingly set in motion, those who did not pay got a taste of being strangers, helpless before the legal system. Most poignantly, they were being initiated into the classic dissenting experience of radical difference from those they considered to be their brethren. Yet their act also made the Quakers metaphoric strangers in broader American society, their former image of rectitude now overshadowed by sharply negative images of lack of patriotism, indifference to the plight of the frontier settlers who were under Indian attack, and of hypocrisy (since as citizens they still enjoyed the protection of a military they were unwilling to support).

Through Friends' collective sacrifice of power for the sake of principle, it could be said that Woolman experienced at least a partial fulfillment of the dissenter's dream: he maintained his position, and his community altered to embrace it. Of course, all but one of Woolman's major writings were composed after 1755, so his views were likely shaped by as well as an agent of these events.[13] It seems significant, however, that, reflecting on the events of the mid-1750s, in the *Journal,* Woolman shifts from the first-person singular to the plural voice:

> It requires great self-denial and resignation of ourselves to God to attain that state wherein we can freely cease from fighting when wrongfully invaded. . . . Whoever rightly attains to it does in some degree feel that spirit in which our Redeemer gave his life for us, and through divine goodness many of our predecessors and many now living have learned this blessed lesson. But many others . . . do manifest a temper distinguishable from that of an entire trust in God. (PM 84)

The "we" and "our" in this passage are assertive, as if they celebrate a momentary triumph over the isolation of dissent through collective learning of the "blessed lesson" of sacrifice. It is a "we" that forces the reader to locate him or herself, to either join a restored community of experiential knowledge, or remain outside.[14]

The achievement of such a positive plural voice in the *Journal* is an important marker in Woolman's discourse, but in his life it was not a lasting one. Resolution of the war-tax issue did not resolve the larger issues of slavery and economic injustice about which Woolman was concerned. Friends had moved a step towards Woolman's position, but, in the years following the crisis of the 1750s, he kept moving ever further along the road of dissenting identity in both his message and outward behavior. To cite only one example, in 1761 he developed "scruples" about clothing with what he saw as "hurtful dyes," and got a beaver hat "the natural colour of the fur," and eventually began to wear undyed clothing. Looking quite literally strange did much to further Woolman's sense of isolation, particularly since he did not initially feel led to explain his motivation to others and it was easily misinterpreted as a form of vanity (PM 120-121).

At the end of his life Woolman had the ironic experience of being most truly a "stranger in the earth" in England, which despite the political tensions of the era he identified without ambivalence as his mother country. In June of 1772 he arrived in London and in his odd attire "went straightway" from the ship (where he had been travelling in the steerage) to the Yearly Meeting of Ministers and Elders (PM 181). According to a well-known anecdote circulated by John Greenleaf Whittier, the English Friends initially regarded him with disapprobation, and when Woolman presented his certificate from Philadelphia Friends endorsing his ministry, someone remarked cuttingly that "perhaps the stranger Friend might feel that this dedication of himself to this apprehended service was accepted, without further labour, and that he might now feel free to return to his home" (quoted in AMG 126-127). While it is impossible to know whether these were the exact words used, the oxymoronic designation of Woolman as "the stranger Friend" is fitting. Never was he a more subject, suffering, marginal being than at that moment. He is said to have been hurt to the point of tears by this unexpectedly cold reception, but eventually he preached and proved his spiritual propriety through the power of his message. Though swayed by eccentricity, the Quaker community could recognize the presence of authentic speech. Thus the path of singularity gave him the authority that led again to communal belonging.

By going as far as he could into the wilderness of dissenting singularity, Woolman reaffirmed what was most central in his tradition. Fittingly, then, the narrative account of this process and vision in *The Journal of John Woolman* has become one of the defining texts of Quaker identity. Narrative, the anthropologist Victor Turner has pointed out, represents "knowledge . . . emerging from action, that is, experiential knowledge." (The word "narrative" comes from the Latin *gnarus,* "knowing.") Turner argues that narrative has the ability to "rearticulate a social group broken by sectional or self-serving interests," and as such can have an especially important role in times of cultural crisis: "Where historical life . . . fails to make sense in terms that formerly held good, narrative . . . may have the task of poiesis, that is, of remaking cultural sense" (Turner 163-164). Although Woolman wrote in a variety of forms, Turner's ideas suggest that spiritual autobiography is the essential genre for his message: as narrative, it portrays the inseparability of experience and knowledge; as first-person narrative, it models solutions to collective and historical dilemmas that can only be reliably attained on an individual, experiential basis. Live as I live, the *Journal* argues, and you can know what I know. Published two years after his death, the *Journal* would fulfill its narrative purpose to the degree that, reader by reader, it continued to make and remake Quaker history and culture, drawing individual Friends into community with slaves and other strangers, with the persecuted forebears of the first generation, and with each other.

I want to conclude this essay by considering Woolman's most famous dream, which occurred during his illness in the winter of 1769-70, in which he was "brought so near the gates of death that I forgot my name," a vision which takes his identification with the stranger to its furthest point and, less familiarly, may also suggest the possible limits of this identification. In this visionary experience, Woolman finds himself "mixed in with" and indistinguishable in identity from a mass of "human beings in as great misery as they could be and live" (PM 185). Immediately following, Woolman hears an angelic voice saying the words, "*John Woolman is dead*" (PM 186). He describes himself struggling to understand this paradoxical assertion, then quoting the passage from Galatians 2:20,

"I am crucified with Christ, nevertheless I live; yet not I, but Christ that liveth in me," and finally coming to realize that "there was joy in heaven over a sinner who had repented and that that language John Woolman is dead meant no more than the death of my own will" (PM 186). What Woolman intends us to understand here is fairly clear: throughout his writing it is the uncrucified will that brings into existence the selfishness that separates human beings from themselves, God, and compassionate relationships with other beings. To repent, then, means to turn away from that will and that self-enclosure. Here lies the broadest significance of Woolman's paradoxical life as "stranger Friend": while he comes to the death of his will through the process standing out as a dissenter amongst Friends, the angels attest that his life is not the singular journey but rather a representative and universal model, the fulfilled conversion story of a Quaker Everyman.

However, despite Woolman's assertion that the angel's words signified "no more than the death of [his] will," as I read them these words do suggest an additional dimension. The import of "that language John Woolman is dead" is very much *in* its words, which Woolman quotes twice; the message is also, I would suggest, *about* the power of words, specifically of the proper name. Standing at the threshold of death, he is recalled to his name for the purpose of witnessing its effacement. What dies is not the man John Woolman, who recognizes himself "alive in the body" (PM 186), but rather "John Woolman." The personal name is, of course, a pragmatic marker of division between one individual and another. More important, however, one's proper name is the signifier of one's possession of legal selfhood; it is the distinction between having and not having property (or even further, in the case of slaves, *being* someone's property) that most distinctly marks who is and who is not the "stranger" within the Anglo-American legal and economic system. The name signifies an individual's link with the patriarchal order; it is what gives one title to inherit, hold, and bequeath all other forms of property.[15] It is of course no accident that this relation to the proper name was a fundamental right denied to slaves, on whom was imposed the family name of their master, if indeed they were granted a last name at all. To have or not to have a name thus marks one's very existence as an individual in a profound political sense. To embrace the death of one's name, then, requires the profoundest sacrifice not just of will but of the place one holds in the social order; it might well be seen as the most radical embrace of stranger status a land-owning white male such as Woolman could conceive.

But does Woolman merge with the mass of the dispossessed as entirely as this releasing of his name would indicate? Woolman's vision has another section that may point towards an unacknowledged underside of his perspective. The account of it is contained in a paragraph located between the description of his initial vision and his account of how, lucid once more, he comes to understand that vision:

> I was then carried in spirit to the mines, where poor oppressed people were digging rich treasures for those called Christians, and heard them blaspheme the name of Christ, at which I was grieved, for his name to me was precious. Then I was informed that these heathens were told that those who oppressed them were followers of Christ, and they said among themselves: "If Christ directed them to use us in this sort, then Christ is a cruel tyrant." (PM 186)

Intriguingly, in his commentary that follows Woolman says nothing about this second section of the vision. It is not adequately accounted for in his death-of-the-will insight, and my sense is that it remains problematic in ways he cannot fully integrate. While "John Woolman" may be effaced, there is one name that remains very much alive in Woolman's universe: the name of Christ. This section of the vision suggests that this name has a more problematic relationship to the ideal of selfless merging. In contrast to the generalized, abstract mass of humans in misery in the first part, there is a seeming specificity to this scene of oppression.[16] What he appears to be witnessing is a pattern played out innumerable times in the history of European colonialism both before and after his time, in which so-called "heathen" (the name itself dehumanizes them) labor to serve those who authorize their domination through their Christianity. For all the earnest desire Woolman expresses throughout his work to know feelingly the pain of outsiders, here he witnesses to something he records nowhere else: the voice of non-Christian victims of oppression, voices filled with resentment and rage, "blasphem[ing]" the name of Christ.

In their understandable rejection of the Christ of empire as a "cruel tyrant," these "heathens" confront Woolman with a final, wrenching paradox: while it is only through Christ that he can die to the separateness signified by the name "John Woolman," the name of Christ itself creates division. There is no question for Woolman that true Christianity should have no part in oppression; clearly, much of the pain in this passage comes from Woolman's recognition of the damage done by those who, estranged from the true nature of the gospel, have distorted it into an instrument of tyranny. But what Woolman specifically says is that he "was grieved, for [Christ's] name to me was precious." Here is one critical name he cannot deny, one prized property he cannot surrender. Surely Woolman perceives at some level that, so long as he speaks the name of Christ, from the "heathens'" perspective he speaks in the oppressor's language. What his deepest grief arises from, I would propose, is his semiconscious recognition that, while diversity of human languages may pose no barrier to communion, the fact that he speaks the language of Christianity means that he can never transcend all difference, can never escape an identity grounded in Western history and culture and carrying the weight of its baggage. With all the good will in the world, at some level he must remain a stranger to these strangers, and they likewise strangers to him.

I expect that some readers of this essay will feel that at this point I have gone too far in my interpretation, or that I task Woolman too sharply. But as a scholar trained in an age of multicultural awareness, I am compelled to voice the areas of my own uneasiness with Woolman's rhetoric of identification between dissenters and the oppressed. Woolman's quotation of the words of these (imaginary) "heathen" reminds me that throughout the *Journal* and his other writings he almost never records the actual voices of the "strangers" for whom he presumes to speak, though he tells us about their suffering and entreats us to imagine their perspective. The course I have taken in this essay is dangerous if we let ourselves forget for even a moment that Woolman's experiences as a witness, and even the sufferings of early Friends—all of which were the consequence of freely-chosen beliefs and actions—were not comparable with the involuntary sufferings of slaves and other oppressed classes. To point to the white middle-class privilege implicit in Woolman's assumption that equations could be made is not to discredit the power and humanity of these connections he forged, nor to accuse him of being anything other than a representative member of his time and society. Surely Woolman was aware at some level of the difficulty of relating his experience to that of the truly oppressed strangers in his world, but it was a difficulty to which he could scarcely have admitted surrender.

To do so would have been paralyzing and silencing, creating doubts he could not afford if he were to keep acting as he felt called to.[17]

I am committed to interrogating the limits of Woolman's moral vision and practice from a contemporary vantage point precisely because I am convinced that what he offers remains so relevant today. Contemporary Friends will recognize that some of us live lives that echo those of the comfortable, assimilated Friends of eighteenth-century Philadelphia, and we are the inheritors of their dilemma concerning spiritual renewal. In broader terms, all relatively secure, relatively mainstream people motivated by social conscience face a not unrelated challenge. We know we must speak out against oppression and injustice, but what inward authority empowers us to do so? Further, we face a public sphere frequently dominated by the language of "identity politics"—that is, positions grounded in categories of identity relating to race, class, gender, or sexual orientation, etc., which are seen as essential determinants giving rise to perspectives and experiences often felt to be exclusive and untranslatable. While in my view we must credit the concreteness of such politics and their capacity to testify to lived experience, how can we overcome their implicit divisiveness?

John Woolman, it seems to me, offers a meaningful alternative in what might be called his "politics of empathy." The hope Woolman offers is that, though the most crushing forms of oppression may not be part of our experience, we may (and must) nonetheless use our own experiences of difficulty and need as a starting point for learning compassion, since they are the best—and only—point we have. And if we lack sufficient experience, then challenging ourselves to speak out in ways that may be uncomfortable—indeed, that in extreme moments may feel like death itself—will be a place to start. There is something here, I am convinced, more challenging and empowering than the liberal guilt in which so many of us get trapped. Critically, too, the *Journal* makes the case that empathy cannot be just a rhetorical stance but to carry authority must be embodied as fully as possible—must be experiential, narrative knowledge. But in addition we must recognize the need for humility in forms that even Woolman could not fully appreciate. It is always dangerous to speak for the other, even with the best of intentions. And we may be called on to go even further than Woolman in letting go of all our "precious names"—whether they are the name of Christ or any other categories of identification and meaning that feel essential to us—when these concepts evoke pain in the people to whose experiences we are trying to attend.

Whether or not this vision remains something we want to put into use, in historical terms the Quaker example offers important broader insight into the continuing possibilities of dissent in America. At a time when other Protestant groups had begun to use a rhetoric that blurred Christian faith with an emergent American nationalism, Woolman and other Quaker reformers of the mid-1700s drew from Friends' past and present a vision of meaningful marginality that offered an alternative to the seemingly all-embracing sweep of American destiny. In so doing, they kept alive the model of conscience-driven estrangement within a society whose norms of individualism and materialism grew increasingly harder to discern and to resist. As Woolman recounts his ever-renewed struggle to speak and act as his conscience demanded, his writing teaches us that the sufferings produced by the anxiety of social nonconformism are not less vivid for being internal, and that it may take as much courage to become eccentric within one's own community as it does to confront institutions of outward domination. In his private battles against his own fear and reluctance, Woolman offers us a starting point to tell the story of middle-class dissent in the modern age, the story of the quiet heroism exacted when there is no escape from belonging, no place to start afresh, no wilderness more terrifying than the human heart.

NOTES

[1] Although influenced by a number of sources, this characterization of dissent is basically my own; it is elaborated in my dissertation, "'Called Out': Languages of Dissent in Early America" (University of Chicago, 1993). For a somewhat related view, see Kendall, *The Drama of Dissent.*

[2] On the history of Quakers in the colonies, see Jones, *The Quakers in the American Colonies* and Worrall, *Quakers in the Colonial Northeast.*

[3] In discussing the *Journal,* I do not distinguish what happened to Woolman and how he chooses to represent those events in his later writing. Although this is a significant question in considering the *Journal* as a work of autobiography, the distinction is not critical to this essay. For a sensitive analysis of

composition of the *Journal*, see Shea 45-84. For a more recent discussion of the relationship of experience to representation in Woolman, see Meranze, esp. 73-74.

[4] Meranze offers a provocative reading of the dynamics of experience, em-bodiment and conscience in Woolman; it appeared after this essay was completed and intersects in intriguing ways with a number of my arguments here.

[5] The Biblical text Penn is discussing is 1 Peter 2.

[6] The entirety of the lengthy Psalm 119 is suggestive as a first-person portrait of a faithful believer in a heedless world. The speaker stresses his longing for God's judgments, his desire for faithfulness to God's "testimonies," and his belief in the need for inward renewal. It is easy to see how Woolman would have felt personally addressed by this psalm and been influenced by its language.

[7] For further discussion of these associations, see Cheyfitz, *The Poetics of Imperialism,* chapter 1 and *passim.*

[8] This discourse also plays a prominent role in "Considerations on Keeping Negroes: Part Second," in which Woolman reviews the history of Israel's relation to the stranger. He struggles to refute the apparent support for slavery in the Mosaic Law, as in the command that "of the children of the stranger that do sojourn amongst you, of them shall ye buy and of their children which are with you which they beget in your land. And they shall be your possession; . . . they shall be your bondmen forever" (Lev. 25:45). Through a dense exegesis, Woolman argues that such commands must be understood as applying only to the individuals purchased, not to their descendants as a class. See PM 216, 217.

[9] There appears to be, if not a pun, at least an overlap in meaning in the original passage between being "under a government" in the political sense, and being under a hard-hearted master's "government" in slavery or other forms of servitude.

[10] On the history of the jeremiad and its function in America as a "ritual of consensus," the lamentory tone of which should not be taken literally, see Bercovitch's *The American Jeremiad.* In his introduction, Bercovitch discusses Perry Miller's earlier analysis of the jeremiad in Miller's essay "Errand into the Wilderness" and his *The New England Mind,* which together established the groundwork for contemporary understanding of the subject.

[11] The complex events and conflicting interests surrounding this crisis have been reconstructed by numerous historians; among more recent sources, see James, Bauman, and Marietta. On the history of the Quaker peace testimony in the colonial context, see Worrall, chapter 8.

[12] Representative of the critical tenor of this view is Alan Heimert's comment that "Woolman's formula ['a quietist rejection of the world's ways as the only means of preserving the vitality of the inner life'] represented a confession that the course of American history could not be made compatible with piety. It was of course this very concession that Edwardean religion refused to make" (Heimert 386n).

[13] As an individual, Woolman himself felt the pressure of the shifts he had been involved in promoting. 1756 was the year in which he felt called to give up retailing altogether, although he had been "thoughtful of some other way of business" as early as 1743 (PM 35). Woolman discusses his decision only in private terms, but the chronology is impossible to ignore. See also Couser 30-31 and 34.

[14] In support of his claim that "in autobiography as in life, Woolman needed to merge with the community as well as to subordinate his will to God's," Couser claims that, beside using the passive voice, Woolman used "frequent substitution of the first-person plural for the first-person singular" (Couser 39). Aside from the committee-written documents Woolman incorporates in his text, I do not find a communal use of the plural at all frequent in the *Journal.* In the one example Couser cites, "we" refers specifically to Woolman and his travelling companion, "my beloved friend Isaac Andrews" (Couser 36). Unity with chosen fellow ministers implies nothing about merging with the community as a whole.

[15] It should be noted that it was largely free *men* in whose names these privileges were vested; married women in this period lost both their names and their individual legal status.

[16] Woolman refers to seeing the mass of humans in misery "between the south and the east," which suggests a connection with slavery in the southeastern part of the colonies (PM 185). In the vision of the "heathen" mine-workers, however, he is evidently describing a setting of imperial domination in Africa or Latin America.

[17] Woolman indicates that what happened during his illness provoked a temporary crisis in his ministry, commenting that following his illness he did not speak in meeting for worship for almost a year, although he goes on to say that during this period his "mind was very often in company with oppressed slaves," and that he exercised his ministry through "abundance of weeping" (PM 187). Moulton quotes Woolman's tantalizingly unclear handwritten comment on this passage from the original manuscript: "though I think I never felt the spring of the min[istry] opened in me more powerfully, yet feeling a [*illeg.*] and in the live [*illeg.*] to speak, yet the gift had a way in my heart in contrition" (PM 187n14). I cannot help wondering, just what is the focus of Woolman's "contrition" here?

WORKS CITED

Bauman, Richard. *For the Reputation of Truth: Politics, Religion, and Conflict among the Pennsylvania Quakers, 1750-1800.* Baltimore, MD: Johns Hopkins University Press, 1971.

Bercovitch, Sacvan. *The American Jeremiad.* Madison, WI: University of Wisconsin Press, 1978.

Cheyfitz, Eric. *The Poetics of Imperialism: Translation and Colonization from the Tempest to Tarzan.* New York: Oxford University Press, 1991.

Couser, G. Thomas. *American Autobiography: The Prophetic Mode.* Amherst, MA: University of Massachusetts Press, 1979.

Heimert, Alan. *Religion and the American Mind: From the Great Awakening to the Revolution.* Cambridge, MA: Harvard University Press, 1966.

James, Sydney V. *A People Among Peoples: Quaker Benevolence in Eighteenth-Century America.* Cambridge, MA: Harvard University Press, 1963.

Jones, Rufus. *The Quakers in the American Colonies.* New York, NY: Russell and Russell, 1911.

Kendall, Ritchie D. *The Drama of Dissent: The Radical Poetics of Nonconformity.* Chapel Hill, NC: University of North Carolina Press, 1986.

Marietta, Jack. *The Reformation of American Quakerism, 1748-1783.* Philadelphia, PA: University of Pennsylvania Press, 1984.

Meranze, Michael. "Materializing Conscience: Embodiment, Speech, and the Experience of Sympathetic Identification." *Early American Literature* 37.1 (2002): 71-88.

Miller, Perry. "Errand into the Wilderness." In *Errand into the Wilderness.* Cambridge, MA: Harvard University Press, 1956.

Miller, Perry. *The New England Mind: The Seventeenth Century.* Cambridge, MA: Harvard University Press, 1954.

Myles, Anne G. "'Called Out': Languages of Dissent in Early America." Unpublished dissertation. University of Chicago, 1993.

Penn, William. *No Cross, No Crown: A Discourse Shewing the Nature and Discipline of the Holy Cross of Christ.* Philadelphia, PA, 1882.

Shea, Daniel B. *Spiritual Autobiography in Early America.* Revised edition. Madison, WI: University of Wisconsin Press, 1988.

Tolles, Frederick B. *Meeting House and Counting House: The Quaker Merchants of Colonial Philadelphia, 1682-1763.* Chapel Hill, NC: University of North Carolina Press, 1948.

Turner, Victor. "Social Dramas and Stories about Them." In *On Narrative.* Ed. W.J.T. Mitchell. Chicago, IL: University of Chicago Press, 1981.

Woolman, John. *The Journal and Essays of John Woolman.* Ed. Amelia Mott Gummere. New York, NY: The Macmillan Company, 1922.

4

Spirit and Substance: John Woolman and "The Language of the Holy One"

Lisa M. Gordis[1]

JOHN WOOLMAN'S ATTEMPTS TO EXPRESS SPIRITUAL TRUTH in flawed human language shape and animate his writings. Such efforts were rooted in Woolman's understanding of the relationship between divine language as perfect and pure, and human language as corrupted by the distortions of self, flesh, and earthly Babel. This understanding was shaped by Woolman's Quaker predecessors, and in negotiating the relationship between divine and human language, Woolman adapted strategies used by earlier Friends. Conscious of the imperfections of human language, Quaker writers often attempted to minimize its obstruction of truth by minimizing its presence altogether, observing Ecclesiastes' exhortation to "Let thy words be few" and striving to make the few words spoken transparent to divine "openings."[2] At other times, however, Quaker writers strove to close the gap between human language and its divine counterpart, investing great energy in the project of purifying human language, and attending to its details in ways that rendered it less transparent than substantial. The tension between transparent and substantial language energizes Woolman's writings and his attempts to reform education, influencing his narrative accounts, his approach to pedagogy, and his use of metaphor.

This tension is most pronounced when Woolman struggles to express divine perfection in the flawed medium of human language. At such moments, Woolman often attempts to minimize his own language, a tricky endeavor for a journal writer. And yet he often manages to create an impression of effacing himself and his own words from accounts of his speech.[3] Early in his *Journal*, Woolman devotes a paragraph to two incidents in which he confronts this challenge. Woolman treats the first occasion as an instance of failure: "[U]nder a strong exercise of spirit," Woolman reports, "I stood up and said some words in a meeting, but not keeping close to the divine opening, I said more than was required of me."[4] Woolman emphasizes the intrusion of self here, using first-person pronouns emphatically to emphasize his error: saying "more than was required of me" was "my error" and produced "my distress" (PM 31).

Like many of Woolman's experiences, however, this failure proves instructive. Woolman closes the paragraph by reporting his progress in the aftermath of this failure, allowing him to say "a few words in a meeting" and "[find] peace":

> [A]s I was thus humbled and disciplined under the cross, my understanding became more strengthened to distinguish the language of the pure Spirit which inwardly moves upon the heart and taught [me] to wait in silence sometimes many weeks together, until I felt that rise which prepares the creature to stand like a trumpet through which the Lord speaks to his flock. (PM 31)

Here, Woolman describes a paradigmatic "opening." Having been "humbled," he learns to distinguish "the language of the pure Spirit which inwardly moves upon the heart" from verbiage that is merely the outpouring of the human ego. The prophet's ability to communicate the "language of the pure Spirit" is closely tied to human silence; only after disciplined periods of "wait[ing] in silence" can he serve as God's vehicle. And in that moment, both self and human language are effaced. Woolman sets aside the first-person pronoun "I," instead describing "the creature" who is prepared by God to serve as his "trumpet." The words spoken by Woolman at this meeting are not reported, for they are, in this moment, transparent to God's communication. Indeed, the image of the trumpet suggests that Woolman's "opening" moves beyond words into the realm of music, transcending human language altogether.

Throughout his *Journal,* Woolman often treats language as similarly insubstantial, privileging language that approaches a state of transparency. He uses words of mass—"matter," "weight," "substance"—to describe ideas or issues which concern him, but separates the "matter" from the words in which it is conveyed.[5] Thus Woolman finds spiritual concerns "heavy," and describes "weighty matters" and the burden of "a matter fixed on [his] mind" (PM 32, 92, 38). Yet although Woolman describes the act of public speaking in similarly substantial terms, he often treats language itself as less solid. While Woolman has "occasion to consider that it is a weighty thing to speak much in large meetings for business," that weight does not stem from the specific language of the speaker's utterance (PM 95). Consequently, in describing statements he has made in other settings, Woolman paraphrases his remarks, rather than quoting them verbatim, introducing his paraphrases with the phrase "I said in substance as follows" (PM 92). Here, Woolman, suggests, the specific words he may have used do not matter—they are distinguished from the "substance" of his remarks. Similarly, he separates "the substance pointed at in . . . figure[s]" from the figures themselves (PM 176).[6] In such instances, Woolman treats figures and words as transparent to the "matter" which they communicate.

At other times, however, Woolman blurs or even collapses the distinction between language and matter. When describing language that is spiritually powerful, Woolman often treats words as solid and substantial. So, for example, he calls a spiritually productive meeting a "solid meeting," and terms a discussion "under which [he] felt [his] soul bowed in reverence before the Most High" a "solid conversation" (PM 67, 158). In Woolman's account of silent worship in a late essay, silence, language, and solidity are oddly blurred. "In real silent Worship," Woolman writes, "the Soul feeds on that which is Divine; but we cannot partake of the Table of the Lord, and that Table which is prepared by the God of this World."[7] In silence, true substance "feeds" the soul, in contrast to the unsubstantial repast offered at the "Table which is prepared by the God of this World." Yet this feeding begets not further silence, but instead language that is divine and nourishing: "If Christ is our Shepherd, and feedeth us, and we are faithful in following him, our Lives will have an inviting Language, and the Table of the Lord will not be polluted" (PM 510). In instances of real spiritual power, language can be substantial, even when it is rooted in silence.

Woolman describes such an occasion early in his *Journal.* One night, while visiting other Friends, Woolman experiences a powerful vision:

> It was yet dark and no appearance of day nor moonshine, and as I opened my eyes I saw a light in my chamber at the apparent distance of five feet, about nine inches diameter, of a clear, easy brightness and near the center the most radiant. As I lay still without any surprise looking upon it, words were spoken to my

> inward ear which filled my whole inward man. They were not the effect of thought nor any conclusion in relation to the appearance, but as the language of the Holy One spoken in my mind. The words were, "Certain Evidence of Divine Truth," and were again repeated exactly in the same manner, whereupon the light disappeared. (PM 58)

In this instance, words become real and substantial to Woolman. They "fill" the "whole inward man," suggesting that they have an almost physical existence. Moreover, the words *are* what they represent. Woolman is offered no argument; no "thought nor any conclusion" is involved. Because this is "the language of the Holy One," the words "Certain Evidence" function as the evidence itself. Whereas elsewhere Woolman distinguishes between the language of statements and their "substance," in this example of divine speech, the distinction between *verba* and *res* collapses. English words become transparent to "Divine Truth," and, in embodying their own meanings, bear substance that ordinary human language lacks.

Phyllis Mack suggests that such special "new, authentic language" is found in the "prayers and prophecies of" someone "who had erased the self, or flesh, and exposed the soul."[8] But although tensions between transparency and substance are most pronounced when Woolman describes the interplay between divine and human language, the same tensions affect day-to-day utterances as well. Woolman shared early Friends' concern with human language in its most routine manifestations. Like the first-generation Friends who called themselves Publishers of Truth, Woolman often emphasized the limitations of human language, striving for language transparent to the divine will, capable of communicating the Inner Light unobstructed by human intervention. Yet as Woolman negotiated between God's voice within him and his own human language, he frequently invested language with a substantive reality of its own, sharing with earlier Quakers an intense preoccupation with the minutiae of language, with details such as pronoun use, spelling, and syllabification.

This preoccupation dates back to the writings of George Fox, who composed numerous texts which treated matters of day-to-day usage as spiritually significant. Perhaps the best-known language crusade of seventeenth-century Friends was their insistence on the use of *thee* and *thou* as singular forms of the second person pronoun, a rejection of shifts in pronoun use which had occurred over the previous few centuries. Until the thirteenth century, the distinction between *thou* and *you* was straightforwardly one of number. In the thirteenth century, however, perhaps influenced by usage in French court circles, plural pronouns *ye, your,* and *you* began to be used when addressing superiors in rank. This usage spread, in the words of Albert C. Baugh and Thomas Cable, "as a general concession to courtesy until *ye, your* and *you* became the usual pronoun of direct address irrespective of all rank or intimacy. By the sixteenth century, the singular forms had all but disappeared from polite speech" (Baugh 242). Kathleen Wales suggests that *thou* was preserved as a "special status form," used in religious contexts (as in the Authorized Version of the Bible) and in association with intimacy and heightened emotion.[10] For example, Hugh Barbour explains, "Seventeenth-century English used *thee* and *thou* within the family, among intimate friends, and to social inferiors, and this form was common among farmers."[11] Moreover, nineteenth-century systematic dialect grammars show that "*thee* forms were standard in the North and West of England, especially in Yorkshire, Lancashire, Westmorland, and Cumberland, and in Devon and Somerset; presumably they had been even more common two centuries earlier" (Barbour 164). Thus, Barbour notes, "It was precisely in the areas where Quakerism arose and was most strong that men used *thee* forms instinctively between equals, whereas in other parts of England *thee* was an insult except to inferiors" (Barbour 165).

Fox addressed the use of *thee* and *thou* in several of his texts, including the exhaustive, even obsessive, *A Battle-Door for Teachers & Professors to Learn Singular & Plural,* a work on which Fox seems to have collaborated with John Stubbs and Benjamin Furly.[12] In this polemical polyglot grammar, Fox, Stubbs, and Furly argue that pure language preserves a distinction between *thou* and *you,* presenting numerous examples from more than thirty languages to buttress their case.

The *Battle-Door's* preface, attributed by some scholars to Fox, reflects the skepticism about human language that Fox expresses elsewhere:

> All Languages are to me no more than dust, who was before Languages were, and am come'd before Languages were, and am redeemed out of Languages into the power where men shall agree: but this is a whip, and a rod to all such who have

> degenerated through the pride, and ambition, from their natural tongue, and Languages, and all Languages upon the earth is but Naturall, and makes none divine, but that which makes divine is the Word, which was before Languages, and Tongues were. (*Battle-Door* A2v)[13]

For Fox, human language was a "degenerated" expression. He shared with other seventeenth-century Protestant radicals an interest in human language in its earliest and purest form, widely conceived as the language spoken by the biblical Adam before the Fall.[14] Drawing on the writings of German mystic Jacob Boehme, whose works were translated into English in the mid-seventeenth century and read by many radical Protestants, Fox celebrated the purity and power of Adam's speech as embodied in his ability to name the animals of creation "according to their name and virtue."[15] In the preface to the *Battle-Door,* however, Fox instead emphasizes the gap that remains between divine language and Adamic language—human language at its most pure:

> Men, crying up Tongues to be the Original, and they have degenerated from the Tongues which they call the Originall, which is not the Originall, which be the Naturals, I look upon the natural Languages no more than men to learn to dress a horse, or women to sweep a house, as to divine things; For in the beginning was the word, which was before Natural Languages were. (*Battle-Door* A2v)[16]

Although Adam's language represented human language in its purest form, it was nevertheless "Natural," and thus not "Originall." Even Adamic language was not "the word, which was before Natural Languages were."

Yet the remainder of the *Battle-Door* advocates the use of *thee* and *thou* by drawing upon the very Babel which Fox decries. The *Battle-Door,* with each section its own battledore, or hornbook, demonstrates through a consideration of more than thirty languages, ancient and modern, that the proper second-person singular pronoun is *thou.* The text is remarkable in several ways. First, the *Battle-Door*'s copiousness is staggering. Indeed, it initially strikes even a sympathetic reader as obsessive and vaguely mad in its accumulation of examples, with evidence from Greek, Latin, French (ironically the source of the loss of *thou* in the first place), German, Hebrew, Arabic, Caldee, Syriack, Aethiopick,

Egyptian, Samaritan, Edomite, and some twenty others. The enormous substance generated by the desire to make language more transparent, less obstructed by human intrusions, is striking.

But Fox does suggest that these languages can be rendered transparent to divine language, at least in structural terms. The logic behind the *Battle-Door* is that the babelish proliferation of tongues is incidental. By attending to the structural similarity of pronoun forms in all of these languages, one can determine the true and pure form of the second-person pronoun. Moreover, the *Battle-Door*'s authors attempt to see through Babel to Adamic purity by privileging the ancient languages, especially those "found" in the Bible, as less corrupted forms. In contrast, they suggest that English may be the most corrupt language, for although English schoolmasters require their students to use proper second-person pronouns when they study Latin, French, and Hebrew, these corrupt schoolmasters rebuke those who would maintain the same standard in their own tongue (A2r).

At the same time, given the energy devoted to amassing conjugations and examples from all of these languages—indeed, cutting the type for the text must have been a significant endeavor in its own right—the authors treat the relationship among languages as remarkably fluid.[17] Here, as in Fox's primer, *Instructions for Right Spelling,* translation is treated as transparent.[18] Even though Fox's preface calls attention to Bible translators who distinguish properly between *thou* and *you,* the text of the *Battle-Door* treats the process of translation as largely irrelevant (A2r). So, despite careful attention to reproducing conjugations and declensions in various languages, translations of translations are repeatedly used without comment as examples of other languages. For example, though the text's authors show the alphabet of "The Ægyptian Language" later in the text, in the *Battle-Door*'s first section, they provide the following example of "Egyptian Language":

> And *Pharaoh,* King of *Egypt,* was *thee'd* and *thou'd,* and *you* was used; so *Plural* and *Singular,* the *Egyptians* Language, which the Spiritual *Egyptians,* which is grown into a Monster, cannot abide it; *Pharaoh thou'd Jacob,* and said how old art *thou? Pharaoh, the'd Joseph,* Gen. 48. and *Pharaoh thou'd* and *thee'd Joseph,* and *you'd* the people; go to *Joseph,* and he will shew *you,* what he says to *you,* Gen. 42. (second page 1, [first page] 2)

Here, an English translation of a Hebrew account of Pharaoh's words stands as an example of Egyptian language. Just as distinctions between English and Egyptian "spiritual Egyptians" melt away, so too do the particulars of the various languages. All of these details, it seems, are incidental to the larger point that can be gleaned from examining them en masse. By wading through all of these particulars, the *Battle-Door*'s authors render them both massive and transparent; this babelish profusion of languages promises insight into the true language that preceded them, enacting Fox's description of the Word "redeemed out of Languages into the power where men shall agree" (*Battle-Door* A2v). What Woolman would later describe as "the language of the pure Spirit" emerged, for Fox, from pure grammar (PM 31).

Fox's concern with language was not limited to the use of *thee* and *thou.* Rather, he showed a consistent concern with details of proper language use, even with apparently minor issues, from the content of primers and social greetings to spelling and syllabification.[19] Moreover, this was not Fox's private quest. Fox reports that the *Battle-Door* was well received, even among non-Quakers:

> And some of them was given to the King and his council: and to the Bishops of Canterbury: and of London: one apiece: and to the universities: and many bought them up: and the King said it was the proper language to all nations.
>
> And they asked the Bishop of Canterbury what he thought of it: and he was so astonished at it as he could not tell what to say to it, for it so confounded people that few after was so rugged against us for saying "thee" and "thou" to a single person: which before they was exceeding bad against us for: and in danger many times of our lives: and often beat for using those words to some proud men who would say: "Thoust 'thou' me thou ill-bred clown," as though their breeding lay in saying "you" to a singular: which was contrary to all their accidence and grammar and all their teaching books that they had taught and bred up youth by. (*Journal* [1998] 306)

That contemporary readers were "astonished," in Fox's words, by the *Battle-Door*, is less surprising than his claim that it sold well and swayed the Friends' opponents, making them less hostile to Fox's program of purifying language. If Fox's representation is accurate, it testifies to the extent of interest in language reform among his contemporaries, Quaker and non-Quaker alike.

Quaker writers in fact produced a large body of polemical texts on pure and proper language. In addition to the *Battle-Door*, Fox published texts including *Concerning Good-Morrow and Good-Even; An Epistle to All Christians to keep to Yea, Yea, and Nay Nay, and to fulfil their Words and Promises* (1682); and *Instructions for Right Spelling, and Plain Directions for Reading and Writing True English, With several delightful Things, very useful and necessary both for Young and Old to read and learn.*[20] Several of Fox's colleagues embraced the project as well. Stubbs and Furley collaborated with him on the *Battle-Door*, while others such as Richard Farnsworth produced their own accounts of *The Pure Language of the Spirit of Truth, Set Forth for the Confounding False Languages, Acted out of Pride, Ambition, and Deceit. . . .*[21] The second generation of Quaker leaders continued to publish on this question, including William Penn, who took up the use of *thee* and *thou* in *No Cross, No Crown* (1669) and emphasized language "*without any Equivocation or mental R[e]servation, according to the true Plainness, Simplicity and usual signification of the words*" in his consideration of oaths.[22]

John Woolman's search for proper language thus emerges from a rich tradition of Quaker concern with language and its details. Scholars often emphasize changes in Quaker approaches to language and in style in the second generation and beyond, but Woolman's approach to language reveals the ongoing impact of early Quaker concerns.[23] Though the Quaker movement's shift from enthusiasm toward quietism was a significant transformation, the First Publishers' interest in language proved readily adaptable to the new program. Woolman shared Fox's interest in pure language, and in its Adamic roots. Edward Taylor's translation of Boehme's works appears on Woolman's list of "Books Lent," and Woolman's writings echo both Boehme and Fox in lamenting the degeneration of human language from divine purity into an earthly Babel.[24]

In his *Considerations on the True Harmony of Mankind*, Woolman considers the call in Revelation to "Come out of Babylon my people."[25] He observes that

> In departing from an humble trust in God, and following a selfish spirit, people have intentions to get the uper [sic] hand of their fellow-creatures, privately meditate on means to obtain their

> ends, and have a language in their hearts which is hard to understand. In Babel the language is confounded. (AMG 444-5)

Once again, for Woolman issues of language and substance are intertwined, though in this instance the problem is that material concerns interfere with linguistic purity. Woolman associates the "confounded" language of Babel with selfishness and greed, emphasizing that "This Citty is represented as a place of business, those employed in it, as merchants of the Earth" (AMG 445). Similarly, in a late essay on "A Sailor's Life," Woolman asserts that "The Language of Christ is pure, and to the Pure in Heart, this pure Language is intelligible."[26] Yet he expresses concern that "the Love of Money" prevents people from attending to that language. In both cases, however, he suggests that the degeneration of human language is reversible. Just as Christ's language is "intelligible," to "the Pure in Heart," so too can their own language be restored:

> as we faithfully attend to the call, the path of righteousness is more and more opened; cravings which have not their foundation in pure wisdom, more and more cease; and in an inward purity of heart, we experience a restoration of that which was lost at Babel, Represented by the inspired Prophet in the "returning of a pure language." Zeph. iii. 9. (AMG 508, 445)

Woolman thus links spiritual and linguistic purity, opposing both to the obstructions posed by commerce and greed.

Woolman pursued the purification of language actively, joining a long line of Friends involved in reforming language instruction and education more generally. In 1688, George Fox had advocated the establishment of Friends-run schools for boys and girls, beginning a long tradition of Quaker schools.[27] Woolman at several periods in his varied career either ran or helped to run a school for Friends' children, and his account books record fees charged to parents for schooling (and in some cases feeding) their children.[28] Woolman also wrote two essays on schools, in which he emphasized the importance of educating children in a way that does not dim "That Divine Light which enlightens all Men," and which Woolman believed "does often shine in the Minds of Children very early."[29] He cautioned it is needful that we deeply examine ourselves, lest we get entangled in the Wisdom of this World, and, through wrong Apprehensions, take such Methods in Education as may prove a great Injury to the

Minds of our Children" ("On Schools" 391). Among those dangers, Woolman included spiritually inappropriate instructors and methods, such as "cherishing the Spirit of Pride and the Love of Praise," as well as more practical ills, such as classes too large to allow teachers to "attend to the Spirit and Conduct of each Individual" (390-1).

Beyond these general educational concerns, Woolman showed particular interest in language instruction and published a primer entitled *A First Book for Children.*[30] In doing so, Woolman was again part of a tradition initiated by Fox, who had written *Instructions for Right Spelling* to address his objections to the schoolbooks available for children. In the final pages of the *Battle-Door,* Fox and his co-authors had lamented both the inaccurate translations offered by school texts and their reliance on "the Heathens words" (second pagination 1-13). In preparing their own primers, Quaker writers sought a purer language in which *res* and *verba* came closer to converging. In *Instructions for Right Spelling,* Fox blended a primer instructing students in spelling and syllabification with a compendium of basic knowledge, a catechism, and of course an argument for Quaker language practices, such as the distinction between *thou* and *you* and rejection of heathen-derived names for days and months. For Fox, the building blocks of language and faith were not separable; the details of language bore doctrinal weight, as did the ideas which were communicated in the texts. Fox's primer was widely used by early American Friends (Brinton 46). Moreover, many of Fox's brethren took up this project as well; between 1660 and 1840, approximately twenty-five Friends in England and America published primers (Brinton 46-47).

Woolman's primer stands squarely within this tradition, demonstrating the attention to details and material qualities of language with which he pursued his search for pure and transparent language. Woolman drew on Fox's model, paying close attention to details of spelling and division into syllables, but produced a more systematic primer more clearly addressed to children.[31] It runs through in alphabetical sequence the syllables that may be formed with each consonant and vowel, and then gradually increases the lengths of the letter combinations to present lists of longer and longer words. Among the lists of syllables, Woolman presents sentences written with increasingly longer words as well—first a set of sentences composed of two- and three-letter words ("Go not in the Way of a bad Man; Do not tell a Lie my Son" [A3v]), then four-letter words, then five-letter words, and ultimately passages in simple language with words of up to nine letters in length. The primer ends with the story of the Good Samaritan, and with Jesus's injunction "Go thou and do likewise."

Woolman's interest in a spiritually and linguistically pure primer is coupled with a firm practicality, not only in the systematic approach to presenting sounds and words, but also in the presentation of the book as a whole. The book's title page explains that it is intended to prevent waste: "Much useful reading being sullied and torn by Children in Schools before they can read, this Book is intended to save unnecessary expence." The book itself is compact—ten by twelve centimeters—and is intended to survive rough use, for the title page also includes a "Note" that "When the above Alphabet is defaced, this Leaf may be pasted upon the Cover; and the Alphabet on the other side made use of." Here, then, written language in its substance—its letters, its syllables, and the pages upon which it is printed—occupies Woolman's attention, and cannot be fully severed from its spiritual impact. Apparently, this synthesis made *A First Book for Children* at least a modestly successful text; Amelia Mott Gummere reports that it "went through at least three editions," and Janet Whitney notes that "On one occasion [Woolman's] Account Book records selling a hundred of them at once."[32]

Woolman's sense of the connection between spirit and substance in language shapes his use of metaphor as well, leading him to collapse distinctions between literal and metaphorical meaning. In his description of seventeenth-century Quaker style, Jackson I. Cope identifies "a tendency to break down the boundary between literalness and metaphor, between conceptions and things" (726). Woolman's treatment of dyed clothing demonstrates the persistence of what Cope calls a "habit of sliding literalness and metaphor into one another" in eighteenth-century Quaker writing (727). Like many early Quakers, Woolman expresses scruples about clothing which unite spiritual and material concerns, and such concerns are discussed frequently in the *Journal.* Late in his *Journal,* Woolman muses extensively on the spiritual significance of dyeing, and his musings wander between metaphorical aspects of impurity and more literal ones. Dyed clothing, for Woolman, is connected with unnecessary luxury and with waste, for Woolman believes that dyes are "hurtful" to materials (PM 119, 120). Moreover, because dyeing involves the staining of otherwise whiter cloth, it symbolically evokes spiritual impurity.

In Woolman's objections to dyed cloth, the spiritual and the material blur together. Woolman is troubled, he explains, by the material impurity produced by the dying process:

> Having of late travelled often in wet weather through narrow streets in towns and villages, where dirtiness under foot and the scent arising from that filth which more or less infects the air of all thick settled towns, and I, being but weakly, have felt distress both in body and mind with that which is impure. In these journeys I have been where much cloth hath been dyed and sundry times walked over ground where much of their dye-stuffs have drained away. (PM 190)

Here, the damage of dyes is physical as well as spiritual. Woolman links the stain on the ground with his own physical discomfort at traveling in dirty and smelly towns.

The power of the assault on Woolman's nostrils generates spiritual musings as well. At the dye-stained ground, he reports "Here I have felt a longing in my mind that people might come into cleanness of spirit, cleanness of person, cleanness about their houses and garments" (PM 190). Earlier, Woolman has associated dirty garments with spiritual backsliding, expressing "a tender concern that the work of reformation so prosperously carried on in this land within a few ages past may go forward and spread among the nations, and may not go backward through dust gathering on our garments" (PM 188). Here, however, the metaphorical aspects of cleanliness seem to pale before the more physical ones. "Cleanness of spirit" may be privileged, but Woolman's prose is most vivid when he describes the alternatives to "cleanness of person, cleanness about their houses and garments" (PM 190). Woolman laments that

> Some who are great carry delicacy to a great height themselves, and yet the real cleanliness is not generally promoted. Dyes being invented partly to please the eye and partly to hide dirt, I have felt in this weak state, travelling in dirtiness and affected with unwholesome scents, a strong desire that the nature of dyeing cloth to hide dirt may be more fully considered. (PM 190)

The "real cleanliness" described here has both spiritual analogues and spiritual consequences: those who use dyed clothing to "hide dirt" reveal their spiritual uncleanness even as they hide their physical uncleanness. Yet the physical uncleanness is "real" not only in its symbolic or metaphorical sense; indeed, for Woolman it seems perhaps more real in its physical and fleshly reality—especially in its odor. As the literal and metaphorical collapse together, Woolman's prose privileges the physical and the bodily, rather than rendering it transparent to the Inner Light. He reports "distress both in body and mind with that which is impure," but his human language proves more suited for complaining about physical stench than about spiritual impurity.[33]

While this might present Woolman with a narrative problem, he turns it to the service of his spiritual message. The blurring of boundaries between physical cleanness and spiritual cleanness (and their opposites) is itself significant: for Woolman, physical impurity can overwhelm not only physical purity, but also spiritual purity, and this can occur in the realms of both narrative and physical experience. Thus Woolman concludes his discussion of dyes and dyed cloth with a broader statement about the relationship between the physical and the spiritual:

> Near large towns there are many beasts slain to supply the market, and from their blood, etc., ariseth that which mixeth in the air. This, with the cleaning of many stables and other scents, the air in cities in a calm, wettish time is so opposite to the clear pure country air that I believe even the minds of people are in some degree hindered from the pure operation of the Holy Spirit, where they breathe a great deal in it. (PM 190)

Woolman suggests that urban stench can obstruct spiritual purity. His sense of the symbolic spiritual power of dyed clothing is thus inextricably bound up with the fleshly and material consequences of dyeing. Though he defines the "substance" of his metaphor as its tenor, the vehicle of the metaphor proves stubbornly substantial, rather than transparent. Both collapse together as spirit and substance merge into a complex web, thus mirroring in metaphorical structure the broader relationship between the spiritual and physical in Woolman's writings and thought.[34]

This merging of spirit and substance reflects the relationship between transparency and substance in Woolman's account of divine language and human language as well. On the one hand, human language should ideally approach a condition of transparency to divine truth. Yet metaphors of solidity and substance suggest spiritual power for Woolman, so that he is striving paradoxically for moments of "solid" transparency, when the "matter" on his mind can be expressed in language. Such moments offer Woolman the writer and would-be prophet "a restoration of that which was lost at Babel," a taste of the power and purity of Adamic language and an opportunity to close the gap between his own language and "pure Language" of Christ (AMG 445, 508). Indeed, in such moments of perfect transparency, words themselves can bear substance, can be "Certain Evidence" of the Truth which Woolman strives to know and communicate.

NOTES

[1] I thank Michele Lise Tarter and Bill Sharpe for helpful comments on this essay, and Anne Myles for her generosity in sharing her copy of John Woolman's *A First Book for Children.* Earlier versions of this essay were presented at the Modern Language Association Convention, 28 December 2000, and the Society of Early Americanists Biennial Conference, 9 March 2001. I am grateful to members of both panels and to the assembled audiences for their responses and suggestions. Funding for this project was provided by the National Endowment for the Humanities, the Folger Shakespeare Library, and Barnard College.

[2] Eclesisastes 5:2, "Be not rash with thy mouth, and let not thine heart be hasty to utter *any* thing before God: for God is in heaven, and thou upon earth: therefore let thy words be few." (Authorized Version, from Quickverse for Windows version 3h, copyright 1992-1994 by Craig Rairdin and Parsons Technology.)

[3] Daniel B. Shea describes this dynamic in his chapter on Woolman in *Spiritual Autobiography in Early America.* He identifies "the two most striking features of Woolman's *Journal*" as "its essential statement that, as self diminishes, the experience of divine love increases; and Woolman's habitual conscientiousness of expression, which strives to reveal Truth without distortion or dilution" ([Madison, WI: U of Wisconsin Press, 1988] 47).

[4] John Woolman, *The Journal of John Woolman* (1774), in *The Journal and Major Essays of John Woolman,* ed. Phillips P. Moulton (Richmond, IN: Friends United Press, 1971) 31, hereafter PM.

[5] See, for example, PM 32, 38, 42, 67, 71, 92, 93, 110, 161.

[6] See also PM 175.

[7] John Woolman, "On Silent Worship" (1773), *The Journal and Essays of John Woolman,* ed. Amelia Mott Gummere (New York, NY: Macmillan, 1922) 510.

[8] Phyllis Mack, *Visionary Women: Ecstatic Prophecy in Seventeenth-Century England* (Berkeley, CA: University of California Press, 1992) 7.

[9] Albert C. Baugh and Thomas Cable, *A History of the English Language* (Englewood Cliffs, NJ: Prentice-Hall, 1978) 242.

[10] Kathleen M. Wales, "Thou and You in Early Modern English: Brown and Gilman Reappraised," *Studia Linguistica: A Journal of General Linguistics* 37.2 (1983) 107-125. Wales cites Brown and Gilman's claim that "reaction against the radicalism of the Quakers" was "a likely factor in the disappearance of *thou* in English; simplified verbal inflection . . . is the only other 'force' they mention" (R. Brown and A. Gilman, "The Pronouns of Power and Solidarity" (1960), reprinted in *Communication in Face to Face Interaction,* eds. J. Laver and S. Hutcheson (Harmondsworth: Penguin, 1972) 115-6.

[11] Hugh Barbour, *The Quakers in Puritan England* (New Haven, CT and London, England: Yale University Press, 1964) 163-4.

[12] George Fox, John Stubbs, and Benjamin Furly, *A Battle-Door for Teachers & Professors to Learn Singular & Plural* (1660). English Linguistics 1500-1800 No. 115 (Menston, England: Scolar Press, 1968), hereafter *Battle-Door.*

[13] William C. Braithwaite notes that "Fox's name was not put to the Preface, but it is evidently by him" (*The Beginnings of Quakerism,* [London, England: Macmillan, 1912] 497n.2).

[14] On seventeenth-century interest in Adamic language, see Hans Aarsleff, "The Rise and Decline of Adam and his Ursprache in Seventeenth-Century Thought," *The Language of Adam / Die Sprache Adams,* ed. Allison P. Coudert (Wiesbaden, Germany: Harrassowitz Verlag, 1999) 277-295.

[15] For discussion of Boehme's influence, see Aarsleff 282; Jackson I. Cope, "Seventeenth-Century Quaker Style," *PMLA* 71.4 Part I (September 1956): 739.

[16] Fox describes a 1648 vision in which he regains Adamic language: "Now was I come up in spirit through the flaming sword into the paradise of God. All things were new, and all the creation gave another smell unto me, than before, beyond what words can utter. I knew nothing, but pureness, and innocency, and righteousness, being renewed up into the image of God by Christ Jesus; so that I say, I was come up to the state of Adam, which he was in, before he fell. The creation was opened to me: and it was showed to me, how all things had their names given them, according to their nature and virtue. And I was at a stand in my mind, whether I should practise physick for the good of mankind, seeing the nature and virtues of the creatures were so

opened to me by the Lord. But I was immediately taken up in spirit, to see into another or more steadfast state, than Adam's in innocency, even into a state in Christ Jesus, that should never fall. And the Lord showed me, that such as were faithful to him in the power and light of Christ, should come up into that state, in which Adam was before he fell: in which the admirable works of the creation, and the virtues thereof may be known, through the openings of that divine word of wisdom and power, by which they were made. Great things did the Lord lead me into, and wonderful depths were opened unto me, beyond what can by words be declared: but as people come into subjection to the spirit of God, and grow up in the image and power of the Almighty, they may receive the Word of wisdom, that opens all things, and come to know the hidden unity in the Eternal Being" (George Fox, *The Journal,* ed. and intro. Nigel Smith. [New York, NY and London, England: Penguin, 1998] 27-8, hereafter "*Journal,* [1998]").

[17] Braithwaite suggests that type for the more obscure languages had to be "cut, no doubt, expressly for the book" (497).

[18] G[eorge] F[ox] and E[llis] H[ookes], *Instructions for Right Spelling, and Plain Directions for Reading and Writing True English, With several delightful Things, very useful and necessary both for Young and Old to read and learn* (London, England, 1673).

[19] See, for example, G[eorge] F[ox], *Concerning Good-morrow, and Good-even; the Worlds Customs: but by the Light Which into the World Is Come, by it Made Manifest to All Who Be in the Darkness* (London, 1657). Concern with syllabification was common to other seventeenth-century radicals, especially those influenced by Boehme. In his *Mysterium magnum,* Boehme argued that individual syllables and even letters had spiritual significance, for example tracing each of the five vowels to the Tetragammaton and explaining their "inward understanding" (*Mysterium Magnum, or an Exposition of the First Book of Moses Called Genesis Concerning the Manifestation or Revelation of the Divine Word. . . .* [1623], trans. John Ellistone and J. Sparrow. [London, 1656]) 228.

[20] G[eorge] F[ox], *An Epistle to All Christians to keep to Yea, Yea, and Nay Nay, and to fulfil their Words and Promises* (London, England, 1682).

[21] Richard Farnsworth, *The Pure Language of the Spirit of Truth, Set Forth for the Confounding False Languages, Acted out of Pride, Ambition, and Deceit. . . .* (London, England, 1655).

[22] William Penn, *No Cross, No Crown, or, Several Sober Reasons against Hat-honour, Titular-respects, You to a Single Person, with the Apparel and Recreations of the Times* (London, England, 1669); (William Penn)], *Reasons Why the Oaths Should not be made A Part of the Test to Protestant Dissenters.* (London, 1683) 7.

[23] See, for example, Hugh Ormsby-Lennon, "From Shibboleth to Apocalypse: Quaker Speechways during the Puritan Revolution," *Language, Self, and Society: A Social History of Language,* eds. Peter Burke and Roy Porter, Afterword by Dell Hymes (Cambridge, England: Polity Press, 1991) 72-112, esp. pages 98-100. See also Cope's assessment that "As Quakerdom passed on into the third quarter of the seventeenth century, this mode of viewing life as *scriptura rediviva,* like the 'incantatory' style, withered and disappeared" (749).

[24] Frederick B. Tolles, "John Woolman's List of 'Books Lent,'" *Bulletin of Friends Historical Association* 31.2 (Autumn 1942): 80, 81. The first reference on the list is to "Behman," which seems to correspond with a copy of Boehme in Edward Taylor's edition found in the Quaker Collection, Haverford College Library, bearing Woolman's signature and the date 1747 on page 218 (80, 80n.22, 75n.6). The second reference is to "Edward Taylors Works," which Tolles suggests is "Probably Edward Taylor's edition of Boehme" (81, 81n.26).

[25] John Woolman, *Considerations on the True Harmony of Mankind and How It Is to Be Maintained* (1770), *The Journal and Essays of John Woolman,* ed. Amelia Mott Gummere (New York, NY: Macmillan, 1922) 444; Woolman's quotation is from Revelations 18:4.

[26] John Woolman, "A Sailor's Life"(1773), *The Journal and Essays of John Woolman,* ed. Amelia Mott Gummere (New York, NY: Macmillan, 1922) 508.

[27] Howard H. Brinton, *Quaker Education in Theory and Practice* (1940; revised and republished as Pendle Hill Pamphlet 9, Wallingford, PA: Pendle Hill, 1958) 23.

[28] Amelia Mott Gummere, "The Journal of John Woolman: Biographical Sketch," *The Journal and Essays of John Woolman,* ed. Amelia Mott Gummere (New York, NY: Macmillan, 1922) 101-105.

[29] John Woolman, "On Schools" (1758), *The Journal and Essays of John Woolman,* ed. Amelia Mott Gummere (New York, NY: Macmillan, 1922) 390. A similar essay stands as chapter 14 of *A Plea for the Poor, or A Word of Remembrance and Caution to the Rich* (1793), *The Journal and Major Essays of John Woolman,* ed. Phillips P. Moulton (Richmond, IN: Friends United Press, 1971) 263-266.

[30] John Woolman, *A First Book for Children.* Philadelphia, PA n.d.

[31] For an analysis of the evolution of Quaker catechisms in terms of shifting attitudes toward children, see Jerry W. Frost, "As the Twig Is Bent: Quaker Ideas of Childhood," *Quaker History* 60.2 (Autumn 1971): 83-87.

[32] Gummere 16; Janet Whitney, *John Woolman: American Quaker* (Boston, MA: Little, Brown and Company, 1942) 333.

[33] Some early Quakers expressed the collapse of distinctions between the metaphoric and the literal by acting out their meaning, rather than creating written texts. See Richard Bauman's discussion of "going naked as a sign." (*Let Your Words Be Few: Symbolism of Speaking and Silence Among Seventeenth-Century Quakers* [New York, NY: Cambridge University Press, 1983] 86-94).

[34] Mike Heller discusses the importance of metaphor in Quaker worship, the role of central metaphors in the Quaker community, and Woolman's use of "clusters of controlling metaphors" in "The Keeping of Negroes." See "'There is a Principle . . .': Argument in Woolman's 'Some Considerations on the Keeping of Negroes,'" in *Soft Persuasion: John Woolman's Rhetoric of Non-violence,* book ms.

WORKS CITED

Aarsleff, Hans. "The Rise and Decline of Adam and his Ursprache in Seventeenth Century Thought." *The Language of Adam /Die Sprache Adams.* Ed. Allison P. Coudert. Wiesbaden, Germany: Harrassowitz Verlag, 1999. 277-295.

Barbour, Hugh. *The Quakers in Puritan England.* New Haven, CT and London, England: Yale University Press, 1964.

Baugh, Albert C. and Thomas Cable. *A History of the English Language.* Englewood Cliffs, NJ: Prentice-Hall, 1978.

Baurman, Richard. *Let Your Words Be Few: Symbolism of Speaking and Silence Among Seventeenth-Century Quakers.* New York, NY: Cambridge University Press, 1983.

Boehme, Jacob. *Mysterium Magnum, or an Exposition of the First Book of Moses Called Genesis Concerning the Manifestation or Revelation of the Divine Word. . . .* 1623. Trans. John Ellistone and J. Sparrow. London, England, 1656.

Braithwaite, William C. *The Beginnings of Quakerism.* London, England: Mac-millan, 1912.

Brinton, Howard. *Quaker Education in Theory and Practice.* 1940. Wallingford, PA: Pendle Hill, 1958.

Brown, R. and A. Gilman. "The Pronouns of Power and Solidarity." 1960. Rpt. *Communication in Face to Face Interaction.* Ed. J. Laver and S. Hutcheson. Harmondsworth: Penguin, 1972. 103-127.

Cope, Jackson I. "Seventeenth Century Quaker Style." *PMLA* 71 (1956): 725-54.

Farnsworth, Richard. *The Pure Language of the Spirit of Truth, Set Forth for the Confounding False Languages, Acted out of Pride, Ambition, and Deceit.* . . . London,England, 1655.

Fox, George. *The Journal.* Ed. and intro. Nigel Smith. New York, NY and London, England: Penguin, 1998.

Fox, George. *Concerning Good-morrow, and Good-even; the Worlds Customs: but by the Light Which into the World Is Come, by it Made Manifest to All Who Be in the Darkness.* London,England, 1657.

—. *An Epistle to All Christians to keep to Yea, Yea, and Nay Nay, and to fulfil their Words and Promises.* London, England, 1682.

Fox, George and Ellis Hookes. *Instructions for Right Spelling, and Plain Directions for Reading and Writing True English, With several delightful Things, very useful and necessary both for Young and Old to read and learn.* London, England, 1673.

Fox, George, John Stubbs, and Benjamin Furly. *A Battle-Door for Teachers & Professors to Learn Singular & Plural.* 1660. English Linguistics 1500-1800 No. 115. Menston, England: Scolar Press, 1968.

Frost, Jerry W. "As the Twig Is Bent: Quaker Ideas of Childhood." *Quaker History* 60.2 (Autumn 1971): 67-87.

Gummere, Amelia Mott. "The Journal of John Woolman: Biographical Sketch." *The Journal and Essays of John Woolman.* Ed. Amelia Mott Gummere. New York, NY : Macmillan, 1922. 1-150.

Heller, Mike. "'There is a Principle . . .': Argument in Woolman's 'Some Considerations on the Keeping of Negroes.'" *Soft Persuasion: John Woolman's Rhetoric of Nonviolence.* Book ms.

Mack, Phyllis. *Visionary Women: Ecstatic Prophecy in Seventeenth-Century England.* Berkeley, CA: University of California Press, 1992.

Ormsby-Lennon, Hugh. "From Shibboleth *Language, Self, and Society: A Social History of Language.* Ed. Peter Burke and Roy Porter. Afterword by Dell Hymes. Cambridge, England: Polity Press, 1991. 72-112.

Penn, William *No Cross, No Crown, or, Several Sober Reasons against Hat-honour, Titular respects, You to a Single Person, with the Apparel and Recreations of the Times.* London, England, 1669.

[Penn, William]. *Reasons Why the Oaths Should not be made A Part of the Test to Protestant Dissenters.* London, England, 1683.

Rairdin, Craig. Quickverse for Windows version 3h. Parson Technology, 1992-1994.

Shea, Daniel B. *Spiritual Autobiography in Early America.* Madison, WI: University of Wisconsin Press, 1988.

Taylor, Edward, ed. *Jacob Behmen's Theosophick Philosophy Unfolded in Divers Considerations and Demonstrations. Also the Principal Treatises of the Said Author Abridged.* London, England, 1691.

Tolles, Frederick B. "John Woolman's List of 'Books Lent.'" *Bulletin of Friends Historical Association* 31.2 (Autumn 1942): 72-81.

Wales, Kathleen M. 'Thou and You in Early Modern English: Brown and Gilman Reappraised." *Studia Linguistica: A Journal of General Linguistics* 37.2 (1983): 107-125.

Woolman, John. *A First Book for Children* Philadelphia, PA, n.d.

—. *Considerations on the True Harmony of Mankind and How It Is to Be Maintained.* 1770. *The Journal and Essays of John Woolman.* Ed. Amelia Mott Gummere. New York, NY: Macmillan, 1922. 438-458.

—. *The Journal of John Woolman.* 1774. *The Journal and Major Essays of John Woolman,* ed. Phillips P. Moulton. Richmond, IN: Friends United Press, 1971. 23-192.

—. *A Plea for the Poor or A Word of Remembrance and Caution to the Rich.* 1793. *The Journal and Major Essays of John Woolman,* ed. Phillips P. Moulton. Richmond, IN: Friends United Press, 1971. 238-272.

—. "A Sailor's Life." 1773. *The Journal and Essays of John Woolman.* Ed. Amelia Mott Gummere. New York, NY: Macmillan, 1922. 505-508.

—. "On Schools." 1758. *The Journal and Essays of John Woolman.* Ed. Amelia Mott Gummere. New York, NY: Macmillan, 1922. 390-392.

—. "On Silent Worship." 1773. *The Journal and Essays of John Woolman.* Ed. Amelia Mott Gummere. New York, NY: Macmillan, 1922. 508-510.

5

Preparing the Heart for Sympathy: John Woolman Reading Scripture

Michael L. Birkel

In the spring of 1772, John Woolman set sail for England, his final journey before his death in York. He spent this voyage not in the comfortable cabins with other passengers but in steerage, the cramped quarters of the poor sailors whose life he grew to understand. His time on this ship offered him opportunity for observation and meditation. On May 28, 1772, John Woolman wrote a rich but complicated entry to his sea journal which would become chapter 11 of his published *Journal* (PM 174-177). It offers us a glimpse into John Woolman's inward life and suggests something of his experience of the interrelatedness of reality, of a universe deep in multiple and mutually enriching meanings, evidenced through his understanding of the inner meaning of Scripture. This *Journal* passage also sheds light on how Woolman understood his own spiritual experiences and therefore what he considered the nature of spiritual growth.

Through a study of that entry, we can see a side of Woolman's thinking not often made public in his writings, namely, his densely-imaged typological imagination. The entry makes it possible (1) to explore how Woolman uses Scripture, (2) to consider his metaphors for spiritual renewal and transformation, and (3) to ponder relations between imaginative reading and imaginative ethics. For John Woolman, these three come together as "sympathy": reading Scripture under the guidance of the Spirit that gave them forth brings one into sympathy with the Biblical characters, and a sympathetic reading of Scripture prepares one's heart for sympathy with others, which is the fruit of inward transformation.

John Woolman and Scripture

The *Journal* entry is rich in Biblical citations and allusions. It has a density of Biblical layering that makes the passage more difficult than most of Woolman's writings—in part because few readers today would even catch many of John Woolman's allusions to Scripture here. Yet it seems safe to assume that Woolman, who meticulously revised his own writings to achieve a greater clarity, would expect at least some of his readers to hear the Biblical echoes in his words—and to assume that such echoes have a meaning, that they shed light on his intent in writing. Woolman found in Scripture a language to describe the spiritual realities of his own experience, as is evident not only from this passage but from the literally hundreds of references to Scripture in his writings.

In Woolman's writings one can discern different ways of using the Bible: official epistles from Friends' bodies such as yearly meetings are replete with Biblical phrases and passages, often as supporting evidence or at least moral authority for the document's major point (PM 48-49, 98-101, for example). Friends knew how to use the Bible to prove their points in disagreements, as John Woolman does expressing his opposition to slavery (PM 63, 213-221), payment of war taxes (PM 90), and sleight-of-hand tricks (PM 139). Scripture was of course quoted, less disputatiously on the whole, in vocal ministry in meetings for worship, and John Woolman on two occasions mentions the Biblical passages on which he was led to speak.[1] Some Biblical passages seem to have become Quaker commonplaces, that is, they assumed a meaning of their own which no longer necessarily had any direct connection with the larger literary context in which they were written in the Bible. Some candidates include Nahum 1:7, "The Lord is good, a stronghold in the day of trouble," quoted without reference to the larger context of gloom and doom but instead as consolation (PM 43, 69). But there was at least one other way of using the Bible, and that was reading it in a meditative fashion, expecting an encounter with God.

Robert Barclay, whose *Apology* had, by John Woolman's time, achieved an authoritative status among Friends, offers helpful clues for understanding how Quakers read the Bible in this manner:

> God hath seen meet that herein [that is, in the Scriptures] we should, as in a looking-glass, see the conditions and experiences of the saints of old; that finding our experience answer to theirs, we might thereby be the more confirmed and comforted, and our hope of attaining the same end strengthened. (Barclay, Proposition 3, Section 5)

To read the Scriptures is to look in a mirror and find one's own inner life reflected in the lives of spiritual forebears. Reading the Scriptures is an experience of growing self-knowledge. The life experiences of Biblical characters are analogous to our own; their spiritual conditions are ours. Reading the Bible is an event of self-discovery, taught by the same Spirit which inspired the written words of Scripture. To read is to be read.

Barclay's words suggest that the act of reading Scripture is approached with an anticipation of an encounter with the Spirit. Reading the Bible with this expectation becomes a reverential act, akin to meeting for worship. The Bible becomes a kind of meetinghouse, where one listens inwardly. The Biblical words are received in the same spirit as vocal ministry, since both originate from the same source.

The Biblical story is recapitulated in the life of the believing reader. Each has his own exile, her own exodus. Samuel Bownas, an elder contemporary of Woolman, writes in *A Description of the Qualifications Necessary to a Gospel Minister* that "all these things that happened to Israel in Egypt, through the Red Sea and in the wilderness, have a true resemblance of believers traveling from a spiritual Sodom and Egypt, so called" (47).[2] The events of the Biblical narrative or "history," in Scripture "have a meaning to believers in the mystery," that is, in the interior life. To understand Scripture, the reader "ought first to experience the veil that is in the history of the letter, taken away by the operation of Christ's Spirit in his own heart, and the substance of the figures under the law given to him in experience" (Bownas 48).[3] Reading Scripture is itself a worshipful act. It requires waiting upon the Spirit to understand its meaning for us.

This sort of reading is obviously not modern speed reading. It is done deliberately, meditatively, spaciously. The pace is attentive and generous. Friends of course did not invent reading Scripture this way. In some important ways it is close in spirit and perhaps practice to the meditative reading practiced for centuries in Christianity and known in the western church by the name of *lectio divina,* or spiritual reading.[4] What Woolman shares with these earlier ways of reading is not simply typology or allegory but rather a layeredness, a free-associative play which suggests something of the inner experience of the interrelatedness of reality, of a universe deep in multiple and mutually enriching meanings. His entry in his *Journal* for May 28,1772, demonstrates an appreciation of the multi-layered meanings of reality that underscore the profound connectedness of all of life. So here we come to a complex relationship: John Woolman read the Bible in terms of his own particular inward experiences, yet he perceived his world in profoundly Biblical terms. His spiritual experiences shaped his reading of the Bible, and the Bible shaped his understanding of his experiences. He did not simply read the Scriptures. He lived them.

John Woolman's understanding of the nature of the religious life did not end with this interior experience alone. For him, religion was always inward and outward, intimate and social. As he wrote of his own convincement experience, "true religion consisted in an inward life, wherein the heart doth love and reverence God the Creator and learn to exercise true justice and goodness" (PM 28). The result of an inward spiritual experience is "a lively operative desire for the good of others" (PM 31). For John Woolman, the mystic's vision brings with it a call for justice. In this respect he is true to his heritage as a Friend.[5]

Crucifying Esau the Heifer: Spiritual Transformation and Three Scripture Passages

As elsewhere in his writings, in the *Journal* entry for May 28, 1772, Woolman sees a natural conflict between the will of God, which is based on love and which promotes universal righteousness, and what he calls the natural will, using "natural" in a sense which he derives from the apostle Paul (as rendered in the King James Version), meaning life apart from the Spirit. This natural will is based in unbounded desire for riches and reputation. This unholy desire is ultimately driven by fear and leads to a life lived in confusion rather than in the clear leadings of the Light. For Woolman, the way out of such a living death is to set aside this natural will. The subjection of the will opens the way to freedom (or separation) from the desire for gain. He calls subjection the "death of [one's] own will" (see PM 176, 186). This death opens the way to new life, to "purity," which in turn prepares one to perceive the nature of divine righteousness and love. It is this process of transformation which is central to Woolman in this passage, and which he explores in a rich, imaginative meditation on Scripture.

Three Biblical texts provide John Woolman with the central imagery for his reflections on inward transformation: a ritual of purification from defilement described in Numbers, the symbolic appropriation of ritual sacrifice to understand the meaning of Christ's death in the Epistle to the Hebrews, and the apostle Paul's description of baptism as a dying and rising with Christ from the Epistle to the Romans. The interplay of these texts provides a complex, even poetic texture. In Numbers 19, the sacrificial death and then burning of a red heifer provides the ashes for what is called the "water of separation." This mixture of ashes and water purifies from sin (Num. 19:9) and cleanses those who have become ritually impure by touching a corpse. In Hebrews 9, the purification rite in Numbers is understood as a foreshadowing of the death of Christ, which purifies the believer's "conscience from dead works to serve the living God" (9:14). In Romans 6, the believer participates in the death of Christ through baptism, which crucifies the "old man" or unregenerate self. Like Christ, the believer then experiences newness of life, becoming a "servant of righteousness" (6:18).

When John Woolman wrote the entry of May 28, 1772, he had been at sea since the first of the month, and so it is possible that his preoccupation with the image of the water of separation may be a metaphor for his own voyage, which he seems to have seen as a journey of purification. He explains, for example, that the leading to travel in steerage was not in his own will (PM 163, 165). He also refers to his journey as a "floating pilgrimage" which "is in some degree bringing me to feel that which many thousands of my fellow creatures often suffer" (PM 173). His travel on the waters of the Atlantic enables him to undergo a further separation from his natural will.

Throughout his journey, Woolman has been reflecting on trade, on what motivates it, on the miserable conditions of the sailors, and on the need to be "redeemed from the love of money and from that spirit in which men seek honour one of another" (PM 173). This extraordinary passage follows a discussion which contrasts the love of gain, prompted by an unrestrained "natural will," and the love of God. Love of God requires the renunciation of the natural will and opens the way to the "pure peaceable government of Christ" among humankind. He then writes:

> In an entire subjection of our wills the Lord graciously opens a way for his people, where all their wants are bounded by his wisdom; and here we experience the substance of what Moses *the prophet* figured out in the water of separation as a purification from sin. [Num.19:13, cf. Heb. 9:9] (PM 175)

The theme of renouncing one's "own will" and conforming to the divine will is dominant in John Woolman's writings (PM 249-50, AMG 484, 487), as is the concept of human wills being bounded by God, that is, God placing appropriate boundaries around human desires (AMG 473, 445; PM 28, 35). Moses is understood as a prophet in his "figuring out," or prefiguring and foreshadowing the truths to be revealed in fullness with the coming of Christ. Such a typological reading of the Old Testament, which sees it not only as a history of God's revelation to the chosen people of ancient Israel but also as a symbolic representation of what was to come in the fullness of God's self-disclosure in Jesus Christ, is also traditional in Christianity, and goes back to New Testament times. Although the overt reference here is to a passage in the book of Numbers, it seems likely that John Woolman took as his starting point the Epistle to the Hebrews, which is a very typological reading of the Old Testament:

> For if the blood of bulls and of goats, and the ashes of an heifer sprinkling the unclean, sanctifieth to the purifying of the flesh; how much more shall the blood of Christ, who through the eternal Spirit offered himself without spot to God, purge your conscience from dead works to serve the living God? [Hebrews 9:13-14]

It seems likely that the journal entry under discussion here began for John Woolman with a meditative reading of this chapter from Hebrews. Although he does not refer directly to Hebrews, many of the key terms in this journal entry are found in Hebrews 9: "heifer," "purification," "figure," "reformation," and the necessity of a death. This suggests that John Woolman read the Bible in an associative, imaginative manner similar to the medieval tradition of meditative reading. The focus of this *Journal* entry is on an inward purification, a purging of the conscience from dead works (understood by Woolman as the unrestrained love of wealth and reputation) to serve the living God.

> Esau is mentioned as a child red all over like a hairy garment. [Genesis 25:25] In Esau is represented the natural will [1 Cor. 2:14] of man. In preparing the water of separation, a red heifer without blemish, on which there had been no yoke, was to be slain and her blood sprinkled by the priest seven times toward the tabernacle of the congregation. Then her skin, her flesh, and

> all pertaining to her was to be burnt without the camp, and of her ashes the water was prepared. Thus the crucifying the old man [Rom. 6:6], or natural will, is represented, and hence comes a separation from that carnal mind which is death [Rom. 8:7]. "He who toucheth the dead body of a man and purifieth not himself with the water of separation, he defileth the tabernacle of the Lord; he is unclean." [Numbers 19:13] (PM 175-176)

The jump from Moses to Esau may strike us as rather abrupt and illogical until we realize that John Woolman has linked in his mind the image of the red hairy Esau with the image of the red heifer. The transition is one of image to image rather than concept to concept. This associative reading is very much in line with the medieval approach to commenting on Scripture.

Esau is described as "red all over like a hairy garment" at the time of his birth [Genesis 25:25]. His uncontrolled appetite brought him to lose his birthright to his younger brother Isaac. In Hebrews 12:16 he serves as a symbol for the ungodly, the "profane person," who "for one morsel of meat sold his birthright." The image of Esau represents the kind of individual whom the apostle Paul might call a "natural" rather than a "spiritual" person (as in 1 Corinthians 2:14: "The natural man receiveth not the things of the Spirit of God.")—and the history of Biblical interpretation has portrayed him in this way.[6] The rest of this paragraph describes the ritual for purifying someone who has been ritually defiled by a corpse.

For John Woolman, the unrepentant will, not conformed to the will of God, naturally brings death, since it is so alienated from the divine source of life. Again he borrows heavily from the apostle Paul, who speaks in Romans 6 of the crucifying of the "old man" or unspiritual self—the "carnal mind" which "is enmity with God" and therefore "is death" [Romans 8:6-7]. The separation from impurity in Numbers becomes for Woolman separation from this deadly carnal mind.

> If one through the love of gain go forth into business wherein they dwell amongst the tombs [Isaiah, c.v.] [Isa. 65:4 via Mk. 5:2], and touch the bodies of those who are dead, if these through the infinite love of God feel the power of the cross of Christ to crucify them to the world [Gal. 6:14], and therein learn humbly to follow the divine leader, here is the judgment of this world—

> here the prince of this world is cast out [Jn. 12:31]. The water of separation is felt; and though we have been amongst the slain and through the desire of gain have touched the dead body of a man, yet in the purifying love of Christ we are washed in the water of separation, are brought off from that business, from that gain, and from that fellowship which was not agreeable to his holy will. And I have felt a renewed confirmation in the time of this voyage that the Lord in infinite love is calling to his visited children to so give up all outward possessions and means of getting treasures that his Holy Spirit may have free course in their hearts and direct them in all their proceedings. To feel the substance pointed at in this figure, man must know death as to his own will. (PM 176)

The above quotation is dense with Biblical allusions, and it is difficult to determine just what echoes Woolman expected would sound in the mind of his reader. At the risk of getting lost in the details of a hypothetical reconstruction, it is useful to try to recapture the Scriptural allusions to try to understand how Woolman's mind might have worked as he wrote this paragraph, since it may shed light on his method of reading Scripture.

To pursue wealth without moral restraint is to become unclean, to touch a corpse, to associate with the fatal "old man." Here Woolman remembers a passage from Isaiah which speaks of a "rebellious people which walketh in a way that was not good, after their own thoughts"—Woolman might say, after their own natural will. Such a people "remain among the graves" [Isa. 65:4]. His notation "c.v." means "chapter and verse," "which Woolman probably intended to look up and insert" (PM 176n58). But Woolman has not recalled the passage quite accurately. Instead he seems to have remembered the Isaiah verse by way of Mark 5, which speaks of the exorcism of a demoniac, a man with an "unclean spirit, who had his dwelling among the tombs" [Mark 5:2-3]. It is perhaps telling that John Woolman seems unconsciously to have remembered a passage about a person possessed with the devil while trying to describe the effects of unbridled greed. Exorcism passes from the unconscious to the conscious when he refers to results of being crucified to the world (again an expression of Paul: Galatians 6:14) as casting out the prince of this world—a reference to John 12:31, "the prince" meaning the devil. The larger context of this verse in John 12 speaks of death and life, and of following Jesus, which may help explain why Woolman's mind turns to this passage at this moment, since Woolman is also speaking of life and death.

Being washed through the purifying love of Christ in the water of separation can be an echo of baptism. In Romans 6 Paul speaks of baptism as a dying and rising to new life with Christ. The inward transformation spoken of here is of the sort that Friends in Woolman's day would have called an inward baptism (PM 314).

When Woolman states that one must know the death of one's own will in order fully to understand this "figure," surely he had in mind his own experience of the death of his will in the vision which he had while suffering nearly to the point of death with pleurisy (PM 185-186). There he again uses the language of dying with Christ and yet living, again from Paul [Gal. 2:20].[7] Although he has not yet told the reader of this vision, the sickness itself occurred some two years earlier, in the winter of 1770. The choice of such powerful images in the *Journal* entry for May 28, 1772—death, corpse, exorcism, and final judgment—underscore the intensity of the experience John Woolman is describing.

Here, coming as it does in the midst of a larger passage on the dangers of greed and of the desire for reputation in the world, "death of the will" seems to mean a release from the illusion that an incessant drive for power, prestige, and wealth affords us any final control over our destinies. For Woolman, the death of the will is followed by resurrection into new and abundant life.

> "No man can see God and live" [Exod. 33:20]. This was spoken by the Almighty to Moses the prophet and opened by our blessed Redeemer. As death comes on our own wills and a new life is formed in us, the heart is purified and prepared to understand clearly. "Blessed are the pure in heart, for they shall see God" [Matt. 5:8]. In purity of heart the mind is divinely opened to behold the nature of universal righteousness, or the righteousness of the kingdom of God. "No man hath seen the Father save he that is of God; he hath seen the Father" [John 6:46]. (PM 176)

The life that follows upon the death of the natural will brings purification and clarity of perception. In fact, the real nature of the divine cannot be understood while in the impure state of selfishness: to see

God, one must be of God. To be of God is to have experienced the death of one's own will. It is important to note that to see God is to behold righteousness. For Woolman, "righteousness" must include the ideal of social justice, as he learned from his reading in the Biblical prophets. Throughout John Woolman's writings, the mystic vision always bears with it an ethical dimension. What is particularly compelling in this paragraph is the organization by images: from life to vision, from vision to purity. The paragraph begins and ends with the image of seeing God.

It is important to emphasize that John Woolman is speaking of his own experience. He knows what it is to be inwardly purified and thus prepared to perceive divine righteousness. On 9th day 10th month 1769, he wrote,

> My heart hath often been affected under a feeling that I have had that the standard of pure righteousness is not lifted up to the people by us, as a Society, in that clearness which might have been had we been so faithful to the teachings of Christ as we ought to have been. And as my mind hath been inward to the Lord, the purity of Christ's government hath often been opened in my understanding. . . . (PM 153-54)[8]

To "consider the purity of Divine Being" is to experience a revelation of the nature of justice.

> The natural mind is active about the things of this life, and in this natural activity business is proposed and a will in us to go forward in it. And as long as this natural will remains unsubjected, so long there remains an obstruction against the clearness of divine light operating in us; but when we love God with all our heart and all our strength [Lk 10:27], then in this love we love our neighbors as ourselves, and a tenderness of heart is felt toward all people, even such who as to outward circumstances may be to us as the Jews were to the Samaritans. "Who is my neighbor?" See this question answered by our Saviour [Lk. 10:25-37]. In this love we can say that Jesus is the Lord [Phil. 2:11], and the reformation in our souls, manifested in a full reformation of our lives, wherein all things are new and all things are of God [2 Cor. 5:17-18]—in this the desire of

> gain is subjected. And employment is honestly followed in the light of Truth, and people become diligent in business, "fervent in spirit serving the Lord" [Rom. 12:11]—here the name is opened. "This is the name by which he shall be called: the Lord our Righteousness" [Jer. 23:6]. (PM 177)

Here John Woolman moves beyond what to this point have been the focal scriptural texts. The Bible has much to say about love, but Numbers 19, Romans 6, and Hebrews 9 do not even mention the word. Yet in Woolman's experience love is an essential ingredient for the process of spiritual transformation which he is discussing. He has already referred to "the purifying love of Christ" as the agent in washing us in "the water of separation." God's infinite love calls us out of greed, as Woolman noted above. The death of that selfishness which gives rise to oppression, the death of the "natural will," opens the way to the love of God and neighbor. And so he remembers and refers to the story of the Good Samaritan, that parable of love for neighbor. Love reshapes all of life into newness. For Woolman, love is what righteousness looks like when it is lived out. And so love is much more than mere sentiment, mere feeling. Love was the "motion" which inspired John Woolman to write his *Journal* (PM 23), to make his famous visit to the Delaware settlement at Wyalusing despite the perils of war (PM 127), and to be concerned for the spiritual well-being of and end of oppression for the poor sailors with whom he was riding in steerage even as he wrote this journal entry (PM 166). Love for him is inextricably linked to righteousness because righteousness is here revealed as the very name and nature of the divine. In addition to the quotations from Romans 12 and Jeremiah 23 at the end of this paragraph, it is possible to hear as well in John Woolman's language echoes of two Biblical texts which were focal earlier in this *Journal* entry: Romans 6:18 ("ye became the servants of righteousness") and Hebrews 9:14 ("purge your conscience from dead works to serve the living God").

> Oh, how precious is this name! [Eccles. 7:1] It is like ointment poured out [Song 1:3]. The chaste virgin [2 Cor. 11:2] is in love with the Redeemer, and for the promoting his peaceable kingdom are content to endure hardness like good soldiers [2 Tim. 2:3], and are so separated in spirit from the desire of riches that in their employments they become extensively careful to give

> none offense—neither to Jews nor heathens nor the church of Christ [1 Cor. 10:32]. (PM 177)

In the above paragraph, the abundance of love language continues. The focus on love and the reference to "name" take Woolman to the Song of Solomon, the Bible's rich collection of love poetry, which he reads in light of the tradition which understands the work as an allegory on the love between Christ and the soul, as his allusion to 2 Corinthians makes clear. Elsewhere he uses this image from Paul to refer to the mind being preserved chaste in resignation to the will of God (AMG 446), which he contrasts with the mind being "corrupted [away] from the simplicity that is in Christ" [2 Cor. 11:3]. The intensity of this love enables the lovers to "endure hardness like good soldiers"—an odd and abrupt change of metaphors, though consonant with John Woolman's emphasis on social reform. In fact, he had also used the expression "enduring hardness" in "Considerations on the Keeping of Negroes, Part II" (PM 212—cf. also AMG 384). He knows that the results of such a spiritual transformation will require difficult, painful changes for the wealthy who have accustomed themselves to a style of living which depends upon injustice and oppression. But their love for God, whose name is righteousness, will strengthen them to endure hardship. Their love for neighbor, "a tenderness of heart . . . felt toward all people," will inspire vigilance to "give none offense"—which is an expression elsewhere used by John Woolman to refer to oppression (PM 128-29, 143).

The nature of this divine love, as opposed to "narrow self-love" (PM 221), is that it is universal in scope and "begets a likeness of itself" where "the mind is sufficiently influenced by it" (PM 202). Natural love, such as love of one's children, is in the final analysis only a branch of self-love and therefore too restricted. Divine love reorders one's life. This wider love is prepared to take risks and to suffer. It loves the stranger, and opens the way to "a feeling sense of the conditions of others" in which one can imagine their lives (PM 31). This love enables one to extend the boundaries of what is called family. What Woolman here calls "love" he calls elsewhere "sympathy." Sympathy for others is the fruit of inward transformation, and the sympathetic reading of Scripture which he has been demonstrating in the *Journal* passage for May 28, 1772, prepares one's heart for this sympathy.

Ethics and Imagination: "A Near Sympathy"

This *Journal* entry offers us some important glimpses into the inward life of John Woolman. It shows us that Woolman practiced a meditative, imaginative reading of the Bible. (At the same time, we must acknowledge that John Woolman himself would not use the term "imaginative" to describe his method of reading. Among earlier Friends, the term "imagination" raised the specter of self-will, or the indulgence of the carnal self.) As in good poetry, image interplays with image, and image yields to insight. There is a powerful link between an imagination cultivated by such Biblical meditation and an imagination which could radically re-envision society as more righteous and peaceable.

John Woolman's sympathetic imagination enabled him to identify with Biblical events and characters, such as King David (PM 157), and the prophets Isaiah (PM 124) and Jeremiah (PM 26).The prophets and the early Christian martyrs are especially important in this regard. His practice of reading and meditating on Scripture in this way enabled him to identify with the oppressed of his day. The fact that he uses the same expression, "near sympathy," to describe his relationship with both prophets and martyrs on the one hand, and with the victims of injustice on the other, suggests that he was aware of the connection between a sympathetic reading of Scripture and the sympathetic love for others that is the fruit of inward transformation. He speaks of "a near sympathy with the prophet" Moses (PM 60). During his visit to the Delaware settlement at Wyalusing, he writes

> . . . I was led to meditate on the manifold difficulties of these Indians, . . . and a near sympathy with them was raised in me; and my heart being enlarged in the love of Christ, I thought that the affectionate care of a good man for his only brother in affliction does not exceed what I then felt for that people. (PM 133-34)

It is, to say the least, rare for one of European descent to express such a depth of love for the native peoples of this land in that (or, sadly, any) time.

Yet such sympathy was, in Woolman's understanding, originally a human inclination. Early on in his *Journal*, Woolman writes of sympathy as a divine gift and a natural human disposition, yet also a delicate gift and one easily lost through inattention:

> [God] whose tender mercies are over all his works hath placed a principle in the human mind which incites to exercise goodness toward every living creature; and this being singly attended to, people become tender-hearted and sympathizing, but being frequently and totally rejected, the mind shuts itself up in a contrary disposition. (PM 25)

For Woolman the cardinal sins of greed and desire for reputation and honor are the chief villains in drawing us away from this sympathizing principle, but he admits that cultural conventions also present obstacles. In "Considerations on the Keeping of Negroes, Part II," he notes that "The blacks seem far from being our kinsfolks" because of their condition as slaves. Therefore an "open friendship with a person of so vile a stock in the common esteem " would be regarded as a disgrace socially because they "have neither honours, riches, outward magnificence nor power, their dress coarse and often ragged, their employ drudgery and much in the dirt, . . . so that in their present situation there is not much to engage the friendship or move the affection of selfish men." Yet, Woolman continues, for "such who live in the spirit of true charity, to sympathize with the afflicted in the lowest stations of life is a thing familiar to them" (PM 226). It is familiar to them because their sympathetic reading of Scripture has prepared their heart for sympathy with the oppressed.

John Woolman's method of reading Scripture offers the understanding that it is only divine love which prepares the heart for sympathy,[9] but to overcome the obstacles which our culture places in the way, it is essential to use the imagination. In his antislavery essays, Woolman encourages his reader to "consider ourselves present as spectators" to the cruelties of slave life: our children stolen, wars in Africa promoted by the slave trade, raiding parties to carry off captives, and so on. Such acts of imagination "move us with grief. And did we attend to these scenes in Africa in like manner as if they were transacted in our presence," we would "sympathize with the Negroes in all their afflictions and miseries as we do with our children or friends" (PM 232-233).

Woolman shows that he has prepared himself for just this sort of sympathetic imagination when, contrary to his own social conditioning within a racist culture, he can identify the slaves of African descent as members of his family:

> The Lord in the Riches of his Goodness, is leading some unto the Feeling of the Condition of this People, who cannot rest without labouring as their Advocates; of which in some Measure I have had Experience: for, in the Movings of his Love in my Heart, these poor Sufferers have been brought near me.
>
> The unoffending Aged and Infirm made to labour too hard, kept on a Diet less comfortable than their weak State required, and exposed to great Difficulties under hard-hearted Men, to whose Sufferings I have often been a Witness, and under the Heart-melting Power of Divine Love, their Misery hath felt to me like the Misery of my Parents. (AMG 499-500)[10]

John Woolman explicitly relates this sympathy to the experience of love toward all, a love which blossoms only after the experience of the death of one's will. Yet we can also see how his sympathy is prepared for this by his practice of the imaginative reading of Scripture.

NOTES

[1]In both of these occasions (PM 123-24), Woolman found solace in assurance of divine protection as he was preparing for his dangerous journey to the Delaware settlement of Wyalusing during a time of war. In the first he speaks on the prayer of Jesus in chapter 17 of the Gospel of John, "I pray not that thou shouldest take them out of the world, but that thou shouldest keep them from evil." In the second he notes that he "was led to speak on the care and protection of the Lord over his people and to make mention of the passage where a band of Assyrians, endeavoring to take captive the prophet, were disappointed, and how the Psalmist said, 'The angel of the Lord encampeth round about them that fear him.'" The references here are to 2 Chronicles 32:20-23 (see also 22 Kings 19 and Isaiah 37) and to Psalm 34:7.

Amelia Mott Gummere records that English Friend Elihu Robinson, in his unpublished Diary, notes that "Our Frd John Woolman from Jersey . . . made sevl beautiful remks in this Meetg and with respt to ye benefit of true Silence, and how Incense ascended on ye Oppening of ye 7th Seal, and there was Silence in heaven for ye space of half an hour, &c. . . ." (AMG 129).

[2]Here Samuel Bownas is alluding to Rev. 11:8, "the great city, which spiritually is called Sodom." In other words, he sees himself as simply continuing a tradition of symbolic or allegorical interpretation already explicit in the Scriptures themselves.

[3]Here again, Samuel Bownas is echoing Scripture, in this case 2 Cor. 3, which contrasts letter and spirit and which speaks of Christ lifting the veil from the heart. Samuel Bownas is writing for ministers, but the concept of how to understand the Bible would have implications for all readers.

[4]For a classic introduction to *lectio divina,* see Guigo II, *The Ladder of Monks.* The *Twelve Meditations* of Guigo, found in the same volume, also show a remarkable similarity to John Woolman's meditative reflections on Scripture, as will be discussed later. It is my intent to pursue the kinship between Woolman's way of reading scripture and that of *lectio divina* in a separate study.

[5]See Hugh Barbour's *The Quakers in Puritan England,* particularly chapter 4, "The Terror and Power of the Light," in which he suggests that the outcome of Quaker religious experience was not so much mystical union as a leading, a divine directive to engage in some action to further the kingdom of God on earth.

[6]See for example Augustine of Hippo, *Enarrationes in Psalmos* 47:4-5 in *A Select Library of the Nicene and Post-Nicene Fathers of the Christian Church* (161).

[7]For a fuller discussion of Woolman's vision while suffering from pleurisy, see my "John Woolman on the Cross," in *The Lamb's War: Quaker Essays to Honor Hugh Barbour* (91-100).

[8]In 1758 he spoke in Yearly Meeting about the injustice of slavery, again noting how God's self-disclosure to the human mind entails a call to justice and righteousness: "My mind is often led to consider the purity of Divine Being and the justice of his judgments. . . . In infinite love and goodness he hath opened our understandings from one time to another concerning our duty toward this people [that is, the slaves], and it is not a time for delay" (PM 92-93).

[9]Cf. Woolman's "On the Slave Trade": "in Divine Love, the Heart is enlarged towards Mankind universally, and prepar'd to sympathize with Strangers, though in the lowest Stations in Life" (AMG 499). Similarly Woolman writes in "A Plea for the Poor": ". . . a person who hath never felt the weight of misapplied power comes not to this knowledge but by an inward tenderness, in which the heart is prepared to sympathy with others" (PM 243).

[10]Woolman goes on to express the same sympathy for young slaves for whom "my Mind hath often been affected, as with the Afflictions of my Children" (AMG 500). Likewise he extends such loving sympathy to the oppressed

sailors while on route to England: "I often feel a tenderness of heart toward these poor lads and at times look at them as though they were my children according to the flesh" (PM 167).

WORKS CITED

Augustine of Hippo. *Enarrationes in Psalmos* in *A Select Library of the Nicene and Post-Nicene Fathers of the Christian Church.* Ed. Philip Schaff. 1st Series. Vol. 7. 1886-90. Grand Rapids, MI: Eerdmans, 1952ff.

Barbour, Hugh. *The Quakers in Puritan England.* New Haven, CT: Yale University Press, 1964.

Barclay, Robert. *Apology for the True Christian Divinity.* 1676. Philadelphia, PA: Friends' Bookstore, 1908.

Birkel, Michael L. "John Woolman on the Cross." *The Lamb's War: Quaker Essays to Honor Hugh Barbour.* Eds. Michael L. Birkel and John W. Newman. Richmond, IN: Earlham, 1992. 91-100.

Bownas, Samuel. *A Description of the Qualifications Necessary to a Gospel Minister.* 1750. Wallingford, PA: Pendle Hill and Friends Tract Association, 1989.

Guigo II, Prior of the Grand Chartreuse. *The Ladder of Monks.* Eds. and trans. James Walsh and Edmund Colledge. Kalamazoo, MI: Cistercian Publications, 1978.

Woolman, John. *The Journal and Major Essays of John Woolman.* Ed. Phillips P. Moulton. 1971. Richmond, IN: Friends United Press, 1989.

6

Thinking About Death: The Companionship of John Woolman's *Journal*

Margaret E. Stewart

JOHN WOOLMAN (1720-1772) WAS NOT ONE TO SETTLE for the surface of things. A devout member of the Society of Friends in the greater Philadelphia area in the period leading up to the Revolutionary War, Woolman looked deeply into matters others did not question. While many accepted slavery and war as part of the natural order of things, Woolman opposed both practices and sought to expose the "routine" attitudes—the racism, consumerism, and greed—that reinforced them. While Benjamin Franklin was urging hard work and linking wealth to wisdom, John Woolman was warning against the spiritual dangers of both overwork and affluence. So if death is the unacknowledged reality lurking beneath the surface of life, then John Woolman would be a good companion to help us approach mortality's deeper truths. Indeed, John Woolman's *Journal,* a spiritual autobiography that has been continuously in printed since it was posthumously published in 1774, shows us that Woolman approached death-encounters with the same probing, get-to-the-bottom-of-things attitude that he took to social issues. And just as with social issues, he let himself be changed and his life be altered by the truths he found.

In its exploration of death's many facets, Woolman's Journal is an appropriate work to consider at this moment in our history. As American society became more technological, the death-familiarity of Woolman's day was increasingly replaced by denial of death, and we are still suffering from that change. Elisabeth Kuebler-Ross writes that death is "taboo" in U.S. culture (6), while Robert Jay Lifton argues that our connection to the life-and-death continuum has been "broken" (The Broken Connection, 5). This impaired relationship with mortality is illustrated by an ambitious effort to encourage people with terminal illnesses and their physicians to discuss dying: despite the help of nurse-advocates funded by the Robert Wood Johnson Foundation, many patients and doctors avoided any mention of death or dying. When patients did express their wishes for their last days, their requests were often ignored (Wheeler). Meanwhile, the vast majority of deaths in the United States continue to take place in institutional settings, removed from the daily lives of healthy people (Ratner and Song). Numerous commentators assert that such avoidance of mortality is tied to the tendencies in our society to value youth over age, the future over the past, progress over cyclical repetitions, and technology over the natural world.[1] Indeed, Patricia Anderson maintains that the inability to accept mortality is at the heart of our way of life—and that it is the source of many ills. "Denial of death," she writes,

> is truly, the fundamental paradigm for how we live. It is the root cause of our inability to accept aging, to abide in the natural world, to tolerate what we don't understand. It has allowed us to proceed unchecked with a merciless, mechanistic, profoundly flawed mythology of progress, and has undermined our best efforts to address resulting societal and ecological ills. (350)

There is a growing reaction in U.S. society, however, against this dissociation from mortality. Signs of such a reaction appear in the establishment of hospices, in the right-to-die and death-with-dignity movements, in the proliferation of conferences and literature on death and dying, in the protests against the trivialization of violence, and in the environmentalist challenge to attempts to alter and dominate nature.[2] Barbara Ehrenreich asserts that death has even become "the ultimate chic" (681). But this reaction against death-denial has not so much transformed our culture as highlighted the need for change: it has become a cliché to say that we should learn that "death is a part of life." But we don't yet have any profound knowledge of what that statement means in practice. What does it mean concretely for death to be "a part of life?" *The Journal of John Woolman* gives us some answers to that question. Woolman's *Journal* is rife with descriptions of death: deathbed scenes, killing, near-death experiences, self-mortification, dreams of death; and appended to the *Journal* is an account of Woolman's own death from smallpox in 1772. Each category of death-encounter is characterized by a mixture of mystery and familiarity, the mystery furnished by the presence of death and the familiarity by conventions of the Quaker tradition. The *Journal* shows that this union of mystery and familiarity is a productive one, yielding emotional energy, ethical insight, and transformative power.

Deathbed Scenes

If our culture is death-denying, Woolman's was death-observing. As a Friend, Woolman belonged to a tradition of recording inspiring deaths. One of the most popular forms of Quaker reading in his era was a collection of deathbed scenes called *Piety Promoted, in a Collection of Dying Sayings of Many of the People Called Quakers, With a Brief Account of some of their Labours in the Gospel, and Sufferings for the Same.* First published in 1701 by John Tomkins, *Piety Promoted* grew and reappeared in numerous editions and forms throughout the next century and a half.[3] The accounts in *Piety Promoted* follow certain conventions: they are brief spiritual biographies that include the individuals' religious development and struggles, their portentous parting words, and their final steadfastness. The deaths thus memorialized are exemplary deaths.

The first deathbed scene that Woolman records, however—the death of a Scottish servant in the house where the young Woolman was an apprentice—is not an exemplary death. "The latter part of his sickness he, being delirious, used to curse and swear most sorrowfully . . . ," Woolman writes (PM 30). Woolman's primary reaction was fear. The night after the burial, he had to sleep in the room where the man had died. "I perceived in me a timorousness," he states (PM 30). He doesn't say whether he was afraid of the man's angry ghost or of the miasma of blasphemy, but clearly the spot where the great transition had occurred, and so acrimoniously, was a disturbingly frightening place. "Nature was feeble . . . ," Woolman writes (PM 30). Nevertheless, he managed to stay in the room all night, comforted by thoughts of his care of the dying man and of his faith in God. He says that "every trial was a fresh incitement to give myself up wholly to the service of God . . ." (PM 30). In his refusal to flee, and in his willingness to "give himself up," Woolman showed a characteristic openness to being touched by the mystery of death, despite the terror. And in his recourse to conventional theology in response to that fear, he also showed an ability to hang onto a familiar concept in the midst of the unknown. At the same time, the encounter changed his accustomed ideas: his sense of God was expanded to include his experience of God's ability to sustain him in the midst of fear, and his sense of himself was likewise broadened to include this proven connection with the divine.

In contrast to the description of this choleric death, the accounts of the deaths of Woolman's sister and father follow the format found in *Piety Promoted*—they tell of spiritual struggle, parting words, and ultimate faithfulness. Woolman mentions his sister's compassionate disposition and his father's religious instruction of his children. However, he also alludes to his relatives' spiritual conflicts. As his thirty-one-year-old sister lies dying of smallpox, she is "disconsolate," remembering the errors of her youth (PM 40). And as his sixty-year-old father succumbs to a fever, he thinks of his "many imperfections" (PM 45). He tells his son that he has experienced the love of God "from time to time"—conveying the obverse implication that he has also, "from time to time," missed that divine connection (PM 45). But both are borne up in their final days, his sister feeling overwhelmed by the love of God, and his father expressing confidence that he is going to a happier life (PM 40, 45).

Expressing as they do the Quaker literary conventions of death as seen in *Piety Promoted,* these last two deathbed scenes implicitly invoke the assumptions of that tradition—that dying is the ultimate test, a burning away of the false, a revelation of the true. It is a transition between the illusory material world and a lasting spiritual reality. The dying, then, may have visions of Truth denied to those who are still in the midst of life. Within these conventions, the memorable words of dying exemplary individuals take on particular importance; this importance accrues to the quotations that Woolman includes from both his sister and his father. Woolman's sister says, "Dear mother, weep not for me; I go to my God" (PM 40). And his father, having read Woolman's first anti-slavery essay, encourages Woolman to publish it. He tells his son, "I have all along been deeply affected with the oppression of the poor Negroes, and now at last my concern for them is as great as ever" (PM 45). Both the sister's pull toward God and the father's concern for the oppressed are presumed to convey an otherworldly understanding, a spiritually privileged view. Death-proximity gives their words a special power that then validates and reinforces Woolman's own Quaker faith and anti-slavery views. Woolman's receptivity to his loved ones' deathbed experiences thus energizes his own deepest values. Their dying messages reinforce his Christianity and his advocacy for the enslaved.

The conventions found in *Piety Promoted* provide a recognizable path to follow into the enigma of dying. In the death of the sister and father, the familiar elements perhaps outweigh the mysterious ones. But in Woolman's other death-encounters, the mystery is not so easily domesticated. Woolman came upon those experiences unexpectedly, with little opportunity to decide upon or prepare a response. And those encounters altered rather than reinforced his sense of himself.

Killing

In one such transformative incident, Woolman was himself the killer. As a child, Woolman was on his way to a neighbor's house when he surprised a robin on her nest. "I stood and threw stones at her, till one striking her, she fell down dead," he writes (PM 24). At first he was exhilarated with his prowess, "pleased with the exploit," but then he was "seized with horror" (PM 24). He realized that he had "in a sportive way killed an innocent creature," that she could have flown away but she had stayed near the nest—within easy stone-throwing range—to be "careful for her young" (PM 24). He thought then of the orphaned nestlings, and, to spare them slow starvation, climbed the tree and killed them, too. (Woolman's conscientious intervention may have compounded his error: robin fathers also bring food to nestlings (Stokes 220).) Confronted with the physical reality of death ("I beheld her lying dead"), Woolman felt new emotions and entertained new thoughts (PM 24-25). He was able to fit his experience into Biblical precedent: "The tender mercies of the wicked are cruel," he thought [Prov. 12:10] (PM 24-25). But categorizing his experience was not enough to calm his agitation; he was "much troubled" (PM 25). He had imagined himself the victor in a contest, boys against birds—but suddenly he saw himself as the villain in a real-life drama, one that highlighted the connections rather than the competition amongst living beings. By killing the robin he had hurt himself; ethics had become a palpable reality. He had learned that kinship could be felt and that violations of it could be felt as well. He concluded, "Thus he whose tender mercies are over all his works hath placed a principle in the human mind which incites to exercise goodness toward every living creature" (PM 25). Through transgression—by crossing the line between life and death—Woolman had stumbled upon a source of ethical energy within himself. And by breaching a bond with a fellow creature he had discovered that such bonds exist.

Near-Death Experiences

Woolman's near-death experiences also led to the discovery of identity-changing power. Both as an adolescent and as a mature man, Woolman had near-fatal illnesses. As an insouciant teenager, he fell seriously ill, and death seemed imminent. He was appalled at thoughts of his past sins and future prospects. "I thought it would have been better for me never to have had a being than to see the day which I now saw," he writes (PM 26). His former sense of himself disappeared. "I was filled with confusion . . . ," he says (PM 26). He describes the experience:

> [I]n great affliction both of mind and body I lay and bewailed myself. I had not confidence to lift up my cries to God, whom I had thus offended, but in a deep sense of my great folly I was humbled before him, and at length that Word which is as a fire and a hammer broke and dissolved my rebellious heart. (PM 26)

Apprehending death, Woolman experienced psychic disintegration, but with a subtle shift. The "confusion" brought about by death-proximity was supplanted by the experience of being "broken" and "dissolved" by "the Word." Meaningless deterioration was thus replaced by purposeful dismantling, while inarticulateness was replaced by "the Word." Speaking gave way to listening—a change that marked a new form of empowerment. What could not come from within came from without—and the image of receptivity offered a new self-concept. The new identity was one of openness to God. Embracing that deferential self-definition, Woolman determined henceforth to "walk humbly before him" (PM 26).

Woolman had numerous spiritual relapses after returning to health, but the sense of himself established on what he thought was his deathbed continued to grow. More than the sum of the old parts reassembled, the new identity was characterized by expansion. "[M]y mind from day to day was more enlightened. . . . ," he writes, "and a universal love to my fellow creatures increased in me" (PM 28-29). This inner expansion had an ethical dimension. Woolman realized that "to say we love God as unseen and at the same time exercise cruelty toward the least creature moving by his life, or by life derived from him, was a contradiction in itself" (PM 28). Connected to this expansive, ethically-coded energy, the "confusion" persisted in the form of experience that could not be defined. "While I silently ponder on that change wrought in me, I find no language equal to it nor any means to convey to another a clear idea of it," Woolman writes (PM 29). Despite its ineffability, however, Woolman could place his experience within a familiar category by connecting it to mystical Scriptural passages. Alluding to Revelations 2:17, Woolman says that his new identity was characterized by a "white stone and new name" (PM 29). Though indefinable, the experience was vital, involving growth, increase, "change." Woolman's new identity sprang from contact with this mysterious dynamism. Slowly, the obliterating mystery of the death-encounter was being incorporated into a new sense of self. Woolman thus established a link between his own mystical experience and his Biblical tradition, between a lost sense of self and a new identity, between "confusion" and a "new name."

In Woolman's mature near-death experience, the dissolution and remaking of the self are likewise pronounced—though here the forces of mystery seem even stronger and the struggle for redefinition more perilous. In 1770, while preparing for a religious trip to the West Indies, Woolman fell dangerously ill. During that illness he had a vision which affected him too strongly for description; in fact, he said nothing at all in meeting for a year afterward. Nevertheless, he wanted to understand the revelation; he was eager, he says, "to get so deep that I might understand this mystery" (PM 186). It wasn't until 1772, shortly before his death, that Woolman felt free to describe the vision. He wrote:

> In a time of sickness with the pleurisy a little upward of two years and a half ago, I was brought so near the gates of death that I forgot my name. Being then desirous to know who I was, I saw a mass of matter of a dull gloomy colour, between the south and the east, and was informed that this mass was human beings in as great misery as they could be and live, and that I was mixed in with them and henceforth might not consider myself as a distinct or separate being. In this state I remained several hours. I then heard a soft, melodious voice, more pure and harmonious than any voice I had heard with my ears

> before, and I believed it was the voice of an angel who spake to other angels. The words were, *"John Woolman is dead."* I soon remembered that I once was John Woolman, and being assured that I was alive in the body, I greatly wondered what that heavenly voice could mean. I believed beyond doubting that it was the voice of an holy angel, but as yet it was a mystery to me. (PM 185-86)

As in his adolescent experience, here, too, death proximity calls identity into question: "Brought so near the gates of death," Woolman wanted "to know who [he] was." Here, too, there is fundamental confusion ("I forgot my name") linked to disintegration (*"John Woolman is dead"*). And here, too, there is reformulation: shown the mass of sufferers, Woolman is told he is "mixed in" with them. As in his adolescent conversion, the "after" self-definition emerges as a more expansive identity than the previous one.

But there is also irony in this vision not present in the earlier experience. The named individual, though "dead," lives on in connection with people who are in "as great misery as they could be and live." Immortality is represented by people who are barely alive. The scarcely-surviving sufferers both mirror the gravely ill Woolman and embody a version of eternal life: there is no separation from the stuff of life, that "mass of matter." And integration into that mass comprises its own ethical imperative: "henceforth [I] might not consider myself as a distinct or separate being."

The implications of that imperative are elaborated further as Woolman beholds a specific subsection of that mass. Describing the next part of the vision, Woolman writes:

> I was then carried in spirit to the mines, where poor oppressed people were digging rich treasures for those called Christians, and heard them blaspheme the name of Christ, at which I was grieved, for his name to me was precious. Then I was informed that these heathens were told that those who oppressed them were the followers of Christ, and they said amongst themselves: "If Christ directed them to use us in this sort, then Christ is a cruel tyrant."
>
> All this time the song of the angel remained a mystery. . . . (PM 186)

Here "separation" from the mass appears in the form of exploitation of the poor, which is also polarization with Christ, as the exploitative "Christians" undermine rather than follow Christ's example. Detachment is revealed to be an illusion: "separation" appears instead as an unholy connection—a kind of parasitism on the poor and a smothering of Christianity in an hypocritical embrace.

The ironies in the vision deepen into paradoxes, formulations that replace either-or perceptions with assertions of the both-and nature of reality. Woolman is dead but alive, dead but perceptive, in the body but in the mines, a distant observer but a "mixed in" participant, in the realm of misery but in the realm of harmony, on earth but in heaven. After returning to "normal" consciousness, Woolman is able, with what feels like divine assistance, to talk out loud. He hears himself quoting Galatians [2:20]: "I am crucified with Christ, nevertheless I live; yet not I, but Christ that liveth in me . . ." (PM 186). This quotation adds to the paradoxes that permeate the vision: Woolman is I but not I, crucified but alive, a companion of Christ but a vessel for Christ. Throughout his account, Woolman stresses his vision's unfathomable "mystery." The paradoxes intensify the mystery—and thus create yet another paradox, that mystery and self-definition should go hand in hand. As Woolman connects the mystery with Galatians, he places it within the familiar framework of his Christian tradition; in turn the mystery animates that tradition. In particular, death-mystery energizes Woolman's practice of Christian asceticism, itself (as the following section will show) a paradoxical loss and assumption of control, an opening up to mystery and an incorporation of it.

Self-Mortification

To Woolman, the self-definition emerging from the mystery of his near-death vision was an ascetic Christian identity. When he heard his own voice quoting Galatians, he writes, "Then the mystery was opened, and I perceived there was joy in heaven over a sinner who had repented and that that language *John Woolman is dead* meant no more than the death of my own will" (PM 186).

I have written elsewhere about how to Woolman the "death of the will" meant the suppression of an individualistic, white-supremacist self and the emergence of a collective, egalitarian identity (Stewart 253-

256). Here I would like to stress as well that this asceticism was part of a dynamic of expansion, that this "death" meant growth. In a letter of 1757 to a friend recovering from an almost-fatal illness (before Woolman's own attack of pleurisy), Woolman discusses the learning that can come from near-death experiences. He writes:

> To forward this work [i.e., the subjection of the personal will to God] the all-wise God is sometimes pleased through outward distress to bring us near the gates of death, that life being painful and afflicting and the prospect of eternity open before us, all earthly bonds may be loosened and the mind prepared for that deep and sacred instruction which otherwise would not be received. (PM 56)

Indeed, Woolman's own "distress" near death brought him "instruction"—the revelation of death-transcendence simultaneously through identity with matter, solidarity with the suffering, and connection to Christ. That larger self did not defeat death; rather, it included death as an essential component. Woolman interpreted the announcement of biological death ("John Woolman is dead") as a symbol for "the death of my own will." Suppression of the will, then, became a way to transcend "distinctness" and "separateness," to acknowledge one's "mixed-in" connections, to reach that larger life. But the symbolism worked in reverse as well. As a referent, as what is symbolized, the death of the will also became a way to understand death itself, to "open" the mystery. And the mystery of death appeared to be part of an identity that knew no bounds, an identity whose limitlessness was expressed in the endless inclusiveness of paradox.

The line between the "distinct or separate" self and the "mixed-in" self was a charged border, a place of disintegration and coalescence. The "death of the will" could lead to the birth of endless connections; the loss of control was an emptying that could lead paradoxically to the fulfillment of expanded life. The location where this exchange occurred was a disturbingly powerful place. Repeatedly, the practice of asceticism permitted Woolman to enter this transformative zone. The familiar paradigm of self-denial provided recognizable stepping stones that led into the mystery.

For example, after his adolescent conversion, Woolman struggled to "bear the cross" of giving up his friends and the amusements that had led him into error (PM 27). He prayed for the strength to do so, and gradually felt "the power of Christ prevail over selfish desires" (PM 28). The power of Christ within soon became a connection to all without: "I looked upon the works of God in this visible creation and an awfulness covered me; . . . a universal love to my fellow creatures increased in me," he writes (PM 29).

Self-denial brought about self-transformation in Woolman's mature life, too. When he gave up his growing business he needed to fight his "natural inclination . . . toward merchandise" (PM 53). But he turned to God, he writes, who "graciously heard me and gave me a heart resigned to his holy will" (PM 53). Through that suppression of his own desires, he brought his life into greater harmony with his fellow beings.

Though Woolman progressively expanded these connections as he moved from adolescence to maturity, he also underwent a cyclical dynamic, a recurrent move from the "distinct or separate" self to the "mixed-in" self and back again. Physical fear, for example, could provoke repeated ascetic struggles. During Pontiac's War in 1763, Woolman felt a "motion of love" to visit the Delaware Indians in northern Pennsylvania. At the same time, reports of settlers killed on the frontier underscored the dangers of the trip. Repeatedly throughout the journey Woolman feared being killed or taken captive. Then he prayed to God, who helped him resign himself to loss of life or freedom. And on the other side of this willingness to sacrifice physical well-being was an increased feeling of solidarity. He became determined "to give no just cause of offense to the Gentiles, who do not profess Christianity, whether the blacks from Africa or the native inhabitants of this continent" (PM 128-129). Woolman writes, "My own will and desires being now very much broken. . . . the difficulties attending the natives in many places, and the Negroes, were open before me" (PM 128). Self-denial broke the self-constricting hold of fear and permitted an upsurge of empathy. But shortly thereafter, news of warriors nearby provoked what Woolman calls "a fresh trial of my faith" (PM 132). He says, ". . . I still found the want of my strength to be renewed, that I might persevere [in God's will]" (PM 132). Drawing on his experience as well as his faith, however, he called upon God, who, he says, "gave me a resigned heart, in which I found quietness" (PM 132). Stronger connections with God and fellow creatures thus came out of ascetic practice. But they were connections that had to be renewed again and again.

Woolman's adolescent conversion, his renunciation of business, his visit to the Delaware in the midst of war—these were dramatic turning-points in his life. But the transformative dynamics of asceticism were something that Woolman was able to incorporate into routine life as well. As a lay minister, Woolman went on numerous religious trips to other colonies and regions, frequently attended both neighboring and outlying Quaker meetings, visited with fellow Friends individually, and regularly remonstrated with slaveholders. These visits were often difficult for him, leading to "trials," "discouragements," and "distress" (PM 47, 149). Meeting what he felt were God-imposed obligations sometimes required "deep exercises that were mortifying to the creaturely will" (PM 107). Quakers, Woolman believed, had a duty "to mortify that which remains in any of us which is of this world" (PM 49). "Mortify" comes from the Latin *mortificare,* and means "to put to death"; it is an active, transitive verb. Putting to death one's own desires, attachments, and inclinations was an active way to take death into one's own hands, to connect with the life-death continuum, and to experience its energizing power. Woolman found that mortifying his disinclination for some of the tasks of his lay ministry catalyzed growth not only for himself but for those he was ministering to. Woolman speaks of hearts "enlarged in the love of our Heavenly Father," of minds "livingly opened," and of connection to "love which is stronger than death" (PM 36, 160, 102). Revitalization appeared in the "springing up of living waters" and in "reviving" and "baptizing" times (PM 41, 151). This rebirth took the form of all-encompassing kinship, in "strong desires . . . for the everlasting welfare of [our] fellow creatures" (PM 122). As an active, interventionist practice, then, self-denial was also paradoxically a form of self-assertion, both a giving up and an assumption of control. In addition, asceticism was a way to move beyond the constrictions of self-centeredness into the limitlessness of mystery—and to take some of that mystery back into the self in the form of energy that animated a larger, "mixed-in" identity.

Through the practice of self-mortification, Woolman deliberately invited transformative experiences into his life. He underwent similar experiences inadvertently through killing the robin and through near-death experiences. Dreams also came unbidden, bringing unsettling effects. But through his willingness to record his dreams and to ponder their meanings, Woolman "invited" his dreams as well, opening himself up to their enigmatic and disturbing power.

Dreams of Death

Sleep has always been an analog for death, and dreams a kind of access to the life beyond. Like dying, dreams inhabit the border between consciousness and unconsciousness, oblivion and memory—and, in the Biblical tradition, between God and human beings. For Woolman dreams were a special way for the inner light to manifest itself; he respectfully recorded a number of his dreams. (His editorial committee removed dreams from the first edition of his *Journal*.) The prose of Woolman's *Journal* is what Mike Heller calls "sincere" (76); it is serious and cautious, given to understatement rather than flights of fancy. It is dense with metaphor, but the imagery is conventionally Biblical ("that Word which is as a fire," "the sure foundation," "the trumpet is sounded," "the gates of death" [PM 26, 122, 160, 185]), so that it draws more attention to a tradition than to an individual imagination. Woolman's straightforward account of his dreams, therefore, inevitably adds strikingly original imagery that provides a poetic contrast to the careful prose. And poetry may be especially suited for discussions of death. "One can turn to scientific medicine to describe death but not to 'frame' it," writes surgical oncologist William B. McCullough. Therefore, he says, "religious thought and much secular thought about death turn to poetry for their expression" (186). According to Robert Jay Lifton, the poetry of our dreams in particular plays a death-transcending role: "We must dream well if we are to confront forces threatening to annihilate us," he writes in *The Future of Immortality* (194). He maintains that in our dreams we find "ultimate concerns," "clue to and expression of the human capacity for good and evil," and "propulsive psychic energy" (*The Future of Immortality* 194, 191). Indeed, the "ultimate concern" of death appears in all of Woolman's recorded dreams: there are the death of a tree, death-threatening fire, fear of death, war, and the execution of an elderly man. Several of those dreams overtly link death with "the human capacity for good and evil" and sources of "psychic energy." Together, the dreams become poetic meditations on mortality, ethics, and vital power.

One such dream paints a portrait of a murderous but self-satisfied society, one that mandates obliviousness to transgression. In that dream, a hunter brings to Woolman's village a mixed-breed animal ("part fox and part cat") whose teeth and claws are particularly "active" (PM 161). Woolman then learns that an elderly Black man has been hanged to feed this animal—and also to feed some hunting hounds. "[H]unting represents vain delights," Woolman comments on this dream (PM 162n8). "Vain delights" were so dangerous to Woolman because of their connection to injustice. In his view, the desire for "superfluities" is the first link in a chain that leads to greed, exploitation, oppression, war. Woolman had called his killing of the robin "sportive"—done for pleasure, not necessity. In the fox-cat dream, too, vanities kill. Here the primordial purpose of hunting—to feed people—has been reversed: now an animal is brought back to eat a person, not to feed one. And the "vanities" in this dream kill not just a fellow creature but fellow feeling.

Indeed, the dream dramatizes an emotionally desiccated environment. One woman says that she was drinking tea when the man was strung up, and that while he was dying, she could not drink her tea. Woolman comments, "[T]ea drinking with which there is sugar points out the slavery of the Negroes, with which many are oppressed to the shortening of their days" (PM 162n8). That the woman must momentarily stop drinking her tea shows that some emotion is struggling to break through. But she reports the interruption as if her discomfort were the main point of the story—and so self-centeredness overwhelms incipient compassion.

Self-centeredness may be reinforced by a desire to fit in. The woman may repress her sympathy and trivialize the dying man because that is what her society expects from her. For in this dream, empathy is quelled by a kind of group consciousness, or group unconsciousness. As Woolman learns about the execution, he is in a house filled with people. From them he hears not only that the man is needed for food but that as an elderly man unable to work he is too expensive to keep. The tea-drinking lady speaks "lightly" of the matter and the others accede to it (PM 161). Woolman is silent as he listens to them, and then he does what the woman does not do: he grieves openly, "lament[ing] bitterly, like as some lament at the decease of a friend" (PM 161). His now-open grief, like his previous silence, sets him apart from the group. He writes that "some smiled, but none mourned with me" (PM 161). Woolman is further isolated from the others when a man speaks up to justify the killing. Woolman wants to reply, he writes, "but utterance was taken from me and I could not speak to him" (PM 161). Something in Woolman, too, has been choked off. And indeed, he is "dead" to the group members, who suppress the feeling he represents. Woolman must feel for them all: "And being in great distress I continued wailing till I began to wake . . . ," he writes (PM 161). Woolman's mourning at the end is not just for his dead "friend," but for his deadened peers, for his inability to make contact with them, for their inability to raise cries of their own, and for the living ties that should have united them all. The powerful feeling the dream evokes, the "wailing," both laments the shared deadness and transcends it: emotion animates both the end of the dream and the awakening dreamer.

A second dream juxtaposes fear of death and war. In this dream, Woolman is walking in an orchard in the afternoon when two lights that look like suns appear in the east. Then streams of fire mix with the air and a firestorm approaches the orchard. Woolman is "calm," in contrast to a distressed acquaintance standing nearby (PM 46). Woolman tells the person, "We must all once die, and if it please the Lord that our death be in this way, it is good for us to be resigned" (PM 46). He then goes into a house, past a group of "sad and troubled" people, into a room with an unfinished floor, where he sits "alone by a window" (PM 46). Out the window he sees that the southern sky is filled with red streaks—huge red streams extending from the earth to the heavens crossed by smaller red bands, with red lines going down from their ends to the earth. He then sees a green plain full of men, some of whom he recognizes, engaging in a military training exercise. As the men come near the house, Woolman writes, " . . . some of them, looking up at me, expressed themselves in a scoffing, taunting way, to which I made no reply . . . " (PM 47).

This dream contrasts Woolman's stance with three different postures. Unlike the fearful bystander, he is "resigned" to his personal death; and unlike the militiamen, he does not prepare for war. Elisabeth Kuebler-Ross writes that war is "a peculiar form of denial of our own mortality" (11). It is, in essence, a war with death, an attempt "to conquer and master it, to come out of it alive" (13). Consistent with this view (put forward by Lifton as well) that death-anxiety is an energizer of war, Woolman in this dream both accepts death and stays aloof from war. The third posture is represented by the downcast people. Woolman goes into the same house with them but does not join them. Instead, he goes into a room by himself where he sees the flimsy construction of the house; he positions himself by a window looking out. What he sees is vast destructive potential, both in the firmament and in the society of men, but he also sees in the red-streaked cosmos something that has not been there before, something unprecedented.

At the heart of that innovation is an energizing optimism, a faith that coincides paradoxically with a sense of impending apocalypse. This dream features two of the Four Horsemen of the Apocalypse, Death and War. There is also an end-time connotation in the afternoon appearance of two suns in the east and the filling of the southern sky with streams of red, as if the cosmos were breaking out in fire or blood. No wonder the people in the house are "sad and troubled." However, Woolman dissociates himself from their perspective, opting instead to look outward. God "hath the command of all the powers and operations in nature," Woolman writes in another passage in which he includes war, along with pestilence, earthquake, and famine, as a "chastisement" available to God for the correction of His children (PM 104). And indeed, there is a sense in this dream, reinforced by Woolman's resignation to God's will, of a mysterious constructive potential at work as well. This potential is underscored by the image of Woolman accepting "taunts" from the militiamen he does not join; this scene epitomizes Woolman's pacifism and part of the price he paid for it. The cosmos may dwarf human beings in its vast and surprising power, it may reveal the inadequacy of their structures, but it does not deprive them of agency. The dream shows humans taking action: a number of men prepare for war while another man persists in peace. Here humans participate in the ambivalent energy of the cosmos—energy whose coding as constructive or destructive is not clear. Is war an evil that pacifism can overcome? Or is war a chastisement chosen by God? Is war a harbinger of the end of this world—or the herald of another? There are no obvious answers to these questions. In this dream, the intertwining of the constructive and destructive strains is shrouded in mystery. Woolman both accepts the (possibly apocalyptic) will of God and through his own example offers an alternative to Horseman War. He casts his vote for what looks like peace. But by resigning himself to his personal death, and to the possible end of the world as he has known it, he relinquishes control of this limited vision. The loss of control is followed by an energizing connection, a yielding to the enigmatically creative powers of the universe.

Taken together, Woolman's dreams are a paean to those creative powers. They portray nature as endlessly protean, able to assume surprising and unprecedented shapes. In addition to the fox-cat, the two afternoon-rising suns, and the red-streaked southern sky, there are in an earlier dream a west-rising moon and a creature, "full of strength and resolution . . . called a sun worm" (PM 24). This innovative capacity reinforces a sense that pervades all of Woolman's writing—that at work within the cosmos are limitless, irrepressible powers that shatter preconception. In "Some Considerations on the Keeping of Negroes," Parts I and II, Woolman writes that slavery and racism can come to seem to be a part of nature, but that we make a mistake if we trust the constancy of this "nature." Looked at truly, there is nothing in "nature" to prevent Whites and Blacks from changing places (PM 198, 202, 225, 237). Shape-changing is latent in an unjust social structure. Woolman sees human nature as likewise malleable. Humans can either heed or ignore intimations of kinship. "[Such intimations] being singly attended to, people become tender-hearted and sympathizing," he writes, "but being frequently and totally rejected, the mind shuts itself up in a contrary disposition" (PM 25). Humans are not the product of some preset template but are shaped by moment-to-moment experiences, responses, choices, and growth—and they grow to cover a vast moral range. Woolman devoted himself to this plasticity—engaging in religious trips and visits, reasoning with slaveowners, opposing war—all in the faith that people could change. His growth was tied to theirs: he felt that the best within him was nourished by the best within them. Truth answers truth, he writes of this interdependent resonance, and "deep answers to deep" (PM 63, 97).

This uncharted creativity and this mutual reinforcement confront society's destructiveness in a third recorded dream, that of a peace mission to a bellicose country. In this dream Woolman is on a religious visit to a foreign country as war is about to break out with a neighboring land. Woolman sets off to visit the neighboring leader, intending to encourage him to find a peaceful resolution. At first people from the two countries greet each other with hostility and fear—but as Woolman tells them of his hopes, they respond with helpfulness and pleasure. Far from being "taunted" by others for his pacifism, Woolman finds that the yearning for peace in his heart evokes the yearning for peace in theirs (PM 297-298). The dream ends before we learn the outcome but not before we get a sense of surprising constructiveness. If the dream of the red streaks hints at the capacity to destroy, the dream of the peace mission suggests the capacity to create. Thus when Woolman writes, as he does in the final section of his journal, "Great reformation in the world is wanting!" (PM 168), his cry must be heard not only as a criticism and a lament, but also as dream-inspired and dream-reinforced faith that reformation, perhaps in a surprising, unheard of shape, could be forthcoming. Woolman's poetically meditative dreams explore the possibility that death-dealing can be matched by peace-making, and that the death of the individual—or even the death of the familiar world—can be part of cosmic creativity. They provide a place for the mysterious to materialize and for the unprecedented to take shape.

Dying

For the same reasons that *Piety Promoted* was published and that Woolman recounted the deaths of his father and sister, those who cared for Woolman during his last illness kept a record of his passing away. While on a religious trip to England in 1772, Woolman contracted smallpox and died outside of York at the home of Thomas and Sarah Priestman, where he was cared for by numerous Friends. Woolman himself recorded the beginning of his illness in his journal, and those around him chronicled the events of his final days (PM 301-306).

"Being now at the house of my friend Thomas Priestman in the city of York, so weak in body that I know not how my sickness may end, I am concerned to leave in writing a case the remembrance whereof hath often affected me," Woolman wrote (or dictated) at the end of his journal (PM 191). He described "a dream or night-vision" of a friend who had passed away some months before (PM 191). Woolman had visited this friend on his deathbed; the dying man had confided something about the "gain of oppression"—and only then did the man feel free to die (PM 191-192). Now on his own deathbed, Woolman thought of how at another time his departed friend had described to him a vision that also touched on the "gain of oppression." With great difficulty, Woolman recorded this dream before the knowledge of it died with him. The dream was of "a great pond of blood from which a fog rose up," with many people, whose clothes had "a tincture of blood in 'em," walking back and forth in the fog (PM 191). To his friend the pool "represented the state of those hardhearted men through whose means much blood is shed in Africa and many lives destroyed through insupportable stench and other hardships in crossing the sea"; it stood for men whose "extreme oppression bring many slaves to an untimely end"

(PM 191). The fog signified to his friend the profit from the slave trade, money which people knew was "the gain of oppression" (PM 191).

Here we see that at the end, the deathbed concerns of others continued to have special force for Woolman, and dreams continued to be a source of Truth. Kinship was a central part of that Truth. One might think that on one's deathbed one would not care much about others' shortened lives. But such was not the case with Woolman. He felt keenly the rightful fullness of African lives. About to experience death himself, the "untimely ends" of others appalled him still. Recording this dream was an act of solidarity with enslaved people; at the end such solidarity was as important to Woolman as ever. Indeed, from Woolman's caregivers we learn that Woolman refused any medicine or pain-relievers that came through "defiled channels or oppressive hands"; he had "a testimony to bear against those things, which he hoped to bear to the last" (PM 303). And Woolman's spirit stayed with the poor: he was aware how tenderly he was cared for in this last illness and how roughly, in comparison, too many poor people fared. It pained him to think of the time and money wasted on "superfluities" when those resources could go to comfort impoverished people in their final hours (PM 305).

As always for Woolman, this solidarity flowered from the root of personal asceticism. It was as important to Woolman in his final illness to suppress his individual will as it had been throughout his adult life. He stressed to his caregivers that he was "perfectly resigned, having no will either to live or die," and that he was "wholly resigned to his will who gave him life" (PM 302). But he did not reach such resignation easily. Despite decades of ascetic practice, at the end Woolman needed to struggle for resignation all over again. The process was as harrowing as any he had endured before. About to experience dissolution of the body, he felt psychic disintegration as well—confusion, horror, and despair. He described the experience:

> O Lord my God! The amazing horrors of darkness were gathered around me and covered me all over, and I saw no way to go forth. I felt the depth and extent of the misery of my fellow creatures separated from the divine harmony, and it was heavier than I could bear, and I was crushed down under it. I lifted up my hand and I stretched out my arm, but there was none to help me. I looked round about and was amazed in the depths of misery. (PM 302)

In this experience, characteristically, Woolman's own misery merges with that of his "fellow creatures," but it is the kinship of isolation. "Separation from the divine harmony," however, invokes a tradition in which such harmony at least exists, however removed. And it was traditional Christian imagery that then helped him to find clarity in the confusion. He described the transformation:

> O Lord! I remembered that thou art omnipotent, that I had called thee Father, and I felt that I loved thee; and I was made quiet in thy will and I waited for deliverance from thee. Thou hadst pity upon me when no man could help me. I saw that meekness under suffering was showed unto us in the most affecting example of thy Son, and thou wast teaching me to follow him; and I said, "Thy will, O Father, be done." (PM 302-303)

Chaotic suffering evolved into purposeful instruction ("Thou wast teaching me to follow him"). Even as he was dying, Woolman was learning; to the end, his asceticism was a catalyst for growth. Still, this deathbed account gives us a sense of the torment Woolman went through ("heavier than I could bear") before he could say, "Thy will, O Father, be done."

As Woolman's death approached, ascetic resignation was joined by other emotions. One was serenity regarding the shape of his life. He said, "I have laboured to do whatever was required, according to the ability received, in the remembrance of which I have peace . . . " (PM 304). Another was an attraction to death. When Woolman was asked if he wanted food, he hesitated to reply, explaining, "I cannot tell what to say to it. I seem nearly arrived where my soul shall have rest from all its troubles" (PM 304). And cautioning the Friend sitting up with him not to cry, Woolman told her, "I sorrow not, though I have had some painful conflicts; but now they seem over and matters all settled, and I look at the face of my dear Redeemer, for sweet is his voice and his countenance comely" (PM 305). Though pronounced at times, such death-affinity was not absolute or final. Woolman later accepted treatment from a non-Quaker apothecary and asked about his chances of surviving. When told that he might indeed pull through, Woolman replied, "[I]f it be his will to raise up this body again, I am content, and if [I] die, I am resigned. And if thou canst not be easy without trying to assist nature in order to lengthen out my life, I submit" (PM 305). On the last morning of his life, Woolman wrote with great difficulty, "I believe my being here is in the wisdom of Christ; I know not as to life or death" (PM 305). His embrace of life was never irreversible, and at the end, his embrace of death was not irreversible, either. "I know not as to life or death"; in his final moments, he detached himself from both in order to be wholehearted about God and thereby remain open to the mystery of the future.

Conclusion

In its descriptions of various death-encounters—deathbed vigils, killing, near-death experiences, self-mortification, dreams of death, and dying—the *Journal of John Woolman* offers a good example of openness to death. But between Woolman's time and ours, that openness has been replaced by denial, though there are many voices in our society today calling for a return to openness. There is no consensus, however, as to what that openness might mean. How might an acknowledgment of mortality affect our lives? In "An *Ars Moriendi* for Our Time," Arthur E. Imhof says that awareness of death should encourage us to strive for "a fulfilled life" (114). He argues that the doubling of the human life span in the past century (he concentrates on Western Europe and the United States) has given us "an amazing chance to realize a life plan" (119); he recommends that people cultivate a variety of interests so that they can enjoy their unprecedentedly lengthy lives (119). In contrast, Robert Jay Lifton maintains that focusing on our individual lives alone will not help us face death. Built into human psychology, he argues, is a need to see our individual lives as part of something larger, "as part of some immortalizing current in the vast human flow" (*The Broken Connection,* 91). Furthermore, unlike Imhof's sanguine view of expected longevity, Lifton's perspective emphasizes the possibility of nuclear war or other catastrophes. "We are haunted by the image of exterminating ourselves as a species by means of our own technology," he writes in *The Broken Connection* (5).

Accepting death to Lifton means acknowledging this ominous possibility. "Just as we know that we must imagine our own death in order to live more fully," he writes in *The Future of Immortality,* "so must we now imagine the end of the world in order to take steps to maintain human existence" (159).

Similarly, there is no agreement about whether our society will in fact leave denial of mortality behind. William J. Bouwsma says that he is "not optimistic" about such a prospect (196), while Howard M. Spiro asserts that the sheer cost of terminal care is forcing our society to acknowledge death (xvi).

In the midst of such conflicting ideas, *The Journal of John Woolman* offers good companionship, showing us specifically what it can mean for death to be "a part of life." In its introspective detail, it helps us to understand death-encounters in terms of the texture of experience—that irreducible element underlying all world views. In particular, it offers insight into an aspect of death on which even contending people can agree—death's mystery.

Woolman discovered that mystery was at the center of death-encounters, and that, paradoxically, it defined his experience. He experienced mystery initially as confusion and dissolution and then as limitless connection. The limitlessness of that connection intensified death's mystery and gave it all-encompassing power. But Woolman also learned that the all-incorporating can be incorporated, that the power of mystery can become life force. Indeed, Woolman found ways to assimilate the mystery of death, to take its energy into himself. He did this partially by trusting in his own imagery, whether derived from his traditions or his dreams, and following where that imagery led. He tied his death-encounters to conventional Christian theology, to Quaker conventions of exemplary deaths, to long-held principles of social justice, to familiar Bible verses, to well-known paradigms of ascetic practice, to his own dreams. He ventured into the unknown, but he took those familiar items with him. They provided a modicum of control with which to approach death, the ultimate loss of control. And they provided the means to assimilate the life force that came out of those encounters.

In particular, that life force appeared in the form of emotional energy, ethical sensibility, and transformative power. Woolman's death-encounters inspired an array of emotions—terror, attentiveness, guilt, confusion, misery, despair, resignation, aesthetic delight, peace, kinship, frustration, mourning, compassion, zeal for justice, enlightenment, love, death-attraction, and trust. Any possibility of the numbness of denial was replaced by a vast range and depth of feeling.

That emotional energy often merged with ethical insight. Out of the confusion of disintegration came a kinship-awareness that animated a sense of right and wrong. Death-proximity made connections palpable—and made violations of those connections palpable as well. Killing the robin, slavery, any form of oppression or selfishness—all felt wrong in the emotional ambiance of death-proximity.

Ethical sensitivity was therefore tied to an awareness of larger connections. Death is often described as the great leveler; for Woolman, death was the great connector. Over and over again, he describes death-proximity putting self-image to the test—and separation from others failing the test. Out of that failure emerged a collective identity that appeared death-transcendent. This larger self and ethical sensibility had mutual repercussions. Kinship led to kindness, but at the same time, conscience compelled a "mixed-in" identity. "Henceforth, I might not consider myself as a distinct or separate being," Woolman had concluded after his near-death vision (PM 185). In this injunction it appears that ever-expanding kinship had become a good in itself, merging ethics with identity. Transgression had become not just a result of breaking a rule, of going too far, but of minimizing connections, of staying too small.

Death-encounters for Woolman were thus inextricably emotional, ethical, and transformative. Ethical insights arose only because death-proximity also gave rise to the power to obliterate one sense of self and formulate another, to transform a "distinct or separate" self into a "mixed-in" one. The very limitlessness that was part of death's mystery turned out to be simultaneously a vitality encompassing endless connections. Indeed, whenever Woolman made death "a part of life," he found that his life became part of Life—that his individuality, including its demise, became part of a vibrant, inclusive whole. Woolman was shaped by his time and place, his experiences and beliefs, just as we are shaped by ours. Nevertheless, we can learn from Woolman's reliance on the familiar as he drew near to the mystery of death. What we love and believe may likewise help us to approach the unknown. Similarly, Woolman's experience of life-changing revitalization can teach us to look anew at our own emotions, ethics, and identities. Perhaps those aspects of our lives can be similarly deepened and transformed through relationship with death.

Like Woolman, we have a great deal of death to deny—more than what Kurt Vonnegut called just "plain old death" (qtd. in Lifton, *The Future of Immortality* 261). While Woolman had to consider the Apocalypse, we must contemplate an unprecedented rate of species extinctions as well as threats of environmental collapse and nuclear war. Indeed, if we ponder our own mortality, let alone the various grim futures which we humans may have created for ourselves, we may feel, like Woolman on his deathbed, covered by "the horrors of darkness" and see "no way to go forth" (PM 302). At that juncture, we may be encouraged by Woolman's example. If we can acknowledge mortality, we may find, like Woolman, that the mystery of death can energize our traditions and dreams, that it can touch the poetry of our imaginations. It may reveal for us, as it did for him, our place in cosmic reality. We may learn, as Woolman did, to "dream well"—to be open to unheard of, improbable transformations. Who knows? We may find, as he did, that the images in our minds are custom-made to incorporate what we discover. We may also experience for ourselves the cosmically creative powers that sustained John Woolman to the end.

NOTES

[1]In addition to the works cited in this essay, see also in particular Philippe Aries's *The Hour of Our Death* (Oxford: Oxford UP, 1991) and *Western Attitudes Toward Death* (Baltimore: Johns Hopkins UP, 1975); Ernest Becker's *The Denial of Death* (NY: Macmillan, 1973); *Death in American Experience* (Ed. Arien Mack. NY: Shocken Books, 1973); Ira Byock's *Dying Well: Peace and Possibilities at the End of Life* (NY: Riverhead Books, 1997); Mary Callahan and Patricia Kelley's *Final Gifts: Understanding the Special Awareness, Needs, and Communications of the Dying* (NY: Avon, 1997); Stanislav Grof and Joan Halifax's *The Human Encounter with Death* (NY: E.P. Dutton, 1977); Jack B. Kamerman's *Death in the Midst of Life: Social and Cultural Influences on Death, Grief and Mourning* (Englewood Cliffs, N.J.: Prentice-Hall, 1988); Jerry Mander's *In the Absence of the Sacred* (San Francisco: Sierra Club Books, 1991); Bill McKibben's *The Age of Missing Information* (NY: Random House, 1992); Carolyn Merchant's *The Death of Nature* (NY: Harper & Row, 1983); Jessica Mitford's *The American Way of Death* (NY: Fawcett Crest, 1963); Sherwin B. Nuland's How *We Die* (NY: Alfred A. Knopf, 1994); and Mary Pipher's *Another Country: Navigating the Emotional Terrain of Our Elders* (NY: Riverhead Books,1999).

[2]Both Patricia Anderson and Lifton argue that this explosion of interest in death and dying is produced in part by death-denial itself. Anderson writes, "The taboo [against death] is so effective, it has created a massive backlog of need for information and comfort about death. As this accumulation of unan-

swered need grows greater and greater it spills over the inhibition the taboo has set in place, like water over a dam" (6). Like Anderson, Lifton also points to a "rebound reaction" against "what may well be the most extreme denial of death that any society has ever evolved" (*The Future of Immortality,* 233). In addition, Lifton mentions five other reasons for the increasing popularity of death as a topic: 1) the prominence in the twentieth century of death by holocaust; 2) historical changes that have attenuated traditional religious or cultural images of death; 3) the increasing ability of the mass media to disseminate images of death and dying; 4) technological advances that obscure the definitions of both life and death; and 5) our "haunting" by the possibility of species self-extinction through the means of our own technology (*The Future of Immortality,* 233-234; *The Broken Connection,* 5).

In addition to the reasons cited by Anderson and Lifton, I would also mention the rise of the environmental movement, which is pushing our culture to rethink its relationship with nature. As nature comes to be seen as less of a necessary evil and more of an essential good, the concept of death undergoes a similar transformation.

[3]J. William Frost describes the process by which each new edition of *Piety Promoted* was prepared:

> Production of each volume was a collective enterprise. The families and friends of the dying gathered around the bedside for parting advice. The monthly meeting commissioned someone to write a memorial to the deceased which was read in the meeting and then forwarded to London where it might be read aloud in a session of the Yearly Meeting. Eventually, the memorial might be incorporated into the next book. (18)

WORKS CITED

Anderson, Patricia. *All of Us: Americans Talk about the Meaning of Death.* New York, NY: Delacorte Press, 1996.

Bouwsma, William J. Conclusion. *Facing Death: Where Culture, Religion, and Medicine Meet.* Eds. Howard M. Spiro, Mary G. McCrea Curnen, and Lee Palmer Wandel. New Haven, CT: Yale University Press, 1996. 189-198.

Ehrenreich, Barbara. "The Ultimate Chic." *Nation* 6 Dec. 1993: 681+.

Frost, J. William. "Quaker Books in Colonial America." *Quaker History* 80 (Spring 1991): 1-23.

Heller, Michael A. "Soft Persuasion: A Rhetorical Analysis of John Woolman's Essays and *Journal*." Diss. Arizona State University, 1989.

Imhof, Arthur E. "An *Ars Moriendi* for Our Time: To Live a Fulfilled Life; to Die a Peaceful Death." *Facing Death: Where Culture, Religion, and Medicine Meet.* Eds. Howard M. Spiro, Mary G. McCrea Curnen, and Lee Palmer Wandel. New Haven, CT: Yale University Press, 1996. 114-120.

Kuebler-Ross, Elisabeth. *On Death and Dying: What the Dying Have to Teach Doctors, Nurses, Clergy, and Their Own Families.* 1969. New York, NY: Collier, 1993.

Lifton, Robert Jay. *The Future of Immortality.* New York: Basic Books, 1987.

—. *The Broken Connection: On Death and the Continuity of Life.* New York, NY: Simon and Schuster, 1979.

McCullough, William B. "Witnessing versus Framing Death." *Facing Death: Where Culture, Religion, and Medicine Meet.* Eds. Howard M. Spiro, Mary G. McCrea Curnen, and Lee Palmer Wandel. New Haven, CT: Yale UP, 1996. 184-188.

Piety Promoted, in a Collection of Dying Sayings of Many of the People Called Quakers: With a Brief Account of Some of Their Labours in the Gospel, and Sufferings for the Same. Eds. William Evans and Thomas Evans. 4 vols. Philadelphia, PA,1854.

Ratner, Edward R., and John Y. Song. "Education for the End of Life." *Chronicle of Higher Education* 7 June 2002: B12.

Spiro, Howard M. Preface. *Facing Death: Where Culture, Religion, and Medicine Meet.* Eds. Howard M. Spiro, Mary G. McCrea Curnen, and Lee Palmer Wandel. New Haven, CT: Yale University Press, 1996. xv-xx.

Stewart, Margaret E. "John Woolman's Kindness beyond Expression: Collective Identity vs. Individualism and White Supremacy." *Early American Literature* 26.3 (1991): 251-275.

Stokes, Donald W. *A Guide to Bird Behavior.* 3 vols. Boston, MA: Little, Brown, 1979, Vol. 1.

Wheeler, David. "Dignity in Death." *Chronicle of Higher Education* 22 March 1996: A8+

Woolman, John. *The Journal and Major Essays of John Woolman.* Ed. Phillips P. Moulton. 1971. Richmond, IN: Friends United Press, 1989.

II.

Literary, Historical, and Economic Contexts

7

John Woolman: The Unconstructed Self

Mary Rose O'Reilley

FOR SEVERAL YEARS I HAVE BEEN TEACHING a university course called "The Rhetoric of Spiritual Autobiography," so I'm used to putting John Woolman at a dinner party, as it were, with Augustine of Hippo, Simone Weil, Thomas Merton, Dorothy Day, and other prototypic spiritual autobiographers. When we study spiritual autobiography in a secular academic context, a number of critical issues emerge that I'll touch on here in a prefatory way. Then I'll get on to more central issues of Woolman's spiritual identity—the uniqueness of which becomes apparent when we hear him speak in company with these other great spiritual seekers.

When we do scholarly work, I hope it is in something of the same spirit that John Woolman sold hair ribbons and mended garments as a Quaker merchant and tailor, that is, aware of congruence between our professional and spiritual identities. Scholarship begins, then, in something like the ancient Quaker query *So what? Why* am I doing this? What's it worth? As I look at some of these critical questions, I hope to carry myself finally into some kind of devotional space. I want my students, as well, to come away from class with the idea that a scholarly question can be *worth your life.* It might have some relevance for our sense of identity and for the good of the human community.

So, I'd like to frame this academic discussion in a query that will resonate, I hope, behind what's written here. As I tell my students, if you just want to think about this query and forget about the rest, our time together will be well spent: *Who are you and what are you doing here?* If we could *really* answer that question—or to the extent we can peck away at an answer to it—many things might change.

Perhaps a second query that I bring to my students has already begun to enter your mind: *How do you know who you are and what you are doing? Can you know who you are and what you are doing? Do you exist at all, or are you merely a construction of people's opinion, a puppet in a social play? To a class, teacher, to a husband, wife, to a child, Mom or Dad. Do you exist at all apart from your social roles?* Trying to answer these questions helps us understand the journey a contemporary scholar must take out of his or her own life into the wilderness of postmodern academic theory. The first query—Who are you and What are you doing here?—elicits autobiography. There are many ways we can frame our lives for ourselves, and therefore many ways to write autobiography. Autobiographies tend to deal with the primary ways a writer views himself or herself: creatures of the social milieu (like Samuel Pepys), people who are featured actors on the stage of history (like Charles Lindbergh), thinkers/feelers (like Virginia Woolf, C. S. Lewis), etc. You can find autobiographies relating to the details of a career, or merely to weird sexual exploits. In spiritual autobiography, such as Woolman's, we read the works of people who understood themselves primarily as spiritual beings, narrating their journey to intelligibility (as Plato put it), to truth, or to God.

However, if the first question—Who are you?—elicits autobiography, the second question—How do you know?—begins to elicit criticism about autobiography as a genre. On the face of it, autobiography seems easy to define. We might say, well, it's a writer's true account of his or her life and times. . . . Simple enough; after all, autobiography is a subspecies of non-fiction. It is not fiction. It is the truth. On this subject, however, critical theorists are usually on the side of Pontius Pilate and not on the side of Jesus. They will always be asking that annoying question, "What is truth?"

The French critic Philippe LeJeune, who has written several critical studies of autobiography, glosses Pilate's question this way: "What illusion to believe that we can tell the truth, and to believe that each of us has an individual and autonomous existence" (qtd. in Miller 10). For the contemporary critic, identity is unstable. Autobiography is best understood as a species of fiction. It's like the old country-western song: "We live in a two story house—she has her story and I have mine." There is no truth, for certain modern critics, only a story. Such critics might say that we construct our identity, settling on a version we can stand to live with.

Yes and no, Socrates might say. Anne Morrow Lindbergh, in her book *Gift from the Sea,* reminds us of his prayer in the Phaedrus that ". . . the outward and inner man be at one" (23). That prayer suggests to me two things: first, that on a bad day you might discover some dissonance between your inner and outer selves; second, that Socrates' God might have an interest in correcting this state of affairs. Otherwise, why pray about it?

In the academic study of rhetoric going back to Aristotle, the identity question asserts itself constantly. The ancient rhetoricians talked about the construction of an ethos: the successful speaker, they taught, needed to present himself in a certain way. He had to construct a persona that the audience would believe in and listen to. Aristotle believed that this constructed persona should be consonant with the speaker's real character. Other rhetoricians thought it permissible to make up an identity that would sell the product. (This second group of rhetoricians have had an enormous influence on the political culture of America.)

Perhaps you think you have an absolutely stable identity. This would be a mainstream Quaker position. Every time I have to give a public address, though, I begin to worry about these Aristotelian questions. It usually begins in a concern about what I should wear and why. My regular, ratty Quaker clothes? Maybe the audience will be insulted, maybe they'll find out I'm a nerd and go home. *Who am I and what am I doing here?* Thoreau, who was so influenced by early Quakerism, said, ". . . beware of all enterprises that require new clothes" (15), but he never had to give speeches at the Modern Language Association.

A first approach, that I have been playfully suggesting, would be to recognize practical issues that arise in the critical study of autobiography, what scholars call issues of the truth, claims of the genre. Much influenced by social construction theory, modern criticism undermines the notion of univocal identity and tends toward the view that the human subject is predominantly a creature of his or her milieu. Below, I'll try to suggest some ways the study of spiritual autobiography in general and of John Woolman in particular responds to these critical issues.

A second approach to the academic study of this genre would be comparative analysis. Certain spiritual autobiographies are, as I said earlier, prototypic; among these we would classify the writings of Augustine, in particular, Dorothy Day, and the young Thomas Merton. To compare them is to realize how easily writers, faced with the daunting problems of writing about spiritual experience, simply fall back on the recipes of their predecessors. Apparently, if you have read enough books on the subject, or enough devotional manuals, you begin to fall into worn-out language as though, to paraphrase George Orwell, you were building a prefabricated henhouse. Prototypic texts, by their nature and the conditions of their publication (the censorship that plagued early Merton, for example) can't help telling you how to have a spiritual life: what the channels are, how to run the video machine. Longing to experience my spiritual life unfettered by the ideas of people more saintly and articulate, I respond gratefully to someone like William Johnston, S.J., who thus paraphrases his colleague Bernard Lonergan's *Method in Theology:* "Religious experience at its roots is experience of an unconditional and unrestricted being in love, but what we are in love with remains something that we have to find out" (12). That is beautifully open-ended, the kind of statement about God that Quakers, inclined to speak from experience rather than orthodoxy, tend to find congenial. By contrast, I can read fifty pages of Augustine and feel he has God pinned down like a butterfly. After enough of that, I can't think or feel any more about God.

Now why am I bringing this to bear on Woolman? Well, because when we invite Woolman to this dinner table conversation, it's interesting to observe how unconventional his comments are (and we can listen to Simone Weil or Virginia Woolf and the expansive mid-life Merton with a similar appreciation for new-minted ideas). In many ways, John Woolman was a unique and uncontaminated spiritual narrator. Not entirely uncontaminated. I wish he hadn't read so many Quaker devotional books, or the kind of standardized spiritual journals which taught him to substitute formulas for details and to suppress the individualizing features of his struggle. In particular I want to know more about his suffering, especially his inner turmoil. It's my own suffering (and my fear of tropical diseases and spiders and panic attacks) that keeps me from acting on the query we started with, *Who are you and what are you doing here?* It would encourage me to know just a little more about the details of John Woolman's mental world, and at what cost to himself he wrought his subversive challenge to the unjust structures of his time.

All Woolman admits to is the occasional bad night. And he doesn't tell us the details. He gives us the kind of formula that we find in thousands of Quaker journals: "I have been much under sorrow, which of late so increased upon me that my mind was almost overwhelmed, and [the Lord] . . . in infinite goodness looked upon my affliction and . . . sent the Comforter" (PM 64).

Well, this is not enough for me. One sleepless night while I was reading Woolman, I happened to have on my bedside table Emily Dickinson's poems. She is quite an idiosyncratic spiritual autobiographer. I quote from a poem of hers (# 280), sometimes printed under the title "I Felt a Funeral in my Brain":

> And then a Plank in Reason, broke,
> And I dropped down, and down—
> And hit a World, at every plunge,
> And Finished knowing—then— (199-200)

There is a woman who *definitely* suffered. I would like to know if Woolman's nights were that bad. I suspect they were, so often does he repeat his formula about being "under sorrow." But I wish he would say more about the funerals, if any, in his brain. In my classes the students write their own spiritual autobiographies, partly to fill in what's left out of Augustine and Dorothy Day and even John Woolman. They tell me a little more about how people experience their lives as spiritual beings—people less hampered by social sanctions against self-disclosure. I want to hear spiritual autobiographies from people who are manic depressive or gay or even just sexual. So much is excluded from the classic spiritual autobiographies, in favor of formulaic pronouncements which hide more than they reveal.

But let me go back to the point that Woolman was a rather uncontaminated petri dish in the spiritual economy. He had read Jacob Boehme, and Thomas à Kempis, and probably John Bunyan, but there is no evidence he read Augustine, the archetypal confessional writer. So what's missing in Woolman are most of the patterns we find in spiritual autobiography influenced by Augustine, and what's present are a lot of interesting things "orthodox" writers leave out.

Missing, first of all, is a conversion narrative. Most great spiritual writers spend years trying to figure it all out. By contrast, Woolman seems to have been one of those rare souls one meets occasionally who seem to have been born into a tender and loving faith community, as we would now call it. He never deserted it, never railed against it, never needed a process of intellectual convincement. As he says: ". . . before I was seven years old I began to be acquainted with the operations of divine love" (PM 23). "Gracious visitations"—the gentle quasi-mystical dreams and experiences natural to children—keep him centered in recollection. As he matures, his father—so different from the tyrannical pagan who terrified Augustine—supports and shares first his spiritual development and finally his antislavery concerns. The father had raised his family, Woolman comments, "to cherish in us a spirit of tenderness, not only toward poor people, but also towards all creatures of which we had the command" (PM 44).

Remove the conversion narrative and you lose a good one half of most spiritual autobiographies, some would say the racier parts. Instead of an intellectual struggle, there is in Woolman a beautiful and quiet unfolding of spiritual destiny. Woolman is so aware of God's loving-kindness that he is able to be gentle with himself and therefore so gentle with slave owners and slave traders and abusers of post boys that they go away from conversations with him changed in heart. Let's follow this thread for a moment by comparing two classic narrative moments in Augustine and Woolman. Both are similar in that they recount adolescent escapades of what? sin? boyishness? Let's see. Here's Augustine:

> Near our vineyard there was a pear tree, loaded with fruit, though the fruit was not particularly attractive either in color or taste. I and some other wretched youths conceived the idea of shaking the pears off this tree and carrying them away. We set out late at night (having, as we usually did in our depraved way, gone on playing in the streets until that hour) and stole all the fruit that we could carry. And this was not to feed ourselves; we may have tasted a few, but then we threw the rest to the pigs. Our real pleasure was simply in doing something that was not allowed. Such was my heart, God, such was my heart which you had pity on when it was at the very bottom of the abyss. And now let my heart tell you what it was looking for there, that I became evil for nothing, with no reason for wrongdoing except the wrongdoing itself. The evil was foul, and I loved it; I loved destroying myself; I loved my sin—not the things for which I had committed the sin , but the sin itself. How base a soul, falling back from your firmament to sheer destruction, not seeking some object by shameful means, but seeking shame for itself! (45)

As many times as I've taught this short text, I've never met anyone who really believed it, who came away convinced of any of the things Augustine wants to convince us of here: his depravity, God's interest in his depravity, Augustine's sincerity about his depravity, the cost of pears in North Africa. Nothing. My students tend to respond to this rhetorical tour de force with the universal student put-down, *get a life*. Then they go on to recount far worse things they have done in their own not-so-distant adolescences. Indeed later, Augustine narrates worse things that he himself has done—he abandoned his concubine, for example, the mother of a son he doesn't seem very much interested in. But he glosses over these things. One of my students, going over to the side of the social constructionists, commented that she thought Augustine was building an idea of himself as a very morally discriminating person. So sensitive that throwing pears to the pigs seemed to him a monstrous deed. A little bit of smoke and mirrors, she thought, to distract us from more serious things that Augustine was in denial about.

Well, I would say at least that Augustine was obsessed with sin. What you focus on expands, and Augustine focuses on—we hear it in the diction: "wretchedness," "depravity," "baseness," "evil," "foulness," "destruction," and "shame." This is a world view tragically influential on certain Christian theologies, notably American Puritanism. By contrast, Woolman narrates a boyish episode that is really quite dark, though his processing of the incident differs significantly from Augustine's.

> . . . once, going to a neighbor's house, I saw on the way a robin sitting on her nest; and as I came near she went off, but having young ones, flew about and with many cries expressed her concern for them. I stood and threw stones at her, till one striking her, she fell down dead. At first I was pleased with the exploit, but after a few minutes was seized with horror, as having in a sportive way killed an innocent creature while she was careful for her young. I beheld her lying dead and thought those young ones for which she was so careful must now perish for want of their dam to nourish them; and after some painful considerations on the subject, I climbed up the tree, took all the young birds and killed them, supposing that better than to leave them to pine away and die miserably, and believed in this case that Scripture proverb was fulfilled, "The tender mercies of the wicked are cruel." (PM 24-25)

Woolman expresses himself "much troubled" by this incident, and says that for a few hours he could "think of little else" (PM 25). He was the son of a conscientious Quaker family, used to the brisk unsentimental cruelties of a farm community, and it seems to me that every aspect of this story reflects balance and sanity—within the terms on which the society is constructed. The principles of kindness abroad in that community would dictate critical reflection on the action, but no sense of shame, foulness, or baseness. Unsentimental clarity demands that the baby birds be summarily put out of their misery, yet this cruel mercy causes him, as well it might, to be "much troubled." At this point, young Woolman seems fully in conformity with the norms of his discourse community. In other words, he was a good Quaker boy.

What happens next, though, seems to be one of those mysterious operations of grace—grace that carries the individual beyond the moral norms of his community and onto the brink of a new prophetic vision.

> . . . he whose tender mercies are over all his works hath placed a principle in the human mind which incites to exercise goodness toward every living creature; and this being singly attended to, people become tender-hearted and sympathizing, but being frequently and totally rejected, the mind shuts itself up in a contrary disposition. (PM 25)

This may not be a new theological insight. Woolman did not discover this inward principle, but he was one of the few who ever acted on it. Acting on it will take the young man on a long journey, carrying the community—carrying us—with him. Unlike Augustine, Woolman does not feel himself to be debased and shamed before an angry God; he simply feels himself to be—what shall we call it?—out of tune.

If you are studying to be a musician, your teacher may ask you to put a tuning fork on your bedside table. Every morning when you awaken, strike your tuning fork and re-collect the sound of A 440. It's quite a beautiful spiritual exercise, and I think it's a pretty good metaphor for what Woolman was engaged in. Let me frame this just for a moment as a mediation of social construction theory: we might explore the hypothesis that the self is a certain way because of the surrounding culture and the roles it is called to play. Did Woolman—do any of us—have a true self or merely an "admonished self"—as I might call it, after rereading some of Woolman's interactions with his father. In one typical parent-adolescent transaction, for example, young John has been sassy and his father has reproved him: ". . . he told me he understood I had behaved amiss to my mother and advised me to be more careful in future" (PM 25). Woolman recalls ". . . I felt remorse in my mind, and getting home I retired and prayed to the Lord to forgive me, and do not remember that I ever after . . . spoke unhandsomely to either of my parents" (PM 25). I suspect that what's going on here is either the transmission of a deep spiritual formation, parent to child, or the creation of a false persona. Probably both processes go on at once; that is, a pious family passes on a model which fits the child, any child, poorly. The child assumes it, suffers inside it, hot and bothered, and eventually either rips it off or grows into its constraints, with luck expanding it to fit.

My experience as mother, daughter, and First Day School teacher is that we are indeed "constructed" or "admonished" selves, but that it is possible to become authentic. How? Woolman's journal suggests the process, often by narrating its early failures. In adolescence, young John resisted grace and "lost ground" (PM 26). As he tells of his "mirth and wantonness" (PM 27), an important idea recurs: he had not yet learned to go "deep enough" to resist the challenges to his true identity: "I . . . did not get low enough. . ." (PM 26); ". . . not getting deep enough to pray rightly, the tempter when he came found entrance" (PM 26). ". . . I was not low enough to find true peace" (PM 27). "To sink down to the seed," "to get low" in the parlance of Quaker journals is to pray deeply, humbly, covered in the spirit. In this contemplative state, in a dance perhaps of grace and discipline, the seeker is able to hear something that transcends the constructions of society. Call it the A 440 of the soul. It is something we can tune to, check ourselves against. And Woolman did exactly that.

I am sure that in the befuddled and stuttering way that all of us approach God, both Augustine and Woolman were crying out to the same "being in love." I don't want to get into discrediting Augustine and trying to prove that my guy is better than their guy. In many years of teaching First Day School, I've noticed that some children seem to be born farther along the path, more sensitive to moral nuance. (Often one can trace this sensitivity to a certain quality of parenting.) It may be that Woolman was such a one; we see in him none of the desperate struggle for intellectual and moral certainty that characterizes Augustine, Simone Weil, and Dorothy Day.

"Sin is behovely" (91) wrote the 14th century mystic Julian of Norwich, that is, "useful." The spiritual crises of youth and adolescence are, for Woolman, events that point him to what his life's real work should be. They challenge his sense of self. They tune him contemplatively to God's mercy. I have at present a First Day School class of nine thirteen-year-olds, five of them boys; in First Day School we refer to this incident as "the famous bird murder." Most of them have bird murders of their own to report. We agree that these crises help us to know who we are (really) .

In this incident, John Woolman seems to discover his innate sympathy as an *instrument of perception.* He will know the world through a lens of tenderness. This is quite a departure from the norms of spiritual autobiography. Most spiritual writers, from Augustine to C. S. Lewis, especially the male writers, examine reality within an analytical framework. Woolman's "principle of tenderness" was a discovery that, once again, seemed to put him further along the spiritual path than those who must climb to God through screeds of argument and consciousness-raising. Both Augustine and Merton found that they had to set aside analytical habits, finally, as not useful to the spiritual quest: "I devoured books making notes here and there and remembering whatever I thought would be useful in an argument—that is, for my own aggrandizement," writes Merton, "in order that I myself might take these things and shine by their light, as if their truth belonged to me" (232). Because of his childhood shock of moral danger, Woolman never seems to have taken on this particular false self.

Academic training teaches us to suspect easy answers, but in the spiritual life our deepest call is often discerned in what is natural and obvious; thus I value Woolman's simple tuning fork. One of my spiritual teachers, Brother Wayne Tesdale, who is a member of Basil Pennington's community, once startled me out of an elaborate problem-solving exercise by quietly saying, "of course, it is always appropriate to be kind." I snapped my jaws shut. You could climb a mountain in India and not be ashamed to carry that wisdom back down. The only problem is applying it.

The applications brought Woolman to his trial of love, to use another Quaker phrase: it led him to preach (how quietly) the abolition of slavery, Native American sovereignty, affirmation of women's ministry, ecological concerns, and finally the rights of animals. Nothing is exempt from the kindness which defined Woolman's spiritual identity. Sailing to England toward the end of his life, still on a direct vector from his earliest moral insight, he worries over the "dunghill fowls" taken on board to feed the passengers. They have stopped crowing, he frets, appear "dull" and seem to be "pining." He concludes that

> . . . where the love of God is verily perfected and the true spirit of government watchfully attended to, a tenderness toward all creatures made subject to us will be experienced, and a care felt in us that we do not lessen that sweetness of life in the animal creation which the great Creator intends for them under our government. (PM 178-79)

Same tune. A 440. Woolman's arguments—those against slavery, for example—could be subtle—but they followed, they did not precede, the motion of the heart. What characterizes Woolman's spirituality is a deep spiritual listening. He knew how to pay attention to the inner currents of feeling, nurtured, one must imagine, in a collected Quaker family and community.

Having unconstructed himself—thrown off the false persona—he was able to turn his attention to constructing the community. This is a prophet's business: not to live within the legalities of things-as-they-are, but to call the community to a higher standard of conduct. I think that Woolman must have been a good logical debater, for there are many instances in the journal where he is asked to lay out a series of complex arguments against slavery: people, after all had reasons—biblical, pragmatic, and even humanitarian—for enslaving others, however specious these arguments seem to us today and to John Woolman then. Jogging along on his horse day after day, Woolman came up with an impressive rational analysis of the peculiar institution.

Yet, as the Buddha said, "People with opinions just go around bothering one another" (qtd. in Kornfield 50). Woolman may have bothered people, but more characteristically he seduced them into his point of view. In some mysterious way he called out to their better natures and co-opted them in their own conversion. When assent has risen within us, rather that being cajoled from outside, how deeply indeed we assent. That is the very nature of conversion.

We see Woolman's characteristic effect when, as a youth, he felt called to labor with the proprietor of a disorderly public house: "I expressed to him what rested on my mind, which he took kindly, and afterward showed more regard to me than before" (PM 32). Such episodes are little mysteries, silences in the text. What did he say? (I felt called to labor with one of my colleagues several years ago and she has avoided me ever since.) We get only occasional hints about his way of discoursing, as in the pivotal moment where he is asked to write up a slave-holder's will, transferring human "property" to an heir. Woolman, in modern parlance, sends "I-messages:" "I cannot write thy will without breaking my own peace" (PM 51). Also, he does not harangue, as I am prone to do, scrambling for the moral high ground. He plants a seed and lets it grow—in this case for years—before more "friendly talk" and the man's decision to free his slaves.

What gave him this charismatic energy? The contemporary Buddhist Jack Kornfield suggests an answer.

> To live a path with heart means . . . to allow the flavor of goodness to permeate our lives. When we bring full attention to our acts, when we express our love and see the preciousness of life, the quality of goodness in us grows. A simple caring presence can begin to permeate more moments of our life. (14)

Simple caring presence doesn't bother people. It radiates, in the best sense, charm. Surely Woolman had this quality. One kind of charm is a product of walking in God's light.

Social construction theory cannot, in the last analysis, account very well for prophecy. The prophet reconstructs society rather that taking on a given role. Not that Woolman didn't try on roles, and not that he wasn't occasionally tormented by some necessity to play them. His favorite role was fool for God: "I find that to be a fool as to worldly wisdom and commit my cause to God, not fearing to offend men who take offense at the simplicity of Truth" (PM 57). He dressed oddly, refusing to dye his clothes with the indigo that depended on slave labor, and suffered even more when that "look" became suddenly fashionable: "In attending meetings this singularity was a trial upon me, and more especially at this time, as being in use among some who were fond of following the changeable modes of dress" (PM 121). He was in a delicate dance with society. He worried about what his friends would think, what the elders would think: "The apprehension of being singular from my beloved friends was a strait upon me" (PM 120). He sometimes surrendered to social pressure. If he had not struggled with fears about making a living, nor wondered why older and wiser Quakers disagreed with him about the treatment of slaves, or suffered extremes of social shyness—well, he would perhaps not have been a prophet but a sociopath. A sociopath merely carries the metaphor of the unconstructed self farther—too far—down the line.

I've talked a little about how social construction theory tends to erode the classical notion of selfhood. Social construction theory also addresses the nature of community. Here again, one of its primary principles is to tell us that all truth is relational. It posits what might be called "usable truth" which keeps people together and functioning in terms of the civic good. This does not *necessarily* lead to godless relativism. For example, we might quote the contemporary theologian Sally McFague in support of a version of social construction theory which does not subvert the transcendent:

> Our lives and actions take place in networks of relationships. To the extent that we know ourselves, our world, and our God, that knowledge is profoundly relational and, hence, interdependent, relative, situational, and limited. (194)

Our experience of culture resonates, surely, with McFague's image of a web of connection. At Plum Village, the Buddhist community where I've lately sojourned, building the sangha is repeatedly stressed: we are lights to each other, and your ardent practice increases the energy of my own. Woolman similarly takes comfort in the company of like-minded Friends: "Some glances of real beauty may be seen in their faces who dwell in true meekness. There is a harmony in the sound of that voice to which divine love gives utterance. . ." (PM 29).

But a web of connection can also throttle.

Woolman's culture, even his Quaker culture, had knitted a pattern in which slavery was justifiable, Native Americans could be robbed of their rights, post boys abused on long coach rides, horses ridden to death, and dung hill fowl left to suffer in their cages until it was time for them to be eaten. At this juncture, the seeker must exchange a rhetoric of prophecy for what we might call a rhetoric of mysticism—a mediation of the inner language of spirit. Woolman periodically enters this mystical space; he talks to God and tells us God's answers:

> The Most High doth not often speak with an outward voice to our outward ears, but if we humbly meditate on his perfections, consider that he is perfect wisdom and goodness and to afflict his creatures to no purpose would be utterly reverse to his nature, we shall hear and understand his language. . . . (PM 105)

Having unconstructed the self—that is, shaken off the baggage of ego and illusion—and having listened to transcendent wisdom, one can perhaps reconstruct society according to a better plan. At least that is the only state in which such an expedition would be marginally possible and not merely an exercise in hubris. Thus Woolman begins his personal crusade against slavery, thus Thomas Merton weighs in against the Vietnam war, thus Simone Weil takes the side of the workers in the Peugeot plant, and Dorothy Day founds her centers for the homeless. The genius of prophecy is in many respects like the genius of poetry, and the prophet faces the social critic with the same ultimate insouciance as the poet faces the literary critic: one creates, the other evaluates what's created (not that this carefree stance insures a favorable review).

I want to try to bring these scholarly questions back to the human and personal, to go back to that earlier query, "So what?" My young colleague, Jan Lindholm, writes of her own struggle with social construction theory:

> I could not reconcile the social constructionist rejection of transcendent truth with my own theological perspective which affirms the presence of a loving God who exists in relationship with human beings and indeed all of creation. On the other hand, neither could I accept naive theories about my ability to know that God. I wanted to find a middle ground, one that acknowledged the human capacity to create worlds through language, but at the same time acknowledged the possibility of our knowing something greater than our own constructions. (1)

Woolman, I think, helps us to station ourselves on middle ground. So, ordinarily, do all great spiritual autobiographers. One way or another, they work from the premise that it is our job to strive for some kind of elusive integrity, to exclaim with Nathaniel Hawthorne at the end of *The Scarlet Letter,* "Be true! Be true! Be true!"

So I will conclude by asking yet again, *Who are you and what are you doing anyway?* What is your deepest and tenderest job description?—

the business of your business or, as John Woolman called it, "the business of our lives" (PM 241)?

WORKS CITED

Augustine of Hippo. *The Confessions of St. Augustine.* Trans. Rex Warner. New York, NY: NAL-Dutton, 1963.

Dickinson, Emily. *The Poems of Emily Dickinson.* Ed. Thomas H. Johnson. Cambridge, MA: Harvard University Press, 1955.

Johnston, William, S.J. *Being in Love.* San Francisco, CA: Harper and Row, 1989.

Julian of Norwich. *The Revelations of Divine Love.* Trans. James Walsh, S.J. New York, NY: Harper and Row, 1989.

Kornfield, Jack. *A Path with Heart.* New York, NY: Bantam, 1993.

Lindbergh, Anne Morrow. *Gift from the Sea.* New York, NY: Random House, 1975.

Lindholm, Jan. "Social Construction and the Language of Faith." Paper delivered at the Conference on College Composition and Communication, 1994.

McFague, Sally. *Metaphorical Theology: Models of God in Religious Language.* Minneapolis, MN: Fortress Press, 1982.

Merton, Thomas. *The Seven Story Mountain.* New York, NY: Harcourt Brace Jovanovich, 1978.

Miller, Nancy K. "Facts, Facts, Facts." *Profession 92.* New York, NY: MLA, 1992.

Thoreau, Henry David. *Walden and Civil Disobedience.* New York, NY: Norton, 1966.

Woolman, John. *The Journal and Major Essays of John Woolman.* Ed. Phillips P. Moulton. 1971. Richmond, IN: Friends United Press, 1989.

8

African Americans and Native Americans in John Woolman's World

Jean R. Soderlund[1]

In June 1763, John Woolman traveled through the mountainous terrain of northeastern Pennsylvania to visit the Indian town, Wyalusing. The rigorous journey awakened in him a realization of "the alterations of the circumstances of the natives of this land since the coming in of the English" (PM 128). The rough passage, punctuated by thunderstorms and rattlesnakes, clarified for Woolman the injustice that the Indians had experienced. They had been forced from the best land or sold it "for trifling considerations," and now had "to pass over mountains, swamps, and barren deserts" to trade. He then connected European oppression of Indians with that of enslaved Africans:

> I had a prospect of the English along the coast for upward of nine hundred miles where I have travelled. And the favourable situation of the English and the difficulties attending the natives in many places, and the Negroes, were open before me. (PM 128)

To obey God, the Quaker minister continued, one must

> give no just cause of offense to the Gentiles, who do not profess Christianity, whether the blacks from Africa or the native inhabitants of this continent. And here I was led into a close, laborious inquiry whether I, as an individual, kept clear from all things which tended to stir up or were connected with wars, either in this land or Africa, and my heart was deeply concerned that in future I might in all things keep steadily to the pure Truth and live and walk in the plainness and simplicity of a sincere follower of Christ. (PM 128-29)

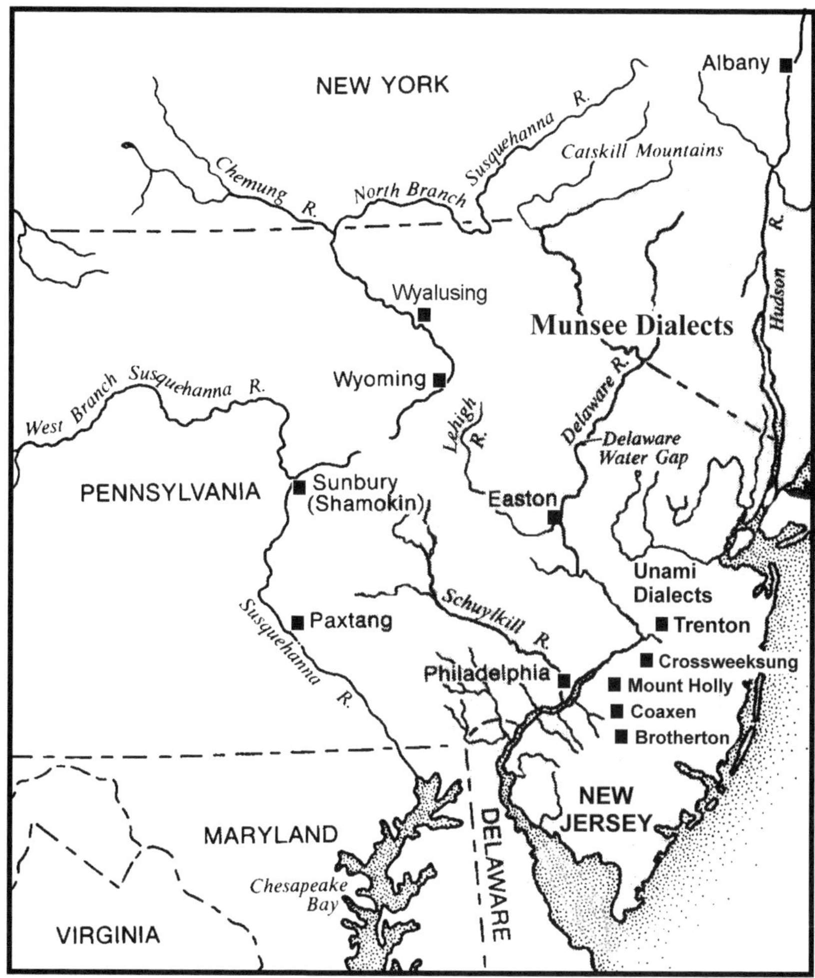

Delaware and Susquehanna Valleys, ca. 1763 (from Ives Goddard's "Delaware," *Handbook of North American Indians,* Vol. 15., 214, with permission of the Smithsonian Institute).

Woolman's meditation, indeed revelation, of the linked oppression of Indians and blacks—which he expanded upon in "A Plea for the Poor," probably written soon after he returned from Wyalusing—expresses a profound understanding of the web of power by which Friends and their neighbors in the Delaware Valley, and throughout British America, were earning their livings and, for some, getting rich. Euro-Americans in New Jersey and Pennsylvania acquired large and small fortunes by producing grain and livestock for the West Indies and southern Europe, while importing molasses and rum, firearms, and luxury goods. Thousands of Africans perished each year in the West Indies raising sugar cane, from which molasses and rum were produced. Merchants sold some of these imports to Native Americans in exchange for furs and large tracts of land. Woolman viewed this Atlantic trading system holistically; he abhorred "luxury and covetousness, with the numerous oppressions and other evils attending them," and warned, with the voice of a prophet, "that the seeds of great calamity and desolation are sown and growing fast on this continent" (PM 129). He insisted, in "A Plea for the Poor," that whites must respect

> that the offspring of those ancient possessors of the country (in whose eyes we appear as newcomers) are yet owners and inhabiters of the land adjoining to us; and that their way of life [requires] much room. (PM 258)

He called for an end to appropriation of new territory until Euro-Americans settled the land they already controlled "so as to accommodate the greatest number of people it is capable of. . ." (PM 258).

How Woolman achieved this unique, fundamental understanding—he was almost certainly the first English writer to do so—remains unclear. He tells only part of the story in his journal. Many scholars have located inspiration for Woolman's thought and social action in the writings of others, yet he emphasized as well the impact of personal experience, particularly while traveling from home (Heller 186-223). Woolman grew up in an area where both African Americans and Native Americans lived, but mentions just a few blacks in his neighborhood, and Indians not at all. To appreciate the magnitude of their oppression, he seems to have found it necessary to leave familiar surroundings, to take long trips into the heart of slavery and war. Even so, examination of the diverse society in which Woolman matured and the tragic events of the 1750s and early 1760s, aspects of his world that he discusses relatively little in his journal, help explain the development of his thought. As he grew up, enslaved blacks labored on the plantations of his grandfather and many neighbors. Hundreds of Native Americans lived in an Indian town, Coaxen, on Rancocas Creek, just a few miles from his house, and in another village, Crossweeksung, thirteen miles to the northeast on Crosswicks Creek. Though this personal contact surely affected him, Woolman stresses in his journal the motif of journey to gain insight from God. The similarity of his experience to the solitary religious quests into the woods by young Indians is remarkable, and perhaps significant, though he is silent on this as well.

Despite Woolman's understanding, by 1763, of the interlocking injustices against African Americans and Native Americans, injustices resulting from the mid-eighteenth-century expansion of the Atlantic economy and white settlement in Pennsylvania and New Jersey, he limited his public witness to the exploitation of blacks. In many respects, Woolman represented what Max Weber called the "exemplary" prophet, whose teaching emphasized "the possession of the deity or the inward and contemplative surrender to God" (Weber 285). Woolman hesitated to preach what he could not fulfill in his own life. During the 1740s, 1750s, and early 1760s, he found ways to distance himself from slavery, from refusal to write bills of sale for slaves to wearing undyed clothes. But when he recognized by 1763 that Euro-American prosperity—indeed survival, for the large proportion of the population who farmed—depended upon the expulsion of the Indians, he could not change his lifestyle without damaging his own well-being and that of his family. While Woolman was no land speculator, grabbing up the property of Native Americans on the frontier, he benefited from the land deals of early West Jersey settlers. Committed to witness by example, his choice was to give up his real estate (and means of support) or remain quiet.

• • •

John Woolman became an ardent opponent of slavery at age twenty-two, much earlier than he expressed concern about the exploitation of Indians. A native of Burlington County in west-central New Jersey, he first spoke against black bondage when his employer directed him to write a bill of sale for an enslaved woman. Woolman complied, but explained to his master and the elderly Quaker who purchased the woman that he "believed slavekeeping to be a practice inconsistent with the Christian religion"; he resolved not to write another "instrument of slavery" (PM 33). Indeed, over the years, Woolman expanded and deepened his witness against involuntary bondage, refusing to write documents such as bills of sale and wills that perpetuated an individual's bondage. He frequently visited slaveholders in his own quarterly meeting and throughout the British mainland colonies and, by 1763, decided to avoid dyes, which slaves produced with their labor. He also gave up shopkeeping, in which he had regularly sold West Indies sugar, rum, and molasses, all slave-labor commodities (PM 32-122; Woolman Papers, Ledger B).

Woolman had been familiar with black bondage since childhood, for significant numbers of African Americans lived in western Burlington County, on prosperous farmlands along the Delaware River. Burlington city, the first English settlement in Burlington County, served (with Perth Amboy) as joint capital of New Jersey, and alternated with Philadelphia, until 1760, as site of Philadelphia Yearly Meeting of Friends. One of several ports on the Delaware River in the early eighteenth century, the town grew as a regional center as Burlington County prospered, particularly during the Delaware Valley's post-1730 economic boom. With success in mixed agriculture and trade, the European settlers of western New Jersey adopted slaveholding. Though they invested in significantly fewer enslaved Africans than did plantation owners in the south, by the early eighteenth century, many affluent merchants and farmers in Burlington city and the surrounding countryside depended upon bondmen and women for domestic service, crafts, and field labor. In 1709, in Northampton Township, where Woolman lived throughout his life, eight percent of households owned enslaved blacks and an additional four percent held Indians, also probably as slaves (Northampton Township Minutes).[2] During Woolman's youth and early adulthood, from 1731 to 1750, about fifteen to twenty percent of Burlington County householders owned slaves (Burlington County Probate Records).[3] The percentage of enslaved African Americans in the county's population was close to the percentage for the colony as a whole; according to the census of 1745, 6.3 percent of Burlington County's population was enslaved in comparison with 7.5 percent in New Jersey (Greene and Harrington 111).[4]

Slavery was thus an integral part of the society in which Woolman matured, including his extended family and immediate neighborhood, though he omits these particulars from the journal. His maternal grandfather, Henry Burr, in 1709 owned Maria, a "Negro" girl aged seventeen (Northampton Township Minutes). Burr apparently freed Maria around 1742, when he wrote his will, for which grandson John was a witness and son-in-law Samuel Woolman, John's father, was executor. Burr bequeathed the now fifty-year-old Maria her bed, other furniture and household goods, a cow, and chickens. John Wills, another Northampton Friend and neighbor of the Woolmans, owned 33-year-old Jenny and 11-year-old Sambo in 1709. When Wills wrote his last testament in 1745, he freed Jenny and instructed his grandson Daniel, who received the plantation, to provide her support. John Wills did not emancipate another woman, Flora, however, but instead bequeathed her to grandson Daniel as long as Jenny lived (Burlington County Probate Records).

John Woolman mentions none of this in his journal, so we cannot be sure that he influenced grandfather Burr to free Maria. It seems instructive, though, that in Woolman's home township during the 1740s, four of six slaveholding decedents freed at least one of their slaves. No Northampton master, at death, had manumitted a slave in the previous decade. In comparison, in Burlington city, home to many members of western New Jersey's political and mercantile elite, more than one-third of the town's decedents in 1731-1750 owned slaves, including wealthy Anglicans as well as such eminent Quakers as Jonathan Wright and Richard Smith, Sr. Wright was the only decedent in the town in the 1730s and 1740s to manumit a slave by will (Burlington County Probate Records; Burlington Monthly Meeting Minutes; Hills).

Woolman knew, of course, that many Philadelphia Yearly Meeting leaders opposed antislavery reform, that the issue still divided Friends in the 1740s. Perhaps he attended, at age seventeen, the 1738 Yearly Meeting in Burlington from which Benjamin Lay was ejected for his "bladder of blood" demonstration. With a sword that he had concealed under his cloak, Lay pierced a book containing a bladder of red juice to dramatize the sins of slaveholders against African Americans. If Woolman did not witness the spattering of "blood," he heard about it and probably read Lay's book, *All Slave-Keepers, That Keep the Innocent in Bondage, Apostates* (1737). Woolman also surely knew the 1715 antislavery tract of John Hepburn, who lived in nearby Freehold, Monmouth County. And, as early as 1746, on ministerial visits and at Yearly Meetings, Woolman likely discussed slavery with members of Shrewsbury Monthly Meeting, in Monmouth County, who by the 1730s had initiated the first emancipation movement in Philadelphia Yearly Meeting (Rowntree 14-15; Drake 43-47; Soderlund 16, 118-19).

Yet in the journal, Woolman chose to emphasize the importance of his 1746 visit to Maryland, Virginia, and North Carolina in heightening his opposition to slavery. While traveling, he became uncomfortable when staying "free-cost with people who lived in ease on the hard labour of their slaves." He condemned the importation of blacks, finding "in these southern provinces so many vices and corruptions increased by this trade and this way of life that it appeared to me as a dark gloominess hanging over the land" (PM 38). As on his later trip to Wyalusing, the Quaker missionary returned from this southern journey using a prophetic voice. By focusing on black bondage outside the Delaware Valley, he reduced the level of confrontation with slaveholding Friends in his own Yearly Meeting, those he most needed to convince to obtain official PYM denunciation of slavery.

Upon his return home in 1746, Woolman wrote his first antislavery essay, titled "Some Considerations on the Keeping of Negroes: Recommended to the Professors of Christianity of Every Denomination." For seven years, however, he delayed submitting it to the Yearly Meeting overseers of the press, a committee dominated by slaveholders until 1751 (Soderlund 34-39). Even after his father Samuel Woolman, on his deathbed, urged him to publish the essay, confiding that "I have all along been deeply affected with the oppression of the poor Negroes, and now at last my concern for them is as great as ever" (PM 45),[5] John Woolman waited three years before approaching the committee (PM 44-45, 47). By 1752, several slaveholding overseers of the press had died, replaced by Anthony Benezet and other antislavery Friends, thus making approval of the essay possible.

The essay, "Some Considerations," finally published in 1754, prodded slaveholders gently to consider the various ways in which slavery was inconsistent with "Truth" (PM 198). Woolman reminded readers that "all nations are of one blood" (PM 200), that the fundamental rule "is not to do that to another which (in like circumstances) we would not have done unto us" (PM 199). Christians must be "faithful stewards" of the benefits God bestowed, not oppress other human beings whose right to liberty equaled their own (PM 201-4). They must provide a better example in educating their children instead of "laying up treasures for them which are often rather a snare than any real benefit" (PM 205). In "Some Considerations," Woolman offered a comprehensive critique of slavery, one that he advanced, in his words, "with reluctance" and "in as general terms as my concern would allow" (PM 199). He focused on individual conscience, but again warned prophetically of dire consequences for violating human brotherhood: "what then shall we do when God riseth up; and when he visiteth, what shall we answer him? Did not he that made us make them, and 'did not one fashion us in the womb?'" (PM 207).

• • •

The young Quaker preacher, dismayed by the blight of human bondage in the southern colonies and in his own neighborhood, resolved to use print, public testimony, and individual persuasion to fight slavery. In these years immediately before the War, however, he had not yet recognized the tragedy that Native Americans experienced as a result of European settlement. Rather, in this first essay against slavery, Woolman described the English domination of the Delaware Valley as a measure of God's benevolence, now imperiled if slavekeepers persisted in sin. "The wilderness and solitary deserts in which our fathers passed the days of their pilgrimage," he wrote, "are now turned into pleasant fields. The natives are gone from before us, and we establish peaceably in the possession of the land, enjoying our civil and religious liberties" (PM 207). He continued, in a passage soon proved wrong by the outbreak of war on the Pennsylvania and New Jersey frontiers, that "while many parts of the world have groaned under the heavy calamities of war, our habitation remains quiet and our land fruitful" (PM 207).

Though Woolman had grown up in the vicinity of several Indian towns in Burlington County, in an area where the Lenape had relatively dense settlements before the Europeans arrived, until 1763 he regarded the oppression of African Americans and Indians as separate issues, with black slavery requiring greatest concern. While most neighboring Lenape lived in their own towns and had freedom to come and go as they pleased, enslaved African Americans had little control over their own lives—in work, place of residence, or creating families. The problems from which Native Americans suffered, loss of lands, decline in population, and impoverishment, eluded Woolman's grasp until after 1754, and perhaps as late as 1763, during his journey to Wyalusing.

Woolman's statement in "Some Considerations," that the "natives are gone from before us, and we establish peaceably in the possession of the land" (PM 207), obscured the near destruction of the Lenape (or

Delaware) Indians in New Jersey and eastern Pennsylvania. While most commentators, from colonial times to the present, have characterized Quaker-Delaware relations as mostly peaceful and just, English settlement in the mid-Atlantic region was no less devastating for its native inhabitants than for the Indians of New England, Virginia, and Carolina. When Dutch and English traders came to the Delaware Valley early in the seventeenth century, about forty Lenape villages were located along streams in what are now northern Delaware, eastern Pennsylvania, New Jersey, and southern New York.[6] Native groups in the area that became Burlington County included the Remkokes, the Atsayonck, the Calcefar, the Mosilian, and the Sankikans, each with one to two hundred men, according to early European traders, who did not count women and children (Goddard 213-16; Merritt 10-11; Samuel Smith 29; Weslager 35-36).[7]

The Lenape interacted with the Dutch and Swedes who built forts and established farms along the Delaware, then in 1677 welcomed the first English settlers at Burlington (Wacker 72-88; Weslager 98-154; Samuel Smith 92-125). The Lenape sachems, or leaders, sold their territory along the east bank of the Delaware to the English and helped them adjust to the land. Mary Murfin Smith, who came as a child in 1678, later recounted "that the Indians, very numerous but very civil, for the most part brought corn and venison and sold [them to] the English for such things as they needed. Soon after, many of the natives died of smallpox; in Mary Smith's account, "God's providence made room for us in a wonderful manner in taking away the Indians. There came a distemper among them so mortal that they could not bury all the dead. Others went away, leaving their town" (Woodward and Hageman 9-11). According to another early Burlington settler, Thomas Budd, some young Lenape blamed the English for the epidemic:

> The Indians told us, in a conference at Burlington, shortly after we came into the country, they were advised to make war on us, and cut us off while we were but few; for that we sold them the small pox, with the matchcoat they had bought of us. (Samuel Smith 100)

The Lenape sachems rejected this argument, stating that the disease had afflicted their people on several earlier occasions, before the English came (Samuel Smith 100).

In 1754, when the Seven Years' War began in the Ohio country and spread through Pennsylvania to the northwestern New Jersey frontier, several hundred Delawares remained in New Jersey, the rest having died or moved west to the Susquehanna Valley, western Pennsylvania, and Ohio. The New Jersey assembly appointed commissioners to investigate the grievances of Native Americans within the colony. After a conference at Crosswicks, Burlington County, to hear the Indians' concerns, the legislature paid off all Delaware claims north of the Raritan River with one thousand Spanish dollars, and exchanged the rights to Indian lands south of the Raritan for a reservation, called Brotherton, in central Burlington County. The idea for the reservation apparently originated with the Presbyterian missionary John Brainerd as a way to safeguard some Indian territory from land-grabbing whites. In 1757, a group of Burlington Quakers formed the New Jersey Association for Helping the Indians to provide financial support, but their money became unnecessary when the assembly purchased the land (Mancall 35-39; Goddard 221-22; Weslager 261-63; Samuel Smith 440-46, 455-83; R. Smith 104-8; C. Woodward 180-88).

By 1763, of perhaps three hundred Delawares living in New Jersey, about one hundred lived at the Brotherton reservation, a 3,000-acre tract with sawmill, dwellings, and Presbyterian meeting house, and forty Indians lived at Coaxen on Rancocas Creek (John Brainerd to Elizabeth Smith, Aug. 24, 1761, published in DeCou 244). Though New Jersey Governor Francis Bernard praised Brotherton as "a tract of Land Very suitable for this purpose, having soil good enough, a large hunting country and a passage by water to the Sea for fishing" (Ricord and Nelson 175), the reservation did not thrive, and by the 1770s only fifty or sixty people remained (Weslager 271; DeCou 246). They lived, according to Quaker minister John Hunt of Moorestown, "in very low Circumstances as to food and Raiment" (DeCou 246).[8]

• • •

John Woolman, like other members of Philadelphia Yearly Meeting, took part in efforts to restore peace with the Delawares during the Seven Years' War and the subsequent pan-Indian offensive called Pontiac's Rebellion. According to the records of the New Jersey Association for Helping the Indians, he was a member and contributed £6 toward the Brotherton reservation (R. Smith 104). He wrote nothing about the association in his journal, however, nor anything about the Indian towns at nearby Coaxen and Crossweeksung, nor about the Brotherton reservation and its decline.

But Woolman did mention his meeting in August 1761 in Philadelphia with the Munsee-speaking Delaware sachem Papunehang and other Indians from Wyalusing, the encounter that led directly to the Susquehanna journey (PM 122-23). Woolman and Anthony Benezet, who also attended the 1761 meeting, were much impressed by Papunehang's religious spirit and desire for peace (AMG 81-83, 86). With approval, both men recorded Papunehang's words, including his belief

> That it was not good to Speak upon matters Relating to the Almighty only from the root of the tongue outward but that in order that their words Should be good they must Come from the good in the heart. (Woolman, "Substance"; see also Brookes 488)

According to an Indian interpreter, as reported by Benezet, Papunehang "was formerly a Drunken man." Upon the death of his father, he "fell into a thought full melancoly state," left his town in search of God, and after five days "it pleased God to appear to him to his comfort, & to give him a sight not only of his own inward state, but also an acquaintance into the works of Nature" (Brookes 484). He became an Indian prophet, founding the town of Wyalusing in 1752. He preached against the Indians' lust for rum and other European trade goods—as well as the greed of white traders—but counseled friendship toward whites. Wyalusing remained at peace during the 1750s and early 1760s (Dowd 31; Merritt 48-50, 239-41).

John Woolman provides little explanation in his journal for going to Wyalusing, beyond his intention to follow up the meeting with Papunehang two years earlier. With the renewal of war, the Quaker surely hoped to reinforce Papunehang's commitment to peace. Yet the most significant result of the journey was its impact upon Woolman himself. Just as his travels in Maryland, Virginia, and North Carolina had sharpened his critique of slavery, his journey to Wyalusing brought into focus the human tragedy that had occurred in New Jersey and eastern Pennsylvania and would continue to occur farther west, he envisioned, unless whites abandoned their greed. He now understood how much the Delawares had lost and that their decline was linked to the oppression of enslaved Africans and the development of the Atlantic economy.

The northern Susquehanna Valley was in crisis when Woolman visited in June 1763. The Six Nations of the Iroquois controlled the territory, but had allowed the Delawares to establish towns. Conflict erupted around one of these villages, Wyoming, in late 1762 and early 1763 when white settlers, sponsored by the Susquehannah Company of Connecticut, began building blockhouses and planting crops.[9] Teedyuscung, the leader of the Delawares at Wyoming, attempted to withstand the Connecticut assault, but was murdered in April 1763 and his town destroyed by fire (Mancall 27-39; Wallace 252-60). John Woolman and his companions traveled through Wyoming soon after many of its residents fled. No wonder the Quaker minister continually reassessed his decision to make the Wyalusing journey at that time (PM 130). On 10 June 1763, early in the trip, Woolman's party met a group of refugees from Wyoming who were "going to settle at another place" (PM 126). After the Quakers reached the burned out town on 13 June, they "visited all the Indians hereabouts that we could meet with . . . in all perhaps twenty," most of whom were preparing to leave within a few days (PM 130). Woolman's journal testifies to the danger he felt as one Indian man threatened with a tomahawk until he understood "the nature of our visit in these parts; and then he . . . soon appeared friendly and sat down and smoked his pipe" (PM 129-30). In discussing the situation at Wyoming, Woolman did not explain the reasons for the town's distress—the invasion by Connecticut settlers and the recent murder of Teedyuscung. One can only speculate why he failed to explain. Perhaps he expected his readers to know about these events, or to remember, at least, Pennsylvania's turmoil at this time. Or perhaps, to Woolman, the details were less important than the journey itself and the insight he gained by going to the Susquehanna.

On 17 June, Woolman arrived in Wyalusing, where he discovered that the Moravian missionary David Zeisberger preceded him, also at the invitation of the Delawares. Woolman preached at religious meetings over the course of five days, but respected the fact that Papunehang and many of his people had already decided to adopt the Moravian faith. Woolman "found some difficulty," as he expressed it, in communicating with the people of Wyalusing, because none of the interpreters "were quite perfect in the English and Delaware tongue. So they helped one another and we laboured along, divine love attending" (PM 133). Zeisberger, on the other hand, was assisted by a Moravian Indian who accompanied him to the town.[10] At the end of his stay, Woolman seemed satisfied that he had gained a respectful hearing from the people and that Papunehang, in particular, "appeared kind and loving to us" (PM 134). The Quaker left Wyalusing to Zeisberger's spiritual guidance, perhaps assured that the pacifist Moravians would give Papunehang the support he needed to avoid war (PM 132-35; Pickett 77-92).

The people of Wyalusing needed that help, for within months more blood flowed in northeastern Pennsylvania. Captain Bull, the son of murdered Wyoming leader Teedyuscung, initiated attacks against white militia and farmers in Northampton County, killing more than fifty people. Next Captain Bull's party headed for Wyoming, where the Connecticut settlers had started to build a town. Warned of the impending assault, most of the whites fled except about thirty-five, of whom the Indians tortured nine to death and took twenty as captives (Merritt 234-39; Wallace 263-64). The Delawares at Wyalusing, many of them now Moravians, including Papunehang, took refuge in Philadelphia. There they were imperiled by the infamous Paxton Boys and local mobs; though protected by the colonial government from such violence, more than fifty-six died from smallpox and dysentery, aggravated by overcrowding in military barracks. Following the hostilities, some of the Delawares who had lived along the East Branch of the Susquehanna returned to Wyalusing, where the Moravians built the town of Friedenshütten, while others joined the Delawares who had already migrated to Ohio. In 1772, the tide of white settlers in northern Pennsylvania forced the people of Friedenshütten to move west (Wallace 265; Pickett 89-92; Merritt 241-42; Dowd 32; Weslager 247-48).

John Woolman did not discuss in his journal the exile and death of so many of the people he had visited in Wyalusing, though he certainly knew of the tragedy unfolding in Pennsylvania. As the concluding paragraph to his Susquehanna narrative shows, the arduous journey broadened his perspective of the problems Indians faced, yet his awareness of their way of life remained limited.

> Between the English inhabitants and Wyalusing we had only a narrow path, which in many places is much grown up with bushes

> and interrupted by abundance of trees lying across it, which together with the mountains, swamps, and rough stones, it is a difficult road to travel, and the more so for that rattlesnakes abound there, of which we killed four—that people who have never been in such places have but an imperfect idea of them. But I was not only taught patience but also made thankful to God, who thus led me about and instructed me that I might have a quick and lively feeling of the afflictions of my fellow creatures whose situation in life is difficult. (PM 137)

Woolman recognized the misfortunes the Delawares had endured—symbolized by the narrow difficult path one must travel between Wyalusing and the Delaware Valley—and valued the understanding he had gained "of the afflictions of my fellow creatures" by making the trip. Still, after such a short visit, his knowledge of Indian culture was fragmentary. He noted prominently among the trials his party faced, that they, like other white travelers through unsettled country, killed four rattlers. Native Americans, in contrast, avoided harming the snakes, which they believed often protected humans rather than threatened them (Samuel Smith 138; Slaughter 220-27). Woolman's reaction, when he heard in 1764 (and recorded in his journal) the graphic details of Indian atrocities (PM 142-43), and his subsequent silence about the people of Wyalusing, suggests an ambivalence toward Native Americans that he did not feel toward blacks. One has the sense that while he sympathized with the Indians and understood the economic mechanisms that were driving them from their homes, he dreaded the violence to which some Delawares resorted and thought their plight well beyond his influence and means. As in the case of slavery, when he wrote "Some Considerations" soon after his first southern journey, Woolman drafted "A Plea for the Poor" upon return home from Wyalusing. This essay and chapter 8 of the *Journal* called upon the most influential men of the Delaware Valley, his fellow Quakers and other Euro-Americans, to curtail trade with the West Indies and stop engrossing Indian land. Woolman's plea remained unpublished until after his death, however, and his personal witness for Indian rights ended there.

John Woolman was an intriguing mix of mortal and saint, a man of his times and beyond them. He opposed slavery from early youth, probably influenced by his father (and mother?), and moved quickly from moral commitment to social action. He knew African Americans as individuals all of his life, hiring and keeping shop accounts with several black men, including Primas, Chap, and Bacchus, and executing the will of Maria, his grandfather Burr's former slave. Woolman's account books and journal provide no evidence of similar relationships with Native Americans though they lived nearby, along Rancocas Creek (Woolman Papers, Ledgers).[11] Until the Seven Years' War, if we can judge from his writings, he thought relatively little about the destruction of New Jersey Indians as a people. On his trip to Wyalusing, however, the linked oppression of Native Americans and African Americans, founded on white greed and played out in the Atlantic trading system, became all too clear. Woolman sought his personal solution in simplicity, in earning only as much income as his family required, yet even that support depended upon the earlier settlement of native lands, leading to the Delawares' decline. Woolman addressed social problems on a personal level, as individual behavior to be changed because God abhorred it, not as social ills to be bemoaned and generally ignored. Because Woolman could not extract himself from the Euro-American economic system without threatening his family's welfare, he refused to criticize publicly the thousands of new immigrants settling the frontier, nor to condemn even the wealthy land-speculating Friends and associates who lusted after domination of North America and the fortunes to be obtained by selling lands.

NOTES

[1]The author wishes to thank Thomas Slaughter, J. William Frost, and Marianne S. Wokeck for their insightful comments on an earlier draft of this essay.

[2]Northampton is the only township in Burlington County for which an early detailed census exists. While this census designated no one as a slave, all "Negroes" and "Indians" lived in white households and lacked last names. All whites, including servants and apprentices, had surnames. Enslaved Native Americans, possibly imported from South Carolina where an extensive slave trade existed early in the 18th century (Merrell 36-37, 66), were much more numerous in Pennsylvania and New Jersey before 1720 than later. Several early Quaker writers, including George Fox, William Edmundson, and John Hepburn, expressed concern about Indian and black slavery (Frost 16, 35, 68, 110), but later abolitionists like Benjamin Lay and John Woolman focused on

enslaved Africans Americans. By the 1730s, in the Delaware Valley, at least, few enslaved Indians were imported and many who remained in bondage had apparently intermarried with blacks. The opposition of the Delawares to importation of enslaved Native Americans prompted the Pennsylvania assembly in 1712 to enact a prohibitive duty (repealed by the British government) on Indian as well as African slaves (Frost 79).

[3]During these years, about one-fifth of Burlington County inventories included slaves. Because propertied decedents were more likely to have their estates inventoried than people with just a few possessions, however, analyses of inventories are likely to be skewed toward the rich. In Burlington County, though, quite a few wealthy estates were not inventoried. Thus, the actual percentage of county households possessing slaves was probably between 15 and 20 percent.

[4]According to the 1745 census, 430 slaves lived in Burlington County.

[5]No evidence exists that Samuel Woolman owned a slave, though he died a relatively wealthy man.

[6]The villages had no unifying hierarchical political organization, but allied with one another against common enemies. The Lenni Lenape were divided geographically and linguistically into two major groups: the Munsee-speaking people who lived north of the Delaware Water Gap and Raritan Valley in what are now Pennsylvania, New Jersey, and New York, and the Unamis who lived to the south on both sides of the Delaware River. While their languages differed, archeological evidence demonstrates that the material culture of these groups overlapped considerably (Cross 207-12). Most English colonists referred to the Munsees and Unamis as Delaware Indians because they originally lived along the Delaware River.

[7]If one uses a multiplier of 5 to compute the total population, each of these Indian groups might have numbered 500 to 1,000 people. Goddard's estimates are lower, based on his conjecture that "the Delaware lived in village bands of a few hundred members each." He estimates that the total population of Delawares declined from 11,000 in 1600 to 3,200 in 1779 (Goddard 213-14). On estimating the population of Native Americans of coastal New York, see Ceci 303-7.

[8]This paper is part of a larger investigation of the history of the Delaware Indians of Burlington County further, including the establishment of Brotherton.

[9]The Susquehannah Company had obtained approval to colonize northern Pennsylvania from the Connecticut assembly, which, on the basis of the Connecticut charter, claimed lands west to the Pacific Ocean. The Pennsylvania

proprietors argued, of course, that the royal charter to William Penn superceded Connecticut's claim (Boyd xxvi, lviii).

[10]The experience of Presbyterian missionary David Brainerd in preaching to the Delaware Indians suggests Woolman's handicap in trying to explain his beliefs without the aid of an interpreter who fully understood what he had to say. Brainerd achieved success in preaching to the Delawares only after he had converted his interpreter, Moses Tatamy (Dwight 210-16).

[11]Because Native Americans in New Jersey often had English names by the mid-eighteenth century, it is possible that Woolman did business with neighboring Indians, though I have not been able to identify them at this point.

WORKS CITED

Boyd, Julian P., ed. *The Susquehannah Company Papers.* Vol. 1. Wilkes-Barre, PA: Wyoming Historical & Geological Society, 1930.

Brookes, George S. *Friend Anthony Benezet.* Philadelphia,PA: University of Pennsylvania, 1937.

Burlington County Probate Records, 1731-1750. Burlington, Chesterfield, Mansfield, New Hanover, Northampton, Nottingham, and Springfield townships. Archives Section, Division of Archives and Records Management, Trenton, NJ.

Burlington Monthly Meeting Records, 1731-1750. Men's and Women's Meeting Minutes. Friends Historical Library of Swarthmore College, Swarthmore, PA.

Cadbury, Henry J. "John Hepburn and His Book Against Slavery, 1715." *Proceedings of the American Antiquarian Society* n.s. 59 (1949): 89-160.

Ceci, Lynn. *The Effect of European Contact and Trade on the Settlement Pattern of Indians in Coastal New York, 1524-1665.* New York, NY: Garland, 1990.

Cross, Dorothy. *Archeology of New Jersey.* Vol. 1. Trenton, NJ: Archeological Society of New Jersey and the New Jersey State Museum, 1941.

DeCou, George. *The Historic Rancocas: Sketches of the Towns and Pioneer Settlers in Rancocas Valley.* Moorestown, NJ: News Chronicle, 1949.

Dowd, Gregory Evans. *A Spirited Resistance: The North American Indian Struggle for Unity, 1745-1815.* Baltimore, MD: Johns Hopkins University Press, 1992.

Drake, Thomas E. *Quakers and Slavery in America.* New Haven, CT: Yale University Press, 1950.

Dwight, Sereno Edwards, ed. *Memoirs of the Rev. David Brainerd: Missionary to the Indians on the Borders of New-York, New-Jersey, and Pennsylvania.* New Haven, CT: S. Converse, 1822.

Fowler, David J. "Egregious Villains, Wood Rangers, and London Traders: The Pine Robber Phenomenon in New Jersey During the Revolutionary War." Ph.D.diss. Rutgers University, 1987.

Frost, J. William, ed. *The Quaker Origins of Antislavery.* Norwood, PA: Norwood Editions, 1980.

Goddard, Ives. "Delaware." *Handbook of North American Indians.* Vol. 15. Northeast. Ed. Bruce G. Trigger. Washington, DC: Smithsonian Institution, 1978.

Greene, Evarts B., and Virginia D. Harrington. *American Population Before the Federal Census of 1790.* New York, NY: Columbia University Press, 1932.

Heller, Michael Alan. "Soft Persuasion: A Rhetorical Analysis of John Woolman's Essays and *Journal.*" Ph.D.diss. Arizona State University, 1989.

Hills, George Morgan. *History of the Church in Burlington, New Jersey.* 2nd ed. Trenton, NJ: W. S. Sharp, 1885.

Lay, Benjamin. *All Slave-Keepers, That Keep the Innocent in Bondage, Apostates.* Philadelphia, PA: Printed for the author [by Benjamin Franklin], 1737.

Mancall, Peter C. *Valley of Opportunity: Economic Culture along the Upper Susquehanna, 1700-1800.* Ithaca, NY: Cornell University Press, 1991.

Merrell, James H. *The Indians' New World: Catawbas and Their Neighbors from European Contact Through the Era of Removal.* New York, NY: University of North Carolina Press, 1989.

Merritt, Jane T. "Kinship, Community, and Practicing Culture: Indians and the Colonial Encounter in Pennsylvania, 1700-1763." Ph.D.diss. University of Washington, 1995.

Northampton Township, Burlington County, NJ. Minutes, 1697-1803. Photostatic copy, Historical Society of Pennsylvania, Philadelphia, PA.

Pickett, Ralph H. "A Religious Encounter: John Woolman and David Zeisberger." *Quaker History* 79 (1990): 77-92.

Pierce, Arthur D. *Iron in the Pines: The Story of New Jersey's Ghost Towns and Bog Iron.* New Brunswick, NJ: Rutgers University Press, 1957.

Ricord, Frederick W., and William Nelson, eds. *Documents Relating to the Colonial History of the State of New Jersey.* 1st ser. Vol. 9. Newark, NJ: Daily Advertiser, 1885.

Rowntree, C. Brightwen. "Benjamin Lay (1681-1759) of Colchester, London, Barbadoes, Philadelphia." *Journal of the Friends' Historical Society* 33 (1936): 3-19.

Slaughter, Thomas P., ed. *William Bartram: Travels and Other Writings.* New York, NY: Library of America, 1996.

Smith, R. Morris. *The Burlington Smiths.* Philadelphia, PA: E. Stanley Hart, 1877.

Smith, Samuel. *The History of New-Jersey.* 2nd ed. Trenton, NJ: W. S. Sharp, 1877.

Soderlund, Jean R. *Quakers and Slavery: A Divided Spirit.* Princeton, NJ: Princeton University Press, 1985.

Wacker, Peter O. Land and People: *A Cultural Geography of Preindustrial New Jersey: Origins and Settlement Patterns.* New Brunswick, NJ: Rutgers University Press, 1975.

Wacker, Peter O., and Paul G. E. Clemens. *Land Use in Early New Jersey: A Historical Geography.* Newark, NJ: New Jersey Historical Society, 1995.

Wallace, Anthony F. C. *King of the Delawares: Teedyuscung, 1700-1763.* 2nd ed. Syracuse, NY: Syracuse University Press, 1990.

Weber, Max. "The Social Psychology of the World Religions." *From Max Weber: Essays in Sociology.* Trans. and ed. H. H. Gerth and C. Wright Mills. New York, NY: Oxford University Press, 1946.

Weslager, C. A. *The Delaware Indians: A History.* New Brunswick, NJ: Rutgers University Press, 1972.

Whitney, Janet. *John Woolman, American Quaker.* Boston, MA: Little, Brown, 1942.

Woodward, Carl Raymond. *Ploughs and Politicks: Charles Read of New Jersey and His Notes on Agriculture, 1715-1774.* New Brunswick, NJ: Rutgers University Press, 1941.

Woodward, Ewan M., and John F. Hageman. *History of Burlington and Mercer Counties, New Jersey.* Philadelphia, PA: Everts and Peck, 1883.

Woolman, John. *The Journal and Essays of John Woolman.* Ed. Amelia Mott Gummere. New York, NY: Macmillan, 1922.

—-. *The Journal and Major Essays of John Woolman.* Ed. Phillips P. Moulton. 1971. Richmond, IN: Friends United Press, 1989.

—-. Papers. Historical Society of Pennsylvania, Philadelphia, PA.

—-. "The Substance of some Conversation with Paponaheal the Indian Chief. . . ." Pemberton Papers, vol. 13, p. 23. Historical Society of Pennsylvania, Philadelphia, PA.

9

John Woolman and the Enlightenment

J. William Frost

1

JOHN WOOLMAN MIGHT NOT HAVE APPROVED of the focus, contents, and conclusions of this article. For it asks the historian's question of whether John Woolman knew the sources of his own thoughts. In spite of all his searchings to feel the motion of God's goodness and to separate it from worldly knowledge, did he, like other eighteenth-century Friends, prove unable to escape his cultural milieu? Scholars correctly describe Woolman as a Christian mystic whose vocabulary, quietist perspective, reform efforts, daily life, and journeys conformed to and helped transform ideals of the Quaker community. It has long been recognized that Woolman's *Journal* contains a selective or partial portrait of the man. This article seeks to determine whether Woolman's writings also show that he was a participant in the eighteenth-century enlightenment—a *weltanschauung* both competing and complementary to Quaker faith and practice. Did Woolman, because he lived in colonial America and was cognizant of rationalist Quaker and non-Quaker apologists for Christianity, echo enlightenment ideas? Were these ideas at odds with his mystical quietism?

Modern interpreters of Woolman's *Journal* and essays show ambivalence in seeing him as an enlightenment Quaker. All insist, quite correctly, that for him the source of true or authentic religion came not from man-made thought, but from an inward experience of God. It would seem that "reason," for Woolman, like "custom," would be a dirty word, signifying a barrier erected by self-will or pride between the believer and the purity of true wisdom. Amelia Gummere in 1922 characterized Rancocas Meeting and the community in which Woolman dwelt as among the most conservative Quaker enclaves in America. Gummere, in comparing Benjamin Franklin and Woolman, insisted that "one can imagine no sympathy between the practical scientist and the Quaker idealist" (AMG 17).[1] Like the prefaces of John G. Whittier ("Introduction" *Journal of Woolman*) and Frederick Tolles ("Introduction") to earlier versions, Phillips Moulton's brief introduction to the critical edition of *The Journal and Major Essays* did not discuss any enlightenment influence. Likewise Michael Heller's analysis of Woolman's rhetoric and methods of persuasion did not list "reason" or "nature" in an index of significant terms or mention any impact of rational religion in style or method of argument ("Soft Persuasion"). Philip Boroughs' careful study of the context and content of Woolman's spirituality included no discussion of the impact of the Age of Reason (58). Moulton, Heller, and Boroughs' writings provide at least implicit support for Gummere's perspective that one need not discuss the enlightenment to understand Woolman.

A few recent commentators are not so certain that Woolman escaped from the Age of Reason. For example, in 1957 Walter Altman in an ambiguous statement hedged that Woolman "cannot have been unaware of the religion of reason; indeed, at some points he seems to have accepted it, consciously or unconsciously" (33). Altman seems to be unwilling to conclude that Woolman, for all his introspection, was not intellectually aware of how much he owed to prevailing norms. Edwin Cady argued that Woolman used a vaguely defined "common intellectual coin of his age" and utilized the "social-contract ideas of the Enlightenment just then so powerfully in the ascendant in provincial America" (94). Paul Rosenblatt was most positive, seeing Woolman and Franklin as "thinkers of the enlightenment," and claiming that Woolman was "a man of reason, a man of the Enlightenment" who saw "divine reason" as "reasonableness" (66-67). Hugh Barbour disagreed, insisting that although Woolman used the language of the Age of Reason, such terms did not influence his fundamental concepts (*Quaker Crosscurrents* 101). In *The Quakers,* I found Woolman in certain passages merging themes of evangelical, quietist, and rational Christianity in a manner possible only in the mid-eighteenth century (Barbour and Frost 132). So many contrary judgments, none of whose basis is described in any detail, are more likely to confuse than to help us understand the concatenation of events which shaped John Woolman.

This article is intended to clarify the relationship between Woolman and the enlightenment by, first, defining what is meant by rational religion and, then, describing its relationship to mid-eighteenth-century Quakerism. Next follows a sketch of some of the major themes of rational religion as applied in the thought of two Quakers, William Penn and Alexander Arscott, whom Woolman is known to have read. Then we will look for similar themes in the earlier antislavery writings of three American Quakers—John Hepburn, John Sandiford, and Benjamin Lay—whose tracts Woolman probably read, although there is no certain evidence. My conclusion is that none of these men specifically utilized themes of the enlightenment. The contrast will be with two of Anthony Benezet's early antislavery writings which depend upon rational themes, and which Woolman almost certainly read. Finally, we will compare the antislavery passages in Woolman's *Journal* and two treatises entitled "Considerations on the Keeping of Negroes" with the earlier non-rationalistic abolitionist and Benezet's contemporaneous rationalist writings. The conclusion is that Woolman was inconsistent, using the language of rational religion in antislavery tracts but rarely in the *Journal.*

2

Two of my Swarthmore College colleagues, in the departments of English Literature and Modern Languages (French), taught a seminar comparing the enlightenment in France and England. They concluded that even when the French and English writers used what appeared to be the same word, there often were very different connotations. Divergent meanings of similar phrases can also occur in phrases used by the British and colonial Americans and there can be a distinctive twist by Friends fitting enlightenment themes to traditional Quaker beliefs. An additional complication is that even before Augustine theologians supported the rationality of Christian revelation and ethical actions using beliefs in reason and natural law derived from Neoplatonism and Stoicism. So when Woolman used the word "reason" he could have had precise ideas derived from either Plato, Aquinas, Locke, or Robert Barclay or just echoed without much thought the common parlance.

Terms also can acquire new meanings over time (one could, for example, write a history of western thought just looking at different connotations to the word "nature") and the English enlightenment lasted a long time. Isaac Newton's *Principia* appeared in 1686; Newton died in

1727, Benjamin Franklin in 1790, and Thomas Jefferson in 1826—all symbolize the enlightenment in their respective countries. Newton also personifies the close relationship between scientific inquiry and theological perspectives in the post-1688 English Age of Reason, for he was interested in the rationality of the Trinitarian formulation and spent many years studying the fulfillment of biblical prophecies.[2]

Unlike the French enlightenment where Voltaire even while praising Quakerism proclaimed against Catholicism, theology, and priests, the British rationalists, including Deists like Matthew Tindal (1657-1733) and John Toland (1670-1722), while attacking what they saw as superstition, sought to strengthen religious commitment and ethical behavior and not to undermine the churches. A so-called latitudinarian party within the Established Church, whose primary spokesmen were Archbishop John Tillotson (1630-1694) and Bishop Benjamin Hoadley (1676-1761), and the Moderate party in the Presbyterian Church in Scotland showed the compatibility of the new ways of thought with either liturgical observances or Calvinism. The Latitudinarians insisted that because the Golden Rule summarized religion, the duty of a Christian was an "inward principle of love of God and goodness" (Tillotson qtd. in Battesin, *The Moral Basis* 19; for background here, see Battesin 14-22; see also Stromberg). God would prefer a good heathen who did charity more than a wicked orthodox Christian who abused his fellows. Denying or down playing original sin, Tillotson argued that "nothing is more unnatural than sin" which arose because of "custom" and could be countered because God planted a seed of benevolence "in the very frame of our Nature" (16-17). Christian charity, defined as an all-consuming virtue and embracing all humanity, led to "a kind of universality in the matter of . . . benevolence" (18). Many American Quakers whom Woolman knew owned the books of Latitudinarian Anglicans, though there is no record that he read them (Tolles, *Meeting House* 169).

For many English thinkers, rationalism's attractiveness lay in creating a system of religious harmony which would end the theological squabbling and fanaticism associated with the Puritan revolution. Some English parish priests and scholars before, during, and after the Puritan revolution sought religious peace through a Neoplatonic emphasis upon the immanence of God's divine reason throughout all creation. Through human reason a person could participate in the divine mind. Robert Barclay, George Keith, and William Penn had associations with the

Cambridge Platonists like Henry More (1614-1687), who debated ideas with Friends at the salon of Ann Viscountess of Conway because he detected a similarity between the Quaker belief in the inward revelation and the Platonic Light of God in nature (Barbour, "William Penn on Religion and Ethics" 250-54). More argued that "the Logos, or steady comprehensive wisdom of God, in which all ideas and their aspects are contained, is but *universal stable reason.*" Like other Cambridge Platonists, More's definition of reason, which he also called "Divine Sagacity," was intuitive and mystical (Stoneburner 24-26; Tullock 303-409). More composed a treatise arguing the compatibility of science and religion. Woolman is known to have read the Platonist John Everard, whose devotional writings were very popular among eighteenth-century American Quakers and reprinted by Anthony Benezet. Everard, a seventeenth-century Anglican clergyman, was more a Platonic mystic relying on intuition of innate truths than a rationalist, but his exaltation of God's immanence in animals and plants led him to advocate treating with care and moderation all of God's creatures. "God's Will is as well accomplishmented in this Tree, as in a Man: for these visible Creatures were made of invisible, and that which is invisible, praised him before, and that praiseth him still" (Everard 119-32). Woolman's dwelling upon living in the guidance of Pure Wisdom, the harmony of all creation, the need for a moderate use of products of this earth, and distress at the abuses of animals reminds one of Everard and other Neoplatonists.

Woolman also had in his library John Locke's *Thoughts on Education.* Locke (1632-1704) was to most educated colonial Americans the seventeenth century's most important English philosopher, political theorist, and apologist for rational Christianity. Locke in *The Reasonableness of Christianity* claimed to discover in reason and natural law a grounding for Christian unity and ethical behavior apart from creeds and the Bible which were subject to subjective interpretation. Although some of his contemporaries questioned Locke's devotion to traditional Christianity, the philosopher did not wish to undermine the authority of the Bible, seeing the miracles of Jesus as a convincing outward evidence of the truth of Christianity. For Locke, like other rationalist apologists, faith was primarily an intellectual assent to a few basic intuitive and self-evident truths (existence of God, Jesus as messiah, life after death, the importance of ethical behavior) which could be derived from nature through reason by intellectuals or through revelation from the

Bible by the common people. Locke's view of the infant as a *tabula rasa,* a blank slate, whose character would be shaped by his environment appealed to Quakers who denied original sin and also saw the child as innocent. His emphases upon practical learning and adapting teaching techniques to the child's personality also were congruent with Quaker norms espoused by Woolman and Benezet (Frost, *Quaker Family* 65-67, 93-95, 114-5; Benezet, *First Book for Children;* Woolman, *First Book for Children*).

Rationalist Christians and post-Glorious Revolution (1688) English Quakers had many ideas in common. Both sought to ground religious truth on something to supplement the words of the Bible, creeds, and liturgy and found a new source of authority within the mind. Both claimed to be impatient with the fine points of formal theology; both sought religious toleration, emphasized the duty of ethical behavior, stressed the importance of moderation, reasonableness, and living according to nature. They supported the educational efforts of the new academies as offering more practical learning than the traditional classical curriculum. Quakers and enlightened Christians participated in scientific inquiry and contributed to the engineering discoveries associated with the beginnings of the industrial revolution. A description of the Moderate Presbyterians in the mid-eighteenth century also applies to many Anglicans and Quakers: they "were determined to show that the cause of science, progress, and genteel culture and the interests of religion were not only compatible, but also necessary to one another. The result was that . . . the potential for conflict between the forces of enlightenment and of religion was greatly lessened" (Sloan 13).

For all their similarities, there was a fundamental difference in ultimate authority insisted upon by even the most rationalistic Quakers. Their Puritan opponents who were supernaturally inclined had long scoffed that the light or seed within derived from the devil. Alternatively, the Puritans claimed that so-called personal inward revelation was produced by a natural faculty: a product of conscience or reason. The rational Christians claimed that the Quaker experience of the voice of God within was enthusiasm or fanaticism, a product of their own emotional state. By contrast, Friends always proclaimed that the Inward Christ was purely of divine origin, a new revelation which communicated infallible Truth. During the meeting for worship, all Friends became quietists. Quietism in which a person stilled her own will and reason prior to feeling the Seed of God provided a religious underpinning guaranteeing the spiritual authority of the Light. In addition, for latitudinarian Quakers the beauty, warmth and attractiveness of the inward motion of God which quickened the mind and led to virtue resembled human participation in the divine logos or light of the Neoplatonists more than the mechanistic reason of Locke. In the eighteenth century Friends' tracts might meld quietist, Neoplatonic, and rationalist themes with little awareness of intellectual inconsistency.

Quakers' first espousal of themes later prominent in the enlightenment such as natural rights originated from their early protests against religious persecution. George Bishop's attacks upon the New England Puritans' persecution of Quakers and attempts to persuade Oliver Cromwell's army and later the Restoration Parliament to allow freedom of worship drew upon theories of the natural rights of freeborn Englishmen first used by the Levelers in the 1640s (Feola-Castelucci 68, 95, 107). In the 1670s William Penn asserted the reasonableness of liberty of conscience. Hugh Barbour has described Penn's odyssey from apocalyptic prophet to liberal Quaker, a transformation originating in his attempts to merge his humanistic education and religious experiences and occasioned by his efforts to persuade the government and people to end religious intolerance ("William Penn: Model of Protestant Liberalism" 156-73).

In the *Great Case of Liberty of Conscience* (1670) Penn employed the full array of rationalist terminology. He labeled religious persecution as "unnatural and antichristian" and against the rights of "freeborn Englishmen" and as destructive to "natural affection." By contrast, Penn pictured toleration as "Christian and rational" and "prudent" and conflated as normative principles "nature" and "principle of reason." Arguing like the Stoics that all peoples can follow God, Penn described an "instinct of the deity" which is "natural" to humanity (*Peace of Europe . . . Other Writings* 154-5), a theme stressed even more in *The Christian Quaker* (1674) which prompted George Keith after he became schismatic to term Penn a deist (*Deism of William Penn*). The following statement from the conclusion of the *Great Case* illustrates the ease with which an enlightenment Quaker could merge history, the Bible, nature, and reason:

> What can be more equal, what more reasonable than liberty of conscience; so correspondent with the reverence due to God,

> and respect of the nature, practice, promotion, and rewards of the Christian religion; the sense of divine writ, the great privilege of nature, and noble principles of reason; the justice, prudence, and felicity of government. (*Peace of Europe* 186)

In the "Fruits of Solitude," Penn created a set of apothegms to serve as a guide to ethical conduct. Here again he proved a man of the enlightenment; so much so that Frederick Tolles in a perceptive essay showed the close relationship between Penn's and Benjamin Franklin's perspectives (*Quakers and the Atlantic Culture* 56-65). The general theme of Penn's maxims is that "All excess is ill" and a reliance upon nature, reason, and moderation pervades (*Peace of Europe . . . Other Writings* 32). Even when discussing religion, Penn blurs the line between God and nature. "Grace perfects, but never spoils nature" (61).[3] There is a strong agrarian bias. "The country is both the philosopher's garden and library, in which he reads and contemplates the power, wisdom and goodness of God" (42). "It were happy if we studied nature more in natural things; and acted according to nature; whose rules are, plain and most reasonable" (26). Passion "may not unfitly be termed the mob of the man, that commits a riot upon his reason" (46).

For eighteenth-century colonial Quakers Penn's writings and example legitimated their concern with political theory, government, science, Native American rights, and enlightenment thought. We do not know how many of William Penn's writings John Woolman had read. He told of reading in the history of early Friends, and his memorandum of books lent listed "No Cross, No Crown" several times and a "William Penn" item once; whether this later reference is to another tract is not clear. The most popular Penn items in colonial Pennsylvania and New Jersey were "The Rise and Progress," "Key to the Scriptures," and "Fruits of Solitude;" only the last of these emphasized enlightenment themes (Altman 71-73; PM 118; Frost "Quaker Books"). So we cannot prove, even though it seems probable, that Woolman was acquainted with Penn's more rationalistic writings.

In the "Some Considerations on the Keeping of Negroes" (PM 203), Woolman quotes from Alexander Arscott's *Serious Considerations Relating to the Present State of the Christian Religion,* one of the few eighteenth-century English Quaker theological works reprinted in Pennsylvania. Arscott (1676-1737) was an Oxford graduate, a convinced Friend, British schoolmaster, and clerk of London Yearly Meeting, who composed his three-part treatise as an attack upon deism claiming to use as evidence only Scripture but in actuality also making liberal use of the tenets of rational Christianity. The book was not directed primarily at Friends and used little distinctively Quaker language, until the last section when Arscott answered his critics who claimed that Friends were deists and/or religious fanatics.

Arscott proclaimed Jesus as a savior whose propitiatory sacrifice on the cross brought salvation. The inward experience of the Holy Spirit brought a sanctification of the will so that the Christian did good work. Arscott attacked the deists for relying exclusively on reason and undermining the Bible; yet at the same time he was an enlightenment Quaker, seeking outward evidence in miracles for the validity of Christianity; i.e. the resurrection of Jesus was a fact which "reasonable" men would accept as truth (14). He quoted John Locke and praised Bishop Tillotson (151-53, 189). Arscott wrote to convince thinking people that "the ways of God are not unreasonable" (22). God creates humans as rational creatures and appeals to their intellect through evidence as well as to their hearts through the Spirit. A rational person after considering the evidence would conclude that God used "rewards and punishments" as his "equal and reasonable foundation" for human behavior (150). A virtuous, religious, and pious life "is reasonable in itself, and tends to our comfort and happiness in this life" and salvation in next life (81). "The divine principle does not act in contradiction, or inconsistency, to right reason" (103, 127, 147). Arscott marshaled evidence so that a thinking person would conclude that Christianity was the truth.[4]

Arscott's tone was very impersonal, almost scientific, in defining terms and presenting evidence to convince readers of the outward truth of Christianity (78) and the utility of religion for "health" and "tranquility" (81). Yet he recognized that reason alone was not sufficient; the real certainty in religion came from the inward experience of the Holy Spirit. The Spirit vivified human reason into a divine reason that transformed a person's will from bare intellectual assent into a Christian life. The good fruits (i.e. ethical behavior) proved that the inward revelation was from God, not the devil or human conscience.

The quietism that plays so great a role in Woolman was at best indirect in Arscott. Like Woolman, Arscott sought the validity of an ethical action from its cause or ground: i.e. earthly or divine. The passage of Arscott's *Serious Considerations* that Woolman quoted emphasized the universality of the Sermon on the Mount as a clear ethical criterion by which to judge actions: "I take it that all men by nature are equally entitled to the equity of this rule and under the indispensable obligation to it" (PM 203). If Woolman accepted Arscott's detached impersonal method of argument, language of rationality, judicial terms, and presentation of evidence—all of which are present in his quotation—he could be seen as an enlightenment Quaker.

3

The three early Quaker antislavery writers John Hepburn, Ralph Sandiford, and Benjamin Lay appear on the basis of their tracts to be well-read. Of Hepburn we know little except that he was an immigrant and tells us that he had opposed slavery but kept silent for thirty years before he wrote in 1714. His opposition towards Quakers holding political office and derision of the Pennsylvania Assembly's decision in 1711 to pay war taxes resembled the Keithians, but, while he had heard of George Keith's antislavery pamphlet, he had not read it and did not identify himself as a Keithian. Like Sandiford and Lay, Hepburn was a man of knowledge. He mentioned earlier antislavery writings by Puritans and Quakers and he cited the historian Eusebius, the early Christian theologian Nestorius, Robert Barclay's *Apology*, and William Penn's *Key to the Scriptures.* Most unusual, Hepburn was sufficiently cognizant of the age of enlightenment to have read Archbishop Tillotson whom he praised as an "excellent man" (qtd. in Frost *Quaker Origins of Antislavery* 84). So his neglect of the language, manner of argument, and conclusions of the age of enlightenment did not come from ignorance.

The only time Hepburn invoked nature as a normative principle was when showing how the vile treatment of the slaves forced them to violate all the Ten Commandments "for the sake of *self-Preservation,* an Instinct of Nature belonging to all creatures of God" (92). Elsewhere the tone of the tract was legalistic, prophetic, and bitter: an early example of decrying the decline of American Quakers from the purity of the founders. Hepburn listed twenty arguments and twenty-two motives against slavery and included a dialogue between a Turk and a Christian, showing the incompatibility of the English opposition to Muslim slavery while keeping Negroes in bondage. The cruelty practiced by the slave masters was searingly portrayed. Masters for the sake of greed violated the Ten Commandments and the law and example of Christ. Hepburn, like Sandiford, Lay, and Woolman, saw the fruits of slavery in its evil origin. Hepburn threatened God's judgment on the slave holders of all denominations, but particularly the Quakers who risked bringing God's wrath on New Jersey and Pennsylvania.

The title page of Ralph Sandiford's *Brief Examination of the Practice of the Time* (1729) did not mention slavery but stressed "how the Devil works in the Mystery." Sandiford related slavery to its original cause, the rebellion of Satan in heaven. Slavery's "natural" root is in evil: "every Principle acts in its own Centre in Nature as the Loadstone [which] draws has Affinity with it self" (25). The European slave trade violated the "Law of Nations" by fomenting wars in Africa to gain humans who have never forfeited their "country and liberty" (38). For Sandiford nature is normally a negative term: natural man is sinful man. Only his proclamation that slavery is not compatible with "Nature, Reason, Humanity, or Morality," (49) much less with Christianity shows any impact of the enlightenment. Like Hepburn, Sandiford's categories of thought are biblical, a lamenting that he must defy the meeting to speak out and mourning that Friends have betrayed the spirit of Christ. "Vengeance is the Lord's and he will repay it in his own time"(65).[5]

Benjamin Lay's *All Slave-keepers Apostate* (1737) continues the apocalyptic tone of the two earlier pamphleteers. (Benjamin Franklin published the tract, but Franklin did not put his name on the title page.) Lay's tract showed that he was a well-read Quaker. Only Francis Daniel Pastorius in early Pennsylvania is known to have had a better library of Quaker books. Perhaps because he was self-taught, Lay provides an extensive list of authors and quotations, many of whom had little relevance to his topic of slavery. Like Hepburn, Lay was so alienated from what he perceived as Quaker hypocrisy that he had trouble concentrating upon slavery. Lay quoted in the text in Latin Ovid and Ames and cited Josephus, the Apostolic Fathers, Milton, Pierre Charron's *Of Wisdom*, histories of the Waldensians and the *Wars in England and Ireland*, Mercurius (Hermes) Trismegistus, Thomas à Kempis, Michael de Molinos, and "some of the best of the Philosophers and others, which I have by me" (125). He mentions at least twenty-four Quaker writers, including Fox's *Doctrinals*, and collected works of Dewsbury, Howgill, and Hubberthorne. Not only did Lay read the First Publishers of Truth, his tract resembles seventeenth-century Quaker apologetics, for it consists of a series of meditations (e.g., "Early this Morning it was given me to see" 136) on various topics which sound like messages spoken in a meeting for worship. The book had no central organization, but was a series of vivid images and denunciations. Like Sandiford, Lay had encountered slavery firsthand and described watching the starving blacks in the West Indies searching through garbage for food or entering a Quaker's house seeing a black hanging upside down as a punishment. Lay pictured the effects of wars in Africa and the slave trade on a black family, provided exegesis of Revelation, declaimed against the spiritual decline of Quakerism, and proclaimed judgment on Quaker ministers who owned slaves. There is only one passage in two hundred seventy-one pages which uses the language of rationalism:

> My Friends, you that practise Tyranny and Oppression for Slave-keeping is such; he that assumes in arbitrary Manner, unjustly, Dominion over his Fellow-Creature's Liberty and Property, contrary to Law, Reason, or Equity; He is a wicked sinful Tyrant, guilty of Oppression and great Iniquity: But he that trades in Slaves and the Souls of Men, does so. (43)

Notice that for Lay slavery is contrary to "Law, Reason, or Equity;" that is, these three entities have only one meaning. God's natural law from which human "Law" takes its validity requires treating people justly; "Equity" is dealing with every people in conformity to natural law standards of fairness; all men of "Reason" will arrive at the universal binding maxims of "Law" and "Equity." So in this one uncharacteristic passage Lay departed from his biblical apocalyptic tone and became an advocate of rationalism.

Twenty years later in 1759, even when he, like Lay, threatened God's judgment on an evil practice, Anthony Benezet in *Observations on the Inslaving, importing, and purchasing of Negroes* sounds different, like a man of the Age of Reason. "When a People offend . . . in a publick Capacity, the Justice of his moral Government requires that as a Nation they be punished, which is generally done by War, Famine or Pestilence" (qtd. in Frost *Quaker Origins of Antislavery* 196). The tone is impersonal. Benezet's God is not a wrathful Jehovah, but a moral judge who summons to his court "People" who collectively have done wrong and are punished through nature or war. Paraphrasing Woolman's "Some Considerations" (1754), Benezet argued that seeking first the Kingdom of God is a "short but comprehensive View of our Duty and Happiness" (194). The slave trade is "inconsistent with the Gospel of Christ, contrary to natural Justice and the common feelings of Humanity" (201). The argument that masters bring slaves not out of avarice but to convert them commits the "absurdity of recommending the Christian Religion by Injustice and disregard to the Rights and Liberty of Mankind" (201-02). Notice the enlightenment language of "natural justice" and the universal rights of all humanity.

Though he was well-read in early Quaker history, Benezet, who in some pamphlets is less author than editor, more frequently quoted travelers who had seen the slave trade in operation than early Friends. This may have resulted from his intended audience of non-Quakers, because Philadelphia Yearly Meeting in 1754 had pronounced against slavery. In *A Caution and Warning to Great Britain* (1763), a tract Woolman cited in the *Journal*, chapter ten (PM 157),[6] Benezet quoted several exemplars of rationalism: the philosopher Francis Hutchinson, the French political theorist Baron de Montesquieu, George Wallis' *System of the Laws of Scotland,* and James Foster's *Discourses on Natural Religion and Social Virtue.* All of these insist that "men and their Liberty are not either saleable or purchasable . . . This is the law of nature, which is obligatory on all men, at all times" (qtd. in Frost, *Quaker Origins of Antislavery* 225). As if to invoke the imprimatur of English Friends for rational Christianity, Benezet quotes the 1758 epistle of London Yearly Meeting "in order to supply the Demands of this most unnatural Traffick, whereby great Numbers of Mankind, free by Nature. . ." (London Yearly Meeting Epistles, in Frost 203). London Quakers again joined Christianity and nature in their 1763 epistle against the slave trade as "evidently destructive of the natural rights of mankind, who are all ransomed by one Savior, and visited by one divine light" (174).

Walter Altman, by comparing passages of Woolman's "Some Considerations" and Benezet's *Observations*, shows that the latter lifted whole sections from his friend's pamphlet; Woolman in his "Considerations on Keeping Negroes: Part II" used Benezet's technique and even quoted the same sources for firsthand accounts of the effects of the slave trade on Africans (Altman 64-65, 256-59; PM 228-30; Frost, *Quaker Origins of Antislavery* 215). The examples of Benezet and London Yearly Meeting provided Woolman as a good Quaker the option of embracing enlightenment motifs as a method of countering slavery.

4

At issue in this article is whether in tone Woolman's slavery pamphlets resemble Hepburn, Sandiford, and Lay in that the argument is essentially biblical and denunciatory or Benezet's where Scriptures and natural religion merge in an attempt to persuade. And if the latter is true, what are the implications for understanding Woolman's quietist theology? A second issue is whether the two slavery pamphlets differ in tone from the *Journal.* There is little evidence that anybody in the eighteenth century except Friends read Quaker journals; so Woolman, like Benezet, sought in antislavery tracts to influence a wider audience who would not have sympathized with Quaker quietism. Both Parts I and II of "Some Considerations" were addressed "to the Professors of Christianity of Every Denomination" (PM 198, 210). According to the *Journal,* Woolman awoke to the evil of slavery when asked as a young man of twenty-two to draw up a bill of sale; however, he wrote his first tract five years later, in 1746, just after he had returned from a religious journey to North Carolina where he experienced southern slavery first-hand. He began writing his journal in 1756, two years after Philadelphia Yearly Meeting printed Woolman's tract as the first official statement of its disapproval of slavery.

The tone of Woolman's first essay on slavery resembled the tracts of advocates of reasonable religion; that is, there is an abstract quality, which was intentional, for he chose not to be "particular." Perhaps that was the reason that the word "slavery" is never used and the title is "On the Keeping of Negroes." Sandiford and Lay told stories of their encounters with the slave system and sought to provoke a passionate response. Woolman provides "hints" (PM 199) in "general terms," a "true search," (PM 209) or an "impartial enquiry" (PM 200) to encourage the reader to engage in "close thinking" (PM 200) or "wise and judicious consideration" (PM 203). "To prevent such error let us calmly consider their [the Negroes'] circumstance" (PM 202). Unlike the earlier tracts, judgment on slave keepers is left to God; "My inclination is to persuade and entreat, and simply give hints of my way of thinking" (PM 207).[7]

The themes provided by earlier Quaker antislavery writers provide the central motifs of Woolman's two essays. Like them, Woolman did biblical exegesis to show that standard defenses of slavery ignored the letter and spirit of the Scriptures. Also like them, he traced the morality of slavery by seeking the ground of the colonists' actions in seizing the Africans, transporting them to America, and keeping them and their posterity in servitude. He concluded explicitly in "Some Considerations on Keeping Negroes, Part II," written fifteen years after his first anti-slavery tract in 1761 and after Philadelphia Yearly Meeting had encouraged emancipation, that the root or ground of slavery was avarice and its fruits destroyed morality and Christian piety for both master and slave. Even if an owner claimed to be keeping the slave for the African's well-being, instruction in knowledge, and conversion to Christianity, Woolman, who did not deny the master's sincerity, suggested that the bad example to others and effects upon his family and the slaves required emancipation.

Support for those scholars who do not see Woolman as part of the enlightenment can be found at the beginning of "Some Considerations" in a disparagement of natural affection or what we call family ties and enjoyment of the world. It was an "instinct" also belonging to each "inferior" creature which "by the ties of nature love self best." Woolman argued that for animals natural affection was a product of "self-love" which substitutes for their lack of "reason" in caring for their offspring. For humans, Christianity checked this "irregular fondness in nature" (PM 198). Unfortunately, self-love reinforced by custom and reason camouflaged the pure truth. The task Woolman set for himself in "Some Considerations" was a careful examination of self-love, custom, and reason as applied to the keeping of Negroes. His language here stood in clear opposition to the enlightenment where self-love and reason became positive principles.

Yet throughout the two antislavery tracts Woolman exalted nature and reason as positive principles. For example, the natural rights of all humans require freedom. "If I purchase a man who hath never forfeited his liberty, the natural right of freedom is in him" (PM 204). To acquire Negroes to teach them Christianity is "a contradiction to reason" (PM 208). "Forced subjection, on innocent people of full age, is inconsistent with right reason" (PM 221). The Negroes are not a "people below us in 'nature'" (PM 221).

> To suppose it right that an innocent man shall at this day be excluded from the common rules of justice, be deprived of that liberty which is the natural right of human creatures . . . is a

> supposition too gross to be admitted into the mind of any person who sincerely desires to be governed by solid principles. (PM 214)

How can an "honest man withhold from them that liberty which is the free gift of the Most High to his rational creatures?" (PM 235). In these passages both style and content are congruent with enlightenment religion. Woolman is appealing to people whose decisions are based upon intelligent weighing of evidence. Humans are "rational creatures" with "natural" rights and Christian ethical standards are in harmony with "right reason" and "nature."

Woolman's conception of nature was not romantic. His writings provided no description of the beauties of the landscape nor claimed religious inspiration from experiencing the wilderness. He was concerned about abuse of nature as expressed in overworking stage coach horses or any other creature, including human laborers. God had so designed the natural world that a moderate use provided sufficient sustenance. By the use of reason, an individual can extract normative ethical standards from nature.

For eighteenth-century advocates of rational religion, God in his wisdom had so constituted the world that following the commandments of God, being truly moral, contributed to the well-being of the person and society. Because of God's benevolence in creating a moral order, the ultimate self-interest was to do good and morality would in the long run result in happiness. Woolman wrote that the Sermon on the Mount "contains a short but comprehensive view of our duty and happiness" (PM 199). (Benezet later echoed this passage.) Man was created to labor: "A supply to nature's lawful wants, joined with a peaceful, humble mind, is the truest happiness in this life" (PM 204-05). Walking in the "path of the just, our case will be truly happy" (PM 205). True Christianity contributes to the physical as well as the spiritual health of humanity. Jesus' life showed "one uniform desire for the eternal and temporal good of mankind" (PM 208). "A life guided by wisdom from above, agreeable with justice, equity, and mercy, is throughout consistent and amiable, and truly beneficial to society" (PM 209). "It is our happiness faithfully to serve the Divine Being who made us. His perfection makes our service reasonable" (PM 221). As these quotations demonstrate, Woolman utilized the eighteenth-century theory of benevolent providence and moral self-interest as leading to happiness.

In passages evoking the major themes of rational Christianity Woolman sounded like Alexander Arscott:

> If the Christian religion be considered, both respecting its doctrines and the happy influence which it hath on the minds and manners of all real Christians, it looks reasonable to think that the miraculous manifestation thereof to the world is a kindness beyond expression. (PM 207-08)

Woolman here endorsed the good results of religion upon what he elsewhere called an "enlightened Christian" nation, stressed the miraculous origins of Christianity, included both evocative terms "happiness" and "reason," and referred to God in abstraction like a "principle" or "wisdom." There is also a kind of implicit complacency implied, as if "God's in his heaven, all is right with the world." After all, it is an eighteenth-century cliché to assume that the experience of the Holy Spirit improves "manners" which even then could have a connotation of etiquette. The "kindness" of God is far removed from the stern judging Jehovah of Benjamin Lay. This passage has a tone quite out of keeping with the radical reform impulse apparent in other antislavery tracts.

Unlike the abstract intellectualism associated with much eighteenth-century rational Christianity, Woolman's use of divine reason and happiness has a pervasive Neoplatonic quality. His was a language of mysticism, harmony, peace, and wisdom with many antecedents from Christian theologians who before Constantine began reading the New Testament with Platonist assumptions. For Woolman temporal "happiness" can be a snare which destroys "the true happiness" because the "highest delights of sense or most pleasing objects visible ought ever to be accounted infinitely inferior to that real intellectual happiness suited to man in his primitive innocence and now to be found in true renovation of mind" (PM 205). Notice that "real happiness" is "intellectual," a product of the mind. In another passage which is less Quaker quietist than Platonic, Woolman argued that true love operated "according to the agreeableness of things on principles unalterable and in themselves perfect" (PM 199). Elsewhere he blended Christian mysticism and Platonism: "For as God's love is universal, so where the mind is sufficiently influenced by it, it begets a likeness of itself and the heart is enlarged towards all men" (PM 202).

The most famous passage in all the Woolman corpus can as easily be interpreted in a Platonic sense of the overflowing of the Logos into the world and humanity as in a traditional Quaker sense as experience of the Inward Light of God:

> There is a principle which is pure, placed in the human mind, which in different places and ages hath had different names. It is, however, pure and proceeds from God. It is deep and inward, confined to no forms of religion nor excluded from any, where the heart stands in perfect sincerity. (PM 236)

For both Platonic mystic and Quaker quietist the experience of God required escape from the cumber of the material world, an ascetic withdrawal so as to participate in the pure "Divine Reason." Woolman's particular gift was to show in his life and writings how to keep a balance between his thirst for inward knowledge, appreciation of outward nature, and quest to create a moral social order.

In the antislavery essays the final effect of Woolman's invocation of mysticism, scripture, divine reason, nature, and happiness was not, unlike many contemporary rational Christians, a complacent acceptance of the status quo; a "Whatever is, is right" and "All evil, [is] good misunderstood." Instead, Woolman used each of these as tools or normative criteria to examine the causes and effects of slavery and led the reader to conclude that forced servitude is contrary to natural reason, subverts the design of God in nature, and opposes the revealed will of God contained in Old and New Testaments. Those readers seeking a pure motion of God will conclude on a basis of rational intelligence and inward prayer that because slavery is grounded in avarice and indulgence originating in excessive self-love, it results in an oppression destroying the religious impulses of the owner and his family and undermining the Negroes' conversion and instruction in civilization.

5

On the basis of the two antislavery treatises, one could easily conclude that Woolman was an enlightenment Quaker. Yet a reading of the *Journal* could easily lead to the opposite conclusion. To be sure, the Platonic emphasis appeared: "as the mind was moved on an inward principle to love God as an invisible, incomprehensible being, on the same principle it was moved to love him in all his manifestations in the visible world" (PM 28). Elsewhere the consistent themes of rational religion are absent. For example, when Woolman bore his testimony against a magician, an opponent "endeavoured by arguments to show the reasonableness of their proceedings therein" (PM 138). Reason was linked with cowardice as in "dark and timorous reasonings." In the *Journal* "reason" (PM 86), "natural will" (PM 176), and "natural part" (PM 112) were consistently used as negative terms and distinguished from the pure feeling of love which comes from God. Woolman's spiritual autobiography contained no emphasis upon the reasonableness of following Christ, no argument from the natural law or God's design of creation, no emphasis upon temporal happiness as resulting from moral action. There are only a few positive invocations of natural laws and these all occur in *Journal* chapter four where Woolman recounted his dialogues with those who defended slavery. Here again, using the arguments from his tracts, Woolman insisted that "liberty was the natural right of all men equally" (PM 61) and claimed that using a weak argument was "unreasonable" (PM 63). In an epistle to Friends in North Carolina, he insisted "To rational creatures bondage is uneasy" (PM 69).

The overall impression gained from reading the *Journal* is that Woolman was either not influenced by or reacting against enlightenment Christianity. And the discrepancy is not only between the slavery essays and the *Journal*. There is considerable emphasis upon reason and nature and a moderate use of creation in keeping with God's design for happiness in the "Plea for the Poor," but almost none of these themes of enlightenment Christianity in "Considerations on the True Harmony of Mankind," and the writings that Amelia Gummere labels "An Epistle" and "Last Essays."[8]

Woolman's inconsistent use of enlightenment religion suggests that he tailored his vocabulary to fit his audience, his genre, and his purpose in writing. So when recounting his spiritual journeys' impact on his religious life and as a traveling Quaker minister, Woolman used traditional language of the Bible, Christian thought, Quakerism, and a mysticism tinged with Platonism—all of which were acceptable in the meeting and to the committees of weighty Friends who edited all publications. Woolman addressed the *Journal* to Friends. Even so, the committees suppressed Woolman's account of dreams and visions, phenomena anathema to the enlightenment rationality. However, when the audience was both Friends and the general community and the topic concerned the right use of the visible creation, then Woolman, like Benezet, willingly used the concepts of rational Christianity. After all, Robert Barclay's *Apology*, a book Woolman owned and which established the parameters of Quaker orthodoxy in the eighteenth century, distinguished between the necessary and right use of reason in outward matters while decrying reason's applicability to spiritual subjects (Barclay, Prop. II 4, Prop. V and VI xvi).

Woolman's antislavery writings are distinguishable from those of Hepburn, Sandiford, and Lay because unlike them he broadened the base of the argument to include reason, natural law, and innate liberty and appeared not as a prophet but a persuader. Yet Woolman was less dependent on and committed to natural right and enlightenment religion than was Anthony Benezet. Moreover, Woolman's application of natural law shows little of the sophisticated analysis he brought to the experience of the light of God, economic inequality, and slavery.

While I am confident that Woolman consciously applied reason and natural law as instruments for reform, it seems unlikely that he was aware of the subtle influence of a rationalistic Neoplatonic Christianity upon his Quaker religious ideas and vocabulary. So my conclusion is that those readers who have found enlightenment themes in Woolman rely on the antislavery essays and others who downplay rational religion's significance emphasize the *Journal.* So in a sense, both interpretations are right and considering them together makes Woolman an even more fascinating writer, aware of the power and wary of the seductiveness of enlightenment Christianity.

NOTES

[1] Gummere was not specific on what she meant by "conservative." I suspect she meant strict in discipline and unwilling to adopt the politically astute and cosmopolitan attitudes more characteristic of Philadelphia's merchμant Friends. Franklin in 1762 published Woolman's "Considerations on Keeping Negroes, Part II."

[2] A good introduction is Mark Wallace, "The European Enlightenment," in S*pirituality of the Ancient Quest.* For more detail see Gerald Cragg, *The Church and the Age of Reason 1648-1789* and Henry May, *The Enlightenment in America.*

[3].The phrase "Grace perfects but never spoils nature" is a quotation from Thomas Aquinas and Penn may have learned it as a schoolboy at Saumur. I am indebted to Hugh Barbour for this insight.

[4]In 1734 Burlington Monthly Meeting ordered a general distribution of books of English Quakers Benjamin Holmes and Alexander Arscott. I am indebted to Jean Soderlund for this information.

[5] Sandiford's invoking against slavery the law of nations and natural law countered a just war tradition defending slavery dating from Aristotle and utilized by Catholic theologians like Francisco Suarez (1548-1617).

[6] In "Considerations on Keeping Negroes, Part II" (PM 224), Woolman also referred to Michel Adanson's *Voyage to Senegal*... (London, 1759), one of the sources on the history of the slave trade used by Benezet in *A Caution and Warning to Great Britain* (215). It is assumed that Woolman took the reference from Benezet who cites it first.

[7] No scholar has addressed the issue of how Woolman learned to write and whether, like Franklin who used the *Spectator,* he relied upon English models. The sermons of Bishop Tillotson, like other esteemed eighteenth-century stylists, relied upon the "close relation between language, reason, and lucidity" (Brown 32). Prose writers relied upon the "cool and persuasive power of reason, the ideal of detached observation and objectivity" (Brown 39). See also Battestin's *Henry Fielding: A Life.*

[8]In his last unpublished writing on slavery, Woolman did not use enlightenment language. Several explanations are possible: (1) he saw no need since others were using the natural rights in antislavery tracts; (2) he saw more clearly the dangers of such language, particularly as applied in a revolutionary context; (3) the audience was only Quaker; (4) the essay was unfinished.

WORKS CITED

Altman, Walter F. "John Woolman's Reading." Ph.D. diss. Florida State University, 1957.

Arscott, Alexander. *Some Considerations Relating to the Present State of the Christian Religion, Wherein the Nature, End, and Design of Christianity, as well as the Principal Evidence . . . In Three Parts.* 3rd ed. London, England: Phillips, 1779.

Barbour, Hugh. "William Penn: Model of Protestant Liberalism." *Church History* 48 (1979): 156-173.

—, ed. *William Penn on Religion and Ethics: The Emergence of Liberal Quakerism. Studies in American Religion.* 2 vols. Lewiston, NY: Mellon, 1991.

—, et al. *Quaker Crosscurrents.* Syracuse, NY: Syracuse University Press, 1995.

— and J. W. Frost. *The Quakers.* 2nd ed. Richmond, IN: Friends United Press, 1988.

Barclay, Robert. *Apology for the True Christian Divinity.* London, 1678.

Battestin, Martin C. *Henry Fielding: A Life.* London, England: Routledge, 1989.

—. *The Moral Basis of Fielding's Art: A Study of Joseph Andrews.* Middletown, CT: Wesleyan, 1959.

Benezet, Anthony. *A Caution and Warning to Great Britain and Her Colonies.* 1766. Ed. J. W. Frost. *The Quaker Origins of Antislavery.* Norwood, PA: Norwood, 1980.

—. *A First Book for Children.* Philadelphia, PA: Crukshank, 1778.

—. *Observations on the Inslaving, importing, and purchasing of Negroes.* Norwood, PA: Norwood, 1980. *The Quaker Origins of Antislavery.* 1759. Ed. J. W. Frost. Norwood, PA: Norwood, 1980.

Boroughs, Philip L. "John Woolman (1720-1772): Spirituality and Social Transformation in Colonial America." Ph.D. diss. Graduate Theological Union, 1989.

Brown, D. D. "Tillotson's Revisions and Dryden's Talent for English Prose." *Review of English Studies* 12 (1961): 32- 39.

Cady, Edwin. *John Woolman.* New York, NY: Twayne, 1965.

Cragg, Gerald. *The Church and the Age of Reason 1648-1789.* United Kingdom: Penguin, 1960.

Everard, John. "The Plus Ultra of the Creatures." *Gospel Treasurers, Or the Holiness of All Unvailing.* 1653. Germantown, PA: Sower, 1757.

Feola-Castelucci, Maryann. *George Bishop: Seventeenth-Century Soldier Turned Quaker.* York, England: Sessions, 1966.

Frost, J. W. "Quaker Books in Colonial Pennsylvania." *Quaker History* 80 (Spring 1991): 1-23.

—. *The Quaker Family in Colonial America: A Portrait of the Society of Friends.* New York, NY: St. Martin's Press, 1973.

—.ed. *The Quaker Origins of Antislavery.* Norwood, PA: Norwood, 1980.

Heller, Michael A. "Soft Persuasion: A Rhetorical Analysis of John Woolman's Essays and *Journal.*" Ph.D. diss. Arizona State University, 1989.

Hepburn, John. *The American Defense of the Christian Golden Rule, or An Essay to Prove the Unlawfulness of making Slaves of Men.* 1715. Ed. J. W. Frost. *The Quaker Origins of Antislavery.* Norwood, PA: Norwood, 1980.

Keith, George. *The Deism of William Penn.* London, England, 1699.

Lay, Benjamin. *All Slave-keepers That keep the Innocent in Bondage, Apostate.* 1737. New York, NY: Arno, 1969.

Locke, John. *The Reasonableness of Christianity.* Ed. I. T. Ramsey. Library of Modern Religious Thought. Stanford, CA: Stanford University Press, 1967.

——.*Some Thoughts Concerning Education.* Ed. S. Yolton. New York, NY: Oxford University Press, 1989.

London Yearly Meeting, Religious Society of Friends. Epistles 1758, 1763. Ed. J. W. Frost. *The Quaker Origins of Antislavery.* Norwood, PA: Norwood, 1980.

May, Henry. *The Enlightenment in America.* New York, NY: Oxford University Press, 1976.

Penn, William. *Peace of Europe, Fruits of Solitude and Other Writings.* Ed. Edwin B. Bronner. Vermont: Everyman, 1993.

Rosenblatt, Paul. *John Woolman.* New York, NY: Twayne, 1969.

Sandiford, Ralph. *A Brief Examination of the Practice of the Times, By the Foregoing and the Present Dispensation. . . .* 1729. New York, NY: Arno, 1969.

Sloan, Douglas. *The Scottish Enlightenment and the American College Ideal.* New York, NY: Teachers College, Columbia, 1971.

Stoneburner, John. "Henry More and Anne Conway." P*erspectives on the Seventeenth Century World of Viscountess Anne Conway. Guilford Review* 23 (Spring 1986): 24-35.

Stromberg, Roland. *Religious Liberalism in Eighteenth-Century England.* Oxford, United Kingdom: Oxford University Press, 1954.

Tolles, Frederick. "Introduction." *The Journal of John Woolman.* Ithaca, NY: Cornell, 1960.

——.*Meeting House and Counting House.* Chapel Hill, NC: University of North Carolina Press, 1948.

——.*Quakers and the Atlantic Culture.* New York, NY: Macmillan, 1960.

Tullock, John. *Rational Theology and Christian Philosophy in England.* Vol. 2. Edinburgh, Scotland: Blackwood, 1884.

Wallace, Mark. "The European Enlightenment." *Spirituality of the Ancient Quest.* Ed. Van Heser. Philadelphia, PA: Crossroads, 1996.

Whittier, John G. "Introduction." *Journal of John Woolman.* Boston, MA: James Osgood, 1871.

Woolman, John. *A First Book for Children.* Philadelphia, PA: Crukshank, n.d. [1774?]

——.*The Journal and Major Essays of John Woolman.* Ed. Phillips P. Moulton. 1971. Richmond, IN: Friends United Press, 1989.

10

On Woolman's "Conversations," Ethics, and Economics

Gerald W. Sazama

THIS PAPER IS AN EXPLORATION of John Woolman's ethics and economics as found in his short essay "Conversations on the True Harmony of Mankind and How It May Be Promoted" (edited by Sterling Olmsted; hereafter referred to as "Conversations"), and a comparison of Woolman's insights with the perspectives of traditional economics as taught in American higher education today.[1] The two great commandments permeate John Woolman's ethics and economics:

> You shall love the Lord your God with all your heart, with all your soul, and with all your mind. This is the great and first commandment. And the second is lit it, you shall love your neighbor as yourself. On these two commandments depend all the law and the prophets. (Matt. 22:37-40)

Quotations from Woolman's "Conversations" are used to show how his ethics and economics are based on these two great commandments. Woolman has a radical Christian view of economics. He has a basic faith that God will provide for all of our wants, if we operate by the two great commandments. According to Woolman, confusion, oppression, harm to the environment, and war all exist because of our failure to live the two great commandments. Woolman engaged in social change that was nonviolent, recognizing Christ within the oppressor, and reaching for that light within by means of courageous and direct dialogue with the oppressor. In contrast, traditional economics is based upon a secular, scientific and rationalistic view of reality, and frequently it views the motives for human behavior as hedonistic and individualistic. For traditional economics, optimum economic outputs is an end in itself, and that end results from the rational use of inputs.

Woolman wrote "Conversations" during the last year of his life, in 1772. While Woolman's "A Plea for the Poor," which was possibly written in 1763, is wider in scope than the shorter essay "Conversations," there is substantial overlap in the concerns Woolman discusses in both essays.[2] However, the style of "Conversations" is much lighter than that of "A Plea for the Poor." Essentially "Conversations" is the supposed reporting of two conversations, one between "Rich" and "Laborer" and the second between "Landholder" and "Laborer." In his search for social justice, Woolman had frequent conversations with prosperous members of the Quaker community, especially on the question of slave holding (Introduction, PM 7-12). Thus, through the dialogue of the laborer we can hear John Woolman challenging the consciences of the rich man and the landowner to be moral in their economic affairs so as to contribute their part to a "higher benefit" for themselves, their families, their employees and tenants, society at large, and the physical environment.

Woolman's Ethics and Economics

Woolman's ethics flow from the two great commandments. His economic concepts flow from his ethics. We find the basis for Woolman's ethics from the following quotation from "Conversations":

> While we love God with all our hearts, and love not ourselves in a love different from that which we feel towards mankind universally, so long the way remains open for that life which is the light of men, to operate in us, and lead us forward in all concerns necessary for us. (15)

In short, following the two great commandments opens us up to the light, and all necessary for us. This is an ethics based in a search for God. Actions toward ourselves and others should be consistent with the inner light. Woolman does not propose a system of ethics based solely on human intellect or feelings, nor is his ethics based on complex abstract philosophical principles. Rather, it is based on a seeking of God's love.

Woolman then considers the implications of following or not following this standard.

> The Love of Christ, which preserves the faithful in purity of heart, puts men into a motion which works harmoniously. . . .

> While we keep to this Standard we are content with a little, but in the love on money and outward greatness the wants of one person may require as much labor to supply them, as would supply ten whose wants extend no further than those things which our heavenly Father knoweth that we have need of. . . .
>
> In the love of money and outward greatness, the mind is perplexed with selfish devices: how to keep! how to defend, from the crafty designs of the proud and envious! and from the desperate attempts of the oppressed!
>
> Now in the bottom of these devices there is unquietness, for where gold or treasures are gathered, and not in that wisdom which is pure and peaceable, the mind in this state is left naked. (15, 16)

In other words, following the two great commandments results in simplicity, harmony, wisdom, and an inner peace. Not following these precepts results in unnecessary effort, being involved with selfish defenses against the envious and the oppressed, and being perplexed.

The concluding sentences of "Conversations" further develop these results:

> The robe of God's righteousness is a Covering, which to them who are Sanctified in Christ Jesus, is an abundant recompense for the loss of that life, with all its treasures, which stood in the wisdom of this world. Under this robe we feel that all things work together for out good; that we have no cause to promote but the cause of pure Universal Love; and here all our cares Center in a humble trust in him who is Omnipotent. (16)

In other words, being sanctified in Christ more than makes up for any loss of worldly treasures. Also, Woolman argues that we find that all things work together for our good when we promote the cause of Universal Love and we trust in God.

Woolman does not develop a formal systematic concept of economics in his "Conversations," but he does raise issues concerning the economy he observed in America of his day, and these can provide insights into our contemporary economy. "Conversations" was written in 1772, a few years before the American Revolutionary War. It was the time of the emergence of capitalism on the North American continent. Internal markets were developing and international trade was increasing. My presentation of Woolman's economic observations is organized around the contemporary economic concepts of: 1) labor, 2) capital and land, 3) markets, both national and international, and 4) the distribution of income and a theory of social change.

First to address labor, throughout "Conversations," Woolman emphasizes the dignity of honest work (8). Although he does not explicitly discuss abstract concepts, like a just wage, surplus, or alienation, he refers frequently to the importance of the laborer's receiving equitable pay (8), to receiving the fruits of his or her labor sufficient for a simple but adequate living for self and family (9), and of the laborer's not being pushed to hurry and to weariness in accomplishing this end (8).

Woolman does say that the fruits of the laborer's work should not be used to satisfy the vanities of the rich (7). He also says that many employments have been invented to gratify the wandering desires of those who have power to turn money into channels of vanity. Such employments are often distressing to the minds of the sincere-hearted people occupied by satisfying such vanities, and these activities have a tendency to weaken in these workers the bands that unite souls in holy fellowship with Jesus Christ that Woolman holds so dear.

> . . . if I put forth my strength in any employ which I know is to support pride, I feel it hath a tendency to weaken those bands which through the infinite mercies of God, I have felt at times to bind and unite my Soul in a holy fellowship with the Father and with his Son Jesus Christ. (8, 9)

It seems to me that Woolman believes that work should be a creative and fulfilling experience in which we produce the necessities for a healthy life. Labor activity should complement, not interfere with the workers unity with God. I must confess that I find in my own work that this goal is hard to realize. It is easy for me to do work to get attention, or to achieve consumption goals, rather than to practice "right livelihood" which develops my person, and places me in harmony with others, nature, and God.

In "Conversations" Woolman does not question private ownership of capital or land; however, he gives many guidelines for owners. He is aware of markets for capital, and of technological change, but he does not discuss capital in the modern economics sense of accumulation of a productive resource that embodies technological change. Mostly, he pays attention to the life-styles of the rich and their accumulative motives, and the impact of this behavior on them, their families, and society. In contemporary terms "the rich" could be members of the owning class, or it could be those who emphasize "the bottom line" over other goals, or those who emphasize the accumulation of things or economic power.

Guidelines for the actions of the rich can be found throughout "Conversations." The "Conversations" are peppered with Woolman's advice. On many occasions Woolman urges that the owner of capital charge a just or fair rate of interest (e.g., 5, 9). Woolman cautions about the bad consequences of the abuse of economic power for the owners of capital themselves, and for their families and society at large. Woolman adds that:

> Gold, where the value fixed thereon is agreed to appears to be attended with a certain degree of power, and where men get much of this power, their hearts are many times in danger of being lifted up above their brethren, and of being estranged from that meekness and tender feeling of the state of the poor, which accompanies the faithful followers of Christ. (13)

According to Woolman, the hearts of the rich are often ensnared by pride and vain desires for delicacies and luxury. Gratification can often lead to a growing exaltation of mind and an imagined superiority. Thus many of them may become separated from true brotherly love and charity (13). In short, their condition closes them off from fulfilling the second great commandment.

With regard to the first great commandment, to love God, Woolman quotes the Good Shepherd from the Bible, "Lay not up for yourselves treasures here on Earth" (13). Later he states that if we trust in humanity, make our flesh our total center, and are estranged from that purified state in which the mind relies on God, we are on the way toward an increase in confusion. This state, even among much gold and riches, is less settled than that of a faithful follower of the lowly Jesus (16).

Woolman also invokes the Quaker goal of a simple life. He suggests to the rich that if their minds were reconciled to that simplicity mentioned by the Apostle, to wit, the simplicity that there is in Christ, they might save a good deal of expenditures on luxuries. By this saving they might help the poor in several ways.

> Your example in a plain life might encourage other rich families in this simple way of living, who, by abating their expenses, might the easier abate the rent of their lands, and their tenants, having farms on easier terms, would have less plea for Shortening the wages of the poor in raising the price of grain than they now have. (7)

Besides providing guidelines to the rich, Woolman considers the impact of their accumulation both on their family and on society. He declares that where people love money, and their hearts are ensnared with imaginary greatness, the disease frequently spreads to their children, who often have wants of the same kind in a much larger degree when they grow up (14). As for society, Woolman asserts that when the rich do not stand upright in the sight of God, but go forth in a way contrary to pure wisdom, it tends to disorder the affairs of society (9). He frequently discusses the effects of the love of money on the distribution of income, the environment, and that people with gold often hire armies, which leads to war (16).

Woolman does not clearly distinguish land and capital as separate factors of production, as is common in modern economics. Rather, he speaks of ownership, the rich, and landholders (from context, large landholders), frequently interchangeably. His guidelines for the landholder are the same as for the rich, or owners of large amounts of capital. However, for the landholder Woolman adds the following words of caution. The consequence of a tenant having to pay too much interest can be too much tilling of the soil, which robs the earth of its natural fertility, and reduces the future output from it (6). Concerning animals: "I have seen poor creatures in distress, for want of good Shelter and plentiful feeding, when it did not appear in the power of their owners to do much better for them, being Straightened in answering the demands of the wealthy" (7). From these observations we see that Woolman had a clear understanding of the links between how we conduct our economic affairs, and our respect for other living creatures and the physical environment. Woolman's insights are as useful and important today as they were in his own time for those concerned with a healthy environment.

While Woolman wrote on the functioning of both national and international markets, he does not work with the clear distinction between demand and supply found in contemporary economics. Rather, for both Woolman and classical economics, which was just emerging in his time, prices are primarily cost driven. Also, Woolman focuses on the immediate practical consequences of the functioning of markets rather than trying to provide a theoretical understanding of how markets function. Accordingly, in discussing regional markets Woolman understands how high interest rates increase the price of grain, meat, and cheese, and the wage of a laborer (5).

Further, Woolman understands the functioning of labor markets under capitalism. For example, Woolman admonishes the landholder for taking advantage of the fact that there were more young men without land at Woolman's time than in earlier colonial periods, that is, there was a relative excess supply of workers. As a result of the competition for jobs from this excess supply of laborers, the landholder paid the laborer less grain, even though an hour of labor time could produce more grain because the fields were already cleared (11).

Here we find Woolman challenging the distributional consequences of a competitive labor market by appealing to a standard of fairness. For a modern economist this becomes a complex issue, because it is at the core of the debate between the medieval concepts of a "just wage" and a "just price" and the increase in total welfare resulting from the "invisible hand" of competitive markets as originally argued by Adam Smith. "Just" wages and prices are always appropriate, but they are especially useful in stable economies. On the other hand, in a dynamic economy rigidly imposed prices and wages could slow change. For example, the lack of opportunities and low wages for farm labor on the East coast was an important incentive to the westward colonization that was occurring at Woolman's time. This debate between balancing fairness and unregulated markets is at the heart of the current debate on the appropriate level for a minimum wage.

With international markets, Woolman sees the increase of income from grain exports causing an increase in the domestic price of grain. This in turn resulted in tradesmen charging more for their wares. These phenomena meant a lower standard of living for the laborer (5, 6). Woolman also frowns on the increase in international trade as a means for landholders to gratify themselves and their families with expensive delicacies. He counsels, "Of things which to me appear convenient, we through divine favor have plenty in our own land" (11). On the other hand, he accepts the validity of international trade: "I believe some trade abroad might be of advantage to us and to some with whom we trade, if that Spirit which leads into error had no part in directing this trade" (12). Thus, we see that Woolman is not opposed to the functioning of markets. Rather, he constantly asks us to evaluate our actions in these markets, and the outcomes of these markets, by some higher moral standard, by our Inner Light.

In some sense all of "Conversations" is about distribution of income and a theory of social change. Woolman does not discuss the subject in any neoclassical sense of systematic payments to factors of production; his concern is equity. According to Woolman, all persons should have the means to raise the necessities of life, with work that is healthy, acceptable to the minds of honest people, and not oppressive. "Laboring to raise the necessaries of life is in itself an honest labor, and the more men employed in honest employments the better" (8). Also, because Woolman uses the standards of love of God and love of neighbor for all economic transactions, he urges the rich to live comfortably with less interest income, which if rightly attained will favor laboring people in obtaining a life "consistent with pure wisdom" (5).

In "Conversations," Woolman views the various parts of society as members in a person's body.

> The members in society appear to me like the members in a man's body, which only moves regular while the motion proceeds from the head. In fits people sometimes have convulsive motions, which though strong, are only mainfestations of disorder. (14)

As for society, the love of money is viewed as the root of evil; it disrupts the true harmony of society (15). Rather than looking for fulfillment in money, Woolman calls for trust in our blessed Redeemer, who is always able to supply our wants, even by miracles when that is consistent with infinite wisdom (13).

Woolman is not naive about economic affairs. He had practical business experience, first he tended a retail shop for the owner, and then he ran his own successful tailor shop (Introduction, PM 4). Based on his experience, Woolman observes and comments on the existence of classes, for example, the rich, landholder, tradesman, and laborer. He does not hold that class harmony existed in his society; to the contrary, on several occasions in this short piece he writes of oppression and oppressors

(8, 14). He recognizes the possibility of violent reactions to oppression when he writes, "In the love of money and outward greatness, the mind is perplexed with selfish devices: how to keep! how to defend . . . from the desperate attempts of the oppressed" (16).

Woolman's proposal for social change is a radical Christian one. In his dialogue with the rich and the landholder he constantly sees the Light, Christ within them. He uses such phrases as "My loving friend and neighbor! . . . let us patiently hear each other, and endeavor to love as brethren" (6). Also, Woolman gives the rich the benefit of the doubt, saying that the intent might have been only to get riches for himself and the hardships of the oppressed may remain unnoticed by him (14, 15). This does not mean that Woolman is not challenging, firm, and direct: "In this state we are dead, and our life is hid with Christ in God. Dead to the love of money. Dead to worldly honor. . ." (16).

Woolman and Traditional Economics

Woolman wrote "Conversations" in 1772, and contemporary traditional economics was crystallized as a separate discipline in Adam Smith's *The Wealth of Nations* in 1776. Smith gave form to the classical school of economics, which sought to understand the emergence of industrial capitalism from feudalism and mercantilism, and to provide a basis for policies that would further that process. By 1860 the market economy and industrial capitalism became the dominant form of economic organization, especially in Great Britain and America. After this point economics reflects the eventual dominance of the industrial revolution and the full transition to capitalism through a shift in focus from classical economics to what is now labeled neoclassical economics. Neoclassical economics is still the dominant economic paradigm in the world. However, as early as the 1820s, starting with the Utopian socialists, a series of alternative economic paradigms were also developed. My objective in this second section of the paper is to explore briefly the ethical basis, and essential concepts of these three forms of economics (classical, neoclassical, and alternative) in order to contrast them with Woolman's approach.

Adam Smith is the principal writer of classical economics. In general, his theological and ethical starting point is representative of the whole school of classical economics.[3] He is a product of the Enlightenment, which held that knowledge was accessible through observation and the application of human reason. In contrast Woolman emphasizes the Inner Light of Christ's revealing to us what we need to know in order to be in harmony with Him and others (16). At the same time Woolman was a keen and practical observer reporting on many details and relationships in the economy (11-13).

Smith and many of his contemporaries were deists, who saw the world as the design of the Deity, which at most levels was a perfectly harmonious system reflecting the perfection of its designer. The analogy of God as watchmaker and the world as an independently functioning watch is often used to summarize the deist's perspective on reality. This deist view of God is in stark contrast to Woolman's faith in a loving God who intervenes in the world on our behalf, "even by miracles when that is consistent with infinite wisdom" (13).

The Theory of Moral Sentiments contains Smith's system of ethics: to be moral an act must be in harmony with the design; to be moral, an act must be in accordance with the intentions of the Deity. In judging one's own act as well as those of others, one must act as an impartial spectator who knows, unbiased by perspective, that the balance of the actor's true sentiments are in harmony with the design (Evensky 451-452). Thus, while Smith sees ethics as based upon the criteria of a rational impartial spectator, Woolman sees ethics as grounded in the two great commandments.

Smith's theological and ethical starting points become articulated into concrete guidelines for economic and government policy in *The Wealth of Nations.* At the core is the theory of the invisible hand: fallen humans, human frailty, leads to distortions in the Deity's design in human social systems, including the economy. However, according to Smith, if everyone follows his or her self-interest under a system of natural liberty, of competition, the result is an invisible hand that minimizes negative social behavior, and results in increasing wealth for the nation and optimal social good. This theory is shown in Smith's discussion of one who employs capital:

> He intends only his own security; and by directing that industry in such a manner as its produce may be of the greatest value, he intends only his own gain, and hi is in this, as in many cases,

> led by an invisible hand to promote an end which was no part of his intention. (Smith 456)

In contrast, Woolman appeals to the goodness in human beings, to Christ within. He asks the rich to respond in love to their fellow human beings. Smith sees humans from a fall-redemption perspective. Smith believes that although people have good characteristics, they also are inherently selfish. Because of his deist perspective, Smith believes that only the invisible hand of competition can keep this selfishness in check.

Whereas, Woolman speaks of the dignity and creativity of work; indeed, balanced work is integral to our coming into unity with God, Smith adjudges people as indolent, seeking to gain from the least effort. According to Smith, work is a laying aside of some portion of ease, liberty, and happiness (Rosenberg 23; Sowell 6, 10).

Woolman is a careful empiricist who observes economic realty in detail, but he also has a profound sense of the mystical. As an example of the empiricist:

> In a time of plenty when great quantities of grain and flour are sent to distant parts, a poor man who labors for hire to get bread for his family, must now do more labor for a bushel of rye than was required for that quantity thirty years past. . . . (13)

And as an example of the mystic:

> This I have learned through the precious operation of divine love, and ardently desire both for myself, and for all who have tasted of it, that nothing may be able to Separate us from it. (9)

On the other hand, Smith was more a produst of a Newtonian system of thought that separated spirit and matter, the latter being the object of scientific investigation

Another stark contrast between Smith's and Woolman's economics is their views on capital accumulation. Woolman constantly counsels the rich and landholder to live simple lives and accumulate no more than is necessary toward that end. While for Smith individual capital accumulation contributes to the general wealth of nations. Of course, a literal application of Woolman's suggestion would result in no private accumulation of capital, which has been so necessary to economic growth and social change under capitalism. Socialist have claimed that capital accumulation without individual greed is possible, if productive capital were owned collectively by a democratic state or cooperatively by the workers. However, such a response accepts the importance of the material goods resulting from economic growth and modern technology. Here Woolman seems to caution us not to invest too much effort in the pursuit of economic goods, even if it were done collectively or cooperatively. This concern of Woolman is partially echoed in the contemporary discussions on the "limits to growth" and "sustainable growth" within the environmental movement.

By the middle of the nineteenth century there was a fundamental shift in the dominant economic paradigm from classical to neoclassical economics. The historical roots for this shift are found in the emergence of industrial capitalism as the principal form of economic organization. With the emergence of industrial capitalism as the dominant economic system, many economists began to search for policies that would increase the system's efficiency, especially for its immediate beneficiaries, and to develop justifications for maintaining it as the dominant system. In my view, these policies and justifications are part of neoclassical economic theory.

Preceding and accompanying these developments in economics were changes in philosophy and the increasing secularization of society. First, there occurred the separation of religion and science, the further separation of the mystical and the material.[4] For traditional economics in its early or classical stages, this meant the invisible-hand theory based on deism. Full secularization began with social Darwinism, whereby competitive behavior filters out the unfit. The complete rupture with religious thought occurred when secular humanism, hedonism, and liberal individualism become the philosophical and ethical foundations of neoclassical economics (Weisskopf 33).

There are many consequences for modern economics from this shift in philosophical base. Virtually every introductory economics textbook throughout the capitalist world of the twentieth century contains a section on how economics is separated into positive and normative economics. Positive economics is economic science, and being scientific it is objective, factual, merely descriptive, and therefore value free. Implicitly, it is not to be questioned. On the other hand, normative economics is the application of scientific economics to policy; consequently, it involves value judgments, ethical considerations that are said to make it subjective and relativistic. According to this distinction, the economist as scientist is objective. Only when the economist moves into a policy area or into applied economics—acts in a political way as any other member of the community might—is he or she to be concerned with ethics. At that point positive economics, that is, economic science has been left behind. This methodological dichotomy between positive and normative economics also is accompanied by a fairly strong demarcation of economic science from sociology and political science, which further isolates neoclassical economics from robust examination of human conditions.

In neoclassical economics the end of economic activity is reduced to the satisfaction of individual preferences based on desires and tastes, mostly directed toward material comforts. Whatever subjective goal is pursued in a rational, efficient systematic fashion is assumed to be given from outside the economic system, and therefore not to be questioned by "objective economic science." Formal, value-free rationality becomes the philosophy of science of economics (Weisskopf 38). How far we have traveled from the ethics and economics of Woolman, or even of Smith!

Additional consequences of the philosophical basis of neoclassical economics is its treatment of work, accumulation, and competitiveness. Work is looked upon as painful, or at least as a loss of leisure. We undertake work to gain income, to have the pleasure of consumption thereby allowed. This may be an accurate description of much work in our current economy, and of the ways in which we frequently seek fulfillment, but it stands in stark contrast to Woolman's notion of balanced, nonalienating work as a fulfilling, creative activity in and of itself. Under neoclassical economics, unbridled accumulation is implicitly approved because capital increases productivity and furnishes more goods for consumption. Again this is very different from Woolman's suggestion to the rich that excessive accumulation of capital may result in estrangement from God and neighbor. The neoclassical model also makes competition central to its analysis; cooperation is virtually ignored, or at best is only an unintended, occasional outcome of the competitive forces. Meanwhile, we see how Woolman urges true brotherly love and charity. Thus, in area after area we find substantial differences between neoclassical economics and Woolman's ethics and economics.

In many ways the ethics of neoclassical economics is a reflection of the values of a capitalist society at large. In another sense the theory of neoclassical economics takes on a life of its own; it becomes an ideology that sustains and reinforces the existing economic system.

Besides the mainstream classical and then neoclassical economics, there are several alternative, competing economic paradigms. These are socialism in its Utopian and Marxist versions, institutionalism, anarchism and the "Small is Beautiful" perspective, and post-Keynesianism.

None of the adherents of these alternative economic schools of thought, except perhaps some of the post-Keynesians, make the neoclassical distinction between positive and normative economics. They see themselves as political economists, and hence they readily admit that they use value assumptions and have an implicit ethical base, even if they might not spend much effort articulating or developing this ethical base.

Virtually all adherents of the alternative economic theories accept some form of secular humanism as the ethical base for at least their economic analysis, and they tend to accept an agnostic form of scientific rationalism as the epistemological basis for their theories. There also is widespread acceptance, with some qualifications, of economic growth of goods and services as an appropriate end of economic activity in and of itself. This occasions an attitude quite unlike the attitude associated with Woolman's spiritually centered approach.

There are some parallels between socialist economics and Woolman's economics. Woolman like the socialists places strong emphasis on the distribution of income, wealth, and economic power. Also like the socialists, Woolman speaks of economic classes, but with such terms as rich, landholder, and laborer, rather than capitalist and proletariat. Indeed, in the late 1890s the Fabian socialists in England printed 10,000 copies of a large portion of Woolman's "A Plea for the Poor" as one of their organizing documents (Introduction, PM 14). However, unlike most of the socialists, for Woolman the source of social change is the spiritual center of individual members of society through openings to the Inner Light. On the other hand most socialists see social change occurring as a result of political struggle to put in place new economic rules and institutions for society as a whole.

There also are important similarities between Woolman's economics as found in his "Conversations" and liberation theology. Liberation theology is the blending of Marxist economic thought and Christian based Bible studies, especially in Latin America during the 1960s and the

1970s. For both liberation theology and Woolman, social justice, the removal of oppression, and spiritual-based social change are central. However, Woolman is nonviolent to the core, while liberation theology has been used to justify armed revolutionary struggle in Latin America.[5]

In summary, classical economics, at least as enunciated by its early adherents, was based on theological beliefs and was explicit about values, even if this theological and ethical base bore little similarity to Woolman's. By the middle of the nineteenth century most traditional economics had shed its theological base, and instead usually worked and still works within the broad context of agnostic scientific rationalism. The dominant neoclassical economics declares itself to be value free, at least in its scientific or positive aspects. In contrast, the alternative economic paradigms acknowledge that they incorporate values into their analysis. These values, however, are for the most part not those expressed by Woolman in "Conversations."

Some Concluding Observations

In some sense the contrast between Woolman's economics and traditional economics is so dramatic and overwhelming that the first impulse is either to write off Woolman or to write off traditional economics.

One temptation is to write off Woolman as economically naive or as a creature of his times. A person might argue that Woolman's thinking may have been appropriate for a relatively simple colonial economy but not for a complex modern economy. Yet, many accept that the modern international economy has serious problems. We believe that it frequently leads to empty alienated lives, and to the oppression of others at home and in foreign lands. We worry about the threat of war abroad and violence at home, and we are increasingly concerned about the impact of endless economic growth on the health of our mother earth. As a result, we are again questioning where modern economics, as well as other contemporary social and moral forces, have led us and will lead us. Woolman presents a radically simple alternative: love of God and neighbor results in harmony with God, ourselves, others, and the globe. But for me at least, it is an awesome, even frightening alternative because of the drastic changes it would require.

The second impulse is to write off the modern economy and traditional economics. I for one like much of what modern technology has given us. It is great to be able to travel long distances in short periods of time. It is comforting to know that food, clothing, and shelter could be within the reach of all. These require a complex industrial economy. Must we sacrifice them to live by Woolman's principles? I believe not, although it seems apparent that we will need to change our personal ethical system and consequently the economic organization of society.

A new economy, a new society, will require many tillers in the field, with many roles. A reunification of science and religious values, of the mystical and the material will be necessary. Caution will be the watchword if we are to achieve a religiously and ethically based economy that does not impose on others in inquisitorial fashion the "correct" economic policy. We will need poetry and the arts, fun and joy to heal and nourish ourselves. Most of all, we will need to follow Woolman's guidance concerning the primacy of the two great commandments: love of God above all else, and love of neighbor as ourselves. This means opening ourselves up to joy and to love of God and creation, about which Woolman speaks frequently and profoundly. It also means the courage to die in our old ways, as Woolman did, so that we can be reborn in God's, Christ's, love. This is not a utopian wish, but a condition of our physical, psychological, and spiritual health.

NOTES

[1] Many helpful suggestions for this paper were received from Sterling Olmsted and Richard Langlois.

[2] "Conversations" is about 11 printed pages, while "A Plea for the Poor" is 34 pages in the Moulton edition.

[3] Material on Adam Smith is largely taken from Jerry Evensky's "The Two Voices of Adam Smith: Moral Philosopher and Social Critic."

[4] For an introduction to these questions in the philosophy of science, see Carolyn Merchant's "Anne Conway: Quaker and Philosopher" and O. Theodore Benfey's "Anne Conway's Interaction with Science Politics, Medicine, and Quakerism." Benfey makes the interesting point that the elite in England during the seventeenth century tended to defend the separation of the mystical and the material "in order to save their jobs and the only form of government they felt would safeguard England's peace and prosperity" (19).

[5] For a further comparison between Woolman's spirituality and liberation theology see chapters 1 and 5 of Philip Boroughs' dissertation "John Woolman (1720-1772): Spirituality and Social Transformation in Colonial America."

WORKS CITED

Baum, Sandra R. "Moral Philosophy, Cognitive Psychology and Economic Theory." *Eastern Economic Journal* 11.4 (October-December 1985): 422-434.

Benfey, O. Theodore. "Anne Conway's Interaction with Science Politics, Medicine, and Quakerism." *Guilford Review* 23 (Spring 1986): 14-23.

Boroughs, Philip. "John Woolman (1720-1772): Spirituality and Social Transformation in Colonial America." Ph.D.diss., Graduate Theological Union, 1989.

Evensky, Jerry. "The Two Voices of Adam Smith: Moral Philosopher and Social Critic." *History of Political Economy* 19.3 (1987): 447-468.

Heilbroner, Robert L. *The Worldly Philosophers.* New York: Simon and Schuster, 1953.

Merchant, Carolyn. "Anne Conway: Quaker and Philosopher." *Guilford Review* 23 (Spring 1986): 2-13.

Rosenberg, Nathan. "Adam Smith and Laissez-faire Revisited." *Adam Smith and Modern Political Economy.* Ed. Gerald P. O'Driscoll, Jr. Ames: University of Iowa, 1979.

Smith, Adam. *The Wealth of Nations.* Eds. R. H. Campbell, et al. Vol. 1. Oxford: Clarendon, 1978.

Sowell, Thomas. "Adam Smith in Theory and Practice." *Adam Smith and Modern Political Economy.* Ed. Gerald P. O'Driscoll, Jr. Ames: University of Iowa, 1979.

Spiegel, Henry W. "Adam Smith's Heavenly City." *Adam Smith and Modern Political Economy.* Ed. Gerald P. O'Driscoll, Jr. Ames: University of Iowa, 1979.

Tool, Marc R. "Equational Justice and Social Value." *Journal of Economic Issues* 17.2 (June 1983): 335-344.

Weisskopf, Walter A. "The Moral Predicament of the Market Economy." *Markets and Morals.* Eds. Gerald Dwrokin, et al. New York: John Wiley, 1977.

Woolman, John. *Conversations on the True Harmony of Mankind and How It May Be Promoted.* Ed. Sterling Olmsted. Philadelphia: The Wider Quaker Fellowship, 1987.

—. *The Journal and Major Essays of John Woolman.* Ed. Phillips P. Moulton. 1971. Richmond, IN: Friends United P, 1989.

11

"Be Ye Therefore Perfect": Integral Christianity in "Some Considerations on the Keeping of Negroes"

Christopher Varga

READING JOHN WOOLMAN'S FIRST ESSAY, "Some Considerations on the Keeping of Negroes," which is counted among the most important antislavery writings produced in colonial America, one is surprised by how few references it makes to the practice against which it is directed. The words "slave" and "slavery" appear not at all, and the essay's title is the only direct reference to the institution of slavery. Woolman uses the synonym "servitude" twice, the first time in inviting his readers to empathize with the slaves' "circumstance" (PM 202) and the second in a reference to "the case of Israel" in Biblical times (PM 206). Although he frequently uses pronouns—we/us and they/them—that clearly refer to the agents and subjects of involuntary servitude in the colonies, slaveholders are overtly designated only once—"them that keep Negroes" (PM 200), and slaves only twice—"these poor Africans" (PM 200) and "Negroes" (PM 202). The absence of these central terms is indicative of the subtle and indirect way in which Woolman presents his antislavery argument in "Some Considerations."

Yet this indirectness did not diminish the essay's effectiveness. It probably found more readers than any antislavery tract before it (PM 13; Drake 56), and it seems well established that the essay, along with Woolman's personal missions to Friends who owned slaves, contributed to the ultimate success of the antislavery movement among Friends (PM 12-13; Nash and Soderlund 53). (Some have further argued that it was indirectly influential in the wider abolition movement (PM 13-14; Nash and Soderlund 80, 138; Soderlund 4).) We can be certain that Woolman consciously chose to employ this indirect strategy. The pains he took in writing the essay are documented in his *Journal* (PM 44-47)—its inspiration during his first journey in the southern colonies in 1746, its subsequent review by his father, his dying father's encouragement in 1750 that it be submitted for publication, and its completion and publication by the Philadelphia Yearly Meeting in 1754. These eight years of contemplating and writing and revising the essay were undoubtedly sufficient to bring the work into accord with its author's intentions, and we cannot suppose that Woolman, an extremely deliberate and conscientious thinker and writer, released it before he was satisfied that it accurately expressed his views.

So Woolman's choice of an indirect antislavery argument must be explicable somehow. One possible explanation is that he realized that such an argument would be most likely to persuade his readers, but it seems unlikely that Woolman was so artful. "Some Considerations" conforms to a favored Quaker style of argument through "quiet kindly persuasion" (Drake 51) and to Woolman's usual persuasive practice, described in the *Journal* and reflected in all of his public writings, of "understat[ing] facts [and] reserving his full force for the declaration of principles" (Reynolds 90). It was simple good fortune that the way in which he chose to express himself coincided with an argument that could be more persuasive to his readers than one which more overtly condemned slavery. First, by minimizing reference to slavery per se, "Some Considerations" evaded to a significant extent the reactions of readers who would reflexively reject an explicitly abolitionist message. Second, by restricting the substance of his message to the primarily religious, Woolman was able to recast the antislavery argument, which in political and economic terms would be for many readers disturbingly radical, as one that was consonant with the most cherished and fundamental belief of the time: Christianity.[1]

The Christianity that Woolman presented to his readers was especially effective in service of the antislavery argument because it was what might be called "integral." It is integral—from the Latin *integer*, meaning intact, entire, pure—in two related senses. First, it does not compartmentalize religion as a sphere of life separable from "worldly" concerns but seeks to integrate all aspects of thought and action, forming a coherent whole consistent with Christian principles. Second, it regards the entire New Testament as moral law governing human conduct. Woolman, unlike many, did not ignore the more difficult or less practical injunctions of the Scriptures—for example, "Give to every man that asketh of thee; and of him that taketh away thy goods ask them not again" [Luke 6:30]—or explain them away as metaphors or utopian ideals. He strove to live in accordance with them—to live, as his *Journal* states, "in the real substance of religion, where practice doth harmonize with principle" (PM 88). And he was moved by a sense of spiritual obligation to encourage others to do the same. "Some Considerations" was a product of this sense of Christian duty. In urging its readers to adopt this integral conception of Christian belief and conduct, it transcended the expected terms of an antislavery argument and became a powerful document in the battle against human bondage.

While the impact of "Some Considerations on the Keeping of Negroes" on the Quaker community has been the focus of most attention, it is important to note that it is addressed not just to the Society of Friends, but to "the Professors of Christianity of Every Denomination" (PM 198). Quakers did not see themselves as an "elect," as did the Calvinists. They believed that what they called Principle or Truth or Inner Light existed in every person. It "penetrat[ed] the deeps of every soul" and, "if responded to, obeyed, and accepted as a guiding star, would lead into all truth . . ." (Jones xvii). The Quaker's role was to proclaim the Truth and to live in accordance with it, so that it might "make its way through the [human] race" and engender a "world-religion of the Spirit" (Jones xiv). Although Woolman was concerned with the plight of the slaves, he directed his arguments towards all those who owned or dealt in slaves. He wanted them to examine their consciences and to come to understand that their lives were out of keeping with the Truth that applied to all. Most slaveholders were of course non-Quaker Christians, and in many cases their churches taught that slavery was an institution ordained by God and "unalterable unless by a new revelation" (Taylor 3). Woolman's contention was that basic, nonsectarian Christian doctrine as already revealed, integrally considered, was sufficient to bring one to an antislavery conclusion.

Throughout his essay, Woolman stresses three central tenets of integral Christianity in his effort to induce his readers to examine their consciences in its light: he reminds Christians of their duty to put religious principles ahead of custom, worldly opinion, or economic benefit; he carefully demonstrates scriptural affirmation of the equality of all persons; and he likewise derives a Biblical doctrine of human fellowship and unity.

In his introduction, Woolman cites Matthew 6:33—"But seek ye first the kingdom of God, and his righteousness; and all these things [food, drink, clothing] shall be added unto you"—and recommends it as "a short but comprehensive view of our duty and happiness" (PM 199). Slavery in Woolman's view was, like all the evils in the world, primarily perpetuated by the supersession of Christian ideals by worldly concerns and secular norms. He understood that many of his readers had probably never thought clearly about slavery in light of Christianity. Like any institution that was justified by tradition and custom, slavery was not subjected to rigorous moral scrutiny. But tradition and custom could not replace the Christian's duty "to humbly apply to God for wisdom, that we may thereby be enabled to see things as they are and ought to be" (PM 203). Woolman rejected the idea that religion was one facet of life and social and economic activity another and called upon Christians to "forego customs and popular opinions" and to subject all facets of their lives to "the infallible standard: Truth" (PM 198). This call to reaffirm religious values and to put them ahead of convention was the essential prerequisite of his argument. As long as Christians could effectively segregate social and economic activity from religion, Woolman's assertion that slavery was inconsistent with Biblical principles would have no effect.

The reason people owned slaves was, as Woolman notes, "for the sake of earthly riches" (PM 208). Christians rationalized their participation in slavery by maintaining a distinction between "meetinghouse and countinghouse" (to use Frederick B. Tolles's terms). Slavery was a matter of business and therefore unrelated to religion in many minds, but Woolman's integral vision allowed for no such distinction. Material wealth and all the "alluring counterfeit joys of this world" (PM 208) he accounts not only irrelevant to true happiness but actually destructive to it. The "pursuit of gain" is "a dark unfruitful toil," he writes in the introduction (PM 199), and those who too eagerly seek wealth and too jealously guard it "miss the true fountain of happiness and wander in a maze of dark anxiety, where all their treasures are insufficient to quiet their minds" (PM 209). Instead, Christians should put their spiritual well-being first; they should "be principally looking to that city 'which hath foundations, whose maker and builder is God' [Heb. 11:10]" (PM 205).[2] Seeking satisfaction in material things is not only a vain employment that distracts from the true purpose of life, it can also be actively corrupting. Woolman cites for example children "educated in fullness, ease, and idleness" among whom "evil habits are more prevalent than is common amongst such who are prudently employed in the necessary affairs of life" (PM 205). Indeed, those who find themselves the beneficiaries of a "liberal distribution of favours from heaven," are in Woolman's view under an even greater obligation than others to live in accordance with Christian principles, lest God find them ungrateful (PM 201). In contrast, the opposite condition can be of benefit spiritually: "such who are intended for high stations have first been very low and dejected, that Truth might be sealed on their hearts, and that the characters there imprinted by bitterness and adversity might in after years remain, suggesting compassionate ideas . . ." (PM 206).

Woolman also saw as false and inconsistent with integral Christianity the accepted idea that wealth and other "outward circumstances" were a valid basis for a "distinction betwixt us and them," that is, between the colonists and the slaves. Such a concept led to "fond [foolish] notions of superiority" (PM 200). Again and again in "Some Considerations on the Keeping of Negroes," Woolman reminds his readers that all souls are equal before God and therefore should be so before all Christians. To illustrate this principle, he recounts the Apostles' lesson in equality: how they as "the Jewish Christians" were "astonished" to learn, in a revelation from the "Most High," that the Christian Gentiles were their moral and spiritual equals, that "God was no respecter of persons," and that "the Father's love was unlimited" (PM 201). Woolman's integral Christianity teaches that all, regardless of status or nation (or what we would call race), are equal before God, both in this world and the next, "are subject to the like afflictions and infirmities of body, the like disorders and frailty in mind, the like temptations, the same death and the same judgment; and that the All-wise Being is judge and Lord over us all" (PM 200).

At times in "Some Considerations," Woolman promotes the idea of human equality in terms not strictly limited to those of integral Christianity, but he does this so subtly, presenting related ideas that seem to emanate from religious ideals, that the reader's perception of the essay as a purely religious document is undisturbed. He invokes logic in exposing the circular reasoning by which whites cited the conditions that slavery imposed on Africans as justification for the Africans' enslavement. After describing the injustices and deprivation endured by the slaves, he asks the reader to consider that their "habits appearing odious to us" have been caused by their treatment *as slaves* and that, "being free men," they might not seem particularly distinct from the colonists themselves (PM 202). At one point, Woolman asserts a "natural right of freedom" in everyone (PM 204), a phrase resonant with eighteenth-century ideas about natural rights that is nevertheless squarely in line with integral Christian belief as Woolman understood it.

An even more radical element of Woolman's assiduously Christian world view is the proposition that to "consider mankind otherwise than brethren, . . . plainly supposes a darkness in the understanding" (PM 202). Citing Genesis 3:20, he asserts that "all nations are of one blood" (PM 200). In the introduction, Woolman cautions that "Natural affection [meaning love of self and of those who are "a part of self" by virtue of being blood relatives] needs a careful examination." He owns that this affection is a good thing "with proper limitations, but otherwise is productive of evil by exciting desires to promote some by means prejudicial to others" (PM 198). That is to say that even the closest bonds of intimacy among human beings should be subordinated to the precepts of Christ, which recognize and privilege the higher fellowship of all Christians, with God equally the father of all. Christians ought therefore to regard all humanity as their family and each person as a brother or sister. Likewise, each person, irrespective of his or her worldly status, should be seen as standing in equal relationship with God and, consequently, as equal in value to oneself and one's loved ones. These Christian principles of universal equality and fellowship are fundamental to Woolman's antislavery argument and are reflected in the Biblical verse he chose as the epigraph to the essay proper: "Forasmuch as ye did it to the least of these my brethren, ye did it unto me" [Matt. 25:40] (PM 200).

In promoting the ideal of human equality and unity, Woolman moves beyond the family metaphor to a more mystical concept of the ultimate unity of all beings. "Our duty and interest is inseparably united," he writes, "and when we neglect or misuse our talents we necessarily depart from the heavenly fellowship and are in the way to the greatest of evils" (PM 208). Christians must not "through a stupid indolence conceive views of interest separate from the general good of the great brotherhood" (PM 207), but must understand that when one neglects or injures another, one neglects or injures the whole of creation. Likewise, one who "rightly advocates the cause of some thereby promotes the good of all" (PM 208). "God's love is universal," and the individual mind, when "sufficiently influenced by it," can share in that universal love, "and the heart is enlarged towards all men" (PM 202).

These integral Christian concepts of human equality and unity give Woolman a remarkable ability to empathize with the slaves and to encourage his readers to do the same, which is a very powerful rhetorical device. In "Some Considerations" this imaginative empathy provides Woolman some of his most potent points in the antislavery argument. He considers the purchase of one who is to be kept "in servitude and ignorance" and asks, "How should I approve of this conduct were I in his circumstances and he i[n] mine?" (PM 204). He invites his audience to empathize with the enslaved Africans, to "calmly consider their circumstance, and . . . make their case ours." After giving a brief description of the woeful circumstances of the slaves' lives, Woolman asks whether the colonists, in like circumstances, would "be less abject than they now are?" (PM 202). Clearly, "Therefore all things whatsoever ye would that men should do to you, do ye even so to them" [Matt. 7:12] was more than an ideal for Woolman; it was an issue "worthy of our most serious consideration" (PM 199).

Woolman's focus in his antislavery essays on slaveholders rather than slaves has drawn some criticism. Forrest G. Wood, in a chapter entitled "Quakers and the Arrogance of Humility" (277-87) has criticized the Quaker reformers, including Woolman, for their emphasis on the moral status of slaveholders instead of the spiritual and physical condition of slaves. This critique is inaccurate in the case of Woolman. Early in "Some Considerations on the Keeping of Negroes" he expresses "real sadness" over "the general disadvantage which these poor Africans lie under" in the colonies (PM 200). He vividly describes their plight in his appeal for his readers to empathize with the slaves, and furthermore, he writes of his concern that the slaves are being deprived of "a Christian education and suitable opportunity of improving the mind" (PM 206) and of "the sweetness of freedom (which, rightly used, is one of the greatest temporal blessings)" (PM 208). It is, however, entirely reasonable that Woolman should place greater emphasis in his essay on those who owned or dealt in slaves rather than the slaves themselves. Slaveholding colonists were his intended audience. He knew that he had to persuade those who held blacks in bondage of the error of their conduct in order for the condition of the enslaved to improve, and he understood that slaveholders would be moved more by concern for their own souls than by compassion alone. Furthermore, Woolman was genuinely, and legitimately, concerned with the moral state of the slaveholders. From his standpoint, the slaves were victims of oppression in this world and could be released from that oppression by their masters, while the masters were subject to God's "heavy displeasure, whose judgments are just and equal, who exalteth and humbleth to the dust as he seeth meet" (PM 201).

Woolman took up the cause of the slaves even more overtly in "Considerations on Keeping Negroes, Part II," which was written in 1761 and published the following year.[3] This second essay treats much more explicitly of the issue of slavery, building on the themes presented in the first essay and countering common Biblical justifications for slavery. But it goes far beyond the first in its denunciation of the violence involved in the slave trade and in slaveholding as contrary to the integral Christian principle of non-violence. The barbarity of procuring and transporting slaves is vividly described in several long and terrible excerpts from contemporary descriptions of the slave trade in Africa (PM 228-30). Woolman then goes on to condemn such acts in forceful terms: "such proceedings are contrary to the nature of Christianity" (PM 232), and "it belongs not to the followers of Christ to be parties in such a trade . . ." (PM 233). He puts less emphasis on the violence involved in slaveholding, perhaps to avoid offending his audience by indicting them too directly, but he does caution that "Forced subjection, on innocent persons . . . , is inconsistent with right reason," because "to be subject to the uncontrollable will of a man liable to err, is most painful and afflicting to a conscientious creature" (PM 221), and that the righteous opposition of the slave to his or her oppression might lead to "terrifying" tortures and executions (PM 222).[4] But he rejects the argument that procuring and trading in slaves rather than owning them is the greater sin, calling it a "nicety of distinction" (PM 234), and alerts slaveholders to their moral complicity in the barbarities of the slave trade:

> He who with view to self-interest buys a slave made so by violence, and only on the strength of such purchase holds him a slave, thereby joins hands with those who committed that violence and in the nature of things becomes chargeable with the guilt. (PM 233)

Thus in "Part II" Woolman adds violence to his catalogue of slavery's violations of integral Christian principles.

The effectiveness in the antislavery effort of Woolman's antislavery writings and their application of a rhetoric of integral Christianity has been the subject of some debate. Earlier scholars of Woolman's life and work were more apt than recent ones to assign him a pivotal place in the Quaker antislavery movement. For example, while Amelia Mott Gummere ascribes the almost total absence of slaveholding among New Jersey Friends by 1800 to Woolman's efforts (397), others have pointed out that Woolman's own Quarterly Meeting of Burlington, "lagged far behind some other New Jersey Meetings in freeing slaves and conformed only after the Yearly Meeting made manumissions mandatory" (Barbour and Frost 131; see also, Soderlund 49). Moulton contends that the antislavery movement within the Society of Friends lacked only "an inspired leader" before Woolman came along and that "Some Considerations" "was largely responsible for the progress against slavery made at the Philadelphia Yearly Meeting of 1755" (PM 12-13). But Nash and Soderlund cite evidence that Woolman's religious antislavery arguments met with only limited success: the moderate progress after 1754 in reducing slaveholding among Friends in the Philadelphia region came to a halt in the late 1750s because of a widespread shortage of labor (55-56). Thus, "religious belief and economic interest interacted in the growth of abolitionism among these Friends" (Soderlund 5).

Woolman's contribution to the effort to combat slavery beyond the Society of Friends is controversial also. Wood says that the Quakers' efforts were "overwhelmed by . . . the economic and political power of those who profited from slavery" (380), and the fact that Christians in the South persisted in owning slaves far longer than did Christians in the North suggests that religious arguments met with limited success when up against economic self-interest. But Soderlund, whose estimate of the effectiveness of Woolman's work within the Society of Friends is conservative, nevertheless asserts that after the Philadelphia Yearly Meeting forbade its members to own slaves in 1776, "Many Friends then helped to foster the growth of abolitionism in American society at large" (4). Slavery may not have been ended in the United States until 91 years after John Woolman's death, yet mid-nineteenth-century abolitionists who helped to bring about emancipation, including William Lloyd Garrison, were influenced by his ideas (PM 13-14).

It is perhaps not fair to try to assess the import of John Woolman's life and work by external effects, because worldly success was never his motive. As Moulton writes, Woolman's

> sense of security in the divine love provided a solid basis for the moral imperative—the conviction that one must do the right, come what may. [His] was not a prudential ethic, in which the judgment of right and wrong is determined merely by foreseeable consequences. In social action he was not so much a strategist working for specific goals as he was a faithful witness to the revealed truth of God. (PM 7)

The author of "Some Considerations on the Keeping of Negroes" was not an activist or a protester as we might use those terms today. The essays reveal a writer who was greatly humble and not egotistically opinionated. He did not rail against slaveholders and categorically demand immediate manumission of slaves. He simply reaffirmed what for him was the highest truth—integral Christianity—in Moulton's words, "trusting [that it would] open the hearts and lives of others to the disturbing power of God" (PM 7). And in this "Some Considerations" was undoubtedly successful.

NOTES

[1] Further insight into the genesis of Woolman's antislavery position and his way of expressing it can be found in the *Journal*. On being asked to write a will for a man who owned slaves, Woolman is reluctant to express his disapproval of slavery and to refuse to write the will, saying that "offending sober people is disagreeable to my inclination," but he does so "in the fear of the Lord." As a result, he enjoys "a fresh confirmation that acting contrary to present outward interest from a motive of divine love and in regard to truth and righteousness, . . . opens the way to a treasure better than silver and to a friendship exceeding the friendship of men" (PM 45-46).

[2] In "Considerations on Keeping Negroes, Part II," Woolman gives an even stronger warning against the evil of materialism: "He who professeth to believe in one Almighty Creator and in his son Jesus Christ, and is yet more

intent on the honours, profits, and friendships of the world than he is in singleness of heart to stand faithful to the Christian religion, is in the channel of idolatry"; that is to say, in potential violation of the First Commandment (PM 210).

[3] Woolman's *Journal* divulges no reason why he deemed an elaboration of his antislavery view necessary, but considering that he spent the intervening years traveling to confer with slaveholding Friends, we can surmise that "Part II" was inspired by the conversations that occurred during his missions. He probably learned from his interlocutors what needed to be added to his argument. Indeed, Phillips P. Moulton calls the second essay "an even more forceful document" than the first (PM 13). In 1774 both antislavery essays were reissued with the first edition of the *Journal.*

[4] That Woolman was aware of the violence and deprivation that slaves in the colonies were subject revealed in a passage in the *Journal* written after a visit to Virginia in 1757:

> Many whose labour is heavy being followed . . . in the field by a man with a whip . . . have in common little else to eat but one peck of Indian corn and salt for one week with some few potatoes. . . .
>
> The correction ensuing on their disobedience to overseers or slothfulness in business is often very severe and sometimes desperate. Men and women have many times scarce clothes enough to hide their nakedness. . . . (PM 65)

WORKS CITED

Barbour, Hugh, and J. William Frost. *The Quakers.* Richmond, IN: Friends United Press, 1988.

Drake, Thomas E. *Quakers and Slavery in America.* New Haven, CT: Yale University Press, 1950.

Gummere, Amelia Mott. "The Early Quakers in New Jersey." *The Quakers in the American Colonies.* Ed. Rufus Jones. 1911. New York, NY: Norton, 1966. 355-413.

Jones, Rufus. *The Quakers in the American Colonies.* 1911. New York, NY: Norton, 1966.

Nash, Gary B., and Jean R. Soderlund. *Freedom by Degrees: Emancipation in Pennsylvania and Its Aftermath.* New York, NY: Oxford University Press, 1991.

Reynolds, Reginald. *The Wisdom of John Woolman.* London, England: Allen, 1948.

Soderlund, Jean R. *Quakers and Slavery: A Divided Spirit.* Princeton, NJ: Princeton University Press, 1985.

Taylor, Ernest E. *The Challenge of John Woolman.* London, England: Friends Tract Assn., 1916.

Tolles, Frederick B. *Meetinghouse and Countinghouse: The Quaker Merchants of Colonial Philadelphia, 1682-1763.* Chapel Hill, NC: University of North Carolina Press, 1948.

Wood, Forrest G. *The Arrogance of Faith: Christianity and Race in America from the Colonial Era to the Twentieth Century.* New York, NY: Knopf, 1990.

Woolman, John. *The Journal and Major Essays of John Woolman.* Ed. Phillips P. Moulton. 1971. Richmond, IN: Friends United Press, 1989.

12

"A Perfect Redemption from this Spirit of Oppression": John Woolman's Hopeful World View in "A Plea for the Poor"

Michael P. Graves

JOHN WOOLMAN'S "A PLEA FOR THE POOR" is a challenging essay, although its major implications are only too clear. Like his more famous *Journal*, the essay demands moral responses of its readers, responses that may result in some reconsideration of their own lives. Put less delicately and more personally, "A Plea for the Poor" places moral demands on me as a reader.

When I first encountered the John Greenleaf Whittier edition of the "Plea" as a young and "financially challenged" newly-convinced Quaker in the 1960s, I was impressed with its arguments. I thought it "radical" since it got to the "root" of so many economic and political problems that have persisted since Woolman's time. Returning to that same text today as a middle-aged father and grandfather, I still find Woolman's essay "speaking to my condition," but now in ways it could not three decades ago. I am intrigued that a text published more than two hundred years ago (1793) has the capacity to insinuate itself once again into my personal life and prompt a reappraisal of my spending, saving, and giving.

The present essay was initially motivated by a personal response to Woolman's essay, and although I will deal here with the "Plea" in a somewhat more analytical mode than my personal enthusiasm for Woolman and his ideas might encourage, I trust my analysis will betray my admiration for the man and more than hint at my continuing personal struggle with the moral demands of his rhetoric. Furthermore, I hope to use Woolman's essay to reveal some of the virtues and inherent challenges in a particular approach to criticism. If the essay succeeds, in some sense Woolman will be seen as having dialogue with secular rhetorical critics.

The version of "A Plea for the Poor" chosen for analysis here is the John Greenleaf Whittier Edition text (reprinted 1961). While I acknowledge the excellent scholarly work of Phillips P. Moulton, who edited the modern edition of the essay (1971; reprinted 1989), I have turned my attention rather to the Whittier version of the "Plea" for three reasons. First, I am a rhetorical rather than a literary critic, meaning that I am interested primarily in the capacity of texts to invite certain readings in historically-situated interactions and among actual audiences/readers. My aim is to look at the text most people actually had read before 1971, the text Moulton himself calls "the famous one" (PM 273).[1] My second reason for choosing the Whittier text is its rhetorical integrity. The Whittier text ends with "Section XII" (chapter thirteen of the Moulton text) and does not include the sections "On Schools," "On Masters and Servants," and the final chapter devoted to the keeping of slaves (chapters fourteen, fifteen and sixteen of the Moulton text). Nevertheless, the Whittier text seems "rounded" and complete.[2] My third reason for choosing the Whittier text is perhaps most important and it is personal. As I noted, I first encountered Woolman's essay in the reprinted Whittier edition. Thus, this analysis of that text is as much a personal journey of rediscovery—a return visit—as it is a scholarly trek.

In this essay I intend to apply to Woolman's "Plea for the Poor" a critical tool called "cluster criticism," first introduced by Kenneth Burke and later developed by others. The essay will be divided into the following sections: (1) introduction of the concept of cluster criticism; (2) presentation of the results of a cluster analysis of the Whittier text of Woolman's "Plea"; and (3) conclusions, with consideration of some implications of this type of analysis for our understanding of Whittier's edition of Woolman's essay.

1

Typically, we read an essay such as "A Plea for the Poor" from start to finish, allowing the "argument" to develop through the rational and psychological effects of the accumulation of "reasons" (arguments and evidence) and emotional or figurative appeals. Cluster analysis, while not denying the value of sequential reading, does not rely on it, except in its initial phase. It allows the reader to "step back" from the inevitable and temporal flow of the essay and chart its pattern of associations among key terms relatively undominated by their sequence. This approach to analysis holds the promise of uncovering associations among key terms in a piece of discourse about which the original writer was not necessarily aware.

In *Attitudes Toward History,* Kenneth Burke proposed cluster analysis as a method to discover what elements or terms are associated with what other elements or terms in the mind of the author, given the evidence discovered in the text under examination. In the cluster approach, the critic endeavors to find "what subjects cluster about other subjects (what images *b, c, d* the poet [essayist] introduces whenever he talks with engrossment of subject *a*)" (232). "By charting clusters," Burke says,

> we get our cues as to the important ingredients subsumed in 'symbolic mergers'. We reveal, beneath an author's 'official front', the level at which a lie is impossible. . . . If a man talks dully of *glory,* but brilliantly employs the imagery of *desolation,* his *true subject* is desolation. (233, emphasis in original)

The idea of clusters was further developed by Burke in 1941 in *The Philosophy of Literary Form:*

> Now, the work of every writer contains a set of implicit equations. He uses "associational clusters." And you may, by examining his work, find "what goes with what" in these clusters—what kinds of images and personalities and situations go with his notions of heroism, villainy, consolation, despair, etc. And though he be perfectly conscious of the act of writing, conscious of selecting a certain kind of imagery to reinforce a certain kind of mood, etc., he cannot possibly be conscious of the interrelationships among all these equations. (18)

Burke thus proposed cluster analysis as a means of discovering linguistic associations that could offer potential insight into an author's mind or worldview as presented in a specific text. This approach to rhetorical analysis and criticism has been used insightfully by several contemporary critics (e.g., Berthold, Foss, Marston and Rockwell, and Reid). Their experience with cluster analysis normally involves the following steps, as described by Sonja K. Foss in *Rhetorical Criticism:* (1) identifying key terms, (2) charting clusters around the key terms, and (3) discovering patterns in the clusters (65-66). Key terms are discovered not merely by tabulating a record of their frequency or repetition in the discourse, which is the starting point of the process, but also by a subjective assessment of their qualitative significance or "intensity." The steps of charting clusters of key terms and discovering patterns among the clusters are to a large extent based upon the critic's subjective assessments of associations among key terms and clusters with reference to proximity and deduced relationship.

Frequently, as Foss points out, the discovered key terms are god or devil terms, the ideal or perfect vs. the "ultimate negative or evil for the rhetor" (65). The concept of "god terms" was introduced in Kenneth Burke's *A Grammar of Motives,* published in 1945, where he refers to "god terms" as "names for the ultimates of motivation" (74; see also 355-356).[3] However, it was Richard Weaver who analytically developed the concept of "ultimate terms" in his *The Ethics of Rhetoric,* published in 1953. Weaver's analysis of ultimate terms is particularly relevant to this consideration of Woolman's "Plea" because it offers an approach which emphasizes a rhetor's moral framework.

Within his discussion of "ultimate terms," Weaver defined "god term" as "that expression about which all other expressions are ranked as subordinate and serving dominations and powers. Its force imparts to [other terms] their lesser degree of force, and fixes the scale by which degrees of comparison are understood" (212). In the milieu of early 1950s America, Weaver argued that "science," "progress," "modern," "efficient," "American," and "allies" functioned as god terms (215-222). Conversely, Weaver wrote that "devil terms" are "terms of repulsion" or "prime repellants" (222). "Devil terms" often point to enemies or scapegoats, such as the terms "Nazi" or "Facist" in World War II or "Communist" in the early 1950s (222-223). Weaver also presented the concept of "charismatic terms." These terms, he says, "seem to have broken loose somehow and to operate independently of referential connections." They are terms "of considerable potency whose referents it is virtually impossible to discover or to construct through imagination" (227). In the culture of 1953 America, Weaver offered "democracy" and "freedom" as examples of charismatic terms (228). Weaver believed that by charting the ultimate terms in the rhetoric of a culture, it was possible to discern

> a system of relationship among the attractive and among the repulsive terms, so that we can work out an order of weight and precedence in the prevailing rhetoric once we have discerned

> the rhetorical absolutes—the terms to which the highest respect is paid. (212)

As will be seen, in this cluster analysis of Woolman's "Plea," Weaver's conception of ultimate terms proved to be a useful conceptual tool, although, not surprisingly, nothing approximating a "charismatic" term was discovered in the essay. I will argue, however, that god and devil terms are present and, by implication, help us "work out an order of weight and precedence" in Woolman's essay.

Those who have employed cluster analysis have also discovered that, whether or not they use Weaver's concept of ultimate terms, cluster analysis frequently leads the critic into an "agon analysis"—"the examination of opposing terms"—particularly helpful because it may suggest "a conflict or tension in a rhetor's worldview that must be resolved" (Foss 66). Agon analysis also proved its usefulness in this study, although it will be seen that Woolman is sophisticated in his conceptual pairings, and what may seem on the surface to be an irreconcilably agonistic opposite, may be reconcilable or act in harmony under certain conditions.

With this basic sketch of the operations of cluster analysis, we are now ready to proceed to a consideration of the results of cluster analysis of Woolman's essay.

2

Cluster analysis of Woolman's "Plea for the Poor" reveals that it is a complex linguistic mosaic that draws rhetorical strength from five clusters of terms: (1) Rich/poor, (2) Oppression/Love, (3) Usefulness/Luxury, (4) Reason/Feeling, and (5) Children. Woolman's use of terms in the Rich/Poor cluster, while potentially antagonistic, does not necessitate an agonistic relationship between the terms as long as their relationship is mediated by Love rather than Oppression. However, Oppression, a *devil* term, is always agonistically related to Love, a *god* term. Similarly, Usefulness and Luxury are agonistically opposed *god* and *devil* terms in the "Plea," while Reason and Feeling—seemingly opposed terms—are seen in Woolman's framework as working in a mutually beneficial tension. Finally, the Children cluster, which evolves over the length of the essay, in the end names the proper relationship of persons to God, one that allows Love to displace Oppression and mediate between the otherwise opposed terms, Rich and Poor.

Rich/Poor. It comes as no surprise that Rich is opposed to Poor in Woolman's essay; cluster analysis is hardly required to arrive at this conclusion. The poor are consistently seen with sympathy while the rich or "wealthy" come in for strong criticism, vigorous admonition, but also occasional sympathy. "Rich" or "riches" appear only seven times. However, a variation of "wealth" appears an additional eleven times. Also, the presence of words such as "luxury," "superfluities," "grandeur," "possessions" and several like terms indicates the significance of the concept captured in the term "rich" as a key element in the essay. Significantly, the essay itself begins with the word "wealth" and makes an initial assertion linking wealth with selfishness and opposing the desire for wealth to the growth of virtue: "Wealth desired for its own sake obstructs the increase of virtue, and large possessions in the hands of selfish men have a bad tendency . . ." (224). Notice here that "wealth" and "possessions," per se, are not condemned by Woolman, only wealth "desired for its own sake." Also, "possessions" coupled with "selfish men" do not automatically equal evil, but present a "bad tendency." The conclusion is clear: riches combined with selfishness produce a potentially corrupting combination, one that "tends" to stunt the growth of virtue.

"Poor" is a prominent word in the essay's title, of course, but also appears in some form (e.g., in plural form) an additional fifteen times in the essay. The presence of other terms associated with poverty, such as "labor(s)," "toil," "straighted," and "distressed circumstances," taken together, add quantitative weight as well as qualitative shading to the term "poor" in the essay. The poor are viewed consistently with sympathy and often as victims: "To be busied in that which is but vanity and serves only to please the insatiable mind, tends to an alliance with those that promote that vanity, and is a snare in which many poor tradesmen are entangled" (225). Here the compliance of the poor with the demands of the rich leads them to fall into a trap set by vain rich persons. The idea that the poor are victims of the rich figures prominently in the following quotation as well, where the rich are seen as breaching the moral demands of love in a world where the poor are viewed as persons possessing rights simply because they are cohabitants of the earth whose true owner is God:

> Though the poor occupy our estates by a bargain, to which they in their poor circumstances agree . . . if our views are to lay up

> riches, or to live in conformity to customs which have not their foundation in the truth, and our demands are such as require from them greater toil or application to business than is consistent with pure love, we invade their rights as inhabitants of a world of which a good and gracious God is the proprietor. . . . (226)

Interestingly, the rich are also occasionally portrayed as victims, as in this passage:

> One person continuing to live contrary to true wisdom commonly draws others into connection with him, and . . . their proceedings are like a wild vine which springing from a single seed and growing strong, its branches extend, and their little tendrils twist round all herbs and boughs of trees within their reach, and are so braced and locked in that without much labor and great strength they are not disentangled. (244-245)

The idea that the rich are victims of "entanglement" also appears in another key passage where the accouterments of wealth are linked with selfishness. Here, Woolman invokes the image of the "Prince of Peace" and his "example of humility and plainness," concluding with a question as to whether people can even remember that they are Christ's disciples "without feeling an earnest desire to be disentangled with everything connected with selfish customs in food, in raiment, in houses and in all things else" (240).

Both rich and poor, then, are seen as victims in the "Plea": the poor because of their circumstances and forced dependence upon bargains they must strike with the rich to secure employment; the rich because they become "entangled" in choking vines that result from their sowing seeds of selfishness, contrary to Christ's example of "humility and plainness." The poor are victims of the rich, while the rich are victims of their own acts.

Cluster analysis underscores the connection, in the passage just quoted and the entire essay, between wealth and "selfishness." Some variation of the root of the term "selfishness" ("self-pleasing," "self-seeking spirit," "self," "selfish men," "self-exaltation," "all that is selfish," and "selfishly loved") appears seventeen times, while associated terms or phrases—"increase to extreme," "not satisfied," and "greater share" appear an additional one time each. Woolman points an accusatory finger at a "wealthy man . . . not satisfied with being supported in a plain way" (230) and asserts that "every demand for money inconsistent with Divine order, hath some connection with unnecessary labor" (232). "When our eyes are so single as to discern the selfish spirit clearly," Woolman says, "we behold it the greatest of all tyrants" (238). This quotation is followed by a lengthy passage that lists some of the terrible effects on society of such tyrants as Domitian and Nero, who, Woolman tells us, "appear as . . . tyrant[s] of small consequence compared with this selfish spirit" (239). This is an arresting conclusion: that the cumulative effect of the tyrannical "selfish spirit" is more devastating on society than the effects of some of history's most infamous villains. Woolman goes on to catalog the "havoc that is made in this age," including "miseries," "hardships," and slavery, and concludes "that self is the bottom of these proceedings" (239-240). "Holding treasures in the self-pleasing spirit," he says, "is a strong plant, the fruit whereof ripens fast" (241). Here again, Woolman turns to an image drawn from the venue of plant cultivation to capture the idea that seeds produce plants that mature and bear fruit. His readers might have been reminded of the Biblical warning: you reap what you sow. Woolman's world is not pinioned by pessimistic necessity, however, for he invites us to envision a future time when, after having disentangled ourselves from the effects of the selfish spirit, "the serenity of our minds may never be clouded by remembering that some part of our employment tends to support customs which have their foundation in the self-seeking spirit" (246).

Oppression/Love. While the opposition of "rich" and "poor" is pivotal in the essay, Woolman also extensively employs the inherent polarity of the *devil* term, "oppression," and the *god* term, "love." The statistics with respect to their employment in the essay are remarkable: some form of the word "oppression" is used a surprising twenty-seven times and "power" (in a negative context) is used an additional nineteen times. By contrast, the idea of "love," both Divine and human—the latter a reflection of the former—is invoked thirty-three times in the essay.

However, it is not merely the *quantity* of these terms that makes them so significant in the essay. The negative effects of oppression and power made possible by accumulated and inherited wealth are so powerful, in their potential and actual evil effects, that only a more powerful force can be enlisted to counter the negative effects of *oppression*, the ultimate negative term in the world of Woolman's essay. Woolman invokes the force of the *god* term, universal *love*.

In the world of colonial America, as well as that of the readers of the Whittier edition right up to our own time, the interests of the rich and powerful are central, while the concerns of the poor and the powerless are marginal. "Money talks," while poverty is silent. Woolman's answer to this recurrent situation is not to reverse the respective places of rich and poor, oppressor and oppressed. Instead, he places *love*, itself a marginalized concept amid the hard-nosed world of economics, squarely into the center and expects its influence to bring about "a perfect redemption from this spirit of oppression" (249)

> Wealth, [writes Woolman] is attended with power, by which bargains and proceedings contrary to universal righteousness are supported; and hence oppression, carried on with worldly policy and order, clothes itself with the name of justice and becomes like a seed of discord in the soul. (241)

In Woolman's view, this kind of "oppression" is very subtle. It begins as a "seed" and grows. It takes the form of customs and comes clothed with dignity, refinement, even taste. It is habitual, seems right, and is constantly reinforced by the economic structures of mainstream culture, thus its full visage is seldom viewed head-on. Nevertheless, Woolman argues, oppression with a refined and habitual appearance is still oppression: ". . . oppression in the extreme appears terrible; but oppression in more refined appearances remains to be oppression, and when the smallest degree of it is cherished it grows stronger and more extensive" (249). We are reminded that the essay is an appeal or entreaty, not a protest. Its title presents a "plea" for the poor, not a "remonstrance," a linguistic choice that indicates that the poor are in a weak position compared with the rich, however benignly "oppressive" they may be. The rich still hold the power of oppression over the poor.

"Love," on the other hand, operates quite differently from "oppression." Given an opportunity to flourish, "love" is striking rather than subtle in its effect: "Divine love which enlarges the heart towards mankind universally is that alone which stops every corrupt stream and opens those channels of business and commerce in which nothing runs that is not pure . . ." (246).

The opposition of "oppression" to "love" is most acute in sections of the "Plea" where the two are found in close proximity. For example, in a paragraph in which Woolman asserts that God is the "true proprietor" of the earth and that His right to the earth has not diminished over time, he calls the oppressors *usurpers*: "... nor can any apply the increase of their possessions contrary to universal love, nor dispose of lands in a way which they know tends to exalt some by oppressing others without being justly charged with usurpation" (243).

Perhaps there is a hint here at potential Divine judgment for "usurpers" who resist the demands of universal love and act as if they are owners rather than stewards of possessions and lands.

In an earlier passage that juxtaposes "oppression" and "love," one dealing with the significant and potentially volatile topic of inheritance, Woolman invites his readers to see a vision of a society where, under the influence of love, inheritance does not simply enable one's children to be lazy or place in their hands the power of oppression, however subtle:

> . . . when we look towards a succeeding age with a mind influenced by universal love, instead of endeavoring to exempt some from those cares which necessarily relate to this life, and to give them power to oppress others, we desire that they may all be the Lord's children and live in that humility and order becoming his family. (237)

Significantly, in three key places where Woolman writes about the "great business" of human life, he links this powerful phrase either to "love" or to "oppression." Early in the essay we find Woolman's most positive context for the phrase "great business": "... to turn all we possess into the channel of universal love becomes the business of our lives" (227). Here is an example of Woolman placing *love*, an often marginalized concept in the world of commerce, in the center of his readers' commercial and spiritual lives. Possessions thus metamorphose into channels of love; the process of such change becomes one's "business." These are radical prescriptions, indeed.

Later, at the beginning of Section VIII, he writes:

> To labor for an establishment in Divine love, in which the mind is disentangled from the power of darkness, is the great business of man's life; the collecting of riches, covering the body with fine wrought, costly apparel, and having magnificent furniture, operate against universal love and tend to feed self.... (236-237)

Notice here that the negative notion of "entanglement" is once again invoked, a term which we have noted is often clustered with "riches," as it is here. This time, however, "entanglement" is employed with specific details about what kinds of things "entangle": riches, expensive clothing, fine furniture. Apparently Divine or universal love is not easily established because of rich persons' "entanglements." Love's establishment demands "labor." Notice also in the passage the term "self," which we have already noted above characteristically clusters with the term "riches."

At the conclusion of the Whittier edition of the essay, Woolman once again uses the phrase "great business," linking it this time directly to "oppression": "To labor for a perfect redemption from this spirit of oppression is the great business of the whole family of Christ Jesus in this world" (249). The two concepts, "love" and "oppression," are inextricably linked in agonistic relationship in Woolman's essay so that the "great business"—the purpose of human existence—is both to establish Divine love and to be redeemed from the spirit of oppression. The implication is that one cannot occur without the other—or without labor. But there is hope, as Woolman reminds us at the outset of the essay, for there are people who are well off, but still treat the poor in the spirit of "universal love": "Men who have large estates and live in the spirit of charity . . . regulate their demands agreeably to universal love, being righteous on principle, do[ing] good to the poor without placing it to an act of bounty" (225). Such persons "are removed into that state of being in which there is no possibility of our taking delight in anything contrary to the pure principle of universal love" (235).

Usefulness/Luxury. A fundamental opposition between the *god* term, "usefulness," and the *devil* term, "luxury," runs throughout the "Plea." Woolman argues that useful work or possessions are simple, plain, moderate, stay within bounds, and tend to the common good or interest. On the contrary, luxuries, by their very nature, are excessive, break boundaries, tend to elevate some individuals socially regardless of their personal merit, and are immoderate. Unfortunately, the habit of social custom tends to reinforce the selfish demands of luxury rather than the moral and altruistic demands of a commitment to "the right use of things." Usefulness and luxury are at opposite moral poles in Woolman's "Plea."

Some form of "useful," "usefulness," or "right use of things" is discovered sixteen times in the essay. "Simplicity," or terms close to it conceptually (such as "singularity"), appear nine times. "Moderation," or closely associated terms such as "sustenance" or "boundaries," appear fifteen times. "Plain(ness)" appears nine times while some form of "equity" (or its conceptual equivalent such as "dividing equally" or "common interest") is found nineteen times.

On the other hand, "luxury," in some variation, appears ten times, but we must add that "superfluities," "grandeur," and other concepts or terms denoting some aspect of "luxury" (e.g., "curious carvings," "magnificent furniture," "fares sumptuously," and "bestows lavishly") are also linked with the terms "rich" or "wealth" discussed above. In this sense, "luxury," which clusters with the term "rich" in opposition to "poor," also clusters with other terms that indicate excess and stand in opposition to the "right use of things."

The concept of "usefulness" as opposed to immoderate living is introduced in the first sentence of the essay where Woolman asserts that "large possessions in the hands of selfish men" results in a situation where "too small a number of people are employed in useful things" (224), whereas wealthy people who "live in the spirit of charity" offer a positive example by "avoiding superfluities" in their own lives. Also, by "not exacting what the laws and customs would support them in [they] tend to open the channel to moderate labor in useful affairs" (225). The significant term "custom(s)" is found fifteen times in the essay and is usually associated with habits that are expensive, excessive, or selfish. Of course, people observe customs out of habit, normally with little conscious thought of their short or long term consequences on themselves or others.

In some passages, the cluster of terms indicating the basic opposition of "usefulness" to "luxury" is striking:

> Were all superfluities and the desire of outward greatness laid aside, and the right use of things universally attended to, such a number of people might be employed in things useful as that moderate labor with the blessings of Heaven would answer all good purposes. . . . (226-227)

"Moderate labor," in Woolman's vision, involves proper apportionment: ". . . either too much or too little action is tiresome, but a right portion is healthful to the body and agreeable to an honest mind" (227). Here, Woolman seems to be envisioning an approach to work that is neither excessive, especially when accomplished simply to achieve the possession of luxuries, nor lethargic, but just the right proportion. His *Journal* indicates in several places his own struggle to pare down his business to keep it from "growing too cumbersome" (see, for example, PM 53ff.). Woolman, it seems, was not only out of step with prevailing profit and growth motives of his times, but of our time as well—perhaps of all times—and we might have cause to consider that he discovered a way to lower stress, keep labor within bounds, and free up time for "the great business" of life.

In another passage, Woolman essentially lays out the path of sacrifice to which he calls his wealthy readers, a path in opposition to the habitual "customs" of luxury and excess:

> To treasure up wealth for another generation by means of the immoderate labor of those who in some measure depend upon us is doing evil. . . . To labor hard or cause others to do so that we may live conformably to customs which Christ our Redeemer discountenanced by his example . . . is to manure a soil for propagating an evil seed in the earth. They who enter deeply into these considerations . . . will feel these things so heavy and their ill effects so extensive that the necessity of attending singly to Divine wisdom will be evident; and will thereby be directed in the right use of things in opposition to the customs of the times; and will be supported to bear patiently the reproaches attending singularity. To conform a little strengthens the hands of those who carry wrong customs to their utmost extent. . . . (233)

Woolman's path is not an easy one as the language in the paragraph above indicates: "feel these things *so heavy*," "ill effects *so extensive*," "bear patiently the *reproaches*." However, the moral demands motivating the change, along with the reference to the example of Christ, are clearly stated and seemingly unavoidable: "To treasure up wealth . . . by means of the immoderate labor of those who . . . depend upon us *is doing evil*. . . . To labor hard or cause others to do so that we may live conformably to customs which Christ our Redeemer discountenanced by his example . . . is to manure a soil *for propagating an evil seed* in the earth." Once again, we are reminded, an evil seed produces entangling vines and evil fruit.

Reason/Feeling. One of the most surprising findings of cluster analysis is the discovery of a state of tension in the essay between clusters related to the use of "reason" and those concerned with the place of "feeling." When I compared references to "reason," including terms such as "reflect," "understanding," or "considers" with references to "feeling," such as "heart," "tender-hearted," or "feeling knowledge," I found the references to be even, at thirty each. Clearly, Woolman holds that decisions on the part of the rich with respect to the poor may be prompted through sound argument. Indeed, "A Plea for the Poor" moves carefully through a series of arguments regarding the condition and treatment of the poor. However, it is also clear in the essay that reasoning alone will not be sufficient to effect the necessary changes; it is the "heart" that must first be touched. Woolman says that, although "the direction of pure wisdom is obligatory on all reasonable creatures" (226), it is "men of large estates, whose hearts are . . . enlarged" (227) and are "kind and tender-hearted" (228) who actually respond with moral behavior and are thus valorized by Woolman.

Woolman's reluctance to trust reason alone as a motivational force in human affairs reflects a long tradition in Quaker thought. The human, to early Quakers, was possessed of faculties that could be exercised for good or evil. Because of degenerate human nature, inherited through Adam and Eve, human reasoning power had become corrupted along with the faculties of understanding and judgment. Although some early Quakers held that human ability to reason should govern in the natural realm, some doubted this. All would agree, however, that the faculty of reason, when unaided by immediate divine revelation, could lead only to apostasy in the spiritual realm. For example, Robert Barclay asked: "Why need we set up our own carnal and corrupt reason for a guide to us in matters spiritual, as some will needs do?" (*Apology* 21), but later asserted that reason was fit to "order and rule man in things natural" and "may be useful to man even in spiritual things, as it is still subservient and subject to the other [the 'Seed' or 'Light'] . . ." (85). The same sort of balance seems to function in Woolman's "Plea."

In Woolman's world, "a right feeling of the laborers' condition" (228) must be discovered. He invites a consideration of query-like probes in a blend of appeals for empathy and reasoned self-appraisal:

> It is good for those who live in fulness [sic] to *cultivate tenderness of heart*, and to improve every opportunity of *being acquainted with* the hardships and fatigues of those who labor for their

> living; and thus to *think seriously* with themselves, Am I influenced by true charity in fixing all my demands? Have I no desire to support myself in expensive customs, because my acquaintances live in such customs? (228, emphasis added)

The passage is an interesting blend of an appeal to become empathetic through direct observation and acquaintance with the trials of the poor, at least potentially an emotionally-charged experience, and an appeal to become self-reflective. He invites the reader to respond to two "queries" which tend to provoke a somewhat dispassionate reappraisal of one's motivations and behaviors.[4]

The appeal to empathize is strongly stated in the essay. Woolman writes of a "duty of tenderness to the poor" and counsels, following Moses, to "know the heart of a stranger" (229) in order to "come to a *feeling knowledge* of the straights and hardships which many poor innocent people pass through in obscure life" (230, emphasis added). Woolman seems to say that there is "knowledge of the head" and "knowledge of the heart," but that the latter is crucial. When empathy is awakened, people are able "To see their fellow-creatures under difficulties to which they are in no degree accessory [and that kind of vision] tends to awaken *tenderness* in the minds of all *reasonable* people" (231). Again, the blend of reason and feeling is obvious.

The same blend of reason and feeling once again is captured in Woolman's counsel that otherwise pious, wealthy people who "increase labor beyond the bounds fixed by Divine wisdom . . . may so consider the connection of things as to take heed" (233). "Consider[ing] the connection of things" is a process of causal reasoning, but Woolman concludes the same passage with a section referred to previously that tips the scales toward *feeling:* "They who enter deeply into these considerations and live under the weight of them will feel these things so heavy and their ill effects so extensive that the necessity of attending singly to Divine wisdom will be evident; . . ." (233). Reason, then, has an undoubted place in the process of persuasion, particularly self-persuasion, but it is empathetic feeling that unlocks the door to "Divine wisdom."

Children. References to some aspect of "family"—including "children," "family," "brotherhood," and "fathers," appear forty times in the essay, but the use of the term "children," at twenty-six, outweighs all the other terms numerically. This choice is significant because it links humankind together conceptually as fellow children with familial ties and a special relationship to a father.

In "A Plea for the Poor," Woolman carefully builds toward the conception of humans as children. The first reference in the "children" or "family" cluster has been noted above, when Woolman refers to wealthy people "whose hearts are . . . enlarged" as "fathers to the poor" (227). Yet these persons are not just "fathers." They also look over "their brethren in distressed circumstances." The result of their kind treatment of their laborers is that the poor, knowing that the rich persons might have taken advantage of them, yet chose not to, "behold [their conduct] lovely and consistent with brotherhood" (228).

Woolman then points out that "Divine love" operates in such a way that people can be "awakened" through a "witness in [their] own conscience" to the "true design of living," because "Divine love imposeth no rigorous or unreasonable commands, but graciously points out the spirit of brotherhood and the way to happiness" (229). Thus far, the path of personal identification with the poor in Woolman's terminology moves from wealthy people seen as "fathers of the poor" to their identification with the poor in the bonds of "brotherhood." This move is fully consistent with the plea for empathy or "tenderness" of heart noted above in the "reason/feeling" clusters.

There remains yet one more level of transformation in the process of the wealthy identifying with the poor: from the level of "brotherhood" to the level of universal relationship as "children" in submission to a common father. Woolman notes that "When he [God] saith unto his people, 'Ye are my sons and daughters,' no greater happiness can be desired by them, who know how gracious a Father he is" (237). Submission to the Father and to the influence of "universal love" is intended to have profound effects on the "children." For example, "universal love" instructs people with respect to the exercise of their right to leave their estate to their children—which, in fact, may give the children "power to oppress others." "Universal love" would have people choose not to follow the "custom" of unthinking inheritance and "desire that they may all be the Lord's children and live in that humility and order becoming his family" (237). In essence, Woolman surmised that the realization that one was linked spiritually and familially to persons in addition to and beyond one's blood relatives would have practical effects on one's attitudes and behaviors. Woolman's principles of inheritance for the wealthy are very clear: "Obedient children who are intrusted with much outward substance," he observes, "wait for wisdom to dispose of it agreeably to His will, 'in whom the fatherless find mercy'" (238). Put plainly, the rich begin to act mercifully, not merely from the acceptance of blind custom; they begin to act, in fact, like children of a merciful God. There is more than a hint in the "Plea" that riches are God's gifts and subject to forfeiture. Woolman warns that the gift of Divine beneficence is "conditional, for us to occupy as dutiful children and not otherwise; for He alone is the true proprietor" (242).

From Woolman's perspective, the linguistic transformation from wealthy humans as "fathers," to all humans as "brothers," to all humankind united as "dutiful children" in relationship to a heavenly father, involves a huge dose of humility and mutual submission to God. Families do not live in harmony when children are rebellious and arrogant. Conversely, family harmony abounds when parents love their children with a divine-like love and when children willingly submit to their parents. Significantly, Woolman turns to the larger term "family" to end his essay: "To labor for a perfect redemption from this spirit of oppression is the great business of the whole family of Christ Jesus in this world" (249).

3

A cluster analysis of "A Plea For The Poor" brings into clearer focus the complex interweaving of Woolman's thought as experienced by readers of the Whittier edition. Cluster analysis of Woolman's "Plea" reveals a deeply agonistic relationship between the *devil* and *god* terms, "oppression" and "love." Similarly, the *god* and *devil* terms, "usefulness" and "luxury" are deeply opposed. Clearly, Woolman has chosen terms that invite a choice of "love" over "oppression" and "the right use of things" over "luxury." There simply is no place given in the essay for the justification of oppression or the accumulation of "superfluities" under any circumstances. Does this polarized view mean that Woolman saw the world as a black or white reality? Not at all, and that fact is born out in his treatment of "rich" and "poor."

The relationship between "rich" and "poor" in the essay is more ambiguous than that of "oppression/love" or "usefulness/luxury." Woolman's choices here invite sympathy for the poor, but do not universally condemn the rich, as long as they live within the constraints of "universal love" and do not use the "power" of inheritance to perpetuate "oppression." Once again, "love" and "usefulness" are *god* terms in the essay while "oppression" and "luxury" are *devil* terms. There is never ambiguity with regard to the valences of these four terms.

The interesting tension between "reason" and "feeling" in the essay may reveal, in Foss' terms, "a conflict or tension in [Woolman's] worldview that must be resolved" (Foss 66). Beyond the results of cluster analysis on this topic noted above, Woolman throughout the essay seeks to appeal to his reader through the use of evidence and reasoned inference, yet the excitation of feeling—empathy or "tenderness" for the poor—is also evinced through his imagery and illustrations, including his litany of the effects of historical tyrants (239), reference to the treatment of Native Americans (243-244), and, particularly, the hypothetical illustration of the island population under the effects of selfish decisions made by a minority (247-249). Perhaps, rather than merely illustrating a "tension" between reason and feeling in the essay, Woolman has proposed linguistically a model of "harmony" in which reason and emotion, the head and the heart, team together to help make possible a new and "perfect" redemptive way of looking at and ultimately reconstructing economics.

The choice of terms forming a cluster around "children" is not only significant, but crucial with respect to accomplishing the daunting task of "redemption" from the "spirit of oppression." By identifying humankind with children, Woolman is able to move farther away from the proprietary implications of the term "fathers of the poor," a phrase he used at the beginning of the essay that tends to perpetuate the inequity between rich and poor. If, however, all humans are "children" and God is the "Father," then life can be lived differently because all are "brothers" and "sisters." From this perspective, the political and economic implications of the notion that God is "Father" and "Proprietor," and humans are all "dutiful children" and "tenants," are radical indeed.

Perhaps, though, this hoped for transformation from a strictly proprietary to a richly familial relationship, is not a new thing after all. It is clear that Woolman is addressing what he sees as a fallen age and is attempting to point out a path to regain its golden age, its lost state of "equity" and "universal love." In Woolman's world, by displacing an ideal existence based on "equity" and "universal love" with one based on selfishness aided by the "customs" of extravagant living and imprudent inheritance, humankind has become divided between "poor" and "rich." Generally, the former are weak and "oppressed" by the latter. The rich live their lives according to the dictates of "self" and unthinking "custom" resulting in a taste for "luxury" rather than an effort to produce universal employment at "useful things."

In order to overcome this situation—to attain, in Woolman's terms, "a perfect redemption from this spirit of oppression" (249), the demands of "universal love" must overcome "oppression" through the humility of seeing ourselves as "dutiful children" living in obedience to a heavenly "Father" who seeks to "awaken" us through a "witness in our conscience." Using Weaver's language, the *god* term, "love," would then have achieved dominance over the *devil* term, "oppression," and the moral universe of Woolman's discourse would be put in order.

Specifically, the rationalizations that are used to justify the existence and operations of business, property, inheritance, and power must be offset by, and come into balance with, the insistence on empathy and "tender-heartedness" on the part of the rich, an approach that Woolman also calls "feeling knowledge," or "the duty of tenderness to the poor" (229). Such a benevolent and enlightened attitude would have the effect of making humankind once again conscious of an alternative perspective: that we are all "children" with a common inheritance in "the whole family of Christ Jesus in this world" (249).

NOTES

[1] While I greatly admire the scholarship in Moulton's edition of Woolman's "Plea" as a reflection of "Woolman's final intentions" (PM 197), I am interested in the Whittier text as a valuable *rhetorical* artifact, because of the effects it had on a reading "audience" beginning in the nineteenth century and continuing through the readership of the 1961 reprint. We may discover insights about Woolman's mind through careful manuscript comparisons and other scholarly means, but original readers of the Whittier version assumed that they were reading what Woolman had intended to say and, more significantly, were variously influenced by the rhetorical choices discovered in that particular text.

[2] One can argue that the added chapters in the Moulton text come across as just that—added chapters. Moulton himself appears to support this conclu-

sion to a degree when he remarks that "at one time [Woolman] apparently considered Chapters 1-13 [Sections 1-12 in the Whittier text] a complete work" (PM 197). Furthermore, he observes regarding one of the key manuscripts of "A Plea": "Chapters 1-13 in MS 'Plea' seem to constitute a distinct unit. The final sentence of Chapter 13 is a fitting close. A gap then appears (not typical of previous chapter divisions), and Chapter 14 begins on the next page . . . in ink of a different color" (PM 320). Moulton concludes his discussion of the two main extant manuscripts of "A Plea" with an observation about "the inconclusive nature of the evidence" as to what Woolman actually intended, and makes the "conjecture" that "he died without having finally prepared either manuscript for the printer" (PM 321).

[3] In 1950, five years later, Burke again deals with "god terms" in a section of *A Rhetoric of Motives* titled "Rhetorical Names For God" (298-301).

[4] On the importance of queries among Quakers, Margaret Hope Bacon writes: "[The queries were] questions which the monthly meeting asked themselves on a regular basis. The queries were first used as a form of gathering information about the Society, but gradually became a form of self-examination" (81). Queries dealt with whether meetings were convened for worship; whether there was expression of love and unity; whether children were being trained properly; whether trade and business were being conducted in an honest manner; whether vain amusements were avoided; and other factors important in Quaker life. Rufus Jones added that "The 'Queries' called for an examination of the life from at least a dozen moral and spiritual view-points, and tended to present a concrete moral ideal for the daily life at home and in business occupations" (146).

WORKS CITED

Barclay, Robert. *An Apology for the True Christian Divinity*. . . 13th ed. Manchester, England: William Irwin, 1869.

Bacon, Margaret Hope. *The Quiet Rebels*. New York, NY: Basic Books, 1969.

Berthold, C. A. "Kenneth Burke's Cluster-Agon Method: Its Development and an Application." *Central States Speech Journal* 27 (1976): 302-09.

Burke, Kenneth. *A Grammar of Motives*. 1945. Berkeley, CA: University of California Press, 1969.

—-. *Attitudes Toward History*. 1937. Revised 2nd ed. Los Altos, CA: Hermes Publications, 1959.

—-. *The Philosophy of Literary Form: Studies in Symbolic Action.* 1941. Revised ed. New York, NY: Vintage Books, 1957.

—-. *A Rhetoric of Motives.* 1950. Berkeley, CA: University of California Press, 1969.

Foss, Sonja K. *Rhetorical Criticism: Exploration & Practice.* 2nd ed. Prospect Heights, IL: Waveland Press, 1996.

—-. "Women Priests in the Episcopal Church: A Cluster Analysis of Establishment Rhetoric." *Religious Communication Today* 7 (1984): 1-11.

Jones, Rufus. *The Quakers in the American Colonies.* 1910. New York, NY: Russell & Russell, 1962.

Marston, Peter J. and Bambi Rockwell. "Charlotte Perkins Gilman's 'The Yellow Wallpaper': Rhetorical Subversion in Feminist Literature." *Women's Studies in Communication* 14 (1991): 58-72.

Reid, Kathaleen. "*The Hay-Wain:* Cluster Analysis in Visual Communication." *Journal of Communication Inquiry* 14 (1990): 40-54.

Weaver, Richard M. *The Ethics of Rhetoric.* 1953. Chicago, IL: Henry Regnery, 1965.

Woolman, John. "A Plea for the Poor or A Word of Remembrance and Caution to the Rich." *The Journal and Major Essays of John Woolman.* Ed. Phillips P. Moulton. 1971. Richmond, IN: Friends United Press, 1989.

—-. "A Plea For The Poor." *The Journal of John Woolman and A Plea For The Poor.* The John Greenleaf Whittier Edition Text. New York, NY: Corinth Books, 1961.

III.

Issues of Oppression, Social Change, and Education

13

John Woolman and Structural Violence: Model for Analysis and Social Change

Vernie Davis

ONE HAS TO MARVEL at the visionary way in which John Woolman's analysis and approach to social change in the mid-18th century is appropriate to our current condition. At first glance our world seems as distant from his as the difference between traveling by horseback and airplane. Woolman (1720-1772) lived at the very verge of the industrial revolution. His concerns were the plight of the poor, slavery, and causes of the Indian wars—issues that seem remote to our lives today. We live in what Robert B. Williams, one of my colleagues in economics, calls a "seamless society" in which our economic relations go beyond the horizon and are often invisible to us. For us the questions might be whether the clothes we wear were produced in sweat shops by oppressed workers in another country; whether we benefit from investments in our managed retirement funds used to promote working conditions or products we would not choose to support if we were more fully aware; or how we as individuals might act in our complex, interconnected world to promote a more humane, just, and righteous economic order. John Woolman provides a model which eloquently addresses important questions of this and every age: How should we live our lives in our economic relations with others (including those we never see directly); how do we promote social change toward a more humane world?

Woolman's approach to these issues is especially useful because it challenges the popular view that the individual is powerless to affect social change. By analyzing the structural roots of social injustice, Woolman identifies individual responsibility in a way that seeks not to point blame but to provide appropriate and meaningful ways in which the individual has the *ability to respond.* At the same time Woolman's approach is consistent with nonviolence.[1] This essay will explore the methods of analysis and approaches to social change Woolman used in the 18th century so as to examine their relevance in responding to structural violence in today's world.

Structural violence, the term used by social scientists to describe the harm caused by structures of culture (socio-economic, political, and/or belief systems), is one of the major problems facing the world today. An infant dying or suffering irreversible brain damage from malnourishment when adequate resources are available or a worker suffering from exposure to pesticides or other toxic chemicals in her job because the employer refuses to provide protective gear are examples of structural violence. Many instances of "starvation and malnutrition, both of which restrict life chances, are seen as violence resulting from an inequitable world economic system and repressive regimes in various nations" (Wehr 14). The harm that comes to an individual who suffers starvation may not be caused by direct behavioral action of another person or group of persons, yet its consequences are no less injurious or debilitating to the person suffering. When this harm results from the withholding of necessary food or resources because of systemic social organization it is termed structural violence.

The harm and suffering of structural violence are sufficiently disturbing, but unfortunately the unjust and inequitable distribution of resources are also responsible for bringing still greater suffering into the world in the form of terrorism and military repression. Many of the oppressed and poor turn to hatred and violence as a way to win back their land or free themselves from oppressive working conditions, while the wealthy and powerful invest in military armaments to defend themselves and the status quo.

Although the social science use of the concept "structural violence" was developed by Johan Galtung in "Violence, Peace, and Peace Research," the concept behind the term has been around much longer. Certainly the problems which drew John Woolman's attention in the 18th century, the plight of the poor, the landless Indians, and the slaves, are examples of what we would now term structural violence. In the last decade there has been much more concern among social scientists to study and better understand structural violence.

Structural violence is not the only cause of behavioral violence, but it is a significant cause. As an anthropologist, I am struck that the most simple societies are also the most peaceful. The most nonbelligerent, peaceful societies in which war is absent are those in which sharing and cooperation are stressed and in which resources are equitably distributed. These societies demonstrate that peace is systemic and permeates all aspects of social interaction. This pattern is true of most hunting and gathering societies, which characterize all human societies up until the domestication of plants and animals about 10-12,000 years ago. Thus approximately 99% of human existence is characterized by the predominance of cooperation and sharing as opposed to stratification where a few amass and control the wealth of others. Likewise, it appears that this period was marked by less warfare and violence than occurs today (see, for example, Wright, Lenski and Lenski, Montagu, and Bodley). This is not to idealize pre-state societies as never engaging in violence. However, as Bodley points out in his book *Anthropology and Contemporary Human Problems,* "Military conquest is a form of economic growth that helps sustain wealth inequality" (177). Bodley notes that the issue of equality is critical to an understanding of the differences between tribal cultures and state societies. "No one in an egalitarian society is denied access to the means of production. . . . Land, water, and game are always open for use" (172). This cross-cultural evidence offers a hopeful message in terms of human capability, but it still leaves us with the problem of where to go from the stratified situation in which we now find ourselves.

There are several responses to the existence of structural violence. One is the use of direct behavioral violence mentioned earlier: the oppressed can use violence and terrorism in an attempt to overthrow the existing social order and/or the rich can invest in more military hardware and use repression in the search for security to protect their disproportionate share of the wealth. Another approach is social action through the method of community organizing developed by Saul Alinsky in *Rules for Radicals.* The tactics developed by Alinsky have been very popular as a way for the oppressed to organize and use power against those viewed as the oppressors without using direct behavioral violence, and they have been widely emulated by many community organizing campaigns in the U.S. Furthermore, Alinsky's methods fit nicely with the sociological theory of conflict theory (see, for example, Mills and Dahrendorf), which holds that social change is produced by the clash of groups such as social classes defending their own interests against another.

By polarizing the groups Alinsky refers to as the "haves" and "have-nots" and by mobilizing the "have-nots" to use social, economic, and political power against the "haves," Alinsky hopes to force the "haves" to lose some of their power and make concessions to the new power of the organized poor. This method avoids the use of behavioral violence—no blood is spilled. The advocates of this method also can argue that no structural violence occurs since the "haves" are wealthy enough to absorb loss of wealth without physical suffering. Yet this method fails to be nonviolent as defined earlier. It is not an action that seeks to further love and good will by actively rooting out harm and injustice, and its polarization of the "haves" and "have-nots" challenges the belief that all human life is sacred. Alinsky supports his method of dehumanizing the opposition by claiming that the end justifies the means.

There have also been some truly nonviolent movements among the oppressed. These are best epitomized by the movements led by Gandhi and Martin Luther King, Jr. Unfortunately, it is difficult for those of us living among the wealthy to send the message to those living under oppression to use nonviolence while we continue to live in comfort. Somehow the message of the value of suffering for the nonviolent approach loses some of its credibility when it comes from those of us able to partake of the comforts of life whenever we choose to return to them. Imagine how much of Christ's message would have been lost if he had been a Roman landowner who gave his sermons but still maintained luxuries unobtainable by the mass of people. The fact is that, now, those who call ourselves Christians are often responsible for holding the excess wealth and amassing military power to protect it. This makes teaching a Christian response to oppression more difficult.

I find John Woolman's approach of encouraging ministry among the wealthy and powerful to offer an exciting model for today. While he explores the structural roots of poverty and injustice, he does not accept that the individual is powerless to affect social change. Nor does he accept the perspective one might infer from Paulo Freire in *Pedagogy of the Oppressed,* that change can only be initiated by the oppressed. Both Woolman's analysis and his methods of addressing the problem are rooted in religious experience. He reverses the means/end perspective of Alinsky because for Woolman the means are the end. The moral imperative for Woolman is to do what is right regardless of the outcome. Moulton captures this aspect to Woolman's approach when he notes that:

> In social action he was not so much a strategist working for specific goals as he was a faithful witness to the revealed truth

> of God. His imperative was not primarily to show results but to testify in what he said and did, trusting to open the hearts and lives of others to the disturbing power of God. Yet he held the conviction that doing right would somehow be validated in the total economy of the universe. (Introduction, PM 7)

This represents a radical contrast to most other approaches of addressing oppression. Its focus on the means *as* the end and its religious base of universal love offers a peaceful approach to social change. It maintains and promotes nonviolence while promoting social change.

Woolman's approach has five essential ingredients: a systemic analysis of all facets of our lives, the recognition that the roots of war are greed for wealth and power, the subordination of personal will to divine will, reliance on universal love, and direct ministry with the wealthy to change their behavior.

The first aspect of Woolman's approach, inward self examination to increase one's conscious awareness of the implications of various parts of one's life, is central to develop a full understanding of the problem. In social science jargon, Woolman is asking us to take a systemic approach to examining our lives. Systems analysis examines the relationships between various elements of a system, e.g., how economic patterns connect with religious beliefs or political practices in a sociocultural system. Systems theory rejects the notion that each of these aspects of society or culture can be studied separately without regard to influences among them.

As the Quaker sociologist Paul Zopf notes, "An examination of these intricate ties in the social affairs of people provides at once the most revealing and the most complicated insights into social life" (2). Social scientists also recognize that systemic analysis as called for by Woolman is not an easy task. In the first place it is difficult to question what already exists and is commonly accepted (see, for example, Berger and Luckman). Furthermore, the complex, many faceted, highly specialized, and segmented society in which we live adds to the difficulty of understanding the systemic relationships among parts of the system even when we choose to engage in such analysis. John Woolman faced both of these problems in his own analysis.

A further obstacle to systemic analysis is the fact that there is resistance to modify a currently accepted belief or understanding. As John Woolman observed about people's inability to see slavery for the evil it was, the fact that the slave trade was an accepted practice that so many Christians were involved in made people "less apt to examine the practice" than if it were just now being proposed as a new idea (PM 211-212). It is difficult to question something which is currently accepted—especially when it is not only accepted but appears to be in our self interest if we are to maintain our present way of life. Imagine what it would be like for eighteenth-century plantation owners who were dependent on slave labor to consider seriously the ethics of slave holding. The recognition that they were dependent on slave labor to maintain the life they had grown accustomed to and the recognition that slave holding was contrary to the laws of God would be impossible to hold simultaneously. Cognitive dissonance theory in social psychology holds that when faced with two conflicting pieces of cognitive information, the human response will attempt to bring these into harmony by modifying one or the other. The temptation in this case was to somehow rationalize an ethic to support slave holding. As we look at the reaction to slavery in its historical context, it is easy to see the pattern of rationalization to provide justification for the owning of other human beings. Woolman recognized the attempt to rationalize unreasonable behavior to attain cognitive consistency. In response to the argument that slavery protected Africans from wars in Africa and that Africans were better off as slaves, he noted that "The love of ease and gain are the motives in general of keeping slaves, and men are wont to take hold of weak arguments to support a cause which is unreasonable" (PM 63).

We might benefit from asking ourselves if we also fall prey to this affliction of reason. Are we really motivated to assist the economic development of other regions when we invest in companies hiring workers at subminimal wages and dangerous working conditions or are we motivated by self gain for our investments? Are we really convinced that working conditions of companies cannot be included in company reports along with data on assets and economic return to stockholders or would we rather not know? Addressing the issue of slavery, Woolman says

> If compassion on the Africans in regard to their domestic troubles were the real motives of our purchasing them, that spirit of tenderness being attended to would incite us to use them kindly, that as strangers brought out of affliction their lives might be happy among us . . . . (PM 62)

Might Woolman ask of us, if our economic investments abroad are really intended to improve the living conditions of others, ought we not pay more attention to the actual conditions of workers and their families rather than to the national figures of economic growth and to the profits generated by corporations?

Transcending the personal difficulty of recognizing the vice in one's own practices is only the beginning of the problem. As Woolman points out, "they who labour to dissuade" others from participation in practices that accord with their material interests will be faced with social ostracism and will "have many difficulties to encounter" (PM 212). Again, from a cognitive dissonance perspective, one way to eliminate dissonance is to label persons who present views that challenge our current understandings as somehow beyond the fringe so that we can dismiss their message. Woolman's effectiveness in addressing these issues with Quaker slave holders might in part be credited to his ability to appeal to their core values, which made it more difficult for his message to be dismissed without creating other dissonance. Furthermore, Woolman himself was spared much of the personal difficulty in dealing with social ostracism because of his personal acceptance of divine will (see aspect three below).

Woolman's call for us to take seriously the inward self-examination of our lives to increase the conscious awareness of the implications for others is even more perplexing now than in Woolman's day. We share the same difficulty as the slave holders of the 18th century in that the implications would severely dislocate our lives. The challenge is compounded by the fact that it is more difficult for us to see the interconnections since our society is more complex in its division of labor. As a result we are frequently unaware of the sources of the clothes we wear and the food we eat. We are, thus, unable to see the relationship between our lives and the lives of the impoverished in the Third World countries, which as Elise Boulding points out, should be called more appropriately "the two/thirds world" (Boulding 1988). John Bodley, in his book *Anthropology and Contemporary Human Problems,* notes that one of the structural problems facing contemporary society is that our reliance on imports causes us to be less aware of the consequences of our consumption on the countries that provide the goods we use (40). It takes more effort to come to realize how corporations that are putting fresh fruit and vegetables on our tables may be pushing peasant families off their land to develop the plantations for export crops, that workers producing goods we consume may be subjected to inhumane working conditions, or that these practices might be encouraged by companies driven to maximize profits for us as shareholders in mutual funds that lack social screens. Furthermore, because of our cultural assumption that growth is a sign of economic health, we interpret increases in gross national products as positive signs of development even though the consequences may produce poverty and inequality. Perhaps this cultural bias is similar to the eighteenth-century European perspective that they were taking what they perceived as "unproductive" land from the Indians and making it more productive.

A clear demonstration of this problem was presented in the classic study by Gross and Underwood in Northeast Brazil. They studied the effects of a plantation which took land that had been used for local food production and converted it to grow sisal, a plant fiber used in the U.S. as twine for bailing hay in the beef and dairy industries. The people who formerly produced food for their own consumption on this land are now paid less than they need to meet their families' nutritional needs.

Gross and Underwood concluded that although sisal production has raised GNP by bringing more individuals into a money economy, the change has resulted in a hierarchical system that pays inadequate wages to the sisal workers. Their study found that wages paid to sisal workers were inadequate to buy sufficient food for their families, leading to malnutrition and attenuated growth rates in their children. Thus while the change may have been helpful to the economic statistics of Brazil's economic "development" as measured by GNP, the overall effect was deleterious to the health and well being of the local families involved. Malnutrition among sisal worker families in Brazil is directly linked to the American food system:

> . . . we should be aware of the contributions which production of sisal and other items make to the welfare of the developed nations which import them at extremely low prices, enforced to a large degree by the political pressure they can bring to bear on producer countries. Sisal, for example, contributes to milk and beef production in North America and Europe since it is used to bind animal fodder on grain fields. Thus sisal production is part of a system whose effect is to expropriate energy in the

> form of manual labor in one part of the world and apply it to the general welfare of another people thousands of miles away. (Gross and Underwood 737)

Similar circumstances are occurring elsewhere in the world. Lappe and McCallie documented the increase in malnutrition in the Philippines as banana plantations took over land that was previously used for subsistence agriculture. Rachel Kamel in an AFSC publication, *The Global Factory: Analysis and Action for a New Economic Era,* explores the causes and consequences of plant closings in the U.S. as well as the impact of substandard working conditions and wages in plants in the *maquiladoras* along the U.S./Mexico border and in the Philippines. Recent news stories have called into question the sweatshop working conditions of the off-shore apparel industry (see, for example, Krouse E1). If we were to take seriously a thorough examination of our global economic interconnections, how many other links might we discover of situations in which we gain from oppressive working conditions abroad?

Woolman also encourages us to look at the full systemic impact of our actions and not dismiss our responsibility if we are a beneficiary but not the direct perpetrator of the injustice. He argues, in "Considerations on Keeping of Negroes, Part II," that those who would reject personally taking arms to capture a slave from his native land by plunder cannot in good conscience deny that they are helping perpetuate that plunder and spilling of blood when they purchase the slave:

> . . . we are not joining against an enemy who is fomenting discords on our continent and using all possible means to make slaves of us and our children, but against a people who have not injured us. . . . He who buys the slave thus taken pays those men for their wickedness and makes himself party with them. . . . For were there none to purchase slaves, they who live by stealing and selling them would of consequence do less at it. (PM 233-234)

Woolman's systemic analysis led him to personal rejection of benefiting from the products of slave labor as well, and he wore undyed cloth to avoid the use of indigo dye which was produced from slave labor.

Although better understanding of these relationships may be difficult, Woolman suggests that we need to make this examination. Woolman asks that we think through how we would feel if conditions were reversed and we were laboring for the other person, or that we consider the case as if we had a son or daughter living in the same conditions. "In Considerations on Keeping Negroes, Part II," Woolman points us to the grief we feel when our own children suffer ill health or we face the death of a friend, and he calls on us to use the same criteria in our concerns for others.

> And did we attend to these scenes in Africa in like manner as if they were transacted in our presence, and sympathize with the Negroes in all their afflictions and miseries as we do with our children or friends, we should be more careful to do nothing in any degree helping forward a trade productive of so many and so great calamities. Great distance makes nothing in our favour. To willingly join with unrighteousness to the injury of men who live some thousands of miles off is the same in substance as joining with it to the injury of our neighbours. (PM 233)

It is often said that Gandhi presented this same criteria when he responded to the question, "What will it take to achieve world peace?" Gandhi is reported to have replied that peace will not be achieved until the life of the child born fifty miles outside New Delhi has the same value as the child born fifty miles outside New York City.

The second aspect to Woolman's approach is the recognition that war has its roots in greed for wealth and power. Woolman believed all wealth to be the gift of God and that, in distributing it, we should act as God's stewards and redistribute it without regard to selfish attachment: "Did we so improve the gifts bestowed on us that our children might have an education suited to these doctrines, and . . . we might rejoice in hopes of their being heirs of an inheritance incorruptible" (PM 205). In his understanding of the Indian wars, he recognized that the greed for land of the whites rather than a satanic spirit of the Indians was responsible for the Indian wars in the colonies. He saw that the plight of the Indians brought about by the unjust loss of their land led them to see war as their only alternative. Economic exploitation and militarism go hand in hand. The way for the colonies to protect their accumulated wealth from Indian uprisings was to increase their military preparedness. At times this relationship between wealth and wars was, and still is, recognized by those who support strengthening the military as well. James Logan, whom William Penn had appointed to represent his colonial proprietorship in Pennsylvania, criticized the Friends for their lack of support for the voluntary militia in Pennsylvania. He wrote in 1747: "Our Friends spare no pains to get and accumulate estates, and are yet against defending them, though these very estates are in great measure the sole cause of their being invaded" (qtd. in Jonas 73).

Jonas notes that the difference between Woolman and Logan is that ". . . having come to the same insight, Woolman saw no alternative to eschewing wealth (which did not mean embracing poverty), while Logan insisted on accumulating wealth (even at the risk of war)" (73).

In "A Plea for the Poor," Woolman recognized that the roots of war lie in desire for personal wealth and the love of dominion, and he pleads with his contemporary readers (and all of us) to recognize this:

> Oh that we who declare against wars and acknowledge our trust to be in God only, may walk in the Light and therein examine our foundation and motives in holding great estates! May we look upon our treasures and the furniture of our houses and the garments in which we array ourselves and try whether the seeds of war have nourishment in these our possessions or not. (PM 255)

Although today European Americans and Native Americans are not at war, we are facing increased social unrest, armed conflicts termed "low intensity wars" (many of which include U.S. involvement), and terrorism. Can we compare the commonly held belief of Woolman's day that the Indians were satanic to the current prejudices and misconception by some people in the U.S. about fundamentalist Moslems? We might do well to consider Woolman's recognition that social inequality not only supports structural violence but contains the seeds of war, terrorism, and military repression. Terrorist activities and attempts at revolution as well as militarism and violations of human rights are forms of overt violence that are a direct corollary of this principle.

The third aspect of Woolman's approach is subordination of personal will to divine will. This is perhaps the most important aspect of his orientation: this theme runs throughout his journal. His subordination to divine will is expressed very powerfully in his report of the vision he had late in his life when he was sick with pleurisy. He reports having heard what he believed to be the voice of an angel saying the words, *"John Woolman is dead."* As he later recognized himself to be alive, he puzzled to understand this mystery, and he came to the realization that "that language *John Woolman is dead,* meant no more than the death of my own will" (PM 186).

His faith in divine will freed him from being concerned about the personal cost of his witness. His faith did not depend upon an assumption that he would escape harm or suffering himself but, as Phillips Moulton writes, "on the assurance that even suffering and death could not ultimately harm one who lived 'in pure obedience to God' " (Introduction, PM 10). His reliance on being guided by divine will also gave him strength to face social ostracism for views and activities that were out of sync with social beliefs of the time. This strength is illustrated by an account in his *Journal* in which he explained to the brother of a dying Friend why he wished to be excused from writing a will that included inheritance of slaves. He records in his *Journal* that he felt the brother was displeased with him, however,

> In this case I had a fresh confirmation that acting contrary to present outward interest from a motive of divine love and in regard to truth and righteousness, and thereby incurring the resentments of people, opens the way to a treasure better than silver and to a friendship exceeding the friendship of men. (PM 46)

Elsewhere, when planning to wear a hat of undyed wool, he notes,

> . . . the apprehension of being looked upon as one affecting singularly felt uneasy to me. And here I had occasion to consider that things, though small in themselves, being clearly enjoined by divine authority became great things to us, and I trusted the Lord would support me in the trials that might attend singularity while that singularity was only for his sake. (PM 121)

For Woolman, reliance on divine guidance protected him from the cognitive dissonance of being seen by others as marginal in his views. His experience may serve as a model for us to consider the source of our own support when faced with social ostracism of others for our singular views. Woolman's *Journal* provides a powerful testimony of one who is spiritually centered in his work.

Subordination of personal will to divine will also decreases the overwhelming and unreasonable feeling of individual responsibility to solve a complex social problem on one's own and may allow for others to contribute their part. Woolman relates an incident in which he felt great weight of concern to address Simons Creek Monthly Meeting during which he felt agitated regarding the condition of slaves but did not feel his way clear to speak. He reports, ". . . In this condition I was bowed in spirit before the Lord and with tears and inward supplications besought him to so open my understanding that I might know his will concerning me, and at length my mind was settled in silence" (PM 70). After some time a member of the meeting addressed the concern that was on Woolman's mind and made a proposal that addressed the concern.

His reliance on divine guidance is the spiritual basis that provides the foundation for the other aspects of Woolman's approach. Were it not for his complete willingness to give up his personal will to follow the divine will it is unlikely he could have expressed the universal love that permeates his work with slave holders and those who benefit from slave labor. Perhaps we would do well to emulate Woolman in this regard as well and find the spiritual basis for allowing ourselves to be guided by divine will rather than what we think might be most effective. Woolman teaches us that it is not possible to demand or expect personal success. Woolman did not rely on himself to bring about change, but rather he sought to open others to the disturbing power of God. If we base our actions on the right rather than the expedient, we have to be willing to accept the outcome with a faith that what we do is worth doing even if we do not see our goals being achieved.

The fourth aspect of Woolman's approach is the belief that true harmony is dependent on universal love. This theme emerges strongly in Woolman's works. Frederick Tolles has described the love of John Woolman as "Pure love, heavenly love, universal love. . . , a tender pulsing sympathy with all mankind and all created things, arising from a secret inward spring" (v). The universality of Woolman's love even obliterated any bitterness toward those following paths he considered responsible for causing suffering. As Moulton writes,

> His primary aim, of course, was to ease the plight of slaves. Sensitive to hardships of any kind, he was keenly aware of what they suffered. Yet he also sympathized with the spiritual plight of the slaveholders, believing that to treat a person as

> a slave dimmed the owner's vision and depraved "the mind in like manner, and with as great a certainty, as prevailing cold congeals water" (PM 237). (PM 7-8)

Universal love, as modeled by Woolman calls attention to the suffering of the oppressed, and it also gives us an understanding of the oppressors. The capacity to love all and to see all life as sacred is a prerequisite for a fully nonviolent approach and is the basis for the next aspect of Woolman's orientation to social change.

The fifth aspect of John Woolman's approach to deal with structural violence is to minister among the wealthy and the powerful; that is, he speaks directly to slave holders to try to get them to examine their own lives. This ministry is supported in two ways: 1) Woolman believes that the vice of one's behavior must be discovered by that person individually, and 2) he is concerned that the "participation in slavery by church members tended to prejudice slaves and other sensitive persons against the faith" (Moulton, Introduction, PM 8).

In "Consideration on Keeping Negroes, Part II" Woolman is very explicit about the fact that judgement of other persons is to be done by God and not by us. He is convinced, however, that people cannot be held responsible for indirect oppression they do not understand. Using an example of idolatry, he says, "Real idolatry is to pay that adoration to a creature which is known to be due only to the true God" (PM 210).

> Whatever a man does in the spirit of charity, to him it is not sin; and while he lives and acts in this spirit, he learns all things essential to his happiness as an individual. And if he doth not see that any injury or injustice to any other person is necessarily promoted by any part of his form of government, I believe the merciful Judge will not lay iniquity to his charge. Yet others who live in the same spirit of charity from a clear convincement may see the relation of one thing to another and the necessary tendency of each; and hence it may be absolutely binding on them to desist from some parts of conduct, which some good men have been in. (PM 211)

It is very clear how this belief leads to Woolman's activity of meeting with the wealthy and powerful to labor with them so that *they can see* the misguided direction of their lives and then choose to change those practices.

Woolman was concerned because those who called themselves Christians were leading practitioners of oppression and exploitation which resulted in discouraging the further spread of Christianity. He recounts a vision in which he says:

> I was then carried in spirit to the mines, where poor oppressed people were digging rich treasures for those called Christians, and heard them blaspheme the name of Christ, at which I was grieved, for his name to me was precious. Then I was informed that these heathens were told that those who oppressed them were the followers of Christ, and they said amongst themselves, "If Christ directed them to use us in this sort, then Christ is a cruel tyrant." (PM 186)

He was concerned that actions by seemingly virtuous Christians could be especially damaging: "to conform a little to a wrong way strengthens the hands of such who carry wrong customs to their utmost extent; and the more a person appears to be virtuous and heavenly-minded, the more powerfully does his conformity operate in favour of evil-doers . . ." (PM 247).

Elsewhere he observes that

> To trade freely with oppressors and, without labouring to dissuade from such unkind treatment, seek for gain by such traffic tends, I believe, to make them more easy respecting their conduct than they would be if the cause of universal righteousness was humbly and firmly attended to by those in general with whom they have commerce; and that complaint of the Lord by his prophet, "They have strengthened the hands of the wicked" [Ezek. 13:22], hath very often revived in my mind. . . . (PM 157)

He was thus concerned that Christians who set a bad example mislead and hinder the religious growth of others.

This raises the question for us of what it means to minister among the wealthy and powerful. The message that "virtuous and heavenly-minded" Christians might "operate in favour of evil-doers" is not easily heard by those in power. But nonviolent protest movements from the oppressed can only be effective if those in power finally choose to give up militarism and repression. In other words, the powerful finally have to come to recognize this oppression themselves. There is no way to peaceful resolution without that recognition. Meanwhile, repression discourages the development of nonviolent resistance. The fact that many Christians are benefiting from this oppression and are willing to look the other way plays into the hands of those who argue that the whole Christian message is a sham to help keep the oppressed from rebelling. This tremendously discourages the adherence to nonviolent principles among the oppressed.

Can we persist in communicating to the managers of our pension funds that we are solely concerned with maximizing our return without attempting to consider the social consequences of our investments as well? Is the so-called pragmatist's warning that "we cannot know all that is necessary to use social criteria for our investments" comparable to the argument faced by Woolman that no one can know that Africans would be better off if left in Africa rather than traded as slaves? Would those who present the argument that it is not practical to pay attention to social criteria for investments really be willing to invest in companies that used slave labor? Are there really no limits to constrain our investments?

Woolman provides us with a model which does not leave us feeling powerless in the face of structural forces that seem too large to be affected by individual action. Yet, his approach is not an easy prescription for social change, and it cannot promise success of a particular goal we may hope to see. Its success must be measured by the means of how we live our lives rather than by the attainment of specific goals we had hoped to achieve. While this approach can be supported by social science theory and research, ultimately the decision to choose this approach must be based on an inward search for what is right. As John Woolman wrote in his *Journal,* "Deep-rooted customs, though wrong, are not easily altered, but it is the duty of everyone to be firm in that which they certainly know is right for them" (PM 50).

NOTE

[1] Nonviolence is here defined as "a positive philosophy of action that seeks to further love and good will by actively rooting out harm and injustice. It is not a particular set of tactics but a way of life predicated on the belief that all human life is sacred" (Davis 547).

WORKS CITED

Alinsky, Saul. *Rules for Radicals.* New York, NY: Vintage, 1971.

Berger, Peter, and Thomas Luckman. *The Social Construction of Reality.* Garden City, NY: Anchor, 1967.

Bodley, John. *Anthropology and Contemporary Human Problems.* 3rd ed. Mountain View, CA: Mayfield, 1996.

Boulding, Elise. *Building a Global Civic Culture: Education for an Interdependent World.* Syracuse, NY: Syracuse University Press, 1988.

Dahrendorf, Ralf. *Class and Class Conflict in Industrial Society.* Stanford, CA: Stanford University Press, 1959.

Davis, Vernie. "The Significance of Meaning in Violence and Nonviolence." *Applied Systems and Cybernetics: Proceedings of the International Congress on Applied Systems Research and Cybernetics.* Ed. George Lasker. Elmsford, IL: Permagon, 1980. 547-52.

Freire, Paulo. *Pedagogy of the Oppressed.* New York, NY: Seabury, 1968.

Galtung, Johan. "Violence, Peace and Peace Research." *Journal of Peace Research 3* (1969): 167-91.

Gross, Daniel, and Barbara Underwood. "Technological Change and Caloric Costs: Sisal Agriculture in Northeastern Brazil." *American Anthropologist* 73.3 (1971): 725-40.

Gummere, Amelia Mott, ed. *The Journal of John Woolman.* New York, NY: Macmillan, 1922.

Jonas, Gerald. *On Doing Good: The Quaker Experiment.* New York, NY: Scribner's, 1971.

Kamel, Rachel. *The Global Factory: Analysis and Action for a New Economic Era.* Philadelphia, PA: American Friends Service Committee, 1990.

Krouse, Peter. "Sweatshops: Exception or Rule?" *Greensboro News and Record.* July 14, 1996: E1.

Lappe, Frances Moor, and Eleanor McCallie. "Agribusiness in the Philippines: Banana Hunger." *Food Monitor* 3 (1978): 11-138.

Lenski, Gerhard, and Jean Lenski. *Human Societies.* New York, NY: McGraw, 1970.

Meeker-Lowry, Susan. *Economics as If the Earth Really Mattered: A Catalyst Guide to Socially Conscious Investing.* Philadelphia, PA: New Society, 1988.

Mills, C. Wright. *The Power Elite.* New York, NY: Oxford University Press, 1956.

Montagu, Ashley. *Learning Non-Aggression: The Experience of Non-Literate Societies.* New York, NY: Oxford University Press, 1978.

Tolles, Frederick B. "Introduction." *The Journal of John Woolman and a Plea for the Poor.* Ed. Frederick B. Tolles. Secaucus, NJ: Citadel, 1961.

Wehr, Paul. *Conflict Regulation.* Boulder, CO: Westview, 1979.

Woolman, John. *The Journal and Major Essays of John Woolman.* Ed. Phillips P. Moulton. 1971. Richmond, IN: Friends United Press, 1989.

Wright, Quincy. *A Study of War.* Chicago, IL: University of Chicago Press, 1942.

Zopf, Paul. *Sociocultural Systems.* Washington, DC: University Press of America, 1978.

14

The Figure of John Woolman in American Multicultural Studies

Susan Dean[1]

WHEN PETER CRYSDALE INVITED US TO TAKE PART in a series of Pendle Hill lectures on "The Presence of John Woolman," he proposed that I might speak on Woolman's influence upon American literature and culture. This suggestion made good sense. American literature and culture is my general field of research, and one of my regular teaching commitments is a chronological survey that takes a four-semester journey every two years across the terrain of myths and chronicles, songs and stories, memoirs and manifestoes that is American literature—or as some prefer to say, American literatures. Often, in the course of this journey, I think about the influence of Quaker culture upon our nation's slow-growing sense of social justice.

One of the best ways for a non-Quaker to understand the influence of Quakerism is to watch it working from within, at individual range; and a good way to do that is to read the *Journal of John Woolman*. For it can be said that the testimonies for social justice that Woolman made to the Society of Friends in the American colonies—especially his nearly thirty-year testimony against slavery—was a major factor in the Society's divesting itself of slaveholding by the end of the 1770s. And since it is widely accepted that the broad Abolitionist movement led by members of other Protestant denominations in the nineteenth century got its inspiration primarily from the example of the Quakers in the eighteenth, then it is not too great a leap to say that John Woolman has had a significant influence upon American society—an influence for the good.

Once one becomes alert to such issues of cultural influence, one can find many other instances of common direction, and other surprising points of near agreement, that connect Woolman to other figures and groups in American culture. But although I have a professional interest in these points of cultural history, I decided to defer them once I sat down in Fall 1994 to write my remarks. (Some of them, though, appear at the end of this essay). To explain my shift in focus, I will open with some personal reflections that grow out of my commuting-journeys between home and work over the past ten years, reflections that I hope will accord with the reflections of others.

• • •

Beneath the immediate concerns that fill our minds from day to day, we carry a sense of uneasiness at the disturbing inequities and social contradictions of contemporary life. The survival-of-the-fittest ethic that dominates the business world is increasingly pushing into all aspects of our lives, leaving little space for compassion and help for those who cannot keep up. No one is immune to the anxiety raised by this win/lose pressure; it pushes upon us all, making us run faster, even as we notice the casualties of the race falling around us. We are weighed down by a sense of helplessness at the difference between our private awareness that the social system is not working and the public consensus on these things. The malaise of which I speak is a low-lying phenomenon; it is possible to forget it or deny it; but I believe the burden of it is real and telling. Little by little, by degrees, we have come to define our own welfare narrowly, separating it from the welfare of others; and in this process we are narrowing our common humanity. In my judgment, only a renewed and sustained surge of fellow-feeling can overcome and heal this social divide that is also a self-division. "In the deserts of the heart / Let the healing fountains start . . ." wrote the poet Auden in 1939, in his elegy "In Memory of W. B. Yeats." I believe John Woolman can show us again how to feel and how to act on our feelings. He can be a presence, a voice, a friend, "tending to lead out of that under which the creation groans" (PM 174).

• • •

The survey-course that I am teaching this semester (Fall 1994) carries an ambitious title: "American Literature from the Creation to 1860." We are using new textbooks that deliberately set out to present a picture that includes more than the traditional European perspective; and so we begin with creation stories of the Native American Indians of South and Central America, creation stories that record visions of nature and spirit, human nature and human spirit, that inspired human beings on this continent before the arrival of European Christians.

My students, who were moved and astounded by those strange and rare opening texts, were troubled when we went on to read accounts of the losses that took place when European cultures met indigenous cultures. We read of how native peoples were mistaken from the beginning as "Indians" and from then on mistaken in almost every other way. They were assaulted physically by technologically-ingenious weaponry and by diseases that the invaders carried with them and that they had never developed resistance to. And they were assaulted psychologically by the intolerant colonizing attitudes of most of the invaders—who appropriated their lands and resources and treated them as savage brutes, sub-humans lacking minds and souls, cheap labor for the settlers and planters who followed the explorers and conquerors. And their religious beliefs and practices, too, were assaulted and desecrated—by persons who did not even notice the sacrilege they were committing.

The hardest thing for the students—and for me—to behold was the way the Europeans seemed to have made themselves psychologically invulnerable to feelings of compassion or remorse. They used the Bible and religious and secular law with sophistry, to make a case for subjecting the world and its creatures to their will. In continuing the dehumanization of other human beings, they seemed to us, as we read their words and lives in 1994, to have lost their own humanity through what I call "a severance of felt connection."

We should say, and in our class we remembered to say, that it is important to be careful, when reading back over the centuries, not to impose our sense of values and morals (itself a shifting sense) upon a period that looked to different standards. And yet perhaps it is right and timely for us to give critical consideration to this attitude of detachment, of a separation of feelings from words and action manifested over the long history of European expansion onto other continents, since it is still prevalent in our society's response to social dislocations today, when supposedly we look to more enlightened, more humane standards. Most of us are familiar with the explanation that is given for the present-day suffering that exists all around us, to be encountered everywhere we walk (if we look for it), between our era's humane ideals and non-humane practices. That explanation goes something like this: "It is unfortunate—tragic!—that there must always be some who lose and suffer, some casualties from the world's great motions—but the world has always moved in this way—that seems to be the price of progress—try not to let it get to you."

Some of us may remember hearing this line of reasoning from older relatives; but more likely it would have been a part of our formal schooling, when we first learned about the sufferings inflicted upon non-European populations after Europeans moved to the Western hemisphere as explorers, finders and founders, enslavers and "savers." The survey courses that many of us remember from school or college would have begun, not with the point-of-view of the peoples who were dispossessed of their lands and bodies, but, rather, with the subjective feelings of the Europeans who "found" them and founded new colonies and nations. Now, as I indicated earlier, many of those courses are changing.

What is happening in our schools is a part of a larger social change that has taken place over these last thirty years in our nation's self-understanding. The change was initiated by our collective experiences with social movements that protested our majority culture's values, assumptions, and methods of claiming consensus: the Civil Rights movement, the anti-war movement, the cultural pride movements, the environmental movement.

This change (and it may not be over-speaking to call it a "sea-change," since it is almost as significant as the European discovery of new continents across the seas, five hundred years ago; and since, indeed, it corresponds to that earlier change, a counter surge to that great wave) is making students and teachers re-analyze our history and re-assess our cultural heritage. We are beginning to appreciate how plural and complex this heritage is, and to scan it for examples of peace and understanding across cultures, examples that can hearten and help us as we live our own chapter of this immense story.

In working through the recently-published multicultural anthologies with students, I am finding that the culture of Quakerism, as it manifests itself in texts of the eighteenth and nineteenth centuries, can be a useful piece of "usable past" to highlight and work with. For the policies of the Quakers toward Indians and Africans stand out as a small bright candle in the dark colonial record of church-sanctioned intolerance and inhumanity. And the example of Quakerism (along with other exceptional sects and individuals) is evidence that Western Europe can generate unorthodox voices within itself, voices that broaden the range of choices inherited by subsequent generations.

• • •

I want to narrow my focus, now, to the *method* of address that John Woolman adopted as a social critic, reformer, and prophet. For I think that his method speaks directly to the problem that disturbs me and disturbed my students: the separation, the detachment, the apparently uncrossable divide that blocks our feelings of sympathy and empathy and prevents them from directly affecting our actual actions in the world—the gap that characterized colonial culture in Woolman's day and that still prevails in public life in our society today.

Woolman wrote as a member of a Society of Friends which was itself in a privileged position in England and America. In the seventeenth century Friends endured decades of persecution on both sides of the Atlantic; but in the eighteenth century they enjoyed toleration from the English government, lands that welcomed them in the mid-Atlantic colonies of New Jersey, Pennsylvania, and Delaware, and in general, a new esteem from many non-Quakers. Friends were increasingly seen as setting a good example and tone for the rising middle class, since they strove to live in consistency with their principles of simplicity, truth, and peace, and thrived from this consistency.[2]

Yet Woolman does not affix the noun "oppressors" upon his neighbors, eighteenth-century members of the Society of Friends in English-speaking America. He speaks of them and to them as true Friends with whom he has common cause, interests, concerns, and at the same time, as Friends "entangled in the spirit of oppression" (PM 165). Despite this tangle, they are persons who have in themselves good intentions, good will, and a sympathetic love of the creation that can be appealed to.

Thus, when Woolman uses the word "we" in his *Journal* and epistles, he refers to a reading audience of Friends who are both privileged and principled. But he pushes this audience: its "we" is implicated in oppression. It is true that Friends have themselves suffered oppression in the past (notably so in the second half of the seventeenth century):

those sufferings are part of their conscious memory and group identity. But Woolman sees that in their time, in the eighteenth century, by virtue of the fortunate and privileged position that their principles have brought them to, Quakers partake in and benefit from a system that oppresses others.

I see a continuum between the contemporary Friends whom Woolman expected would read the *Journal* after his death, and his many later readers outside the Society of Friends, whom he probably did not anticipate. For agreement with Woolman's views does not seem to be a necessary condition to dialogue with him. The *Journal* shows repeatedly that Woolman's ideas of goodness appeared eccentric and unrealistic to many of his fellow-Quakers. But rather than abandon a conviction of truth once he had prayerfully arrived at it, Woolman would keep bringing his testimonies before those he thought should and could act on them. He would persist, in a spirit of mutuality (differing finite readings of infinite Truth, mutual love of it and need for it), until eventually his testimonies came to be tolerated and (sometimes) accepted and adopted.[3]

His words, as they come through in the writings, always seem to expect, and to be appealing to, "Friendly" qualities in his audience: their good will, their concern for their fellow-beings, their desire not to inflict injury to "that of God." It is this "Friendly spirit" in his "we" that kept him from giving offense to his contemporaries and that has continued to appeal to subsequent generations. Even today (perhaps especially today) his address has the power to put us in touch with our better thoughts and feelings and to move us to suspend disbelief and indifference.

• • •

In this section I will lift out of the *Journal* a number of passages that allow me to describe the "motion of love" that Woolman makes to those he approaches as Friends. I will set them in three groups in order to explain the three steps (psychological and logical) that I see him taking.

I. The first set of quotations shows Woolman's characteristic way of looking at social problems and needs: he sees them not as separate entities, self-contained rights and wrongs, but as *influences*, helpful and harmful.

> (1) . . . for the promoting [of] his peaceable kingdom in the world [they] are content to endure hardness like good soldiers, and are so separated in spirit from the desire of riches that in their employments they become extensively careful to give none offense—neither to Jews nor heathens nor the church of Christ. (PM 177)

Why should a desire for superfluities beyond one's basic needs, and the acquirement and display of them, be so offensive to a Quaker? Such a desire is *unFriendly*, hurtful in its effects upon others. These superfluities attract attention; they instill confusion, envy, and unhappiness in those whose sense of self-sufficiency ("content," "fulfillment") is shaky and who look to their Quaker neighbors for examples of how to live their lives.

> (2) As the least degree of luxury hath some connection with evil, [then] for those who profess to be disciples of Christ and are looked upon as leaders of the people, to have that mind in them which was also in him, and so stand separate from every wrong way, is a means of help to the weaker. (PM 54-55)

This is the principle, a psychological principle of simplicity that necessitated separateness, which most Quakers saw clearly in the early days of their movement, but which was lost sight of as the Society prospered and as succeeding generations moved to pass their prosperity on to their heirs.

> (3) Friends in early times refused on a religious principle to make or trade in superfluities, of which we have many large testimonies on record, but for want of faithfulness some gave way, even some whose examples were of note in Society, and from thence others took more liberty. Members of our Society worked in superfluities and bought and sold them, and thus dimness of sight came over many. At length Friends got into the use of some superfluities in dress and in the furniture of their houses, and this hath spread from less to more, till superfluity of some kinds is common amongst us. (PM 184)

> (4) . . . I had at several times in my travels seen great oppressions on this continent, at which my heart had been much

> affected and brought often into a feeling of the state of the sufferers. And having many times been engaged, in the fear and love of God, to labour *with those under whom the oppressed have been borne down and afflicted,* I have often perceived that a view to get riches and provide estates for children, to live comfortable to customs which stand in that spirit wherein men have regard to the honours of this world—that in the pursuit of these things I had seen many entangled in the spirit of oppression, and the exercise of my soul been such that I could not find peace in joying in anything which I saw was against that wisdom which is pure. (PM 164-65, emphasis added)

Look at the double action here, as Woolman speaks of being moved to feel the "state of the sufferers" *and* to labor feelingly with those under whom they suffer. He looks in both directions as a *Friend*, never in a manner that would divide, isolate, measure fault or misery, or publicly shame. He focuses, and helps others to focus, upon the tendencies of a practice or attitude or situation, and its ongoing effects. He shows his readers and neighbors how susceptible to one-another's influence all human creatures are: the borders of our individual selfhood are so much more permeable and porous than we realize, and we observe, compensate for, and often imitate one another's actions and attitudes beneath the level of consciousness. In this great chain of conductive influence, no one is unconnected to the sufferings of another, and no one is free of the tangle of being partly responsible for those sufferings. The English Friend who has gotten into the use of luxurious superfluities is connected to the suffering of African slaves in the Carolinas and in Barbados, as well as to the underground labor forced upon native miners in Uruguay. The frontiersman who moves onto territories in western Pennsylvania to which the Indians had been guaranteed exclusive use by Penn's descendants through solemn treaties is implicated in the violent wars of reprisal engaged in by those Indian tribes, since he covets their land and sells them whiskey to cloud their judgments so that they will sign it away. Yet this same frontiersman has been pushed West by more civilized citizens—some of whom are Friends—in the East, who have raised the cost of real estate with their rising standard of living, and pushed their rough and red-necked countrymen out to seek cheaper lands.[4]

There is always a danger that a vision which shows the entangling effects of evil and oppression may itself generate despair and discourage resistance. Where is one to start, how is one to start, in a tangle that one is part of, whose knots reach across physical distances and down into the psyche? But Woolman does not despair because he is able to draw comfort from the movings of the Holy Spirit, whose breathings are as close to him as his own. (Brought up in the culture of the Society of Friends, he has been taught and he has become sensitized to such movings.)

> (5) . . . I have felt tender breathing in my soul after God, the fountain of comfort, whose inward help hath supplied at times the want of outward convenience; and strong desires have attended me that his family, who are acquainted with the movings of his Holy Spirit, may be so redeemed from the love of money and from that spirit in which men seek honour one of another that in all business by sea and land we may constantly keep in view the coming of his kingdom on earth as it is in heaven, and by faithfully following this *safe guide,* may show forth *examples tending to lead out of that under which the creation groans!* (PM 173-174, emphases added)

The points at which we can sense creation groaning, these are the points at which to labor, to explain; they can become places for help and comfort now, and in the future, positive examples of how human beings may become cultural agents working with the creation, helping extricate, alleviate, liberate.

In the next group of quotations a second step can be read. In addition to recognizing that we are mutual influences upon one another across the spaces that separate us, we must look deep within our own selves to the power that makes creaturely connections possible—that is, to the Creator who made us all and whose word dwells deep within each soul; and we must take that source as our primary influence. This is the "safe guide" that will help us find points of opening for the Spirit in the world.

II. One makes contact with this "safe guide" by attending to the voice of the Creator deep within and by bringing its testimony into conversation with all the voices and influences of the rest of creation.

> (6) . . . many look at the example of one another and too much neglect the pure feeling of Truth. Of late years a deep exercise

> hath attended my mind that Friends may *dig deep,* may carefully cast forth the loose matter and get down to the rock, the sure foundation, and there hearken to that divine voice which gives a clear and certain sound. . . . (PM 184, emphasis added)

In the next-to-last chapter of his *Journal,* which records the mental and spiritual "exercises" that he was under during his voyage to England, Woolman tells us how one attains such closeness with the fountain of comfort, God in one's soul, that one breathes and moves in the Spirit. One must feel it.

The water of separation is felt. . . . (PM 176, emphasis added)

It is God's fluid, melting, dissolving power. It puts us in touch with the Creator's love for the creation. We love too, and we wish for the well-being of all, without presuming to understand the mystery and diversity of the forms and motions of this All. We are separated from separateness, and we love not only the sufferers who have been borne down by oppression, but also those who are so "entangled in the spirit of oppression" as to bear them down, those whose minds have become divided and set against the principle of tenderheartedness and sympathy implanted in them at birth. Creation includes and embraces all.

> (7) In an entire subjection of our wills the Lord graciously opens a way for his people, where all their wants are bounded by his wisdom; and here we experience the substance of what Moses *the prophet* figured out in the water of separation as a purification from sin. (PM 175, Woolman's emphasis)

> (8) . . . if these through the infinite love of God *feel* the power of the cross of Christ to crucify them to the world, and therein learn humbly to follow the divine leader, here is the judgment of this world—here the prince of this world is cast out. *The water of separation is felt;* and though we have been amongst the slain, and through the desire of gain have touched the dead body of a man, yet in the purifying love of Christ we are washed in that water of separation. . . . *To feel the substance pointed at in this figure,* man must know death as to his own will. (PM 176, emphases added)

Why must the individual will, the individual ego, be stilled, "subjected," to the love of God? It is because of the tendency of "unsubjected" human beings (even Friends—perhaps especially Friends!) to be purposeful and active, to busy themselves at their worthy purposes, until their entire attention is so dominated by the motions of their own projected "business" that they become desensitized to the motions of God within. "Subjection," then, has as much to do with the problem of perception as with the issue of authority.[5]

> (9) The natural mind is active about the things of this life, and in this natural activity business is proposed and a will in us to go forward in it. And as long as this natural will remains unsubjected, so long there remains an obstruction against the clearness of divine light operating in us; but when we love God with all our heart and with all our strength, then in this love we love our neighbours as ourselves, and a tenderness of heart is felt toward all people, even such who as to outward circumstances may be to us as the Jews were to the Samaritans. . . . In this love we can say that Jesus is the Lord, and the reformation in our souls, manifested in a full reformation of our lives, wherein all things are new, and all things are of God . . . —in this the desire of gain is subjected. (PM 177)

It follows that when one subordinates one's will and attention, suspends one's busy purposes so as to be open to fresh promptings from love, one will be filled with, led by, tender feelings of sympathy and empathy. For Woolman the gap between feeling and acting exists to be crossed. Again and again God's fountain helps him do it. *"The water of separation is felt."* It is God's water, and so it floats us free from the grip of the business that would separate us from others, and from all the separateness and isolation. We feel the whole of creation, feel the groaning chains of oppression but also the creative potential they cannot contain, the spirit tending to "lead out."

III. In what I see as the third and closing step in Woolman's approach, he leaves us with examples of how to keep open the way, once it has been cleared, to the inner waters that are our contact with oneness and wholeness. He shows us how he himself goes about "digging deep." Consciously, attentively, ongoingly, he undertakes mental and spiritual exercise with the social needs that he encounters. At the same time he opens himself to promptings, divinings, intuitions, intelligence from below the level of consciousness so that the whole self is engaged. He records his most telling dreams in detail (see PM 24, 161, 186, and 257-58), without pinning down the exact meanings that they bore for him when he dreamt them or when he set them down in writing. His treatment allows the mysterious suggestiveness of the dreams to continue to offer new messages for him and for his readers. They speak inexhaustibly to his ministry of love and concern.

Let us look at one of Woolman's dream-visions, that of an injured, groaning creation that appeared to him two and one half years earlier and that he reflects upon in a 1772 *Journal* entry. The dream opens with a view of a massive shape, perhaps suspended in space, a shape which on closer approach proves to be a mass of humanity.

> (10a) In a time of sickness with pleurisy a little upward of two years and a half ago, I was brought so near the gates of death that I forgot my name. Being then desirous to know who I was, I saw a mass of matter of a dull gloomy colour, between the south and the east, and was informed that this mass was human beings in as great misery as they could be and live, and that I was mixed in with them and henceforth might not consider myself as a distinct or separate being. (PM 185)

> (10b) I was then carried in spirit to the mines, where poor oppressed people were digging rich treasures for those called Christians, and heard them blaspheme the name of Christ, at which I was grieved, for his name to me was precious. Then I was informed that these heathens were told that those who oppressed them were the followers of Christ, and they said amongst themselves: "If Christ directed them to use us in this sort, then Christ is a cruel tyrant." (PM 186)

This powerful image anticipates the picture of colonialism and imperialism that students of American culture are assembling from the new multicultural readings, the troubling picture that I spoke of at the opening of this essay. Modern textbooks present us with a picture of a world racked with fever; Woolman's dream catches that illness with full force, and then goes on to imagine and experience a spiritual cure for it.

> My tongue was often so dry that I could not speak till I had moved it about and gathered some moisture, and as I lay still

> for a time, at length I felt divine power prepare my mouth that I could speak, and then I said: "I am crucified with Christ, nevertheless I live; yet not I, but Christ that liveth in me, and the life I now live in the flesh is by faith in the Son of God, who loved me and gave himself for me" [Gal. 2:20]. Then the mystery was opened, and I perceived there was joy in heaven over a sinner who had repented and that that language *John Woolman is dead* meant no more than the death of my own will. (PM 186, Woolman's emphasis)

Let me try to translate this "cure" into faith-language that can be accessible to the full spread of readers of this essay, those who share Woolman's Quaker beliefs and those with beliefs that require suspension while his reasoning is followed. The dreamer who lacks the power to speak, who waits until moisture is released and wells up to his tongue, is experiencing yet again "the waters of separation"—the waters of feeling that separate, release, creatures from their separateness. When the oneness of creation is *felt,* the barriers of finite will and understanding are dissolved; the perceiver is no longer caught in the apparent finality of oppression, surrendering to the gap that oppression makes us believe is the law of life, but is released into the solution, to experience the love that makes life possible. Deep love is the vital intelligence that Woolman holds out today to individuals who despair at the vision of cultural oppressions that they see themselves born into.

I think this intelligence is one that many of us are seeking at this time in our history, as we work to respect cultural relativism and to be suspicious of false universals, but at the same time yearn to experience again a oneness beyond the reach of oppression.

To fill out this section, here are three simply-stated articles of faith, or faith-principles, that Woolman inscribes in the early pages of his *Journal* and that set the tenor for the story that follows:

> (11) Thus he whose tender mercies are over all his works hath placed a principle in the human mind which incites to exercise goodness toward every living creature; and this being singly attended to, people become tender-hearted and sympathizing, but being frequently and totally rejected, the mind shuts itself up in a contrary disposition. (PM 25)

> (12) I . . . was early convinced in my mind that true religion consisted in an inward life, wherein the heart doth love and reverence God the Creator and learn to exercise true justice and goodness, not only toward all men but also toward the brute creatures; that as the mind was moved on an inward principle to love God as an invisible, incomprehensible being, on the same principle it was moved to love him in all his manifestations in the visible world; that as by his breath the flame of life was kindled in all animal and sensitive creatures, to say we love God as unseen and at the same time exercise cruelty toward the least creature moving by his life, or by life derived from him, was a contradiction in itself. (PM 28)

> (13) I found no narrowness respecting sects and opinions, but believed that sincere, upright-hearted people in every Society who truly loved God were accepted of him. (PM 28)

In these three statements of faith, love of the creation, for Woolman, dissolves every divisive classification. These faith-principles give us the assumptions that guide Woolman during the conversations and meditations, teaching and writing that make up the unpretentious narrative of his life. The principles, the quiet narrative, the revelatory images in the dream-visions, and the Friendly manner in which he "tenders" his social criticism: these form a vitally living word, still capable of speaking to our need today, a word which enlarges and releases our sense of hope and possibility.

• • •

In the broad project of comparative cultural studies that is under way in our time, Woolman's *Journal,* as an expression of Quaker culture, invites comparison with writings produced from cultures coming out of other American religions. Within English Protestantism, Woolman's "Friendly" purity contrasts with that of the seventeenth-century Puritans, as does his kind of separatism with that of the New England Separatists (separation *to,* separation *from*). His inconspicuous ways of working for the public good can be usefully compared with those of his contemporary, Benjamin Franklin; his faith in the deep intuitions of the individual soul, with those of the nineteenth-century Transcendentalists. Woolman's willingness to put feelings prominently into his discourse, so as to move the public to sympathize with the sufferings of others and to support social reforms, connects him to some of the reform-minded women writers in the nineteenth-century, such as Harriet Beecher Stowe and Rebecca Harding Davis, Pauline Hopkins and Zitkala-Sa. As for his unselfconscious androgyny, the flowing tears that are as important as the reasoning in his spoken and written testimony: when these stylistic features are removed from context and put next to the "objective," impersonal style of the twentieth-century modernists, Woolman can appear sentimental and oddly "feminized"; but when his style is set alongside the more open, and openly gendered subjectivity of our own postmodern times, its powerful fluency comes clear.

From such acts of comparison a remarkably contemporary figure emerges, whose writings speak to our present-day cultural situation. As we look for positive images that stand out from five dark centuries of colonial history, Woolman can be seen to represent not only Quakerism but also liberal European Protestantism at its best, a figure to remember alongside Bartolome de las Casas in the Roman Catholic tradition.

But let us extend the cross-cultural conversation further, beyond the voices of the European tradition. Let us compare Woolman's principles of spiritual and economic democracy with those that have held together the cultures of Native American peoples since long before the arrival of Europeans and that hold many of them together still, despite the tirelessly expansionist efforts of "civilization."

Woolman's three faith-principles (quoted above) express his belief in "that of God" in all creatures, a belief we know he held consistently (e.g., the concerned attention he gives in his *Journal* to the cooped-up fowls on shipboard and to the abused post-horses in England). But in these statements he does not mention bodies of water and earth as life-forms alive with spirit and sentience. Here Woolman's imagination, which is otherwise so free of European tendencies to stratify by class, religion, nationality, race, and species, slips into a view of land as an inert substance, a "field" for human development, that is traditionally European.

In "A Plea for the Poor," chapters 11-13, Woolman argues that God is the Original Proprietor of the earth who grants life-holdings of land to his faithful children and their descendants. These property-grants are loans, says Woolman: the loans can be renewed so long as the tenants use the properties "properly"—-i.e., cultivating them in a spirit of simplicity and mutual charity, avoiding possessive and oppressive ways. A property-right stops being a "right" when it is used wrongly. Woolman uses this imagery to remind Friends that they owe their commonwealth to the Creator, and to "plead" that they remember to share their wealth with the needy. The Old Testament vision beloved by Quakers, of a peaceable kingdom where the lion lies down with the lamb and where economic inequality does not create discord and suffering, still lies in the future; the colonies founded by Penn in New Jersey and Pennsylvania have only moved a little ways toward it. The gap, the need that still obtains, this must continue to be addressed by countless liberal efforts of friendly persuasion, such as we see Woolman performing in his writings.

Native Americans also argue that the earth cannot be possessed by humans, but they do so on a more thoroughgoing, radical basis. God, the Great Spirit, has created all bodies—including the body of the earth—with living spirit. Land is not a commodity to be divided, settled, developed, "owned" as personal, private property. In the twentieth century they have used with increasing urgency the resonant metaphor "Mother Earth" to make clear the relationship that they want to maintain toward the land. Since all creatures are the children of Mother Earth, it is wrong for humans to own or exploit one another (an idea Woolman shared) or to own or exploit other species (an idea Woolman would have been drawn to) or to own or exploit Mother Earth herself (an idea that would have seemed revolutionary to Woolman). Though Native American social and economic arrangements differ greatly according to the situation and history of each tribe, yet they show, under their variety, a common set of attitudes toward the land: basic human needs (foods, medicines, shelter, fuel) are gathered communally and distributed evenly so that plenty and scarcity are shared by the group, and so permanent classes of "rich" and "poor" do not arise; decisions affecting the group are arrived at communally, by consensus; stable, non-expansionist economies carefully keep the needs and size of the human populations in balance with the other life-forms around them.

• • •

In 1763, when his labors against slavery were nearing completion, Woolman made a long, dangerous journey to visit the Delaware Indians at Wyalusing on the northern frontier of Pennsylvania. The Delawares and Woolman had to communicate through interpreters, in short sentences only; but they did appreciate one another's tone, attitude, spirit. ("I love to feel where words come from, " said the chief Papunehang, after a meeting at which Woolman spoke [PM 133].)

I like to imagine that if Woolman were alive today, he would again be drawn into cross-cultural dialogue with Native American peoples. Given his ability to look for the effects, the tendencies, of things, Woolman would notice, I believe, that the human characteristics promoted by the Native American spiritual-economic beliefs—simplicity, contentment, harmony, mutuality—are the very ones that Quakers are called to and that he, Woolman, re-called them to. And given his steady emphasis on the motive power of human feelings, Woolman would appreciate, I believe, the comfort and joy, as well as the motive power—the sense of relatedness and of responsibility—that are released when humans can put the "New World" assumption that the environing earth is a good mother together with the "Old World" belief that the heavens above house a good father.

Where this cross-cultural conversation would take Woolman, we can only imagine. But such a conversation is being urged upon us today, for even business-as-usual is having to pay attention to the voices that are rising from all directions, calling attention to the destruction that business-as-usual is wreaking on the natural world and upon the indigenous peoples in America and on other continents who identify with, and stand alongside, the natural world. This conversation demands that we draw upon perceptions and feelings and spiritual ideas that our secular culture has socialized us to regard as sentimental, immaterial. Woolman can help us to recover our feelings and to labor with them, digging deep until we arrive at the waters of separation that will bring us into unity with the creation.

NOTES

[1] As a part of the autumn 1994 Pendle Hill Monday evening lecture series on John Woolman, Anne Dalke and Susan Dean gave companion talks on the same evening (Dodson 8-20), since they have much in common, both being Americanists, both teaching in the same department at Bryn Mawr College, and both belonging to local monthly meetings.

[2] A useful discussion of the changes brought about by Quaker prosperity can be found in Frederick B. Tolles' *Meeting House and Counting House: The Quaker Merchants of Colonial Philadelphia, 1682-1763* (Chapel Hill, NC: University of North Carolina Press, 1948).

[3] This is a good point for me to register my personal response to the concern that Anne Dalke has raised about Woolman's "singleminded certitude." How may we understand it?

I do think it is possible—though difficult—to keep hold simultaneously to certitude and incertitude. And I myself think Woolman kept hold of both. He is certain about some basic principles—he has to be. (As occasions change, the application of those basic principles will also change, so that what was a sufficient expression of them at any given time will probably be insufficient at another time, place, and occasion.) But his belief that the principles are true—the Truth, unchanging beneath historical changes—is, in my opinion, importantly steadying for John Woolman. It gives to him and to other would-be-Friends-of-Truth a sense of an inner light to go by.

In the secular world and the secular institutions that most of us work in, the principle of Truth is not equated with the principle of Love. In fact, in many institutions of higher learning almost the opposite assumption holds: there is a non-equation, an instinctive doubt that the two principles could be identical, a suspicion that Love is not a strong truth in our universe and that the Truth is not loving. But for Woolman and for many Quakers, there is a conviction that the principles of Love and Truth are in harmony, have been in harmony throughout creation, and will always be in harmony, beneath every change of circumstance and occasion.

Both assumptions can take the form of convictions, "certitudes."

Can Woolman's "religious certitude" be introduced into classrooms in institutions where skepticism is the dominant mode of inquiry and where there is a disposition, not only to distinguish Truth from Love, but to distance them from one another? I believe that these two ways-of-seeing and speaking can co-exist fruitfully in a secular classroom. Here is how I imagine their conversation: a teacher in the Woolman mode might announce, "This is the proposition that I assume; let me explain why I think it is relevant here"; the response from the academy would be: "We [the difference in pronouns is deliberate] are suspicious of your proposition, but you may articulate it here and it will be considered, like any other hypothesis, on the basis of the particulars and reasoning that you attach to it and on the problems that it illuminates." The secular academy's ideal of Truth (an endlessly free play of ideas and speech) means that its certitudes can be challenged; the final word has not been spoken. The same can be said of Woolman's certitudes.

[4] See Woolman's trip to visit the Delaware Indians at Wyalusing, Pennsylvania (PM 122-37), when he ponders the encroachments upon tribal lands by "people on the frontier."

[5] Woolman's account of an "unsubjected," "natural mind" seems to me more clear, and thus more accessible to outsiders, than the account of the "fallen" nature of "natural man" that is passed on in orthodox Christian cultures under the doctrine of "Original Sin."

There is a clear contrast in the pictures of "nature" and "nurture" that are developed in these different faith-traditions. Because Quakers believe that God is a living presence in nature, the work of "nurture," as they see it, is "pro-active": to promote a supportive group-culture that will be attentive to the motions of that inner life, able to form and re-form in motion with them. In orthodox Christian denominations that begin with a perception that all forms of nature are fallen, born with a proclivity to fall, "nurture" tends to be set in reaction to this perceived problem. Nurture's work is to save nature from itself, repress its proclivities, and control its motions; much of this work has traditionally been assigned to regulative institutions—the offices of the church, the school, the law, the state.

WORKS CITED

Brinton, Howard H. *Friends for 300 Years: the History and Beliefs of the Society of Friends Since George Fox Started the Quaker Movement.* 1952. Wallingford, PA: Pendle Hill Publications, 1964.

——. *Quaker Journals: Varieties of Religious Experience among Friends.* 1972. Wallingford, PA: Pendle Hill Publications, 1983.

Dodson, Shirley, ed. *John Woolman's Spirituality and Our Contemporary Witness.* Philadelphia, PA: Philadelphia Yearly Meeting Religious Education Committee and Pendle Hill, 1995.

Galeano, Eduardo H. *Genesis.* New York, NY: Pantheon Books, 1985. Vol. 1. of *Memory of Fire.* Trans. Cedric Belfrage. 3 vols. 1985-88.

Gill, Sam D. *Mother Earth: An American Story.* Chicago, IL: University of Chicago Press, 1987.

Lauter, Paul, et al., eds. *The Heath Anthology of American Literature.* 2nd ed. 2 vols. Lexington, MA: Heath, 1994.

Mander, Jerry. *In the Absence of the Sacred: the Failure of Technology and the Survival of the Indian Nations.* San Francisco, CA: Sierra Club Books, 1991.

Tolles, Frederick B. *Meeting House and Counting House: The Quaker Merchants of Colonial Philadelphia, 1682-1763.* Chapel Hill, NC: University of North Carolina Press, 1948.

Woolman, John. *The Journal and Major Essays of John Woolman.* Ed. Phillips P. Moulton. 1971. Richmond, IN: Friends United Press, 1989.

Wright, Louella Margaret. *The Literary Life of the Early Friends, 1650-1725.* Intro. by Rufus M. Jones. New York, NY: AMS Press, 1966.

15

"Fully Attending to the Spirit": John Woolman and the Practice of Quaker Pedagogy

Anne Dalke[1]

LIKE SUSAN DEAN, WHOSE ESSAY APPEARS EARLIER in this volume, I draw on Quakerism in general, and on John Woolman specifically, as inspiration for the work I do at Bryn Mawr College.[2] As Americanists, Susan and I find Woolman's *Journal* and essays wondrous guides to our vocation, as we engage with our students with issues of curricular diversification on campus, and with colleagues in various gatherings—which, like all academic decision-making bodies, get fractious at times. I try in particular to bring Woolman's understanding of "universal Light" (PM 264), and Woolman-like practices—such as the evocation of personal witness, the process of mutual correction, and the construction of group authority—into such deliberations.

I find a particular call, and need, to do so because of Bryn Mawr's rather "vexed" Quaker roots. Joseph Taylor, the founder of the college, envisioned it as a "female copy" of Haverford, a place where conservative Friends could send their daughters (Horowitz 106, 111). Its second president, M. Carey Thomas, whose vision really defined the college as it exists today, was raised as an orthodox Friend, professed the faith in order to gain control of Bryn Mawr, and used her Quaker connections to secure her position there (113). But Thomas soon transfigured "what began as a Quaker college for women into a secular and cosmopolitan institution," one that turned decisively away from "adherence to Quaker traditions" (116-117). A friend of mine, whose mother was traveling companion to Thomas, says that she often remarked (in a lowering sort of tone), "Thee knows not Quakers." Thomas saw Friends as obstacles to her ideal of Bryn Mawr: a place where women could succeed at the kind of rigorous academic work that had been offered only to men in this country (119). To mark that vision, the architecture of her school is not plain style, but Jacobean Gothic (118). The scholastic mode is not egalitarian, but hierarchical, with heavy emphasis on bracing intellectual challenge, high standards, and rigorous examination (115).

And yet, because Bryn Mawr is a small school, with small classes and many opportunities for getting to know our students well, the few of us Friends who teach there now have much opportunity to practice a kind of Quaker pedagogy, to be faithful to a vision we see as antecedent to, and in part contributing to, that of M. Carey Thomas. It is a pedagogy well described by John Woolman in "A Plea for the Poor": the "careful and patient attendance of . . . tutors [who are] . . . enabled rightly and seasonably to administer to each individual . . . and gently lead them on . . . fully attending to the spirit and disposition of each" (PM 264).

This essay is an account of my own attempt to put that pedagogical ideal into practice at Bryn Mawr. In this recounting, I draw heavily on the Woolman retreat I attended at Pendle Hill in June 1994. The leaders, Sterling Olmsted, Mike Heller and Mary Rose O'Reilley, helped me into an understanding of Woolman's ideas, but this is my own pedagogical "spin" on what they taught me. As one of the participants said at the close of the weekend, "The definitive edition of Woolman's *Journal* is still being written; it won't be finished until all of us have done our work in the world." What follows is a chronicle of my work as I understand it now, my own particular playing out of Woolman's ideas.

I find four key concepts in Woolman useful in my teaching practice: his counsel against overworking, his counsel to work outward from a motion of love, his conviction of the mutuality of the learning process, and his conviction of the necessity of humility in the teacher. But I also wrestle with Woolman's assumption of the prophetic mode, which I find problematic as a model for a Quaker pedagogy. In the passages which follow, I will address each of these points in order, both the helpful and not-so-helpful (or even dangerous) ones.

First, at Bryn Mawr, which is certainly a breeding ground for workaholics, Woolman's advice against overworking is sound, and much needed, counsel: "To labour too hard or cause others to do so," he says in "A Plea for the Poor," "is to manure a soil for the propagating an evil seed in the earth" (PM 247). In this essay, which is addressed to the wealthy (its subtitle is "A Word of Remembrance and Caution to the Rich"), Woolman repeatedly admonishes his readers to consider whether their own luxurious habits make immoderate demands on the labor of others. To do so interferes with others' "leisure," exhausts their spirits, and drives them to "crave help from strong drink" (PM 240, 246-247, 260).

Although the correspondence between the landowner and the professor is hardly exact, I do try to engage in an activity which is analogous to what Woolman urges, by building time and space for reflection into the syllabus of my classes. Mary Rose O'Reilley's recent book, *The Peaceable Classroom,* is also helpful as a reminder that it isn't possible "to absorb much of anything without silence and rest on either side of the learning" (101):

> . . . it may be useful to retrieve the idea that literary study . . . is essentially a contemplative activity. Therefore, we have to look differently at how we spend our classroom time.
>
> Perhaps we should teach fewer texts or shorter texts.
>
> It requires a long time to take in a few words.
>
> On either side of the word we need a patch of white, of silence. . . .
>
> By and large, our students are relentlessly overstimulated.
>
> Teachers often pride themselves on a challenging syllabus, which usually means that they assign an astonishing amount of reading. Students perceive this as a "tough" course and the teacher a "tough" teacher. Everybody is happy—parents, principals, deans, school boards. . . . (104-106)

But, as Woolman counsels, we might ask ourselves what we accomplish when we place such demands on others, what kind of inward life we thereby discourage.

Following Woolman's observation that "Truth did not require me to engage in much cumbrous affairs" (PM 53), I try, too, to model for my students a life that is not one of frenzied overwork. (This means, of course, that I also need to work at living such a life.) I am careful to speak to students of time off, of down time. I encourage them to use their own fall, winter, spring and summer breaks to take a break. I remind them that academic achievement isn't the whole of life, but only one element in a full and satisfying one; I take care to describe to them the ways in which I try to balance my own work life with family, community and Meeting commitments, and the ways in which I take time for worship and contemplation.

In offering my own life as a possible model for their own, I also find myself enacting what I see as the single most important principle in Woolman: "Love was the first motion" (PM 127). The experience and practice of love are leitmotifs throughout the *Journal,* which begins, "I have often felt a motion of love to leave some hints in writing of my experience of the goodness of God" (PM 23). "There is a love," Woolman says later, "clothes my mind while I write" (PM 57):

> Thus he whose tender mercies are over all his works hath placed a principle in the human mind which incites to exercise goodness toward every living creature; and this being singly attended to, people become tender-hearted and sympathizing. . . . (PM 25)

The *Journal* gives a full account of how Woolman exercises the "first motion" in his interactions with others. Woolman's is a grammar of openings: he uses lots of "-ing" words, verbs of process, of suggestiveness. He describes his own discomfort with certain practices, operating out of his feelings, using "I- statements" rather than "you-statements" of condemnation. He speaks with great compassion, in a language of tenderness and concern for those whom he addresses, those whose behavior he would correct. Assuming what may at first seem a truly paradoxical position, Woolman speaks with unconditional acceptance of those whom he chastises. But he is urging them into a fuller awareness of the universal Light within, into a truer life than the one which currently occupies them.

Perhaps the clearest account of this process at work is Woolman's interchange with the tavern owner, whose place of business he saw as the location of disorder and corruption:

> . . . at a suitable opportunity I went to the public house, and seeing [the master of that house] . . . I went to him and told him I wanted to speak with him; so we went aside, and there in the fear and dread of the Almighty I expressed to him what rested on my mind, which he took kindly, and afterward showed more regard to me than before. In a few years after, he died middle-aged, and I often thought that had I neglected my duty in that case it would have given me great trouble. . . . (PM 32)

Although Woolman is dismayed by the business practice of the tavern owner, and expresses that dismay, what is most striking about this passage is his concern for the fate of the man's soul.

I take both Woolman and O'Reilley (whose book is also a good guide to the practice of being lovingly present to one's students) as models for coming to my students with an attitude of love, in wonder at who they are and expectation of who they want to be. This is true both for the older women whom Susan Dean and I teach in our first-year classes, and for the eighteen-through-twenty-two-year-olds who make up the majority of Bryn Mawr's student population. The non-traditional students are "wonder-full" in their accomplishments, and in their hunger for more; the younger students are full of wondering what to do with themselves. It is a joy to be their "gardener," their "midwife," the "host" to their conversations, to listen attentively to what they have to say, and to draw out of them what they know already but haven't yet been able to articulate, to nudge them into knowing what they haven't yet realized.

I see my vocation as evoking witness in others, helping them to see their truth as their own, directing them to their own sense of who they are now, and who they could become. This is an activity of trust, and it involves a good deal of mindful waiting for their "truth" to unfold. But it is profoundly satisfying to see it happen. To be thus attentive is not only to be amazed at their "this-ness," to be "drenched in their glory" (I take these words from my friend Susan Dean). It is also to be open to being instructed by them.

This brings me to the insight of John Woolman that I find key for teachers in particular: the notion of instruction as a process of mutuality. Trying to find the courage to speak, Woolman tells us,

> . . . after some days deliberation and inward seeking to the Lord for assistance, I was made subject, so that I expressed what lay upon me in a way which became my youth and his years; and though it was a hard task to me, it was well taken, and I believe was useful to us both. (PM 34-35)

On a later, similar occasion, Woolman says, "Here I found a tender seed, and . . . it was a time of mutual refreshment from the presence of the Lord" (PM 63). And yet later:

> . . . a concern arose to spend some time with the Indians, that I might feel and understand their life and the spirit they live in, if haply I might receive some instruction from them, or they be in any degree helped forward by my following the readings of Truth amongst them. (PM 127)

"So they helped one another," he tells us, "and we laboured along, divine love attending" (PM 133).

I try to engage in similar practices of mutual helpfulness in my own classroom. Several years ago, during a month-long course on eldering, I received some good advice on putting such ideals to work. The instructor, Kenneth Sutton, tried to update for the members of my Meeting an old Quaker notion. The idea he developed was twofold: that each of us has the responsibility and the authority to speak up when something in Meeting disturbs us, that we should not wait for a weighty Friend to do the speaking for us. But—and this is the flip side of this same coin—each of us needs to cultivate a sense of humility, knowing that we can also be corrected by others.

With the help of both Ken Sutton and John Woolman, I now understand that these two ideas depend absolutely on one another: we can express with authority the "truth" as we see it in a given moment, knowing that our speaking will provoke others with different viewpoints to correct us. We can feel free to speak, because we know that we will be corrected, that revision is always possible, indeed always necessary. Correcting people is okay, can even be a calling, if rightly fulfilled, as long as we hold ourselves open to correction as well.

The philosopher Susan Bordo explains the same process in postmodern and secular terms:

> It is impossible to be "politically correct." . . . all ideas . . . are condemned to be haunted by a voice from the margins, already speaking (or perhaps presently muted by awaiting the conditions for speech), awakening us to what has been excluded, effaced, damaged. . . . This is, of course, the way we learn; it is not a process that should be freighted . . . with the constant anxiety of "exposure" and political discreditation. (138, 154)

I find this conception—that each of us possesses only partial understanding, a limited vision which invites mutual correction—enormously useful in my work as a teacher. It helps me reconcile myself to the grading, ranking, and evaluating that are built into my job; it helps me feel able to correct others with integrity.

As I correct my students, I also acknowledge my own need for revision, and invite them to help me re-think our common project every step of the way; that is, I invite them to criticize the process and content of our course. This is, of course, seldom a comfortable process. I have had many a talk with Susan Dean about how best to "read" the criticism I invite from my students, for the word of God, as it is mediated by them, can arrive indirectly, be hard to decipher, or, once deciphered, be very hard to accept.

It is for that reason that I find a fourth element, a phrase much used in Woolman's writing, so helpful. This is his language of "keeping low," of being humble:

> . . . I was not low enough to find true peace. Thus for some months I had great trouble, there remaining in me an unsubjected will which rendered my labours fruitless, till at length through the merciful continuance of heavenly visitations I was made to bow down in spirit before the Lord. (PM 27)

Lowliness is the way to "true peace"; paradoxically, it can also be a means of power, an access to glory:

> Deep humility is a strong bulwark, and as we enter into it we find safety and true exaltation. . . . Being unclothed of our own wisdom and knowing the abasement of the creature, therein we find that power to arise which gives health and vigor [to] us. (PM 57)

Not incidentally, humility is also politically astute, Woolman says, for it will enable you to accomplish more in this world. If you keep "low," others will be more able to hear your testimony:

> . . . if such who were at times under sufferings on account of some scruples of conscience kept low and humble and in their conduct in life manifested a spirit of true charity, it would be more likely to reach the witness in others, and be of more service in the church, than if their sufferings were attended with a contrary spirit and conduct. (PM 98)

I know I do not just speak for myself when I observe that such an emphasis on "lowness" is hard for contemporary Quakers to hear, much less to practice. But at the Woolman retreat, Sterling Olmsted came to an understanding of lowness which I found very helpful. This understanding draws on two passages from Woolman. In the first, Woolman says, "I often saw the necessity of keeping down to that root from whence our concern proceeded" (PM 96). The second reads, "as I was preserved in the ministry to keep low with the Truth, the same Truth in their hearts answered it" (PM 63). Sterling suggested that the phrase "being low" might be used in the *Journal* to mean "being on common ground, guided by common principles"; "keeping low" might be a way of expressing and understanding our common source, our common root. To speak with pride and assurance is to forget our interconnectedness, to forget to be in sympathy with one another. To "keep low" is to be reminded of such things.

I also find that the ideal and practice of "keeping low" is a useful way to answer the many challenges I receive from students about relationships of authority in our classrooms. A student who is used to dominating class discussion frets about my authority to enforce her silence; a student who embraces me as a spiritual companion refuses to take an exam I have assigned in a course on feminist spirituality. A student with a devout religious life has a psychotic episode, and writes me from the hospital to complain about my classroom "rules." An older woman, a returning student, describes the similar authority of the class to censor itself, to place limits on what is said in the group. I respond now to such queries with an alternative theory of authority that I learned from Woolman, an ideal which I also see enacted in Friends' business practice. Since, as Helen Hole explains, "in each person there is some element of the Divine, and therefore some potential for access to the Truth," authority in Meeting for Business is not entrusted to any single individual. Agreement grows rather "out of the pooling and sharing" of those involved; the aim is "to discover the Truth, which will satisfy everyone." Friends believe that such satisfaction is possible, for our "deepest self is one which touches that of others: we belong to one vine . . . of which we are all branches" (97-99).

In the "corporate search for Truth" which is Quaker business practice, all members "must accept a kind of vulnerability." They must be willing both to verbalize what they care about, and "try to be open to another's point of view, endeavor to understand it, and even think themselves into it" (Hole 99, 102). As Michael Sheeran points out in his study of the process of Quaker business meetings, participants must be willing to make a spoken contribution: it is of great importance that Friends who feel they cannot speak, "who are diffident about the significance of their share in the Meeting be encouraged to say what they can" (55). "Quiet ones" must accept some blame for decisions made without their input, and "more vocal Friends" need "temper their remarks in order to encourage reluctant speakers" (55-56). All Friends are encouraged to express their opinions "humbly and tentatively in the realization that no one person sees the whole truth and that the whole Meeting can see more of Truth than can any part of it" (56).[3]

Sheeran finds such humility the most striking quality of the Quaker business method: the "tentativeness" of individual speakers, the "artless willingness to face the weaknesses in one's position," the "atmosphere of respectful openness to one another" (56, 59). The atmosphere necessary for this process to work emphasizes "a sense of the partiality of one's own insights, and one's dependence on searching together with the group for better conclusions than anyone alone could have attained" (61). The clerk of Business Meeting needs to exercise thoughtful speaking, attentive listening, and the gift of discernment: "the ability to read the unity of the group" (101), when—and if—it is reached.

I am trying now explicitly to institutionalize this Quaker conception of authority in my classes by modeling them on the practice of Friends' Meeting for Business. I position myself as clerk, as "reader" of the discussions I direct. Every student in each of my classes, like a participant in Business Meeting, has an obligation to speak, and to speak in a certain way: tentatively, and with an awareness of what might be useful for us all. Reflecting on the use of personal experience in the classroom, one of my students, Alisa Conner, distinguished between inappropriate and uncomfortable "confession" and empowering and publicly useful "testimony":

> The language of personal experience turns into "confession" when it becomes self-protective, when it shuts people off from really examining themselves and their discourses . . . "testimony," in contrast, is "toward something," meaningful to other people as well as to the testified. (29)

Our judgment of what counts as "testimony" is constant, ongoing, evolving, adjustable. It always means careful readings of the texts, with attention both to nuances of argument and our vested interests in them; often it means reflecting on classroom dynamics; sometimes it means stories of the choices others have made in their lives, or hopes we have for our own.

The obligation to speak—and this is key—is particularly weighty if a student finds herself in disagreement with the general tenor or focus of the conversation. By insisting that students take the responsibility for fulfilling that obligation, I am trying to counter the homogenizing tendency of secular community-building with what seems to me a more open, and more Woolman-like, sense of our common need for understanding, an understanding that will be incomplete unless each of our perspectives, the "access to truth" which each of us represents, is included.

Many quiet students have told me they are grateful that I insist on their speaking: it's a welcome relief, they say, to know that they must speak, that I respect them enough to assure them the time and space they need to do so. To speak, they come to acknowledge, is to make themselves vulnerable to critique, but it is also to aid our group work towards comprehension; to refuse to speak is to deny both themselves and others the possibility of being educated.

In establishing the classroom as a site for this particular Quaker practice, which locates authority in our common labor, I continually remind my students of their obligation to listen carefully to the testimonies of others. One of my returning students, Lynn Litterine, described her understanding of how this process took place in a course called "Major Texts of the Feminist Tradition":

> What if feminism means listening to the other woman's voice when she talks, instead of our own voice jumping ahead of her with impatience, or with fear, or with prejudice, or with boredom . . . ? What if feminism means a determination to understand women when they speak? Or in their silence? . . . it would be a listening, a careful listening . . . but it would be specifically feminist because it would be listening with an awareness of all the barriers to women being really heard, an awareness of all my own handicaps to hearing . . . . when it comes to women, the whole damn world is hearing impaired. . . . I call my plan "Feminism As Hearing Aid."

> I'm going to miss this class, because it's a safe place to get to know the other women in the room. Here I can practice listening to another person reveal and explain her thoughts. I can slow down the anxious din in my mind and look and listen . . . . my love and connection were clarified and exercised and I now listen to other women within that strong framework.
>
> I'd like [my graduation] to be Q&A. . . .

Listening one another into speech, testifying in ways that help others hear themselves in the story—or hear their exclusion, and so feel called to testify in turn: the touchstone of such teaching is a process of communal "tearning" (that word was coined by Alisa Conner, by splicing two words the thesaurus identifies as antonyms: "teaching" and "learning"). "Tearning" involves the principle of correctability, an authority grounded in humility, and an awareness of our shared need for, and usefulness to, one another.

In a lecture at Villanova University, Paulo Freire reflected on the importance of such a process in academic life. Acknowledging the "scarcity of humbleness" in academia, our "fear of others' intelligence," Freire insisted that tolerance, "giving the testimony of respect to the ways of others," is indispensable to the task of education. It is such humility, and the attentiveness it induces, that I am trying to encourage in my students, when I conduct my classes as if I were clerking Meeting for Business.

I am guided in this pedagogical practice by John Woolman's convictions about both the mutuality of the learning process and the necessity of humility in the teacher. As he says in the *Journal*, "I must in all things . . . be teachable" (PM 119). But I wouldn't be giving an accurate, or complete, account of my reading of Woolman—both the degree to which he has helped me in the practice of Quaker teaching, and the degree to which he has not—if I didn't also acknowledge that there are times when Woolman himself doesn't seem to "keep low." For me, intent as I am on the process of mutual, humble correction in the classroom, the most disturbing of these passages are those in which Woolman dismisses the reactions of others: "I saw at this time that if I was honest to declare that which Truth opened in me, I could not please all men, and laboured to be content in the way of my duty" (PM 52). Woolman also writes,

> I find that to be a fool as to worldly wisdom and commit my cause to God, not fearing to offend men who take offense at the simplicity of Truth, is the only way to remain unmoved at the sentiments of others. The fear of man brings a snare.... (PM 57)

Woolman similarly testifies that "my concern was that I might attend with singleness of heart to the voice of the True Shepherd and be so supported as to remain unmoved at the faces of men" (PM 59). Later he says,

> Traveling up and down of late, I have had renewed evidences that to be faithful to the Lord and content with his will concerning me is a most necessary and useful lesson for me to be learning, looking less at the effects of my labour than at the pure motion and reality of the concern as it arises from heavenly love. (PM 72)

In each of these passages, I hear Woolman's testimony to his faithfulness to the Light, despite resistance from others. I see him actually steeling himself against others' reactions, so as to be true to the Lord.

One of the most remarkable things about John Woolman is that he refused to give up the world for lost. Christ may have said, "Render unto Caesar that which is Caesar's," but Woolman did not. He was a faithful follower of the Truth, and tried to bring it into realization in this world. Like the other eighteenth-century Quakers Jack Marietta describes in *The Reformation of American Quakerism,* Woolman did not think that life could be meaningfully separated into spiritual and political spheres. The religious impulse infused all; all behavior was interconnected. I am moved by such a vision, and try in all humility to affirm and practice it in my own life and teaching.

But when I hear Woolman say, "the worldly part in any is the changeable part, and . . . the Truth is but one," when he favors being "single to the Truth" (PM 49), I am left floundering; I don't know what Truth is, certainly not with the assurance that Woolman seems to have known and experienced it. As a postmodern American intellectual of the late twentieth century, I have been convinced by the multi-discipline of cultural studies that all understanding is inflected by the economic, political, and historical context in which it emerges; it is never autonomous, never free, never independent of material conditions (Berlin viii, xi).

So I do not find the certitude of John Woolman, his conviction that he knows the Truth, very helpful as a model for classroom practice. Perhaps I am simply too much of a postmodern to tolerate the prophetic mode. Certainly, I think we can come to know the "truth" more clearly by testing, in conversation with others, but I do not believe that we can know it truly—or even know if we know it truly. I find it a dangerous position for Quaker teachers to act and speak as if we can.

For all his talk of mutuality and lowness, Woolman relies ultimately and absolutely on the Truth that comes to him inwardly, to a degree I can't countenance (probably, as one of my respondents suggested during the lecture series, because I have never experienced it). This is where we differ, where I find Woolman's work, and his example, not only unhelpful, but troubling as a guide to my teaching. For Woolman, Truth was the moving of the spring of Christ in every person; with him, I affirm such a conception, but I want also to insist that such movement needs always the testing, the guidance, and the affirmation of the larger community, of all of those gathered, for instance, in a classroom "Meeting for Learning" (Palmer 4). I am too conscious of the partiality of individual insight not to insist that we rely, always, on our common dependence on one another, as guides to the Light, searching together for a more adequate understanding than each of us could achieve alone.

NOTES

[1] Portions of earlier versions of this article appear, with permission, both in Anne Dalke's *Teaching to Learn/Learning to Teach: Meditations on the Classroom.* Studies in Education and Spirituality. Vol. 4 (New York: Peter Lang, 2002) and "Outside the Mainstream/In the Well of Living Waters: Toward a Feminist Quaker Pedagogy" in *Women's Studies: An Interdisciplinary Journal* 28 (1999): 469-497.

[2] As a part of the autumn 1994 Pendle Hill Monday evening lecture series on John Woolman, Anne Dalke and Susan Dean gave companion talks on the same evening (Dodson 8-20). At the time, both were Americanists teaching in the English department at Bryn Mawr College and members of Philadelphia area Monthly Meetings.

[3] In these references to Michael Sheeran's *Beyond Majority Rule,* Sheeran is quoting other sources. The first is a quotation from Thomas S. Brown, the second is from James Walker, and the third is from Howard H. Brinton.

WORKS CITED

Berlin, James, and Michael Vivion. *Cultural Studies in the English Classroom.* Portsmouth, NH: Boynton/Cook, 1992.

Bordo, Susan. "Feminism, Postmodernism, and Gender-Skepticism." *Feminism/Postmodernism.* Ed. Linda Nicholson. New York, NY: Routledge, 1990. 133-156.

Conner, Alisa. "Feminist Pedagogy and the Feminist and Gender Studies Program at Bryn Mawr College: Reading the Stories." Senior Thesis. Bryn Mawr College. April 1994.

Dodson, Shirley, ed. *John Woolman's Spirituality and Our Contemporary Witness.* Philadelphia, PA: Philadelphia Yearly Meeting Religious Education Committee and Pendle Hill, 1995.

Freire, Paulo. "The Catholic University: Reflections on its Task." Villanova University. November 20, 1991.

Hole, Helen. *Things Civil and Useful: A Personal View of Quaker Education.* Richmond, IN: Friends United Press, 1978.

Horowitz, Helen. *Alma Mater: Design and Experience in the Women's Colleges from Their Nineteenth-Century Beginnings to the 1930s.* New York: Knopf, 1984.

Litterine, Lynn. Journal. English 280. Bryn Mawr College. Spring, 1994.

Marietta, Jack. *The Reformation of American Quakerism: 1748-1783.* Philadelphia, PA: University of Pennsylvania Press, 1984.

Olmsted, Sterling. "Motion of Love: A John Woolman Retreat." Pendle Hill. June 3-5, 1994.

Palmer, Parker. "Meeting for Learning: Education in a Quaker Context." *The Pendle Hill Bulletin* 284 (May 1976).

O'Reilley, Mary Rose. *The Peaceable Classroom.* Portsmouth, NH: Boynton/Cook, 1993.

Sheeran, Michael. *Beyond Majority Rule: Voteless Decisions in the Religious Society of Friends.* Philadelphia, PA: Philadelphia Yearly Meeting, 1983.

Sutton, Kenneth. Course on Eldering. Radnor Monthly Meeting. Villanova, PA, 1992.

Woolman, John. *The Journal and Major Essays of John Woolman.* Ed. Phillips P. Moulton. 1971. Richmond, IN: Friends United Press, 1989.

16

Answerable to the Design of Our Creation: Teaching "A Plea For The Poor"

Paul A. Lacey

If nothing focuses one's mind on the problems of a text better than preparing to teach it, then absolutely nothing will more sharply focus one's mind than trying to think through how to introduce John Woolman's writings to three hundred students in a required first-year college Humanities course. I work with some very daring colleagues, however, as demonstrated by the fact that we have occasionally taught Woolman's *Journal* and, more recently, "A Plea for the Poor" in that course. Initially, Woolman the journal-keeper gets an unfriendly reception from our students. They think he is morbid: that business with the robins is too bad, but Woolman needs a sense of proportion. He spends too much time trying to make his readers feel as guilty as he does about human failings. How many occasions of sin could he have found in Mount Holly, after all? He is not optimistic enough about people and goes to extremes in living his beliefs. And since he does not talk about family life, and is always traveling on his concerns, he must have been an indifferent parent and spouse who left others to do all his work. But their most telling criticism is that, as one of my students put it, "John Woolman had no individualism, he just did what God told him to do."

Most of those problems of reading and interpretation can be addressed satisfactorily. Students set aside some objections when they learn what readers expected of such a journal in Woolman's time, and how he worked with a committee to oversee the work. If a class can give the *Journal* any kind of open-hearted reading, they will come to appreciate Woolman's tenderness toward slaves, Indians, and the poor, and his honesty in examining what it takes to live consistently. And if there is still resistance to the writing, an English teacher can always fall back on Charles Lamb's praise of Woolman's style: "get the writings of John Woolman by heart" (68).

The problems, and the resistances, are greater when reading "A Plea for the Poor" with first-year college students. Since there is no narrative line, we do not see Woolman struggling directly in his own life with his ethical responsibilities, as we do in the *Journal*. To our students, everything seems to be more abstract, more dependent on religious convictions which are unshared, unfamiliar, or uncongenial to them. Yet the ethical passion of the "Plea" will make its way with them, if they can be helped to see how it is organized and argued. What follows is an attempt to offer a reading of "A Plea for the Poor" which might make it more accessible to a college audience.

Publishing History of "A Plea for the Poor"

Phillips P. Moulton tells us the first known printed edition of "A Plea for the Poor" was published in Dublin in 1793, under the title "A Word of Remembrance and Caution to the Rich," twenty-one years after John Woolman's death (PM 196). We cannot be sure, therefore, that the essay is in what Woolman would have considered a final form, nor do we have any indication that he followed his usual practice of sharing works-in-progress and soliciting advice about them. The essay has been known by two titles, "A Plea for the Poor" and "A Word of Remembrance and Caution to the Rich" (PM 196). Woolman took care to identify the audience he wished a piece of writing to address. "On Keeping Negroes" Parts I and II, for example, were "Recommended to the Professors of Christianity of Every Denomination" (PM 198, 210). His *Journal* seems to have members of the Religious Society of Friends as its primary audience, though he would hope that those who know the inward life and "reverence God the Creator" (PM 28) whatever their denomination, would read it appreciatively.

The two titles for "A Plea" are usefully complementary. Woolman offers the plea on behalf of the poor, addressing the rich, who require not instruction but "remembrance and caution." They are, we may assume, the "professors of Christianity of every denomination" who also have a disproportionate share of the world's goods. Woolman does not expect his audience to be surprised by new ideas, since he believes he is merely reminding them of the implications of principles they and he share.

Woolman's Method of Arguing

The tone of the essay does not feel like a single tightly woven, consecutive argument. Instead, the thirteen brief chapters of the main essay (I read chapters fourteen through sixteen as separate essays) make up a series of linked, recursive meditations on issues of wealth, power and oppression, and how we might free ourselves of their temptations, and on the meanings of stewardship and the obligations to simplicity. Typically the shorter meditations circle back to basic premises, then out to explore their concrete implications, then back to the premises, now enriched in meaning.

We see Woolman's method in the tightly packed, one sentence opening paragraph of chapter one. The first two clauses have simultaneously the feel of the poetry of the Psalms and the condensed balance of epigram: "Wealth desired for its own sake obstructs the increase of virtue, and large possessions in the hands of selfish men have a bad tendency. . ." (PM 238). The theme is stated in the first clause, restated and enlarged in the second. He very carefully describes *tendencies,* patterns which express moral laws. It is not simply that our own wealth, if we desire it for its own sake, will obstruct the increase of our own virtue. True as that may be, Woolman addresses the issue far more broadly. Wealth itself, pursued for the wrong motives, will obstruct the increase of virtue *generally,* affecting the moral lives of both those who grasp for wealth and those they exploit and victimize. Large possessions, held for the wrong reasons, have bad tendencies. He identifies three particular evils which occur by means of large possessions: too small a number of people are employed in useful work; those people, "or some of them," have to work too hard; others would be too underemployed to earn a living without "employments invented . . . only to please the vain mind" (PM 238). Woolman's analysis does not ignore human agency, but he begins by showing the objective consequences of economic process in order to stress the interconnectedness of economic, social, and moral laws: because rent on land is set too high, economic necessity, not wilful cruelty, drives tenants to overwork the oxen and horses they must depend on, and to deny them adequate shelter and care, just as they overwork and deprive themselves. When trapped in debt, they cannot hire the workers they need. ". . . and honest persons are often straitened to give their children suitable learning" (PM 238). Woolman connects luxury, waste, overwork, and alienation of labor as largely unintended but inescapable consequences of wealth pursued for the wrong reasons.

It is useful to recognize that Woolman makes no attempt to convince his readers of the fundamental premises he works from, not because he is dogmatic but because he can be confident that his audience would take them for granted. He even postpones stating them until the second chapter: God is the Creator, to whom the whole world belongs. Human beings are tenants in this world, along with other creatures, and have special obligations as stewards. Christ is the Redeemer of humanity and the creation. These premises do not require arguing or proving, for Woolman's intended audience (PM 239-40).

"Answerable to the Design of Our Creation"

For Woolman it is not necessarily inconsistent with equity or with what he calls "universal love" for humans either to pursue or to possess economic wealth. As a result of their own efforts, and "the agreements and contracts of [their] fathers and predecessors," some people "claim a much greater share of this world than others" (PM 239). But the wealthy stand in relation to God as their tenants stand in relation to them. The primary test of our good tenancy of God's earth is whether ". . . we live answerable to the design of our creation . . ." (PM 239). Those who are righteous on principle, Woolman says, do good to the poor without making it an act of bounty. By avoiding superfluities, they encourage moderation in others. If they do not charge whatever the market will allow for rent of land, nor exact "what the laws or customs would support them in," but instead "regulate their demands agreeable to universal love," their tenants and dependents can engage in "moderate labour in useful affairs" (PM 239).

To shape his reflections, Woolman employs a personal vocabulary which almost takes on the quality of a technical language. "Answerable to the design of our creation," for example, is explicated by such phrases as "universal righteousness," "universal love," "pure wisdom," "pure love" and "divine love." To a modern reader, these seem curiously periphrastic, especially in a writer who writes so simply most of the time, but Woolman prefers to speak of God primarily in those attributes and qualities which remind us of both the design of our creation and of how we should "channel"—a favorite word for him—our actions in accord with God's nature. Righteousness, love and wisdom, universal and pure, are the great standards, the plumb line, and "goodness remains to be goodness," as "oppression . . . remains to be oppression" (PM 262), according to those standards, no matter what contracts and agreements, laws and customs permit or require. His test is goodness, consistency with pure love, not what human laws allow: "Goodness remains to be goodness, and the direction of pure wisdom is obligatory on all reasonable creatures—that laws and customs are no further a standard for our proceedings than as their foundation is on universal righteousness" (PM 240).

The poor may have bound themselves to hard conditions by "a bargain to which they in their poor circumstances agreed." If we require excessive work of them, even though we require less than the letter of our agreement with them allows, "we invade their rights as inhabitants of that world of which a good and gracious God is proprietor . . ." (PM 240).

"The Business of Our Lives"

These thoughts lead Woolman to explore what he calls "the business of our lives"—a phrase which appears in some form three times in the entire essay (PM 241, 250, 262). For him, it is an aspect of the design of our creation that our lives be active. Work is not a curse, therefore, but a gift, an aspect of our nature which we receive from and share with God the Creator. By our design, all human beings are entitled to "a convenient subsistence" and moderate labor to obtain it. When it is neither too much nor too little, work is "healthful to our bodies and agreeable to an honest mind" (PM 240). As a gift from God, useful work is interesting in itself, and to the extent that human beings are influenced by God's love, we must also be "interested in his workmanship" (PM 241). Late twentieth-century theologians, such as Walter Wink, who speak of humans as "co-creators" with God appear to be speaking from a similar insight. Once we understand that our work is to be in harmony with God's, we feel a desire "to take hold of every opportunity to lessen the distresses of the afflicted and increase the happiness of the creation" (PM 241). By our design, then, humans are most fully and richly employed when our work lessens affliction and increases the happiness of the creation. When we realize our common interest with all of creation and with the Creator, we discover our real work: ". . . To turn all the treasures we possess into the channel of universal love becomes the business of our lives" (PM 241).

The Spiritual Imagination: "A Right Feeling of the Labourer's Condition"

Accomplishing the business of our lives so defined requires imagination, and the great test of the moral or spiritual imagination for Woolman is learning how it feels to be the other, the stranger. "To pass through a series of hardships and to languish under oppression brings people to a certain knowledge of these things," he tells us, but those who live comfortably on the labor of others cannot lessen their distresses unless they can get "a right feeling of the labourer's condition" (PM 241-2). Reminding us that Christ calls us to test by our own feeling how we should treat one another, he offers two down-to-earth ways to sensitize our imagination.

First, we may enlarge our imaginations by recalling hardships and oppression of our historical past, to know the heart of a stranger by recalling what it was like to have been strangers in the land of Egypt. But those who are now comfortable might have no sense of such a past or, worse, might justify their present condition by appropriating to themselves a suffering which is only historical:

> He who hath been a stranger amongst unkind people . . . knows how it feels; but a person who hath never felt the weight of misapplied power comes not to this knowledge but by an inward tenderness, in which the heart is prepared to sympathy with others. (PM 243)

Second, in the absence of genuine personal knowledge, we can only try to imagine ourselves into thc laborer's life, to ask, for example, how it would feel for us to be forced to overwork continually for little income, so that others could live in luxury. Woolman's own imagination is so acute that he knows when oxen and horses are overworked, because "their eyes and the emotion of their bodies manifest that they are oppressed" (PM 238).

Feeling "The Weight of Misapplied Power"

From this discussion of the work of the spiritual imagination emerges a definition of oppression as simple as it is concrete: oppression is "misapplied power" (PM 243). This returns us to the essay's beginning: if their poverty requires people to work beyond what is healthful, if they must work at tasks without intrinsic meaning, if they must drive their families and animals as hard as they drive themselves, in order to earn scant livings by creating luxuries for their masters or employers, if they must depend on strong drink to keep themselves working, if their work is a curse rather than a gift from God, they feel the weight of misapplied power.

"Every degree of luxury of what kind soever and every demand for money inconsistent with divine order hath some connection with unnecessary labour" (PM 246). We, on whose behalf others labor immoderately, whose demands divert their labor from useful products and thus create scarcity and inflate the prices of necessities, misapply our power. To oppress is to misapply power. To be oppressed is to feel "the weight of misapplied power" (PM 243).

Stewardship Versus the Selfish Spirit

Having shown his readers how to get a right feeling for the weight of misapplied power, Woolman now begins an extended meditation on stewardship in conflict with the selfish spirit. Taking what might be called a heaven's-eye view on treasuring up wealth for another generation, chapter seven begins with an epigraph "'This kind goeth not out but by prayer' [Mt. 17:21]" (PM 248). Characteristically, Woolman frames his topic by an appeal to our imaginations: suppose a man with a large estate he expected to leave to his children discovered that title to half of it belonged to a number of orphan children, and that, on grounds of virtue and understanding, they were as worthy as his own children. Would he still want to leave everything to his children by blood, or would he recognize his common interest with all the children, including the worthy orphans? (PM 248). The good steward would be happy to share his estate so as to provide sufficiency and moderate labor for as great a number as possible. The selfish spirit, on the other hand, would urge us to favor our own children, to pile up immoderate wealth for them, to free (or deprive) them of the necessity of labor. The selfish spirit loves his children with a short-sighted selfish love. But would we be partial to our children if we could see the long-term outcomes? The good steward considers his children's future under the aspect of eternity.

The Great Family

Woolman leads us first to imagine ourselves as stewards of a great family, then, in chapter eight, as stewards to "the numerous branches of the great family" (PM 251), a phrase for the whole human race which recurs with increased resonance late in the essay. "As Christians, all we possess are the gifts of God" (PM 249). Our only real inheritance is the true felicity in this and our future life, ". . . being inwardly united to the fountain of universal love and bliss" (PM 249). The fruits of that inheritance cannot be passed down from parent to child, however; each of us must earn them by our own work, and that is both the business of our lives and a gift from God. "To labour for an establishment in divine love where the mind is disentangled from the power of darkness is the great business of man's life" (PM 250).

"The Greatest of All Tyrants"

In chapters nine and ten, Woolman offers an analysis of the selfish spirit. He cites the example of the early Church Father Origen to illustrate how it tempts us, through the smallest steps, to practice idolatry. During a time when Christians were being put to death for refusing to cast incense onto the altar-fire as an act of homage to the state religion, Origen took incense in his hand and let "a certain heathen" take his hand and cast the incense for him. Origen could argue that he did not comply with the law but merely remained passive while someone not conscientiously opposed to doing homage used him as an instrument of his own obedience. Origen saved his life, but he came to believe that he had fallen into a worse state. "Thus it appears that a small degree of deliberate compliance to that which is wrong is very dangerous . . ." (PM 254).

For Woolman the selfish spirit is also "the greatest of all tyrants," and the root of all warfare. Nations continually raise and maintain great armies to protect their own wealth and to seize that of others. Great numbers of people are taken out of useful productivity and engaged instead in preparing the materials for war. The labor imbalances thus created lead to scarcity, to overwork for some, and to "fetching men . . . from distant parts of the world, to spend the remainder of their lives in the uncomfortable condition of slaves . . ." (PM 253). Woolman sees a cause and effect relationship that is devastating: "The rising up of a desire to attain wealth is the beginning. This desire being cherished moves to action, and riches thus gotten please self, and while self hath a life in them it desires to have them defended" (PM 255).

"The Seed of War Swells and Sprouts"

His line of argument now brings Woolman to the most sophisticated and pointed analysis in his essay. If we have not noticed before, we become acutely aware how carefully he has been addressing his audience, an audience opposed on Christian grounds to the wars of great nations which needs to face how its own pursuit of wealth and luxury partakes in the selfish spirit which makes war inevitable.

He circles back again to first principles: "Wealth is attended with power," which can impose "bargains and proceedings contrary to universal righteousness" (PM 255). That is misapplied power, by Woolman's definition, oppression. ". . . carried on with worldly policy and order, [oppression] clothes itself with the name of justice and becomes like a seed of discord in the soil . . ." (PM 255). As Woolman develops the implications of his image, the seed of discord becomes "the seed of war." As "holding treasures in the self-pleasing spirit is a strong plant, the fruit whereof ripens fast," the seed of war "swells and sprouts and grows and becomes strong, till much fruits are ripened" (PM 255). These seeds are not planted deliberately but inadvertently and carelessly, as we might accidentally sow beggar's-ticks or thistles in our gardens by carrying the seeds home on our clothes. Wilful, active oppression is terrible, but inadvertent or unexamined oppression is no less injurious. The aim of Woolman's discussion in this section is to bring his readers to self-examination: "May we look upon our treasures and the furniture of our houses and the garments in which we array ourselves and try whether the seeds of war have any nourishment in these our possessions or not" (PM 255).

"There the True Intent of the Law Is Fulfilled"

Chapters eleven and twelve test once more the premises of stewardship under God, this time in relation to how European settlers of North America have behaved toward "those ancient possessors of the country" (PM 258), the Indians. Again Woolman begins by reminding us of what we should know. As servants of God, we hold whatever we have as God's gift, and we are obliged to use the fruits in accord with the Creator's design. The gift is not absolute, but conditional, as confirmed by the law of the Year of the Jubilee, which required the Israelites to re-distribute land every fifty years, "the design of which was to prevent the rich from oppressing the poor by too much engrossing the land" (PM 256). Where people act steadily on "a principle of universal righteousness, there the true intent of the Law is fulfilled" (PM 256). But where people accumulate vast wealth without regard to universal love, even though by completely legal bargains and purchases, they are usurpers. By reminding us that only God has *rights* to the earth, Woolman establishes the framework for his discussion of the idea of property rights and of pressure for Europeans' expansion in North America (PM 257).

Woolman takes us back to the circumstances of the earliest European settlements in North America, when Europe was thickly settled and North America thinly settled. As Europeans came to colonize this continent, he argues, the natives saw advantages to them in the iron tools, other items "convenient for man's use," and "improvements made peaceably" (PM 257), which they brought with them. They therefore "gladly embraced the opportunity of traffic and encouraged these foreigners to settle" (PM 257). To the extent that Europeans came peacefully, negotiated for the land they settled on, and brought conveniences and benefits to the Indians, they were not usurpers. Only to that extent can it be said that God led them to find solutions to their overcrowding by sharing the abundant land with the Indians.

Woolman establishes two necessary conditions which alone can justify Europeans' inhabiting North America: 1) that the "ancient possessors of the country" (which they have been given as stewards under God) granted them the land; and 2) that the Indians are "yet owners and inhabiters of the land adjoining to us" (PM 258), and are entitled to live in the ways transmitted to them by their ancestors, ways which require large amounts of land.

Under the pressures created by accumulation of wealth and indulgence in luxuries, however, the Europeans want to expand into more and more of the Indians' land and to constrain their way of life, "settled by the custom of a great many ages" (PM 258). In Woolman's view, there is no legitimacy in the right of conquest, certainly not in the right of eminent domain, nor in what will later be asserted as the right of "manifest destiny." Woolman insists that the Europeans are obliged to cultivate the land already granted, "to accommodate the greatest number of people it is capable of, before we have any right to plead, as members of the one great family, the equity of their assigning to us more of their possessions and living in a way requiring less room" (PM 258). He accepts the "right to plead" for equity only "as members of the one great family," and then only after the Europeans have practiced the right kind of stewardship and husbandry.

Woolman recognizes that it is possible for people to live plainly solely in order to increase their wealth and power, and though a plain life is always to be preferred, "by living plain in a selfish spirit we advance not forward in true religion." In the case at hand, "living plain" in the right spirit and for the right motives would allow greater numbers of people to live well on the land already granted, would stimulate trade in necessities instead of superfluities, and would keep the Europeans from acting unjustly toward the Indians (PM 259). To live simply is the best way to handle wealth and power so as not to oppress others.

"Oppression . . . Remains to Be Oppression"

In the thirteenth chapter of "A Plea for the Poor," Woolman recapitulates a number of points in order to address the distinctions among the terms "right," "legal," and "just": as individuals and families inherit and accumulate goods over time, wealth, property, and power become unevenly distributed. Even plain living contributes to accumulating greater wealth. Though such uneven distribution of land and wealth "may consist with the harmony of true brotherhood," that "the poorest people who are honest" are entitled to "a certain portion of these profits" (PM 260), is for Woolman indisputable.

God the Creator remains the sole owner of the earth; wherever wealth leads to misapplication of power e.g., rents set too high, people forced to work too hard "this puts the wheels of perfect brotherhood out of order" (PM 260). Consequently, no one has a "right" to property separate from how it is used. Though the word *right* is commonly used to assert a right of property, he says, its meaning derives from the concept of *righteousness*. No one can claim a *right,* no matter how attested to by legal precedents, or gifts and grants "proved by sufficient seals and witnesses," which is at base *unrighteous.* "In this—that is, in equity and righteousness—consists the strength of our claims" (PM 261).

To test his arguments, he sets the following case: suppose twenty men and their wives discover and take possession of an uninhabited island and divide it equitably. Suppose nineteen of those twenty provide for the future equitable distribution of their property in ways "as best suited the convenience of the whole and [tending] to preserve love and harmony" (PM 261), and their heirs follow the same practice in their turn. Suppose, as well, that the twentieth man gives most of his property to his favorite son, making all the other sons his tenants and dependents, and that all subsequent inheritors do the same in their turn. Brothers, sons, and nephews, and all their dependents, are reduced from family to tenants of the favored son. Over time, the island will have one great proprietor over one-twentieth of the land who will also have an increasing influence over the public affairs of the whole island. With that accumulation of riches will come indulgence in luxury, paid for by the increased impoverishment of the disinherited.

Woolman creates this extended image of a ruined family in order to make a radical assertion on behalf of "the one great family." If we traced the claim of the ninth or tenth of these great landlords back to the first possessor, he says, and found the legal claim supported at every step by "instruments strongly drawn and witnessed," we still could not believe anyone had a genuine *right,* under such circumstances, to own so much. In giving them life, Woolman argues, God gave all humans a prior right, a claim on the fruits of the earth which supersedes any great landlord's claim to luxury. And they have such a *right* "though they had no instruments to confirm their *right*" (PM 262).

The essay's conclusion is as tightly packed as its opening sentence, once again drawing the simplest truths together: "oppression in the extreme appears terrible, but oppression in more refined appearances remains to be oppression" (PM 262), for, as the whole essay has taught us, oppression is always at base the same thing, misapplied power. It may start as small as a seed, but where it is cherished it grows stronger and more intensive, like a tangling vine which chokes out all other growth (PM 258-9). Woolman's final clause draws together four dominant themes: redemption; the spirit of oppression, which he has previously identified with the spirit of selfishness; the meaning of labor or "business" in human life; and our connection with "the great family."

> . . . to labour for a perfect redemption from this spirit of oppression is the great business of the whole family of Christ Jesus in this world. (PM 262)

Someone reading "A Plea" for the first time (especially if required to do so for a course) may find it repetitive and therefore hard to follow. On closer study, we can find not only a line of development but a number of entry-points into significant parts of the argument, from which we can follow all the rest. "Goodness remains to be goodness" and "Oppression remains to be oppression" offer one set of frames for the argument. "Answerable to the design of our creation" and "the business of our lives" offer another. The gift of work and the spirit of selfishness stand counterpoised, as do good husbandry and the seeds of war. The essay does not move in a linear fashion; instead it grows out of what Douglas Steere, describing Woolman's *Journal,* called "the scrupulous logic of love" (110). Once any thread of that argument is discovered, it leads us to the whole complex and beautiful fabric.

WORKS CITED

Lamb, Charles. "A Quaker's Meeting." *Essays of Elia and Last Essays of Elia.* New York, NY: Oxford University Press, 1964.

Steere, Douglas. "The *Journal* of John Woolman." *Doors into Life.* New York, NY: Harper, 1948.

Wink, Walter. *Engaging the Powers: Discernment and Resistance in a World of Domination.* Minneapolis, MN: Fortress Press, 1992.

Woolman, John. *The Journal and Major Essays of John Woolman.* Ed. Phillips P. Moulton. 1971. Richmond, IN: Friends United Press, 1989.

IV.

Scholars Who Became Disciples

17

In Honor of Phillips P. Moulton

Mary Moulton

On our first date, Phil and I took the New York subway to see the Cloisters. We became so engrossed in conversation we got no further than the bench outside the building. We continued talking for fifty-two years about what drew us together in the first place, a faith-based imperative to apply Christian ethics to daily living. This concern, inspired by the New Testament and John Woolman, has been the common thread throughout Phil's varied career. My own religious convictions had developed gradually, first as the child of missionaries, and then under the influence of a radical school chaplain. Phil, however, had a Christian conversion at age sixteen. He decided to become a minister, to his father's dismay.

Seeking the best intellectual preparation for his calling, Phil studied hard in college while participating in intramural sports and varsity track. After his sophomore year he became seriously ill while working on a railroad gang. He failed to get adequate treatment and never fully recovered. Despite his illness, he was student body president and valedictorian at Ohio Wesleyan University. During his senior year he and Edward R. Murrow were the two officers of the National Student Federation. Phil eventually went to seminary and in 1948 obtained his Ph.D. from Yale, where he was named University Scholar.

Even before going to seminary, Phil's beliefs became increasingly radical as he studied the New Testament. A student in a course he taught for the Cleveland YMCA, Isabel Needham (later Bliss), loaned him a copy of Woolman's *Journal,* saying "I think you'll find ideas similar to yours." Phil said it was like a homecoming, a validation and a great expansion of what he had been trying to work out by himself. A natural next step was to join the Wider Quaker Fellowship. When we met about ten years later, Phil introduced me to the Friends. I joined the Ann Arbor Meeting during the Vietnam war. Phil later joined the same meeting while maintaining his Methodist ties. He never identified strongly with a denomination. His work with students and in the peace movement, as well as his teaching and writing, cut across religious divisions.

As a college professor, Phil used readings from Woolman, and in 1964 decided to study him in depth during a semester's sabbatical. "Whoever heard of Woolman?" asked Henry Pitt Van Dusen of Union Seminary, when he learned of Phil's plan. Van Dusen wanted Phil to work further on the subject of his Ph.D. thesis, the philosopher A.E. Taylor.

During the leave Phil's training in Biblical criticism and his eye for detail led to an astonishing discovery: much of the Woolman edition currently in use was based on the wrong manuscript and there were many errors in the remainder. He tried unsuccessfully to find someone to work on a new edition. Finally in 1967-68, he took a year's leave of absence without pay. With the help of some grants, an invitation to share Edward Bronner's home, and my obtaining a job, he undertook this labor of love. Both before and after the publication of his work in 1971, for over thirty years in all, he conducted workshops and lectured on Woolman or pacifism at Friends General Conference, monthly and yearly meetings, and Quaker centers in the United States and Great Britain.

Before he went into full-time teaching, Phil was involved in student work for the National Council of Churches and the University of Chicago. For a year he held a temporary appointment teaching religion and higher education at Union Theological Seminary. He then taught philosophy and religion at Simpson College, the University of North Dakota, where he was chairman of an interfaith department, and Adrian College. His major interests were in Christian ethics and in relating other disciplines to religion.

A student in an independent study told Phil, "Dr. Moulton, I could never have done the things I did if I had taken this course first." He referred to some of the less legitimate functions he had performed for the athletic department. Phil had been collecting materials on the ethics of college athletics after reading a thesis on the topic at Union Seminary, and, with this firsthand material before him, decided to write on the subject. Upon retirement in 1976, he became Visiting Scholar at the Center for Higher Education at the University of Michigan. His monograph was titled *Enhancing the Values of Intercollegiate Athletics at Small Colleges*. For a year thereafter Phil consulted with college personnel responsible for athletic policy and took a leadership role in their conferences.

Phil next concentrated on the area that had concerned him since high school days, issues of war and peace. Following a speech he made to the Military Study Group at the University of Michigan, he was asked to join as a regular member. The group was a weekly seminar of professors and outstanding graduate students selected by war academies to pursue doctoral degrees in military history. Phil was given access to military perspectives and materials seldom available to pacifists. During his eight years with the group he wrote *Ammunition for Peacemakers,* winner of the Pilgrim Press Book Competition. In his early eighties he traveled with study groups to problem areas in the Middle East and Central America, staying ten days longer by himself in each place. He also joined a Fellowship of Reconciliation team on a mission to the USSR.

Phil's balanced approach to problems, his diplomatic manner, and careful scholarship made him a valued member of peace groups. He served on advisory committees and boards of such organizations as the Civilian-Based Defense Association and the Fellowship of Reconciliation and Global Peace Service. His lack of physical endurance, however, prevented him from engaging in direct action or writing as much as he wished. Over the years Phil and I balanced each other well; he was the scholar while I was the activist. His pamphlets and articles dealt with higher education, or John Woolman, or presented a pacifist perspective on world issues. Aside from Quaker publications, most of his articles, book reviews and reports appeared in the *Christian Century.*

Phil and I have two children. Kathy Moulton, an English teacher, is married to Alexander Gurevich, a physicist. Lawrence Moulton, a biostatistician, is married to Ann Riley, a demographer; they have two children. We moved to Maryland to be near them and settled happily in Friends Retirement Community in Sandy Spring. Although Phil's activities were curtailed by failing health, he continued to encourage others in a large number of organizations. Until his death in January of 2002 at the age of 92, he remained a gentle compassionate man with a steadfast resolve to advance the cause of peace. Phil wrote: "I am especially grateful to Isabel Bliss for introducing me to Woolman, whose keen analysis of social conditions, faith in divine guidance and challenge to put beliefs into action has profoundly influenced my life."

—Mary Moulton, June 20, 2002

18

The Contribution of John Woolman to Human Betterment

Phillips P. Moulton[1]

WOOLMAN'S ABIDING CONTRIBUTION TO HUMAN WELFARE is profound and multi-faceted. This short essay deals with the relationship between his religious convictions and his ethics, with special attention to his realism and his relevance to our time. His life and thought rested on a solid basis of personal religious experience. He had a deep Christian faith, nurtured by regular Bible reading in his family, by his study of great religious literature, and by the Quaker community to which he belonged. No theological innovator, his beliefs place him in the mainstream of Christian and of Quaker thought.

Woolman had a strong sense of the love of God pervading the universe. As we become aware of God's love for us, he felt, we are called to respond with love to God and all people everywhere. His writings stressed also God's immanence and transcendence, as well as the providence and judgment of God.

Rooted in the love and power of God, Woolman's faith gave him a sense of security. God would certainly care for those who trusted in him and who lived in the power of that trust. Any sacrifice or risk could be accepted with courage by a person "united to him who hath all power in heaven and Earth. And though a woman may forget her sucking child, yet he will not forget his faithful ones" (AMG 441).

Woolman should not be confused with those who hold the facile assumption that if people have enough faith they will escape misfortune. Always realistic, he recognized that the faith of a Christian, far from protecting one from suffering and death, might even bring those misfortunes upon one. But this would not constitute *ultimate* harm to one who lives in pure obedience to God.

This conviction was in accord with the Christian martyrs and with the belief of Socrates that no event or person can inflict ultimate harm on one, for the only basic harm is the deterioration of one's character, one's moral being. This cannot be caused by an external agent, but only by the person oneself. With Woolman this idea was baptized by his belief in a personal God.

While holding very strong convictions, Woolman recognized that valid religious experience is not confined to Quakers or Protestants or Christians. His sense of kinship with those of other faiths, notably Roman Catholics and Native American, is aptly expressed in his statement that "sincere, upright-hearted people in every Society who truly loved God were accepted of him" (PM 28).

Woolman's ethical insight and the action to which it led issued naturally from his religious faith. His sense of ultimate security in God impelled him to express his convictions in action, as he put it, "looking less at the effects of my labor than at the pure motion and reality of the concern as it arises from heavenly love" (PM 72).

Another conviction that gave a sense of urgency to his endeavors was his conception of the divine judgment upon human affairs. Ten times in the *Journal* he warned of the dire consequences if slavery were not abandoned:

> I saw in these southern provinces so many vices and corruptions increased by this trade and this way of life that it appeared to me as a dark gloominess hanging over the land; and though now many willingly run into it, yet in future the consequence will be grievous to posterity! I express it as it hath appeared to me, not at once nor twice, but as a matter fixed on my mind. (PM 38)

A reciprocal relationship existed between his religious faith and his ethics. Not only did his ethics issue from his faith; he was convinced that one's perception of spiritual reality was in direct proportion to the purity and consistency of one's ethical life. Insofar as one lives up to the highest moral standards, one attains greater clarity and depth of perception in spiritual matters; to the extent that one compromises ethically one's spiritual vision becomes obscured. After being impressed by this insight in Woolman, I have noticed the same idea expressed in the writings of others—notably Plato, Augustine, Jonathan Edwards,

Spinoza, Thoreau, Aldous Huxley, and Tillich. Although the thought is not original with Woolman, it is a very pervasive aspect of his philosophy, in support of which he quotes the Beatitude: "Blessed are the pure in heart, for they shall see God" (PM 176).

A notable characteristic of Woolman was his ability to understand varied viewpoints and life styles. This enabled him to establish rapport with slaveowners and others with whom he differed. It also enabled him to deal directly with issues that were important to them, rather than talking past them. Very realistic, he recognized the crucial issues and facts regarding a disputed question, granted whatever validity there was on the other side, and then exposed its weakness. When a chance acquaintance complained of the "slothful disposition" of slaves, adding that they only did half as much work in a day as free white laborers, Woolman did not waste time and lose credibility by contending that the slaves worked just as hard as the free men. He did not dispute the observation of the other, but pointed out that "Negroes, labouring to support others who claim them as their property and expecting nothing but slavery during life, had not the like inducement to be industrious" (PM 61).

During his passage to England, Woolman pondered the miserable conditions in which the sailors lived and the more grievous plight of the slaves as they were transported "frequently in chains and fetters, on board the vessels, with hearts loaded with grief under the apprehension of miserable slavery" (PM 172). He traced the cause of these evils to the desire for profit by businessmen responsible for the slave trade. He did not castigate the traders. He criticized, rather, the "business is business" philosophy that is generally taken for granted by respectable businessmen. He recognized their good intentions. They would like to be ethical, he granted, so long as it did not interfere with pursuing profits. But he reversed the priorities: striving for success may be justified—so long as it does not entail unethical practices:

> In the love of money and in the wisdom of this world, business is proposed, then the urgency of affairs push forward, nor can the mind in this state discern the good and perfect will of God. . . . if we . . . say in our hearts, "I must needs go on, and in going on I hope to keep as near to the purity of Truth as the business before me will admit of," here the mind remains entangled and the shining of the light of life into the souls is obstructed. (PM 175)

Woolman's realistic type of analysis and recognition of how others view a situation helps one understand the repressive acts of the Nicaraguan government in the summer of 1988. Most peace activists and liberals would agree that insofar as the Sandinista government is militaristic and violates human rights, this is largely a response to the aggression of the contras and the threat of a U.S. invasion. With the removal of these threats, the Sandinistas would grant greater freedom to the media, release opposition leaders from jail, and become a more pluralist society. Certainly, by any fair standard of measurement the Sandinista regime is far superior to its predecessor. This is the stock liberal answer and is valid as far as it goes.

Yet a more complete explanation emerges when we realize that the present regime came to power by killing and other types of violence. Considerable truth inheres in the words of Woolman: "Where violent Measures are pursued in opposing Injustice," the result is "Passions and Resentments," as well as "Conflicts productive of very great Calamities" (AMG 384):

> the minds of contending Parties often remain as little acquainted with the pure Principle of Divine Love as they were before. But where People walk in that pure Light in which all their "Works are wrought in God;" and under Oppression . . . abide firm in the Cause of Truth, without actively complying with oppressive Demands, through those the Lord hath often manifested his Power, in opening the Understandings of others, to the promoting of Righteousness in the Earth. (AMG 384)

Woolman does not advocate submission to the oppressor. We are to "abide firm in the cause of Truth, without . . . complying with oppressive demands." But neither are we to be caught in the trap of seeking justice and liberation through violence.

A further example of Woolman's unusual ethical perception was his capacity to discern the long-range or obscure effects of one's conduct and to act accordingly. He wrote with approval of those who "see the relation of one thing to another and the necessary tendency of each," for whom "it may be absolutely binding to desist from some parts of conduct which some good men have been in" (PM 211).

In accordance with such insight he refused to pay the taxes levied to support the French and Indian War. He refrained from using silver eating utensils because of the oppressive conditions in which the miners were compelled to work. Some twentieth-century followers of Woolman abstain from moderate, so-called "responsible drinking" of alcoholic beverages because it provides financial and social support to the beverage industry which is ultimately responsible for excessive drinking and its attendant evils.

Many people in the late twentieth century have expressed deep appreciation for the insight they have gained from Woolman's life and thought. Two aspects of his ethics that are especially relevant to our time may be mentioned in closing. liberation theologians who stress the "preferential option for the poor" might well look to Woolman for inspiration. Throughout his writings, especially in "A Plea for the Poor," he expresses the conviction that God, "who is a refuge for the oppressed will in his own time plead their cause" (PM 63). In a letter to his wife he writes of God "who regards the helpless and distressed and reveals his love to his children under affliction" (PM 107).

But he didn't rely on God alone. He spent his life striving to relieve the burden of slavery from those who suffered from it. People in all walks of life—farmers, tradesmen, stagecoach drivers—who were poor and oppressed, and even beasts of burden, were objects of his compassion. Every aspect of his life underlined his challenge: "To labour for a perfect redemption from the spirit of oppression is the great business of the whole family of Christ Jesus in his world" (PM 262).

An especially important contribution of Woolman to our time is that he provides a much-needed antidote to the hedonism and narcissism that saturates our society. Slick magazines and TV advertisements extol self-expression—withy scarcely a self to express. People resort to noise, speed, and motion to distract their attention from the void at the center of their lives. When Woolman turned self-ward it was to increase his sensitivity to the reality beyond himself. He was other-directed—to the transcendent God and to human beings with whose needs he identified. His ethical insight and inner strength were largely due to his reading of the Bible and devotional classics and to frequent periods of quiet reflection. He was sensitive to the still small voice that gave his life purpose and direction. This practice, integral to his life and to Quakerism at its best, is in direct contrast to some of the most destructive aspects of our society.

With a sound base in the Christian faith, a sure sense of mission, and keen ethical discernment, he combined in superlative fashion the inner life of the spirit with persistent social action. He attacked not only individual sins, but also the systemic evils embedded in the social structure—slavery, economic exploitation, and war. As one who embodied in his personal life the ideas and principles by which he judged contemporary mores, he provides us with a superb example of the Quaker contribution to human betterment.

NOTE

[1] This article is reprinted, with permission, from the *Conference on Quaker Studies on Human Betterment Proceedings, Swarthmore College, June 16-18, 1988*, Ed. Jim Nichols (Philadelphia, PA: Friends Association for Higher Education, 1988) 13-18.

WORKS CITED

Woolman, John. *The Journal and Essays of John Woolman*. Ed. Amelia Mott Gummere. New York: Macmillan, 1922.

—. *The Journal and Major Essays of John Woolman*. Ed. Phillips P. Moulton. 1971. Richmond, IN: Friends United P, 1989.

19

In Honor of Sterling Olmsted

Neil Snarr

STERLING OLMSTED CAME TO WILMINGTON COLLEGE in the fall of 1968 and retired from full-time employment in 1980. It was during his years as Dean and later as Provost of Wilmington College that I came to know and respect Sterling as an educator, a scholar and a person committed to the highest ideals of Quakerism. His influence continues to be felt at Wilmington College and his scholarly work on nonviolent social change and Woolman studies continues to grow. Sterling deserves much credit for nurturing new interest in Woolman studies. It must be acknowledged, however, that Sterling's work cannot be separated from that of his wife Barbara who shares many of these interests and pursuits with him.

Sterling was born in Hartford, Connecticut, in 1915. He was an only child and lost his father prior to his first birthday. As a child he was quite sickly and missed two full years of school. At age eight and weighing in at 42 pounds, he was taken to a specialist who pronounced in his presence that, "He won't live to be fourteen." After enduring grade school he experienced a more positive high school career where he became a debater. He later went to Rollins College in Florida where he graduated in 1936 and soon was pursuing a graduate degree at Yale in English Literature. In 1939 he took a position at Rensselaer Polytechnic Institute in Troy, New York, teaching English. He received his Ph.D. in 1940.

Prior to being married in 1942, Barbara and Sterling, who were both raised in the Congregational Church, began attending the Albany Friends (Quaker) Meeting. Sterling did not seek conscientious objector status and was drafted into the army. About this event Sterling, then very new to Friends, recollects a kind elderly Quaker woman who thought he was a good Quaker boy gone wrong, saying to him, "I am sorry thee has joined the world's people." He learned a great deal from his military experience, but it seemed to direct his interests and energies toward issues of reconciliation rather than confrontation and helped prepare him for his later commitment to nonviolence. After nearly three years in the military he returned to RPI to teach English. There he became deeply involved in exploring the role that the humanities might play in the education of engineers. He concluded his work at RPI with a Carnegie funded study of "Liberal Learning and the Engineer" and also co-authored a work on the *Ethical Problems in Engineering.*

In the fall of 1968 the Olmsteds moved to Wilmington College, a Quaker institution, in Wilmington, Ohio. This move proved to be a turning point in Sterling and Barbara's lives as they became more actively involved in Friends' concerns. For those of us who know Sterling well, it seems appropriate to say that at about this time he became especially sensitive to John Woolman's petition that we "consider the connection of things" ("A Plea for the Poor," PM 247). They joined the Campus Friends Meeting which was a member of both Ohio Valley Yearly Meeting and Wilmington Yearly Meeting. (These two yearly meetings represent both the traditional unprogrammed worship and the more recent and conventional pastoral structure. They also represent a liberal and conservative social and political philosophy.) He and Barbara have worked in a variety of ways to bring these two traditions together through national gatherings and cooperative regional meetings.

Sterling's commitments and values have also found expression in three Quaker organizations, two of which are national and one international. He became deeply involved with the Friends Committee for National Legislation (FCNL) which works in Washington D.C. to bring Quaker values to bear on public policy. He also participated in the early conferences that led to the founding of the Friends Association for Higher Education (FAHE) which meets annually at Quaker schools. For some years he was active in Friends World Committee for Consultation (FWCC), an organization that brings together the diverse Quaker groups throughout the world. He served on the National Executive Committee of FWCC and continues to be active in FCNL and FAHE.

Sterling became deeply involved in the college, first as Dean and later as Provost. He worked hard to mould and clarify the mission and future of this small liberal arts college. In his own words he relates that "I wanted to define what we were trying to do as a Quaker college. A student helped me. He walked into my office one day and announced that he had found out what we were all about. 'What we're trying to do,' he said, 'is to turn out practical idealists.' I hoped this was so and began trying to make it so." This reflects his earlier concern with engineers and liberal learning and has given Wilmington College direction and identity. He was also responsible for the college receiving at least two major grants that gave further clarification and form to the college's image.

Sterling's teaching career spanned some 55 years including 15 years after his retirement. In the 1970s, Sterling was part of a study tour to India that evoked greater interest in nonviolence and Gandhi. He later initiated a course on campus with the title "Nonviolence and Social Change" which continues to be taught. This commitment to Wilmington College and Quaker education was capped in 1992 when he, along with Barbara, helped to produce the book *Partners in Education.* This is a unique volume about the relationship between Wilmington College and Wilmington Yearly Meeting of the Religious Society of Friends.

Although Sterling uses religious language very carefully he would probably refer to this new focus as a "concern," and would explain it much like Woolman did: "I cannot form a concern, but when a concern cometh, I endeavor to be obedient" (Woolman's letter of 16th, 9th month, 1772, *John Woolman: A Nonviolence and Social Change Source Book* 50). Sterling's command of English coupled with his sensitivity to other's feelings and commitment to social justice produce a rare expression of human and Quaker concern. In meetings and on paper he has a masterful way of clarifying and focussing the tasks at hand.

Sterling's life experiences seem to have prepared him in various ways for his later commitment to understanding the implications of John Woolman's life and writings. His approach has been cautious and open to the responses of others. His scholarly works on Woolman have always had lengthy exposure to the critical eyes of many and varied audiences. It might seem as if he does not trust his own intellect, but it is more than this. He seems very much aware of the innumerable ways in which ideas can be interpreted and carry meaning.

Sterling's scholarly work on Woolman is not that of a detached scholar. As his involvement in Quaker groups and social justice attest, the insights he has gained have been applied in his own life. In his pamphlet *Motions of Love: Woolman as Mystic and Activist,* Sterling quotes two passages from Woolman's *Journal* that sound as if they came from Sterling personally. They are "I found no narrowness respecting sects and opinions, but believed that sincere, upright-hearted people in every Society who truly loved God were accepting of him," and "As I lived under the cross and simply followed the openings of Truth, my mind from day to day was more enlightened . . ." (PM 28). With Mike Heller, Sterling recently edited *John Woolman: A Nonviolence and Social Change Source Book* for college courses and the general reader. This volume is to be part of a series of source books on nonviolent social change agents such as Gandhi, Dorothy Day, and Lucretia Mott. Woolman studies were reinvigorated by Sterling's efforts through FAHE and particularly through the Quaker Studies in Human Betterment Conference at Swarthmore College in 1988 which Sterling helped to organize. *Motions of Love, the Social Change Source Book* and his edition of Woolman's *Conversations on the True Harmony of Mankind and How It may Be Promoted,* as well as several other essays, represent a significant contribution to Woolman studies. Of his studies on Woolman and non-violence he said in 1996, "I propose to spend on it whatever time and energy I have left."

Sterling's productive life has been and continues to be committed to those things Quakers hold most precious. These commitments show through in his work on liberal learning and ethics among engineers, his involvement in the local, regional, and international activities of Friends, his crafting of an image and direction for Wilmington College, and more recently his academic work on non-violence and John Woolman. Sterling continues to inspire and motivate others who seek to understand the "connection of things" in our complex and increasingly dangerous world. Beyond understanding, however, is the continuing effort to be actively engaged in this "business of life."

Works Cited

Alger, Philip L., et al. *Ethical Problems in Engineering.* New York: J. Wiley, 1965.

Olmsted, Sterling. *Motions of Love: Woolman as Mystic and Activist.* Wallingford, PA: Pendle Hill, 1993.

Partners in Education: Wilmington College and Wilmington Yearly Meeting of Friends. Wilmington, OH: Wilmington College Study Committee, Wilmington Yearly Meeting of the Religious Society of Friends, 1992.

Woolman, John. "Conversations on the True Harmony of Mankind and How It May Be Promoted." Ed. Sterling Olmsted. Philadelphia: The Wider Quaker Fellowship, 1987.

—— *John Woolman: A Nonviolence and Social Change Source Book.* Eds. Sterling Olmsted and Mike Heller. Wilmington, OH: Peace Resource Center, 1997.

20

Woolman and Gandhi and Human Betterment *or* The Yoga of Peacemaking

Sterling Olmsted[1]

MANY WHO ARE ENGAGED IN THE STUDY OF THE PRINCIPLES and the practice of peacemaking have been greatly impressed by John Woolman's *Journal* and "A Plea for the Poor," and by Mohandas K. Gandhi's *An Autobiography: The Story of My Experience with Truth*. It is my contention that the study of Woolman and Gandhi together, however, takes us one step at least beyond either, and provides insights which may be of value to peacemakers and would-be peacemakers today.

For the past eight years, I have been teaching a course at Wilmington College entitled "Woolman and Gandhi: Non-Violence and Social Change." All students in the course are required to read Woolman's *Journal* and "A Plea for the Poor," and now also Woolman's *Conversations*, as well as Gandhi's *Autobiography* and Jane Bondurant's *The Conquest of Violence*. Each student then does an individual seminar paper and class presentation on one other change agent: Martin Luther King, Jr., Oscar Romero, Helder Camara, Lucretia Mott, Dorothy Day, Adolfo Perez Esquivel, Kenneth Kaunda. The list of seminar subjects changes from time to time, but the intent is always the same: to broaden the study of nonviolent change into other times and places, still using Woolman and Gandhi as reference points.

Most students I believe, learn something from the course, but what I want to focus on is what I have learned from looking at Woolman and

Gandhi together, and how what I have learned relates to what I see as two dilemmas of peacemaking: the dilemma of trying to maintain inner peace in the midst of the struggle for peace in the world, and the dilemma of trying to work for peace and justice at the same time. Can one work actively for social change and still avoid the despair which comes with frustration? Can one indeed find some measure of self-realization in what one is doing, regardless of the outcome? And can one work to reduce violence and destructive conflict and at the same time to achieve greater justice and equity? Can one be advocate and conciliator at the same time and in the same situation?

The first thing I have learned, I believe, from looking at Woolman and Gandhi together is that, in spite of circumstantial differences, they were very much alike. The differences were obvious. Woolman worked primarily as an individual; Gandhi commanded mass movements. Woolman concentrated his persuasive efforts on his fellow Quakers; Gandhi took on the British Empire as well as his very diverse compatriots. Woolman's major concern was for the rights, not of his own people, but of those in slavery; Gandhi's focus was on the rights of his fellow Indians in South Africa and in their homeland, though he was also concerned with an outgroup, the Untouchables, and with the end of communal strife, especially between Hindus and Muslims. Woolman was not much interested in politics; Gandhi was a masterful politician.

The similarities, however, are striking. Taken together they constitute, I believe, a description of the essential characteristics of peacemaking. For both Woolman and Gandhi peacemaking was an integral operation: there was no separation between peace and justice, no giving in on essentials, no acceptance of means which were incompatible with ends. The opponent, whether a slave-holder or rich merchant, a British official or conservative Brahmin, was to be won over, not beaten down or eliminated. For both Woolman and Gandhi this integral operation was not a some-time activity, but a continuing effort, involving words and actions, and ways of living consistent with one's goals. For Woolman, this last meant ridding himself of "cumber," simplifying his wants; for Gandhi it meant not only simplifying wants but developing a "constructive program" which would enable India's millions to become more self-reliant. For both, giving up luxuries entailed some self-suffering: Woolman traveled to England in steerage; Gandhi traveled about India third class. Gandhi, however, made self-suffering an instrument in the struggle; it may also have worked that way for Woolman, but he did not apparently see it as Gandhi did as a means of "melting the hearts" of the opposition (Nanda 113). Finally, for both Woolman and Gandhi, this integral, consistent, and continual peacemaking, went far deeper than technique or attitude change.

The second thing I have learned is that, at this deeper level, the roots of Woolman's and Gandhi's peacemaking, as well as their practices, are, in spite of obvious differences in tradition, very much alike.

Let me begin the comparison with Gandhi, since his religious roots may be less familiar than those of Woolman. In the introduction to his *Autobiography* Gandhi writes:

> What I want to achieve,—what I have been striving and pining to achieve these thirty years,—is self-realization, to see God face to face, to achieve *Moksha*. I live and move and have my being in pursuit of this goal. All that I do by way of speaking and writing, and all my ventures in the political field, are directed to this end. (Gandhi xii)

I find this an astonishing statement. What Gandhi seems to be saying, if we take him literally, is that all his practical efforts have been directed toward a spiritual goal, the attainment of m*oksha*, the fourth and last of the traditional Hindu aims of life. Gandhi's religious tradition is, of course, ancient and very complex; but central to it, as I understand it, is a belief in the presence in every person of a divine element—the Self, the Atman, the Knower-of-the-Field. I can find no better statement of this Knower-of-the-Field than these verses from Gandhi's favorite Hindu scripture, the *Bhagavadgita*.

> It is outside and within all beings. It is unmoving and moving. It is too subtle to be known. It is far away and it is also near.
>
> It is undivided and yet seems to be divided in all beings. It is to be known as supporting all beings and as absorbing and creating them.
>
> It is also, it is said, the light of lights beyond darkness; it is knowledge, the object of knowledge, and the goal of knowledge; it is seated in the hearts of all. (Deutsch 109)

To be united with this Knower-of-the-Field is to achieve *moksha*. There are a number of ways of achieving *moksha*, but they generally involve some form of *yoga*. There are many *yogas*. Every chapter of the *Bhagavadgita* ends with the words, "This is the yoga of ..." The focus in the *Bhagavadgita*, however, is on just three yogas: the yoga of knowledge (*jnana yoga*), the yoga of devotion (*bhakti yoga*), and the yoga of action (*karma yoga*), which is distinguished from other forms of action by its spiritual goal, the attainment of *moksha*, and by its non-attachment to social, political, or other "worldly" ends—though these may be the very ends to which the action is ostensibly directed. It is clear, I think, that in terms of these categories, Gandhi is a *karma yogin*), though I cannot recall any place in which he uses the phrase about himself. His emphasis on "speaking, writing, and all my ventures in the political field" makes it apparent that action is, in fact, his means of attaining *moksha*.

At first glance all this Hindu teaching seems far removed from the thinking of John Woolman, and the thinking and writing of the early Quakers including George Fox. But if we look more closely, we become aware of striking parallels. Central to both traditions is a belief in the presence in every person of the Divine. Quakers, of course, use different words for the Divine, many different words. George Fox calls it That-of-God, the Seed, the Inner Light, Christ, the Teacher within. Woolman is probably less metaphorical. He speaks once of the "Heavenly Instructor" (PM 55), but his favorite term is probably "pure wisdom." He also speaks of the "true witness in the hearts of others" (PM 73), and of "being inwardly united to the fountain of universal love and bliss" (PM 249), but he often thinks in terms of principles, for example, "the inward principle of virtue" (PM 32), or "a principle in the human mind which incites to exercise goodness toward every living creature" (PM 25). And though Woolman had probably never heard of *moksha*, he is very conscious not merely of the presence of the Divine within, but also of the possibility, in fact the necessity, of becoming joined with it. To quote in full the sentence which was quoted in part earlier in this paragraph, "The true felicity of man in this life, and that which is to come, is in being inwardly united to the fountain of universal love and bliss" (PM 249). Conversely, he writes, if "our wills continue to stand in opposition to the fountain of universal light and love, there will be an unpassable gulf between the soul and true felicity" (PM 250). He also notes, speaking of the principle which incites to the exercise of goodness, "this being singly attended to, people become tender-hearted and sympathizing, but being frequently and totally rejected, the mind shuts itself up in a contrary disposition" (PM 25). And though Woolman had certainly never heard of karm*a yoga*, with its principle of non-attachment, he also shows some understanding of it when he writes in the *Journal* of "looking less at the effects of my labour than at the pure motion and reality of the concern as it arises from heavenly love" (PM 72).

When I first noted these similarities between the traditions represented by Woolman on the one hand and Gandhi on the other, I was astonished. Since then, I have found them less surprising. If the central idea of the presence of the Divine in all human beings is present in both, as it should be, if the traditions themselves are to be trusted, then it is not surprising that both recognize it, and that both work out the implications in similar ways. What I am interested in now—and it is the third thing, I believe, I have learned from studying Woolman and Gandhi together—is the way in which the two traditions complement each other, and thus point toward further understanding of what peacemaking is and what it might be.

What Gandhi has to contribute to this larger vision is probably already fairly clear. He saw his kind of social change work—which I see as peacemaking in a very comprehensive sense—as a means to self-fulfillment, a form of yoga. I propose to call it the yoga o*f peacemaking*, since *karma yoga*, of which it is a sub-class, can presumably be practiced in pursuit of a great variety of goals. Indeed, in the *Bhagavadgita*, the *karma yoga* action which Krishna urges Arjuna to perform, with non-attachment to the results, is not peacemaking but war making—at the story level at least. Gandhi, who probably knew the *Bhagavadgita* by heart, who used it in ashram devotions, and who frequently commented on it, proposed his own allegorical interpretation, and thus evaded its war-like implications. I prefer, therefore, to think of peacemaking as a special, but complex kind of activity which may lead to self-fulfillment, in other words as a yoga. Gandhi's view of peacemaking seems to complement Woolman's view. Though Woolman was very close to understanding *moksha* and *karma yoga*, it does not appear that he made a causal connection between his actions for social change and self-fulfillment, his becoming inwardly united to the fountain of universal love and bliss.

I suggest, however, that we explore that connection in our own peacemaking activities. If we could see our own efforts at peacemaking as a kind of yoga, a spiritual activity, as well as an effort at human betterment in the social and political world, we might be less frustrated, less anxious about results, less subject to burn-out.

Woolman's contribution to the larger vision of peacemaking may not be quite so clear. The key to it, I think, is in the phrase, the "true witness in the hearts of others." What he says, stated more fully, is: ". . . I had cause humbly to adore him who supported me through sundry exercises, and by whose help I was enabled to reach the true witness in the hearts of others" (PM 73). The idea of being able not only to address others, but to address the Divine within them has been stated even more forcefully and eloquently by George Fox, in a well known passage in the *Journal:*

> Be patterns, be examples, in all countries, islands, nations, wherever you may come, that your carriage and life may preach among all sorts of people, and *to* them: then you will come to walk cheerfully over the world, answering that of God in everyone. (Nickalls edition 263)

In another passage in the *Journal* Fox moves beyond addressing or answering that of God in others. It is now a matter of bringing people to the Teacher in themselves. After hearing the magistrates say that if they had money enough they would hire him as their minister, Fox writes:

> But when I heard of it, I said, "It is time for me to be gone; for if their eye were so much on me, or on any of us, they would not come to their own Teacher." For this (hiring ministers) had spoiled many, by hindering them from improving their own talents; whereas it is our labour to bring everyone to his own Teacher in himself. (Jones edition 508)

I do not know whether Woolman had ever taken in the full import of these passages, but they are certainly part of his tradition. Reaching the "pure witness in others," "answering that of God in everyone," "bringing everyone to his own Teacher in himself," all point to a kind of peacemaking which operates on a level which is deeper than that of ordinary discourse, a level where people meet each other in that which they have in common. And they all suggest a way of working which not only recognizes the presence of a divine element or principle in all, but also seeks to involve it in the process.

At the beginning of this essay, I raised several questions: Can one work actively for social change and still avoid the despair which comes from frustration? Can one indeed find some measure of self-realization in what one is doing? Can one work to reduce violence and destructive conflict, and to produce greater equity and justice? Can one be advocate and conciliator at the same time, in the same situation? I believe we are now nearer to being able to answer these questions.

If one takes self-realization, *moksha,* as the spiritual goal of one's peacemaking efforts, and if one still pursues peacemaking with all one's might, but without attachment to the political and social results, it may be possible not only to maintain inner peace, but to achieve the kind of self-fulfillment which Gandhi said he was seeking through his efforts. And if one accepts, even tentatively, the religious institutions of Woolman and Fox, Gandhi and the *Bhagavadgita*, one may be able to carry on a kind of peacemaking which enables those who take part to move together toward the "true witness," the Teacher within, the Knower, which the *Bhagavadgita* says is undivided and yet seems to be divided in all beings," and which is seated in the hearts of all. And if one can function both as advocate and conciliator, working simultaneously for greater harmony, greater justice and equity. In fact, it may well be that, only if we pursue peace and justice simultaneously will we be able to achieve self-realization, or to bring others to the Teacher in themselves.

If one accepts all this, this would be a good place to conclude this paper. The questions have been more or less answered: Peacemaking can be a satisfying and fulfilling occupation, which can combine—in fact should combine—advocacy and conciliation. It's all very neat.

But it is also very difficult, even painful. We need to recognize that fact. It is relatively easy to be a mediator, even to practice what Mike Yarrow called "balanced partiality" (Yarrow 165). It is not difficult to be an active partisan. But to try to be both at the time is to stray into No Man's Land. Which side are we supposed to be on? Gandhi, after all, was killed by a fellow Hindu; Oscar Romero who was chosen as Archbishop of San Salvador as a conservative and turned out not to be one was shot while saying mass. But there are other dangers. One may be torn apart. One may lose one's sense of identity. Woolman's life was never threatened, as far as I know, though he was startled during his visit to the Indians at Wyalusing when he was approached by a man carrying a tomahawk. There is no doubt, however, that Woolman suffered. The agonies of his decision-making as he sought to respond faithfully to his inner leadings are in every chapter of the *Journal.* But the climatic account of his inward struggles comes in the last chapter, in which he writes of an illness, two years before, which brought him so near to the gates of death that he forgot his own name. He had a vision of human beings in as great misery as possible and yet live; he saw himself so mixed in with them that he might not henceforth consider himself a distinct and separate being; and he heard the words, "*John Woolman is dead.*" Then he was carried in spirit to the mines where he saw poor oppressed people "digging rich treasures for those called Christians" (PM 186). Next day he asks his wife and the friends at his bedside who he is, and they think he is light-headed, but "at length I felt divine power . . . and then I said: 'I am crucified with Christ, nevertheless I live; yet not I, but Christ that liveth in me,'" and he comes to understand that "*John Woolman is dead,*" means no more than the death of his own will (PM 186).

Was he light-headed? Or is he, at last, after a lifetime of obedience to the drawings and leadings of the spirit within him, becoming inwardly united to the fountain of universal love and bliss?

Is this the self-realization Gandhi was striving and pining for? Is this the *moksha* which one may attain through the yoga of peacemaking?

NOTE

[1] This article is reprinted, with permission, from the *Conference on Quaker Studies on Human Betterment Proceedings, Swarthmore College, June 16-18, 1988*, Ed. Jim Nichols (Philadelphia, PA: Friends Association for Higher Education, 1988) 43-50.

WORKS CITED

Bondurant, Joan V. *Conquest of Violence: The Gandhian Philosophy of Conflict.* Berkeley: University of California Press, 1965.

Deutsch, Eliot. *The Bhagavad Gita.* New York: Holt, Rhinehart and Winston, 1968.

Fox, George. *The Journal of George Fox.* Ed. Rufus M. Jones. New York: Capricorn, 1963.

Fox, George. *The Journal of George Fox.* Ed. John L. Nickalls. London: Religious Society of Friends, 1975.

Gandhi, Mohandas K. *An Autobiography: The Story of My Experiments with Truth.* Boston, Beacon Press, 1957.

Nanda, B. R. *Mahatma Gandhi.* New York: Barrons, 1965.

Woolman, John. *Conversations on the True Harmony of Mankind and How It May Be Promoted.* Ed. Sterling Olmsted. Philadelphia: The Wider Quaker Fellowship, 1987.

—. *The Journal and Major Essays of John Woolman.* Ed. Phillips P. Moulton. 1971. Richmond, IN: Friends United P, 1989.

Yarrow, C. H. Mike. *Quaker Experiences in International Conciliation.* New Haven and London: Yale University Press, 1978.

Contributors

Paul Anderson is Professor of Biblical and Quaker Studies at George Fox University, where he has taught since 1989. He has also served as Friend in Residence at Woodbrooke, a visiting scholar at Pendle Hill, and a visiting professor of New Testament at Yale Divinity School 1998-99. Paul edited the *Evangelical Friend* from 1990-94, and currently serves as editor of *Quaker Religious Thought*. He co-edited Howard Macy's *Truth's Bright Embrace: Essays in Honor of Arthur O. Roberts*. Paul is the author of *The Christology of the Fourth Gospel* and *Navigating the Living Waters of the Gospel of John*.

Michael L. Birkel, Professor of Religion at Earlham College, has published several other articles on John Woolman.Trained as an historian of earlier Christianity, he has published translations of fifth-century monk Nilus of Ancyra and twelfth-century Cathusian Guigo II. His previous books include *The Lamb's War* and *The Inward Teacher*. He is currently writing on Quaker spirituality.

Philip L. Boroughs is a Jesuit priest and Vice President for Mission and Ministry at Georgetown University. His doctoral dissertation explored John Woolman's integration of spirituality and social transformation, and he also has written in the area of spiritual discernment and the Ignation tradition.

Anne Dalke is a member of the English department at Bryn Mawr College, where she coordinates the Feminist and Gender Studies Program. She offers literature courses on the spiritual autobiographies of American women and on historical feminist texts of the western tradition. She is active in the Religious Education Committee of Radnor Meeting, where she is a member.

Vernie Davis is Professor and Director of the Peace and Conflict Studies at Guilford College and the faculty director of the Guilford College Conflict Resolution Resource Center. His current work integrates cultural anthropology with peace studies to apply conflict resolution approaches in multicultural settings.

Susan Dean taught American literature at Bryn Mawr College for 25 years. After retiring in 2000 she moved from Pennsylvania to Tacoma,

Washington, where she continues her study of the confident vision of democracy in Walt Whitman's poetry—with particular attention to the inflow of Quaker culture, gay culture, and Native American culture through that vision. She is working on a book on Walt Whitman's *Leaves of Grass,* in which she explores the influence of minority cultures (including Quakerism and Native American culture) upon Whitman's vision of democracy.

J. WILLIAM FROST is Senior Research Scholar at Swarthmore College. Formerly, he was Howard M. and Charles F. Jenkins Professor of Quaker History and Research and Director of the Friends Historical Library at Swarthmore College. His books include *The Quaker Family in Colonial America, A Perfect Freedom: Religious Liberty in Pennsylvania,* and, with Hugh Barbour, *The Quakers.*

LISA M. GORDIS is Associate Professor of English at Barnard College, where she teaches courses in early American literature and American Studies. She is the author of *Opening Scripture: Bible Reading and Interpretive Authority in Puritan New England.* She is currently working on a book-length study of Quaker theories of language under the working title *Beyond What Words Can Utter: The Power and Limits of Language for Early Quakers.*

MICHAEL P. GRAVES is Professor of Communication Studies at Regent University, Virginia Beach, where he lives with his wife, Darlene, also a professor of creative process and post-secondary education. Michael received the 1985 publication award of the Religious Communication Association for his essay "Functions of Key Metaphors in Early Quaker Sermons, 1671-1700," published in the *Quarterly Journal of Speech,* November 1983.

MIKE HELLER teaches American literature and writing at Roanoke College, where he has served as chair of the English department. He co-edited, with Sterling Olmsted, *John Woolman: A Non-violence and Social Change Source Book.* He has had a long-time interest in the processes of the personal journal and autobiography. He is a member of the Roanoke (VA) Monthly Meeting.

PAUL A. LACEY is Professor Emeritus of English at Earlham College. He works and writes in several areas, among them Quaker education, faculty development, contemporary American poetry, and teaching literature. At present he serves on the boards of the Friends Council on Education and the American Friends Service Committee. He is married to Margaret S. Lacey, a writer, and they have three children.

Mary Moulton was a social worker, retiring in 1988 from a position in a psychiatric hospital. She was an active member of the Ann Arbor Meeting for twenty-two years before joining the Sandy Spring Meeting in Maryland. Peace education has been a major avocation.

Phillips P. Moulton taught at Union Theological Seminary, Simpson College, the University of North Dakota (where he was Chairman of the Department of Religion), Adrian College, and was a Visiting Scholar at the University of Michigan. He edited *The Journal and Major Essays of John Woolman,* and he wrote *Ammunition for Peacemakers* as well as numerous articles, including several on John Woolman.

Anne G. Myles is Assistant Professor of English at the University of Northern Iowa, Cedar Falls, Iowa, where she specializes in Early American literature, with particular interest in the formations of dissenting language and selfhood. She has published essays on Mary Dyer and the seventeenth-century Quaker "New England martyrs," among other topics. She is a member of the Religious Society of Friends.

Sterling Olmsted has served as Dean and taught English and Peace Studies at Wilmington College at Wilmington, Ohio. He wrote the recent Pendle Hill pamphlet, *Motions of Love: Woolman as Mystic and Activist.* He co-edited, with Mike Heller, *John Woolman: A Nonviolence and Social Change Source Book.* Sterling and his wife, Barbara, have been active members of numerous Friends committees.

Mary Rose O'Reilley is Professor of English at the University of St. Thomas, St. Paul, Minnesota. Her books include *The Peaceable Classroom, Radical Presence,* and *The Barn at the End of the World.* She is a member of Twin Cities Friends Meeting.

Gerald W. Sazama is Associate Professor of Economics at the University of Connecticut, Storrs, where his research is on government policy in affordable housing, higher education, and Latin America. He serves on the Board of Directors of the National Association of

Housing Cooperatives, and he is a member of the Storrs Monthly Meeting, Storrs, Connecticut.

Neil Snarr is Professor of Sociology and teaches courses on Global Issues at Wilmington College (Ohio). With Daniel Smith-Christopher he edited *Practiced in the Presence: Essays in Honor of T. Canby Jones* (Friends United Press, 1994) and recently, with his son Michael, co-edited the second edition of their book *Introducing Global Issue* (Lynn Reinner, 2002).

Jean R. Soderlund is Professor and Chair of the Department of History and Co-Director of the Lawrence Henry Gipson Institute at Lehigh University. She is the author of *Quakers and Slavery: A Divided Spirit* and co-author with Gary B. Nash of *Freedom by Degrees: Emancipation in Pennsylvania and its Aftermath.*

Margaret E. Stewart is Professor of English at Washburn University in Topeka, Kansas. In addition to writing about John Woolman, she has also published essays on Herman Melvillc, Viet Nam war literature, teaching methods, social justice, and birdwatching.

Christopher Varga is a graduate of the University of Virginia and the City University of New York. He was an adjunct professor of English at various colleges in the New York area for five years. Now employed in private industry, he continues work as an independent scholar and writer living in Glen Ridge, NJ.

Pendle Hill Acknowledgments

Pendle Hill Publications wishes to thank the following people for helping make this book possible:

Philip L. Boroughs

Daniel A. DiBiasio

Mike Heller

Terry C. Miller

Mary Moulton

Kevin N. Snarr

Neil Snarr

Mary Rose J. Zink

THE TENDERING PRESENCE

was composed on a Power Macintosh 7600 computer using Adobe Pagemaker 6.5 and typefaces from the Adobe Type Library: the Adobe Caslon Collection and Caslon Open Face.1,000 copies were printed in the United States by Thomson-Shore, Inc., Dexter, Michigan in July 2003. It was printed on 60# Gladfelter Recycled, 358ppi.

History of the Typefaces

William Caslon released his first typefaces in 1722. Caslon's types were based on seventeenth-century Dutch old style designs, which were then used extensively in England. Because of their incredible practicality Caslon's designs met with instant success. Caslon's types became popular throughout Europe and the American colonies: printer Benjamin Franklin hardly used any other typeface. The first printings of the American Declaration of Independence and the Constitution were set in Caslon.

For Adobe's Caslon revival, designer Carol Twombly studied specimen pages printed by William Caslon between 1734 and 1770.

Book Design by

Eva Fernandez Beehler and Rebecca Kratz Mays